Redcoats in the Classroom

The British Army's Schools for Soldiers and Their Children During the 19th Century

Howard R. Clarke

Helion & Company Limited

Helion & Company Limited
Unit 8 Amherst Business Centre
Budbrooke Road
Warwick
CV34 5WE
England
Tel. 01926 499 619
Email: info@helion.co.uk
Website: www.helion.co.uk
Twitter: @helionbooks
Visit our blog at blog.helion.co.uk

Published by Helion & Company 2021
Designed and typeset by Mary Woolley (www.battlefield-design.co.uk)
Cover designed by Paul Hewitt, Battlefield Design (www.battlefield-design.co.uk)

Text © Howard R. Clarke 2020
Images © as individually credited
Maps drawn by George Anderson © Helion & Company 2020

ISBN 978-1-912866-47-2

British Library Cataloguing-in-Publication Data.
A catalogue record for this book is available from the British Library.

For details of other military history titles published by Helion & Company Limited
contact the above address, or visit our website: http://www.helion.co.uk.

We always welcome receiving book proposals from prospective authors.

Contents

List of Illustrations

List of Maps

List of Tables

Note from the Editor

It is my sad duty as Series Editor to inform the reader that Howard Clarke sadly passed away from Covid-19 before this book could be completed. It was the wish of his widow Diana Clarke that the manuscript be readied for publication and subsequently published in tribute to Howard. To that end as Series Editor I have attempted to complete and edit the manuscript to the best of my ability. Sadly, I lack Howard's specialist knowledge of the area, but have endeavoured to use my knowledge of the Victorian Army to bring this to fruition. Errors in the understanding of the system of military education are therefore likely to be mine rather than Howard's.

Howard himself had originally asked that the work be dedicated to the memory of Arthur (Art) W. Cockerill of Cobourg, Ontario, Canada who, in Howard's words, 'strove to ensure that the story of the British Army's schools for soldiers and their children would be told and not forgotten.' It seems appropriate that I should also recognise Howard's role in doing the same through his many hours of hard work in preparing the original manuscript.

Christopher Brice PhD
Series and Commissioning Editor
From Musket to Maxim 1815-1914
Helion & Co Ltd

Author Notes

1. Notes on British Army Organisation and Administration in the 19th century

The regiment was the basic unit of the Army throughout the century. Men enlisted in a particular regiment of cavalry or infantry and could not be transferred to another unit without their consent.

There were three regiments of Household Cavalry comprising the First and Second Life Guards and the Royal Horse Guards. There were also three regiments of Foot Guards: the 1st or Grenadier Guards, the 2nd or Coldstream Guards and the 3rd or Scots (Fusilier) Guards. Each regiment had a number of battalions designated 1/1st Foot Guards, 2/1st Foot Guards, 3/1st Foot Guards; 1/2nd Foot Guards, etc.

The cavalry of the line consisted of ten regiments of Dragoon Guards and Dragoons and up to 18 regiments of light cavalry, which at various dates during the century were designated as Light Dragoons, Hussars or Lancers.

The infantry of the line comprised around one hundred regiments of foot each with a designated number which identified that regiment's position of seniority in the Army. During the Napoleonic Wars a second battalion and sometimes a third or fourth battalion was added to many of the regiments, but these were mostly disbanded following the end of hostilities in 1815. The First (Royal) Regiment of Foot retained its two battalions and in 1858 it was decided to expand the Army and the 2nd -25th regiments of foot were regiments were augmented with a second battalion. Whenever a Regiment had more than one battalion, each battalion is identified as follows in the text: 1/1 Foot, 2/1 Foot; 1/2 Foot, 2/2 Foot etc.

In 1782 several regiments of foot were ordered to cultivate a connection with a particular English county with the hope that this would improve recruitment and the regiment adopted the name of that county in its title. For example, the 14th Regiment was designated the (Bedfordshire Regiment and subsequently the Buckinghamshire of Foot) and the 22nd Foot, the 22nd (Cheshire) regiment. The attempt to foster local recruitment was largely unsuccessful and regiments recruited widely across the country enlisting men whoever they could find them. In 1873 the decision was taken to link and localise the infantry regiments of the line. The first twenty-five regiments already had two battalions and the remaining line regiments were linked in pairs, although they retained their titles and numbers. In 1880 the linking system was taken one step further and two battalion territorial regiments were established for most of the infantry. The old regimental numbers were abolished, and the new regiments were each given a title associated with the regiment's locality. This established the system of county regiments, such as the Northumberland Fusiliers, the Durham Light Infantry and the King's Own Scottish Borderers which lasted into the second half of the Twentieth century.

The term 'regimental school' is used throughout the work to identify the schools of the infantry, irrespective of whether a particular regiment had more than one battalion each with its own school.

The Administration of the Regular Army was complex for most of the century with responsibility divided between several government departments and agencies. In essence there was a dual system of governance with a broad distinction between the command of the cavalry and infantry vested in military officers under the Commander-in-Chief at the Horse Guards (although the Master-General of Ordnance was responsible for the artillery and engineers), and its administration and finance in the hands of civilian ministers, including the Lords of the Treasury, the Secretary of State for War and Colonies and the Minister at War at the War Office, who were responsible to Parliament. The dual system was simplified from 1855 with the command and control of the cavalry, infantry, artillery and engineers increasingly concentrated in the hands of the Secretary of State for War. When at various times several government departments and agencies, for example the Commander-in-Chief at the Horse Guards and the Secretary at War at the War Office, were involved in a decision about the Army's school, they are referred to jointly as the 'military departments' in the text.

2. Notes on India Place Names

Throughout the century a large and growing part of the British Army was stationed in India, with King's /Queen's regiments attached to the armies of the Bengal, Bombay or Madras Presidency. There were a large number of military stations in each presidency and the regiments moved at intervals between the stations that were provided with barracks deemed suitable for European troops and their families. The names of many of the military stations were spelt in a number of different ways in documents during the Raj and have changed since India gained independence in 1947. Throughout this work the place names are as they appear in contemporary documents during the Nineteenth century and the spelling has been standardized as used in James Wyld's map of India (1838). The 21st century names follow in parenthesis.

3. Notes on Measurement and Currency

During the Nineteenth century the standard measurements in Great Britain and throughout the Empire were in imperial units.

The imperial units of height, length and distance were inches, feet, yards and miles. There were 12 inches to one foot (305mm), three feet to one yard (0.91m) and 1760yards to one mile (1.61km).

4840 square yards made one acre, which is equal to 4047 square meters and 0.4 hectare.

The unit of currency was in Pounds Sterling. One Pound (£) was divided into 20 shillings(s) and one shilling(s) was divided into 12 pence (d).

In the current United Kingdom decimal currency there are 100p to £1and 5p is the equivalent of 1s or 12d in the old pre-decimal currency

Preface

This volume tells the little-known story of the British Army's regimental and garrison schools, which were established in 1812 to provide some elementary education for soldiers' children and subsequently for enlisted men, some 30 years before the government provided public money for civilian schools in England and Wales.

In this, the first published work on the British Army's schools during the 19th century for almost 50 years, the author takes a fresh approach, placing the narrative within the context of contemporary opinion about the need for educated soldiers and the schooling appropriate for the children of the lower classes, from which the Army predominately drew its recruits. He will also attempt to explain the hitherto neglected, but crucial part played by responsible ministers at the War Office in establishing and ensuring the continuation and development of the schools. This volume breaks new ground by combining material drawn from the archives of more than 40 regiments of infantry and cavalry preserved in their regimental museums and county records offices with contemporary records held in the British Library, the National Army Museum and the United Kingdom's National Archives, to construct an unprecedented account of the workings of the schools during these years.

Acknowledgements

I first became aware that regimental and garrison schools existed in the British Army during the Nineteenth century whilst researching my *New History of the Royal Hibernian Military School, Phoenix Park Dublin* (Yarm 2011). Reference is made to the origins and foundation of the schools and the subsequent arrangements for the training of army schoolmasters in the small number of the histories that were published in the middle years of the 20th century. Since then, other than the occasional journal article and a few unpublished postgraduate dissertations, there has been little interest in the regimental schools and garrison schools and no attempt to provide a comprehensive history.

I started the research for this book by searching in the government and parliamentary papers for material on the formation and subsequent operation of the schools. Much this work was conducted at the British Library, the United Kingdom's National Archives and National Army Museum. I would like to record my thanks for the assistance provided by the staff of these establishments. The National Army Museum inherited much of the documentary material from the archives of the Royal Army Educational Corps following the closure of the Corps museum, but some documents and pictorial material was placed in the Adjutant General Corps' Museum at Winchester. I am especially grateful to the then curator Ian Bailey for allowing me to view and copy material from the museum's reserve collection.

The War Office and the Parliamentary archives contain very little material on the operation of the school before the publication of Lieutenant Colonel Lefroy's Report on the Regimental and Garrison schools in 1859. Fortunately, a great deal of material in the form of standing orders, digests of service and personal diaries and some paintings from the first half of the century has been preserved in the regimental museums and county archives across the United Kingdom. In the course of my research I have visited a number of these archives which are listed in the bibliography and I am indebted to the curators and staff for locating and extracting such a wealth of relevant material. In particular, I would like to thank Colonel John Downham for allowing me to read and quote from the records of the 30th, 40th, 59th, 47th, 81st and 82nd regiments of foot which have been preserved in the Lancashire Infantry Museum at Fulwood Barracks Preston.

A special debt of gratitude is owed to the late Arthur ('Art') W. Cockerill of Cobourg Ontario, the author of *Sons of the Brave—the Story of Boy Soldiers* (London 1984) who provided much encouragement and support in the preparation and publication of my history of the Royal Hibernian Military School . 'Art' Cockerill encouraged me to undertake further research and provide a comprehensive account of the British Army's schools during the 19 Century. Sadly, Art did see the completion of this volume, but most of the chapters have benefited from his constructive criticisms and suggestions for improvements in the text. Any errors of omission and commission in the content and presentation are my own responsibility.

This history of the regimental and garrison schools is the first of two volumes on the British Army's schools in the Nineteenth century, with the second on the Royal Military Asylum Chelsea in preparation.

Howard R. Clarke

Glossary & Abbreviations

Add. MMS	Additional Manuscripts, British Library
AEC	Army Educational Corps
BL	British Library, London
C-in-C	Commander-in-Chief
CO(s)	Commanding Officer(s)
DYRMS	Duke of York's Royal Military School (formerly RMA), Dover
EHR	English Historical Review
HC	House of Commons, Westminster London
HO	Home Office London
H R H	His (Her) Royal Highness
Lt Col	Lieutenant Colonel
NAM	National Army Museum Chelsea London
NLI	National Library of Ireland, Dublin
RAEC	Royal Army Educational Corps
RMA	Royal Military Asylum (subsequently Duke of York's Royal Military School)
RHMS	Royal Hibernian Military School
SP	State Papers
TNA	The National Archives, London
WO	War Office London

Introduction

For most of the nineteenth century elementary education for the vast majority of children in Great Britain was conceived as little more than a preparation for their future roles in life. It was considered sufficient schooling for a child to be able to read a simple narrative, spell common words correctly, write legibly a short and intelligible letter and master some basic arithmetic. It was not envisaged that this schooling would extend much beyond the age of eleven or twelve. There was no provision for older children to continue with their schooling or for adults to return to the classroom and improve their education in order to further their careers.

The Director General of Military Education at the War Office, Major General C.W. Wilson concluded his annual report in 1896 with a reminder that schools for the education of soldiers, enlisted boys and soldiers' children had been established in the British Army in 1811: more than twenty years before the first civilian elementary schools were granted state aid. Although strictly speaking Wilson's claim could only be made with reference to England and Wales, he nevertheless was making an important statement about the place of the Army's school in the history of popular education in the United Kingdom.

Schools providing an elementary education for the children of the lower classes in England and Wales in the early years of the nineteenth century were voluntary bodies often founded and maintained by the Anglican and non-conformists churches and supported by charitable donations and bequests, sometimes supplemented by a small fee payable by the parents. There was a rivalry between the schools supported by the National Society for the Education of the Poor in the Principles of the Established (Anglican) Church founded in 1811 and the schools of the British and Foreign School Society founded in 1808, which provided non-denominational religious teaching and were supported by most non-conformists. Any move by government to establish taxpayer funded schools faced acute political difficulties. Members of the established church argued that any national system must be Anglican based and non- conformists and Catholics fiercely resisted this. In the absence of any consensus successive governments resorted to making grants to existing denominational schools in the hope that these grants would encourage the building of more schools. An Education Committee of the Privy Council was set up by Order in Council in 1839 'to superintend the application of any sums voted by Parliament for the purpose of promoting Public

Education', but it was not until 1870 that Parliament enacted legislation to establish a system of locally administered and publicly funded elementary schools to supplement the work of the grant maintained voluntary schools .

The Army schools which Major General C. W. Wilson referred to in his 1893 report were the regimental schools, which had been established in all the regiments and corps in the British Army from 1811. When the Education Committee of the Privy Council made its first grants for civilian school building in 1839 these Army schools were providing an elementary education of sorts for some 8,500 children and a similar number of serving soldiers at home and throughout the Empire with funds voted annually as part of the Army Estimates by the United Kingdom Parliament at Westminster.

The first part of this volume identifies some of the reasons that were advanced for establishing schools in the British Army and considers why the military authorities in London decided to establish regimental schools at a crucial stage in the Napoleonic Wars. It explains how these schools survived the financial retrenchment that was imposed on the Army by successive governments in the post war years. The military authorities did not go to the expense of establishing a college to train the army's schoolmasters and Commanding Officers (COs) were ordered to select suitable men from within the ranks for appointment as schoolmaster sergeants to run their regiment's school. The study considers the difficulties faced by COs in securing literate and numerate soldiers from within their regiments who were suitable for appointment. It explains the difficulties in keeping open the regimental schools and the challenges faced by even the most competent schoolmasters in effectively teaching their pupils as their regiments moved with regularity between barracks in the United Kingdom and with long journeys to stations across the Empire.

Although the Army's regimental schools were pioneers in the provision of publicly funded elementary education, they were far from perfect and by the 1840s were urgently in need of reform. A CO simply appointed the best literate man who was available to be the schoolmaster sergeant for his regiment and there was often a high turnover of staff. In consequence there were wide variations in standards across the Army and in the progress of pupils at particular schools. The general officers conducting inspections of units in their respective military districts reported on the number of children and soldiers on the school registers and made brief comments about the character and diligence of the schoolmaster sergeants but were not qualified to assess the educational progress of the pupils. COs were provided with regulations governing establishing the schools and in 1812 written guidance that was to be followed by the schoolmaster sergeants in teaching their pupils. The guidance was based on Rev Andrew Bell's 'Madras' monitorial system that had been introduced in the National Society's schools in the 1800s, but little attempt was made in the following years to revise the notes of guidance to incorporate progressive developments that were taking place in the civilian elementary schools.

The second part of this volume explains the reforms that were introduced in the Army's Schools during the 1840s. It examines the background to the establishing of the 'Normal school' at the Royal Military Asylum Chelsea to train a new class of army schoolmasters to replace the schoolmaster sergeants in the regimental schools. It chronicles the long and difficult process of training sufficient schoolmasters to staff all the regimental schools as the size of the British Army increased following the Crimean War (1854-56) and the Sepoy Mutinies and Uprising in India (1856-57). It explains how a succession of Army School Regulations during the 1850s and 1860s established what later became known as the 'Corps of Army Schoolmasters'.

The Education Committee of the Privy Council had recognised that the need for a suitably qualified team of inspectors to see that its grants were not abused and to spread best classroom practice amongst the grant aided civilian schools. The first of 'Her Majesty's Inspectors' (*HMIs* as they were subsequently known) was appointed in 1840 and by 1870 62 inspectors had been appointed to inspect the elementary schools receiving grants in England and Wales. Given the dispositions of the Army at home and abroad, it was impractical to expect the HMIs to inspect the regimental schools and the Army needed to establish its own inspectorate. This part of the book explains the circumstances in which the Army's Chaplain-General, the Rev George Gleig, was appointed to the additional post of Inspector of Army Schools in July 1846. Initially, Gleig was occupied with devising a curriculum for the 'Normal School', selecting students for training as schoolmasters and drafting regulations for their conduct of the regimental schools. He had little time to inspect more than a handful of the Army's schools in Great Britain and Ireland each year.

In 1860 the post of Inspector-General was abolished and the responsibility for appointment, discipline and promotion of the schoolmasters and mistresses and the superintendence and inspection of the Army's schools was vested in a Council of Military Education. In practice the Council relied on the annual reports from the three Assistant Inspectors in the UK and the local inspecting officers in the larger colonial garrisons. Army School Regulations in 1863 created the commissioned rank of Superintending Schoolmaster and these men who were selected from trained and experienced army schoolmasters formed the basis of the army schools' inspectorate. By 1870 Superintending Schoolmasters had been appointed to every military district in Great Britain and Ireland and they had responsibility for inspecting all the Army's schools in their districts.

The final decades of the century saw developments in the Army's schools that remained in place until the outbreak of the Great War. These developments are the subject of the third and final part of this book. Consideration is given to the impact on the Army's schools of short service enlistment and the localisation of the infantry introduced by the Cardwell and Childers' Reforms. There is an examination of the case for replacing the regimental schools with larger garrison schools and why it was decided that the regimental schools should be retained for soldiers' children.

The 1870 Education Act, which committed governments to the provision a national system of elementary education, albeit one that was locally managed, lead to speculation about the future need for the Army's adult schools. The frequent movement of regiments between stations presented serious difficulties in placing soldiers' children in the civilian elementary schools.   Nevertheless, many of the developments in the pedagogy and curriculum at the civilian schools were adopted in the Army's schools and the expansion in the civilian teacher training colleges raised the question of whether the Normal School at Chelsea was the most cost effective way of training the Army's schoolmasters.

Throughout the century the British Army's manpower was raised by voluntary enlistment and until the Army Enlistment Act of 1870, as part of the Cardwell Army reforms, men enlisted for long periods of service. There were always a large number of women and children accompanying the regiments and there were good reasons for the Army's pioneering work in establishing schools for the soldiers' children.

The Army also has a strong claim to being one of the pioneers of adult education. The Army's schoolmasters unlike their civilian contemporaries were in the unusual position of having to teach both children and enlisted soldiers. NCOs were promoted from within the rank and file of each regiment and these men needed to be literate and numerate so that they could effectively discharge their duties. Private soldiers with the potential for promotion often had little elementary education and many COs recognised the benefits of encouraging promising soldiers to attend at their regimental schools. In the second half of the nineteenth century there was a growing recognition that an educated army was more likely to be an effective army and hence that all newly enlisted men should attend school until they had a basic proficiency in reading, writing and arithmetic.

The British Army differed in a number of ways from the armies of the major European powers and this had particular consequences for the organisation and development of the Army's schools. It was a small army by continental standards. The regiments of cavalry and infantry were the core units and very essence of the Army. Individual self-contained battalions of infantry and regiments of cavalry moved regularly between stations at home and garrisons throughout the British Empire. The regimental school therefore remained the default model for the Army's schools for most of the 19th century and when in 1887 garrison schools were established for enlisted men they were retained for the younger children.

The main focus hitherto in what is a sparse historiography of the Army's schools has been on the contributions made by a small number prominent public officials in initiating policy: such as HRH Frederick, Duke York, in establishing the regimental schools in 1811/12 and the Rev George Gleig in connection with the reforms introduced by the War Office in the 1840s and 1850s. This study attempts to provide a more balanced narrative, which also acknowledges the crucial role played by government ministers, such as Viscount Palmerston, Sidney Herbert and Lord Panmure at the War Office in enacting policy and in ensuring that Parliament voted the requisite financial resources.

Throughout the century a large part of the Army was stationed in India. The existing literature does not explain the particular challenges faced by the COs and schoolmasters in keeping open schools when regiments were stationed in the sub-continent, nor does it mention that after the reorganisation of Army education in the 1840s, separate arrangements existed until the 1870s for superintendence and inspection in the three Indian Presidencies of Bengal, Bombay and Madras. This work pays particular attention to the circumstances of the Army's school in India.

Any account of the Army's schools would be incomplete without considering the day to day work of the schoolmasters and schoolmistresses and the difficulties that they faced in teaching soldiers and their children and implementing government policy for the Army's schools at home and abroad.

The 1861 Report of the Commissioners appointed to enquire into the state of Popular Education in England (The Newcastle Commission) quoted extensively from Lieutenant Colonel Lefroy's 1859 'Report on the Regimental and Garrison Schools of the Army and on Military Libraries and Reading Rooms' and acknowledged the work of the Army's teachers and the pioneering work played by their schools in the providing elementary education.

There are no published government reports on the operation of the regimental schools prior to Lieutenant Colonel Lefroy's report and this study has drawn on regimental archives to construct an account of the organisation and teaching at the schools during their early years. These archives include regimental standing orders, digests of service, and personal diaries relating to the period. Whilst the sample of regimental archives consulted has not been scientifically constructed, it has yielded similar material across a broad the range of regiments. This material combined with the factual information in the half yearly inspection reports by general officers in each military district, which can be found in the National Archives at Kew, forms the basis of the accounts of the schools during the first decades of the century when they were staffed and managed by the schoolmaster sergeants.

The responsibility for superintending the regimental and garrison schools and the work of the new class of trained army schoolmasters and mistresses was assumed by the Council of Military Education in 1860 and from 1870 by the Director Generals of Military Education. These bodies published eleven reports on the Army's schools between 1872-96 containing the observations of the War Office's inspectors. The Second Report of the Royal Commission appointed to enquire into Military Education published in 1870 provided additional testimony submitted by COs and serving schoolmasters. The 1882 Morley Report and the 1887 Harris Committee Report on Army Schools and Schoolmasters supplemented the Reports of the Director Generals of Military Education and together these detail the organisation of the schools and the work of the masters and mistresses in the final years of the century.

This book tells the story of the British Army's regimental and garrison schools and the work of its schoolmasters and mistresses in providing an elementary education for serving soldiers and their children during the nineteenth century. It also provides these schools with a place in the social history of the British Army. Moreover, it provides insight into the complexities of the formation and administration of military policy during the period.

Part I

Origins and Early Years of the Regimental Schools to 1846

1

Some Early Influences on the Formation of British Army Schools

The systematic provision of elementary education in the British Army can be traced to several initiatives by the military departments during the Revolutionary and Napoleonic Wars (1793-1815). These culminated in the system of regimental schools, which were established in each battalion and corps from 1812.[1] Various writers have identified some earlier influences, which they claim are important in the development of education in the Army. A review of these claims is relevant, not only for tracing the continuities in the development of army schooling, but also to understand why it was not until the final years of Great Britain's last war with France during the 'long 18th century' that the military authorities decided to provide elementary education for soldiers and their children.[2]

The formation of the British regular army is normally dated from the restoration of the monarchy in 1660,but some writers have dated the founding of army education to a number of measures, sometimes referred to as the 'Cromwellian Experiment', introduced by the generals of the Parliamentary armies during the English Civil War.[3] Both the Royalist and the Parliamentary armies had chaplains to provide for the religious instruction of the soldiers and their respective articles of war stressed the

---

1   The administration of the British Army in the 19th Century was a complex matter. Before the Crimean War there were numerous departments responsible, including the Secretary at War, the Secretary for War and the Colonies, the Foreign Office, the Home Department, the Board of Ordnance. As many as ten different bodies had a degree of responsibility for the Army. After the Crimean War and until the Cardwell Reforms the responsibility was shared inter alia by the War Office and Commander-in-Chief and his staff at Horse Guards. For more information see John Sweetman, *War and Administration: The significance of the Crimean War for the British Army* (Edinburgh: Scottish Academic Press, 1984) & Edward M. Spiers, *The Late Victorian British Army, 1868–1902* (Manchester: Manchester University Press, 1992).

2   T. Bowyer-Bower, 'Some Early Educational Influences in the British Army', *Journal of the Society for Army Historical   Research)*, Vol. 33, (1955), pp.5-12.

3   A. C. T. White, *The Story of Army Education1643-1963*, (London: George G. Harrap &Co., 1963) pp. 15-17.

importance of the attendance at prayers and reading the scriptures. From around 1648 there was a considerable increase in the number of chaplains in the Parliamentary Army. They were well paid and, when appointed to a particular garrison, received regular commissions from the C-in-C. The provision varied at different dates and it was not always easy to recruit the requisite number of regimental chaplains, nor is it clear that the military authorities systematically and continuously sought to procure them. To assist and supplement the teaching of the chaplains, a number of tracts were printed to instruct soldiers. Between 1643 and 1645, Major–General Skipton published three books of devotion addressed to his fellow soldiers and in 1644 Robert Ram, the minister of Spalding in Lincolnshire, published *The Soldiers' Catechism, composed for the use of the Parliaments Army, consisting of two parts (1) the justification and (2) the Qualification of our soldiers.* This explained the lawfulness of the military profession and the justice of the war and described the behaviour that was expected from the ideal parliamentary soldier. More famous is a little pamphlet of sixteen pages published in 1643, entitled *The Soldiers' Pocket Bible,* consisting of a selection of texts drawn from the scriptures under various headings which prescribed the godly behaviour of a soldier. Both works were private productions and had no official sanction, but confusingly they were reprinted in the late 19th century as *Cromwell's Soldiers' Catechism* and *Cromwell's Soldiers' Bible.*[4] These tracts were political weapons useful for the Parliamentarians in supporting their cause and it has been suggested the military authorities systematically distributed these texts to the army and that soldiers' regularly carried copies of *The Soldiers' Pocket Bible.* There is little evidence to support these assertions. Bibles were issued in 1652 to troops in Dublin and Galway and in 1655 two thousand copies were sent to soldiers in the West Indies and in 1658 to the garrison at Dunkirk. In all three cases the government only issued bibles because the soldiers had none or few chaplains to minister to them.[5]

It also has been suggested, although again without citing any evidence, that these publications, which were written and distributed for the guidance of soldiers, produced a 'remarkable increase of literacy' amongst the rank and file.[6] There is a broad consensus that, whereas the volunteer troopers in the cavalry regiments of the New Model Army were often men of 'good points and learning', the rank and file of the infantry, many of whom were pressed men, had very little education and the majority could not write their own name.[7] The tracts issued by the military authorities appear to have been limited to one text per file of six men, which was to be read in their quarters.[8] The expectation, following the practice of the time, was that men who were literate would read out aloud to their colleagues.

4   C.H. Firth, *Cromwell's Army*, (London: Methuen, 1962), pp. 311-28.
5   Firth, *Cromwell's Army*, pp. 329-30.
6   White, *The Story of Army Education*, p. 17.
7   Firth, *Cromwell's Army*, pp. 39 40.
8   Bowyer-Bower, '*Some Early Educational Influences*', p. 6 & Firth, *Cromwell's Army*, pp. 330.

There are no records of any policy to establish schools to provide an elementary education for soldiers in the New Model Army. The distribution of tracts supported the work of the chaplains whose ministry to the rank and file served the religious needs of the soldiery. They also worked to strengthen morale in the Parliamentary armies, which at that time was closely associated with religious faith, and also aimed to make the private men into better soldiers. The latter view persisted into the 18th century and beyond. A book entitled: *A Short Course of Standing Rules for the Government and Conduct of an Army* published in Dublin in 1746 by Lieutenant General (later Field Marshal) Richard Molesworth, 3rd Viscount Molesworth proclaimed that 'A strict attendance on their respective Duties must be required of all Degrees of Officers whatever; not excepting the Chaplains; which officers, well-chosen well directed, and properly employed, might be of notable Benefit to the Army....In short I will venture to affirm that by making your Army Better Men, you make them better soldiers.'[9] Army chaplains were given an important role when regimental schools were established in the early 19th century and this view of the primary purpose of educating the private soldier was strongly held by Rev George Gleig, who was appointed Principal Chaplain in 1844 and in 1846 became the first Inspector of the Army's schools.

For most of the 18th century the British Army expected very little in the way of education from its rank and file. *The Soldiers' Pocket Bible* was reprinted in 1693 under the title of *The Christian Soldier's Penny Bible* and during 'Queen Anne's War' (War of the Spanish Succession 1701-14), Josiah Woodward (1657-1712), an Anglican minister and an author and publicist in the cause of moral reform, published the *Soldier's Monitor.*[10] This short publication, which was sub-titled: *'Being Serious Advice to Soldiers to behave themselves with just Regard to Religion and true Manhood'*, argued that 'the employment of a soldier' was lawful and also expedient, because of the need to protect the nation from foreign aggression. The *Soldier's Monitor* made the case for a regular army in England at a time when a standing army was often viewed as a threat to liberty and the constitution. It also alluded to some of the fears in polite society about the lewd and licentious behaviour of enlisted men and exhorted soldiers to behave in a godly way and to desist from swearing, drunkenness, lustful and cruel behaviour and concluded with a selection of prayers for use at home and on active service. The *Soldier's Monitor* was reprinted in London on a number of occasions during the 18th century and the Society for the Promotion of Christian Knowledge (SPCK) issued five thousand copies to Marlborough's Army.[11] We do not know how this publication was used, if at all, nor does its distribution tell us anything about the level of literacy or the practical advantages that might be gained from providing schooling for enlisted men.

9   Bowyer-Bower, *'Some Early Educational Influences'*, p. 7.
10   Woodward addressed his first edition to The Duke of Marlborough and dedicated the book to Queen Anne. The second edition in 1722 was dedicated to King George I.
11   R. Porter, *English Society in the Eighteenth Century* (London: Penguin Books, 1991), p. 295.

The Royal Regiment of Artillery might be expected to have been interested in securing educated manpower. From the earliest days of the 'trains of artillery' the establishments included gunners and 'matrosses' – a type of assistant gunner. By the 1720s the companies of the regiment also included cadet gunners and cadet matrosses and there was a recognition that promotion to the substantive ranks required knowledge gained through practical experience as cadets. The Royal Warrant establishing the Royal Military Academy for the training of artillery officers at Woolwich in 1741 recognized that it was to be available for the professional education of all 'the raw and inexperienced people' belonging to the 'military branch of the ordnance.' It was envisaged that there would be practical and theoretical schools and the former were to be attended not only the officer cadets, but also by commissioned officers and men above the rank of bombardier, when off duty. Men below those ranks who showed any special talent or capacity for study could also attend.[12]

Throughout the century the military authorities in Great Britain and Ireland began to issue regulations, including orders concerning infantry drill. The drill practiced in each infantry regiment taught the soldier the use of his weapons, the ability to move with regulated order and docile obedience to commands, which when used in combination enabled him to perform complicated manoeuvres and deliver volley fire to order. This was achieved through a practical approach to training and did not require theoretical instruction in a class room.[13] There was nevertheless a growing body of privately published and widely read literature devoted to all aspects of drill and tactics written for serving officers, some of which gained royal favour. This literature was written to assist the officer corps, which at that time had no formal training and very often no active experience of warfare. The literature provided advice which filled in gaps in the regulations. The decision to expand the peacetime army following the end of the Seven Years War (1756-63) increased the number of regiments and hence of the number of inexperienced junior officers and this gave a further impetus for writers address the essentials of managing and training a regiment, including tactics and drill.[14]

The most prolific writer of these publications was Captain Thomas Simes of the Queen's Royal Regiment (2nd Foot) who produced five military works between 1767 and 1780. Although Simes has been accused of plagiarism and his writings were condemned for being long winded and uninspiring, they were widely read and provided young officers with a fairly comprehensive catalogue of their duties, and his publications contributed considerably to their basic schooling during this period.[15] A reading of Simes' publications suggests that there was an expectation during these

12   F. Duncan, *History of the Royal Regiment of Artillery* (London: John Murray, 1872), Vol.4, pp. 104, 108.
13   J.A. Houlding, *Fit for Service* (Oxford: Clarendon Press, 2000), pp. 160-62.
14   Houlding, *Fit for Service*, p. 216.
15   Houlding, *Fit for Service*, pp. 218-20.

years that a non-commissioned officer should be able to read, write and undertake a little arithmetic. When speaking of the duties of a sergeant-major he writes: 'He should be a man of real merit, a complete sergeant and a good scholar ... and must be ready at his pen and expert in making out details and rosters'; and of the corporal that 'He should have a quickness of comprehension with knowledge of reading, writing and accounts necessary to discharge the duty.'[16]

The dispositions of the British Army during the 18th century placed extra demands on the administration of regiments that called for an elementary education in reading, writing and arithmetic from at least some of its non-commissioned officers. In peacetime the 'marching regiments of foot' (the infantry of the line) had no fixed or permanent quarters. They were rotated between garrisons around Great Britain and Ireland to suppress smuggling, riot and public disorder, generally acting in support of the civil powers. Increasingly, as the century progressed, they were sent to stations throughout the overseas territories of the Empire. Within Great Britain units of foot and horse were always on the move and widely dispersed. Since barracks in Great Britain were virtually unknown, troops were billeted in public houses, inns and livery stables. Matters were a little different in Ireland where, by the late 1720s, many of the towns had been provided with barracks and billeting was much less commonly resorted to, except when troops were on the march. Soldiers often moved in small detachments under the command of a sergeant or corporal and used various staging posts to rest during their marches.

Billeting during marches required NCOs to keep account of food and drink (and to calculate deductions from the men's pay), to settle outstanding bills with landlords and to keep a record of payments. This was all in addition to preparing duty rosters, reading hand-written notes and regimental orders, and writing reports for their officers. Commanding Officers could not always rely upon their non-commissioned officers having the requisite literacy and numerical skills. The solution was to establish regimental schools and appoint schoolmasters to produce literate NCOs.

Thomas Simes was an early advocate of regimental schools and in 1767 he observed:

> A Sergeant or Corporal, sobriety, honesty and good conduct can be depended upon, and who is capable of teaching Writing, Reading and Arithmetic, to be employed to act in the capacity of a Schoolmaster, soldiers and soldiers' children are to be carefully instructed; a room to be appointed for use; and it would by highly commendable if this chaplain, or his deputy would pay some attention to the conduct of a school.[17]

16 T. Simes, *A Military Course for the Government and Conduct of a Battalion* ... (London: privately published, 1777), pp. 217, 227.
17 Bowyer-Bower, 'Some Early Educational Influences', p.7. The reference here is to the First Edition of Simes' *Military Medley* published in Dublin in 1767. There was a second revised edition published in Dublin in 1768 which does not contain this reference (For

In a later work he placed a greater emphasis on the role of the regimental chaplain and, in enumerating his duties, he wrote that '...it would be highly commendable in him if he would pay some attention to the conduct of a regimental school and appoint a non-commissioned officer to act as master who is capable of teaching reading, writing and arithmetic, by whom soldiers and their children should be carefully instructed and a place should be fixed upon for that purpose.'[18]

Simes was not suggesting that the military authorities should take the lead in the provision of schooling in the army, but he was optimistic in expecting that the regimental officers would establish and sustain regimental schools. Other than at a few permanent garrisons, the scattered distribution of the companies and troops of the infantry and cavalry in the 1770s and 1780s, and the constant movement of regiments made it difficult to maintain a regimental school. The disposition of the Foot Guards and Household Cavalry was more favourable and except in wartime remained in London and Westminster with detachments at Windsor. The companies of the foot guards were however dispersed among the numerous stations of the metropolis.[19] Very often the Guards were billeted in taverns and inns, but there were also a few larger stations such as the Tower of London, where it is believed the first regimental school in Great Britain was established by the First Regiment of Foot Guards in 1762.[20]

We do not know how many regimental schools were established and flourished before the outbreak of the wars with France in 1793, but without state aid they would have been modest affairs and their curriculum would have been focused on acquiring the basics of reading, writing and arithmetic and such useful knowledge as mastering accounts and writing reports, returns, parade states, etc. Soldiers with an appetite for further learning and advancement would have been left to their own devices. The Standing Orders of the 10th Prince of Wales Own Light Dragoons issued by the command of His Royal Highness at Guilford in January 1797 recommended corporals to improve and perfect their reading, writing and keeping of accounts. Men of conduct who perfected these skills would be recommended for further promotion irrespective of their seniority in the regiment. There was however no mention of a regimental school.[21]

The pamphleteer William Cobbett was able to read when he enlisted in 1784. He recollected that:

details of Simes' writings see Houlding *Fit for Service*, pp. 218 and n. 147, 148; pp. 219-20 and n. 149, 150.)

18 Simes, A *Military Course*, p. 230.
19 Houlding, *Fit for Service*, pp. 32-33.
20 The National Archives (TNA): WO47/59, Board of Ordnance, Minutes of Surveyor General, Vol.126, January 1762, f.42.
21 Horse Power Museum, *Standing Orders of the 10th Regiment, Prince of Wales Own Light Dragoons* (Guildford: unknown 1797), p.110.

I learned grammar when I was a private soldier on the pay of six pence per day; the edge of my berth, or that of the guard bed was my seat to study in; my knapsack was my bookcase; and a bit of board lying on my lap, was my writing table.

He was subsequently promoted Sergeant–Major and took his discharge with this rank on the return of his regiment, the 54th Foot, from North America in 1791.[22] Other soldiers who possessed an elementary education on enlistment saw that this provided an opportunity to earn a little money from their fellows. Roger Lamb enlisted in the 9th Foot in 1773 and was stationed at Waterford in Ireland where he was put into a mess with a number of other recruits. The recruits' non-commissioned officer spent much of their pay on settling his bills at the local public house and Lamb undertook a little clerking and some private tuition to improve his standard of living. In his memoirs he writes 'I had plenty of writing to do for the various sergeants and corporals, in making reports etc.' and 'I was employed by a sergeant and his wife to teach their son writing and arithmetic.' After transfer to the 25th Foot in North America, Lamb was discharged from the Army in 1783 and made his way to Dublin where he was schoolmaster for over twenty-six years at the Methodist Free School in White Friars Street.[23]

Although Thomas Simes' main purpose in recommending the establishment of a regimental school was the education of soldiers, he suggested that the schoolmaster might also instruct their children. The British Army's first known school for children was at Tangier, when the town came into possession of Charles II as part of the marriage dowry of his Queen, Catherine of Braganza. The Tangier Regiment, later to be known as the 2nd Foot (Queen's Royal Regiment), was raised in 1661 to provide the garrison. It remained there until 1684 when the town was abandoned by the King on the grounds of cost. An entry in the Calendar of State Papers dated 17 April 1675 stated:

Whereas we have thought fit to employ Richard Reynolds Master of Arts and Fellow of Sidney Sussex College in our University of Cambridge in our Service as Schoolmaster in our Towne of Tangier…[24]

22 *Life of William Cobbett* (Anon.,1835), p.56 [Quoted in Bowyer-Bower, *Some Early Educational Influences* p.9 and I. Dyck <oxforddnb.com/view/article/5734> (accessed 2/06/2011).

23 R. Lamb, *Memoirs of His Own Life*, (Dublin: privately published, 1811), p. 67 and D.N. Hagist, 'Unpublished Writings of Roger Lamb', *Journal of the Society for Army Historical Research*, Vol .90 (Summer 2012), pp. 86-88.

24 TNA: Calendar of State Papers, Domestic Series, 1661-78, Entry Book, 47, p. 6.

On 30 December 1676, there were 217 wives and 342 children in the garrison of whom 129 and 173 respectively belonged to the army and these were the source of the garrison's school children.[25]

Thomas Simes was a captain in the Queen's Royal Regiment and it has been assumed that he was describing the current duties of the schoolmaster in his regiment in his various military writings.[26] The Queen's Royal Regiment was a part of the garrison at Gibraltar from 1730 to 1741 and at various stations in Ireland from 1741-65; then in the Isle of Man until 1768, a year after he published the first edition of his *Military Medley* in Dublin. It is possible that some type of regimental school may have been established in the Queen's Royal Regiment during these years. Simes was an early subscriber and thereby a governor to the *Hibernian Society for the Orphans and Children of Soldiers* in Dublin and he ensured that this was prominently featured in the front page of the *Military Medley*. This no doubt was calculated to serve Simes' ambitions for preferment, but he was careful to stress the 'inconvenience' and 'ill consequences' of having too many married soldiers on the strength of a regiment. Soldiers' wives, he argued, were too frequently women of 'abandoned character and behaviour' who often occasioned quarrels, drunkenness, disease, and caused desertions or involved their husbands in debt. He was careful to recommend non-commissioned officers and private men not to marry without the consent of their commanding officer.[27]

Some permanent accommodation for quartering troops was available in ancient fortifications such as Berwick on Tweed, Dover Castle, Tower of London and large barracks established at the ports of embarkation: Portsmouth, Plymouth and Chatham, which by the 1780s had the most extensive facilities in England.[28] Some schooling may have been provided from time to time for soldiers' children at these stations. Where army schools were stablished, it was usually through the charity of individual regimental officers and the schools did not receive any official recognition or public funding. In this respect they were typical of the elementary education provided by charity schools established in Great Britain in the eighteenth century.[29] Governments at this time saw no reason to provide schooling for soldiers' children. There was however one exception in Ireland where the *Hibernian Society for the Orphans and Children of Soldiers* was founded in Dublin in 1765 received a royal charter in 1769 and with funding from the Irish Parliament maintained a school in Phoenix Park from 1770. This Irish charity although not part of the British Army provided exclusively for the orphaned and distressed children of soldiers and in the 19th century it would be transformed into the Royal Hibernian Military School.

25 N.T. St John Williams, Tommy Atkins' Children, The Story of the Education of the Army's Children 1675-1970 (London: Ministry of Defence, 1971), pp. 7-8.
26 St John Williams, *Tommy Atkins' Children*, p. 8
27 T. Simes, *Military Medley* (Dublin: S. Powell, 1768), p. 3.
28 Houlding, *Fit for Service*, p. 40.
29 J. Mokyr, *The Enlightened Economy: An Economic History of Britain 1700-1850* (Yale: Yale University Press, 2009), pp. 232-35.

The 18th century British fiscal state saw no reason to establish a system of elementary schools for serving soldiers or their children and where any schooling was provided, it was the product of individual initiative, and as such was want to be disparate and disorganized. These early attempts to educate soldiers and their children did however have some small influence on the introduction of schools in the Army during the Revolutionary and Napoleonic wars.

2

Crucible of War 1793-1810

Great Britain entered the war with Revolutionary France in 1793, as she did the First and Second World Wars, with a small army that needed to be expanded quickly into a much larger fighting force. Throughout the Revolutionary and Napoleonic Wars, recruitment to the armed forces was a continuous problem and successive British governments struggled to recruit and retain sufficient manpower to meet the needs of the army for the defence of the British Isles against invasion and also for expeditions to the colonies and continental Europe. Until the passing of the Defence Act in 1803 the normal age for enlistment into the Army was 18 years. There is however some evidence that in the first years of the Revolutionary War boys of 16 and 17 years were recruited for general service as private soldiers, provided that they were a minimum of five-foot one inch in height and were expected to grow.[1]

The Army experienced heavy casualties in a number of expeditions in the 1790s and disease wasted away large numbers of troops in campaigns in the West Indies. Sir John Fortescue has estimated that at least 5,000 men perished in Sir Charles Grey's expedition to the West Indies in 1794 and that the fatalities for the army in that theatre alone amounted to some 25,000 men during the years 1794, 1795 and 1796. He concluded that when the casualties in Flanders and elsewhere together with those discharged as unfit for further service are included, 80,000 soldiers were lost to the army. Forty thousand of this number had died. Further casualties followed in the West Indies in 1797-98.[2]

The losses suffered by the army in the expeditions to the West Indies between 1793-97 meant that many battalions returned to Great Britain at little more than cadre strength and had to be re-built. The manpower situation was so desperate that in December 1797 six regiments of Foot on the British Establishment (9th, 16th, 22th, 34th, 55th and 65th) were authorised 'because of the difficulty of obtaining recruits of

---

1 P.J. Haythornthwaite, *The Armies of Wellington* (London: Brockhampton Press 1998), p. 50.
2 J.W. Fortescue, A *History of the British Army*, Vol. IV (East Sussex: Naval and Military Press reprint, 2004), pp. 384, 496, 565.

a proper description' to complete 'from lads, who in the course of two or three years, may attain sufficient size and strength to fulfil the duties of soldiers.'[3] These regiments were allowed to recruit boys under 16 years of age who were healthy and free from physical disability and were at least five foot one inch in height. Each regiment was prohibited from enlisting recruits who were above 18 years of age, and was permitted to retain only six older men per company for the purpose of recruiting and assisting in the instruction of the young recruits.[4]

Field Marshal Frederick Augustus, Duke of York and Albany, C-in-C of the Army at the Horse Guards, provided detailed orders to the commanding officers of the six regiments that the boys were to be well cared for and that they should not carry arms until they had acquired some knowledge of military drill, after which they were to exercise with 'light fusilees', before progressing to carrying the standard issue flintlock.[5] He also suggested that the commanding officers of the regiments should consider 'the expediency of establishing a regimental school, for the instruction of such of [the boys] as discover abilities in the necessary qualifications of reading and writing, with a view of their becoming hereafter, useful and valuable non-commissioned officers.'[6] In making this suggestion the Duke of York was echoing a view that had been increasingly voiced by Thomas Simes and others during the eighteenth century that it would be useful to have some soldiers in each regiment and especially non-commissioned officers who were able to read and write.

The 22nd Foot, which was based at Colchester barracks, sent out eight strong recruiting parties to Bury St Edmunds, Birmingham, and Manchester, and as far afield as Exeter, Berwick upon Tweed, Edinburgh, and Aberdeen. This produced an establishment of some 400 men. The commanding office, Lieutenant Colonel James Mercer, issued a regimental order on 18 December 1797, requesting every officer to assist in implementing the Duke of York's plan and cautioning the NCOs and private soldiers against ill-treating the boys.[7] With regard to the provision of a regimental

3   TNA WO 3/17: f. 321,'Letter from the Commander in Chief to Colonels of regiments', Commander-in-Chief Out-Letters. Although the muster rolls of regiments in the 18th century contain instances of boys enlisting as drummer, below18 years of age, the balance of evidence does not support the theory that drummers were usually young boys. A drummer was a substantive rank, which was filled by men of all ages. (S.M. Baule, 'Drummers in the British Army during the American Revolution', *Journal of the Society of Army Historical Research*, Vol. 86 (Spring 2008), pp. 24-28.

4   TNA WO 3/17: ff. 324-327: 'Letter from the Commander in Chief to Colonels of regiments', Commander-in-Chief Out-Letters.

5   TNA WO 3/17: ff. 322-324: 'Letter from the Commander in Chief to Colonels of regiments', Commander-in-Chief Out-Letters.

6   TNA WO 3/17: f. 324, 'Letter from the Commander in Chief to Colonels of regiments', Commander-in-Chief Out-Letters.

7   Cheshire Military Museum,22nd Regiment of Foot, *Digest of Service*, Vol.1, 18 December 1797.

school, Colonel Mercer appears to have anticipated the Duke of York's order, and on 30th October 1797 he had issued a regimental order:

> The Commanding officer wishing to give every soldier of the 22nd (or Cheshire) Regiment an opportunity to read and write, has directed that a school should be established and open to all persons who are desirous to improve themselves, every necessary articles being provided by the regiment. The school to be under the direction of the Sergeant Major and Regimental Clerk, and to commence on Wednesday 1 November – hours from 6 to 8 in the evening – and to be open during the day to such men who are desirous to improve.[8]

The regiment moved from Colchester to Hampshire in early December 1798 and on 29th December sailed from Gosport to join the garrison at Fort George, Guernsey. Major General Sir Hew Dalrymple (1750-1830) who was the Lieutenant Governor of Guernsey when the regiment moved to the island was impressed with the progress in the boys' military training. He inspected the battalion in 1799 and commented in his inspection report that boys had grown rapidly since they came to the island and despite the difficulty in securing sufficient NCOs who were prepared to treat the boys sympathetically (as requested by the Duke of York in his 1797 Order), he had found them to be well disciplined and unusually well drilled.[9] The records of the 22nd Foot however do not mention a regimental school nor any arrangements for teaching the boys whilst the regiment was stationed in Guernsey.

John Shipp, who had enlisted as a boy in the 22nd Foot at Colchester in 1797, does not mention attending a regimental school in his memoirs, but he was trained as a fifer and drummer. He served in this capacity in the regiment's light company and when the regiment moved to India in 1803 he refers to his company Captain 'who generously undertook to assist me in reading and writing of which I knew very little. After a year's close application, I was so much improved that I was able to keep the books of his company, and his own private accounts.'[10]

The 1797 experiment of enlisting boys was a success and in 1800 the 22nd, 34th and 65th regiments were sent to form part of the garrison at the Cape of Good Hope.[11] In July 1801 the scheme was extended to include the 32nd and 45th regiments of Foot and in December 1804, the second battalions of regiments of the line were directed to add

---

8   22nd Regiment of Foot, *Digest of Service*, Vol.1, 18 December 1797.
9   B. Rigby, *Ever Glorious: The Story of the 22nd (Cheshire) Regiment* (Chester: W.H. Evans, 1982), p.104.
10 John Shipp, C.J. Stranks (ed), *The Path of Glory* (London: Chatto and Windus, 1969), pp. 40-1. Shipp was classed as a Drummer when he arrived in India. He realised that this substantive rank provided little prospect for promotion. He approached his Captain and was granted a transfer into the ranks. He was soon promoted corporal and then sergeant, and subsequently gained a commission in the 65th Foot.
11 TNA WO 379/1: Disposition of the Army 1737-1950.

10 boys not exceeding sixteen years of age to each company. On 8th November 1811 a further circular was issued to the COs of the second battalions of 14 regiments of foot granting them the authority to enlist boys.[12] In each case the Circulars from the Horse Guards repeated the instructions and advice for the treatment of the boys that were included as in the 1797 Circular Letter and the COs were exhorted to establish regimental schools with the object of qualifying some of the boys for future promotion as non-commissioned officers.[13] From 1805 there was an annual recruitment of boys into the regular Army and 18,349 had been enlisted by September 1813, which made up almost 14% of total recruitment to the regular army during these years, excluding the volunteers from the militia.[14]

There is no official record of the number of commanding officers who responded to the Duke of York's exhortations and established schools from their own regimental funds, but there is evidence of a growing appreciation of the importance of an elementary education for enlisted soldiers. Lieutenant Colonel James Thewles in his *Standing Orders for the Royal Irish Dragoon Guards*, published in Dublin in 1797, wrote that the Sergeant-Major 'must make himself as good a penman as possible, and keep regular lists of Sergeants and Corporals, with the rosters for their duties, and the roster of the Privates orderly duties.'[15]

A school for the 95th Foot (later the Rifle Brigade) was established in 1800, for 'the instruction of those who wish to fit themselves for the situation of Non-Commissioned Officers.' NCOs were expected to attend 'when not fully masters of the information which is required for their duties.' They were expected to be able to read, write and have mastered the four rules of arithmetic. The Regimental Standing Orders (School Regulations) explained that riflemen with these skills knowledge of these skills would be more likely to achieve promotion.

The schoolmaster in charge of the school was to be a sergeant of good character and would be appointed after having passed a board of three officers. There were three classes in the school: the first for those learning to read; the second for learning to both read and write and the third and highest class for those learning reading, writing and arithmetic. Particular attention was to be paid to copying reports, rosters, and passes. When there were 20 scholars, the schoolmaster was to be assisted by a corporal. Both these NCOs were exempt from other duties apart from church parades and were under

12   National Army Museum (NAM), Records of the Royal Army Educational Corps, Army Education Army Education before 1846, Box 2212, 'Circulars from Horse Guards to Commanding Officers of regiments'.
13   British Library, Hardwicke Papers, 'Commander in Chief to Colonels of regiments', f. 201-3.
14   House of Commons' Journals, LXIX, 635, quoted in J.W. Fortescue, '*The County Lieutenancies and the Army 1803-1814*', Appendix I, (East Sussex: Naval and Military Press reprint, date unknown).
15   'Standing Orders Royal Dragoon Guards 1797', quoted in: Bowyer-Bower, 'Some Early Educational Influences', pp.5-12.

the immediate direction of the Adjutant and Sergeant Major. The school was open every day and in the evening, excepting Sundays and Saturday evenings. When the Corps was stationed for a period in any one location the quarter master arranged for a school room with coals and candles. A register was kept, and the school was to be visited daily by the senior orderly officer and this was to be confirmed in his report. All officers commanding companies were expected to visit the school and encourage their own men and present prizes to the best scholars from the company's charity fund. The school was to be self-financing: Sergeants were charged 6d per week, Corporals and Buglers 4d and Private Soldiers 3d per week. When the school was not occupied by the men of the regiment, the Schoolmaster was ordered to give instruction to its children at a charge to their parents of 2d per week. The Schoolmaster collected these sums from the company pay sergeants every Saturday evening and was required to pay the Corporal not less than one third of his profits. The Standing Orders looked forward to a regular programme of lectures on military subjects and to the provision of a regimental library, similar to that already established in the 18th Light Dragoons.[16]

The 2nd Battalion of the 25th Regiment of Foot had also established a school and on 17 September 1804 adopted Standing Orders, which were similar to those of the 95th. Boys enlisting in the regiment were ordered to attend, and private soldiers were reminded that 'those who have made the greatest proficiency in their schooling will be the first for promotion.' This school was intended to be self-financing with Sergeants paying 3d, Corporals and Drummers 2d and Privates 1d per week. The rank and file were left in no doubt about the importance which the regiment attached to the school. The Standing Orders explained that Schoolmaster in his official capacity was next in rank to the Sergeant Major and that any NCOs or men who were insolent to him or caused any disturbance in his classes would be punished.[17] These examples were followed by other units: in 1807, Lieutenant Colonel Robert Barclay of the 52nd Foot established a school for NCOs and men with weekly fees to purchase, books, paper and pens and for remunerating the teachers.[18] The Standing Orders for the 81st Foot published in 1808, encouraged the rank and file to attend its regimental school and suggested that they would get greater pleasure from improving their reading and writing instead of wasting time 'lounging around the Barracks.' The Non-Commissioned Officers, the orders continued, would be made more independent and not be 'indebted to others for writing out his orders or making his returns.'[19]

16   NAM, Records of the Royal Army Educational Corps, Army Education before 1846, Box 22125, 'Rifle Brigade School Regulations'.
17   NAM, Records of the Royal Army Educational Corps, Army Education before 1846, Box22125, 'Standing Orders of 25th Regiment of Foot, 1804'.
18   'Notes on the School of 52nd Regiment', *Journal of the Society for Army Historical Research*, Vol. 27 (Summer1949), p. 87.
19   Lancashire Infantry Museum, Standing Orders of 81st Regiment, 1808, p. 35.

In the absence of public funding through the army estimates, these schools were established on the initiative of commanding ófficers and survived through the generosity of the regimental officers, occasional charitable donations from private benefactors, and fees charged to cover the costs of tuition. A good example was the Royal Artillery regimental school that was established in August 1797 by Captain Robbie, with the strong support of Major General Francis Thomas Lloyd, the commandant at Woolwich. The school was opened in a building in what later became the Horse Artillery Square. The Duchess of York subscribed 20 guineas for the purchase of books, and this was followed by subscriptions from all the officers at the Headquarters. Given the bureaucratic complexities of the administration of the British Army in the 18th Century, any official involvement in the management of the school would have been undertaken by the Board of Ordnance. A Sergeant named Dougherty was appointed schoolmaster and the institution was so successful that the regimental history relates that the Board of Ordnance was induced to undertake its management and financial support.[20]

There is evidence that a number of regimental schools were established in the auxiliary forces during the 1800s. The county militias in England and Wales were immediately embodied at the outbreak of hostilities and in Ireland the 1793 Catholic Relief Act paved the way for the establishment of an Irish Militia in the same year. Unlike the English Militia, the Irish Militia was almost totally recruited from volunteers and many men were married and often there were almost as many women and children as there were militiamen when the regiments moved between their various stations.[21] The presence of such large numbers of children was a serious matter and in 1807 a Dublin newspaper (*Faulkner's Journal*) observed:

> [E]very military man who has been engaged in a regimental duty and is acquainted with its interior economy well knows to what low vices the children of soldiers reared in barracks are early addicted and that from the promiscuous intercourse of barrack life they receive and imbibe the most licentious habits.[22]

The potential nuisance when large numbers of children accompanied a unit was a good reason to establish a regimental school. It is thought that Colonel John Blagwell of the Tipperary Militia was the first commanding officer to formally establish a regimental school and his example was followed by other units. In 1810 the commanding officer of the Limerick County Militia thought it proper to establish a school and the regiment's standing orders stated that this was 'in order to open the door to promotion and give every soldier in the Limerick Militia an opportunity

20 Duncan, *History of the Royal Artillery*, p. 82.
21 H. McAnally, *The Irish Militia 1793-1816* (Dublin: Clonmore and Reynolds/Eyre and Spottiswoode, 1949), pp. 267, 277.
22 *Faulkner's Journal*, 10 December 1795.

of pushing forward in the world.' Charitable ladies in Ireland gave money for the education of the children of militiamen and in 1807 the officers of the Cavan Militia undertook a regular subscription to teach 40 boys reading, writing and the common rules of arithmetic. They were also instructed in the '...principles of the Christian religion and the duties of morality.'[23]

This emergence of what was no more than a patchwork of schools in the regiments of the regular army probably owed most to the decision to enlist boys into the infantry, but it was increasingly influenced by the need to ensure that a sufficient number of enlisted men were of a calibre suitable for promotion as NCOs. These factors touched on the more fundamental problem of how the army might be organized to recruit and retain a sufficient number of private soldiers of higher social calibre than had hitherto been the case.

Apart from the county militias that were embodied from 1793, there was no system of conscription into the regular army in Great Britain and Ireland and the forces were recruited by voluntary enlistment. Men and boys enlisted for a variety of reasons: some enlisted for adventure, others were few fugitives from justice, and many enlisted to escape unemployment and financial depredation, but after they had enlisted there was no doubting the hardship of service in the ranks. Although the deaths in battle were comparatively few, enormous numbers of men died or were incapacitated by disease. There was general agreement that service in the regular forces was a career that was likely to attract only the most deprived and desperate members of the lower classes, whereas the western European conscript armies had the advantage of enlisting men from higher classes of society. George Scovell, drawing on his experiences during the Peninsular War, was struck by the contrast between the narrow sections of society dredged up by traditional recruiting methods for the British Army and the high quality of many French recruits who were the product of a properly organized system of conscription. Similar comments were made by Francis Seymour Larpent, Wellington's Judge Advocate General in the Peninsula (1812-14) who thought that in all respects, except their courage, the British were inferior soldiers to the French and Germans.[24]

Ways of attracting a better class of recruits were discussed by senior officers in the Army during the 1800s. General Sir Hew Dalrymple had been impressed by the boys of the 22nd Foot whist serving as Lieutenant Governor and commander of the garrison in Guernsey. In June 1800, Dalrymple wrote to Sir Harry Calvert, the Adjutant General at Horse Guards suggesting a scheme, which he argued would improve the calibre of the rank and file in the infantry.[25] Dalrymple agreed that

23   McAnally, *The Irish Militia*, pp. 205-6.
24   M. Urban, *The Man Who Broke Napoleon's Codes* (London: Faber and Faber, 2002), pp. 257,260; Sir George Larpent.Bart.(ed.), *The Private Journal of Judge Advocate Larpent* (London: Richard Bentley, 1854), Vol. I, pp. 258.
25   Sir Henry Calvert had a remarkable long tenure as Adjutant General serving from 1779-1820.

soldiers were recruited from the worst classes of society and that they received little encouragement to better themselves whilst in the ranks. Furthermore, he observed that each regiment was '...accompanied by a crowd of profligate women whose children imbibed licentiousness at an early age'. In these circumstances it was difficult to 'identify a worthy child of a respectable father.' His recommendation was to establish a school in every regiment, which would take the sons of 'meritorious soldiers, where there would be taught reading, writing and accounts and also the theory behind the duties that soldiers and NCOs were required to perform, whether in the ranks, in barracks or other quarters.' The education would qualify young soldiers with ambition for promotion and would make them excellent NCOs. Because units regularly served overseas, he did not think the school could accompany the regiments and suggested instead that it should be established at the regimental depot. He noted that since 1782 a number of regiments of foot had been given county titles but that their depots were often located elsewhere. He proposed that the depots and their regimental schools be located within the counties with which they were associated. Recruits would be trained at these depots and the unit's wounded and sick solders sent there to recuperate. He argued that a properly organised scheme for the localisation of regiments would, as shown by the example of the county militias, engender a strong esprit d'corps. Men would enlist in their county regiment and remain with it throughout their service. Successive generations of men and boys would be trained and schooled at their county depots. Soldiers with a good and meritorious record of service could be certain that their sons would be admitted to the regimental school, recognised and cared for as 'children of the regiment'.[26]

Although schemes for 'localization' were discussed during the 1800s they remained nothing more than a pious hope. It was unrealistic to expect that governments would propose such a radical scheme of military organization to Parliament at a time when the most pressing need was to secure sufficient manpower of any description for the country's regular army. Instead governments relied more and more on transfers from the militias – with some 110,000 transferring between 1800-13.[27]

Dalrymple did not consider making improvements in the conditions of service for the rank and file, such as arranging for the accommodation and welfare of soldiers' families that might make enlistment a more attractive career. Although Dalrymple subsequently earned notoriety, he never the less was one of the first general officers to advocate an official and publicly funded system of regimental schools throughout the army, in place of one that was reliant upon the commitment of individual commanding officers and the charity of the officers and men of their regiments.

26   Claydon Archives, Papers of Sir Harry Calvert, 9/112/6, 'Letter from Hew Dalrymple to Sir Harry Calvert', 20 June 1800.
27   J.E. Cookson, *The British Armed Nation 1793-1815* (Oxford: Clarendon Press 1997), pp. 118-9.

Moreover, he anticipated that these 'regimental' schools would bring positive benefits for the Army.[28]

28   Sir Hew Dalrymple later earned notoriety when in 1808 he countermanded Sir Arthur Wellesley's orders to pursue the French army after the latter's victory at Vimiero and subsequently agreed to the evacuation of the French forces by the Convention of Cintra. Although he was subsequently promoted General he never held another command in the field.

3

Civilian Schools in Great Britain and Ireland in the 1800s and Their Influence on Army Schools

The small number of schools in the regiments of the British Army in early1800s had been founded on the initiative of commanding officers (albeit with in some cases encouragement from the Horse Guards) who could see that improved literacy in the ranks would bring practical advantages to the military service. The schoolmasters who ran these schools were men already serving in their regiments. The regimental pay rolls do not identify their names, because their emoluments were not paid out of the Army Estimates but came from the fees charged to the soldiers and the parents of the children who attended at the schools. In the case of the 25th Foot, the charges were 3d per week for sergeants and 2d for corporals, drummers and privates; whereas the 95th Foot charged sergeants 6d per day, corporals and buglers 5d per day, privates 3d and children 2d per day.[1] The schoolmasters of these schools had not received any training and their education had probably been gained at one of the charity schools that had been established during the previous century.

Although the charity school movement had lost much of its earlier impetus, many schools survived and continued to provide tens of thousands of children with some elementary education. The majority were for day pupils and most were financed by endowments, subscriptions and charity sermons, although some made a small charge for tuition, which was often beyond the financial resources of the poorer working class families. The most significant development in the education of the children of the poor in England and Wales in the last twenty years of the eighteenth century was the Sunday school movement, which is often associated with Mrs Mary Trimmer (1741-1810) who established a school at Brentford in 1786 and subsequently produced a series of publications for use in Sunday schools. The movement was popular because it enabled children to earn a wage during the week and receive some free instruction on the Sabbath and in consequence attracted the charitable support of both businessmen

1   NAM, Records of the Royal Army Educational Corps, Army Education before 1846, Box 22125, 'Standing Orders of 2/25the Foot 1804'; 'Standings Orders of 95th Foot 1802'.

and philanthropists. Some of the fees collected from the scholars at the regimental schools may have been used to purchase copies of Mrs Trimmer's schoolbooks or similar publications, but otherwise the majority of the early army schoolmasters would have relied upon their own experiences at the charity schools to guide them in the organisation and teaching in their regimental schools.

There were large numbers of poor children in England and Wales who did not receive any elementary education, but the success of the charity day schools and the Sunday schools has been seen as the 'triumph of the voluntary principal', because the state played no part in their foundation or operations.[2] Matters were different in Ireland, where some Protestant schools, such as the Hibernian Society for Soldiers Children's school in Phoenix Park Dublin, had for some years received grants from the Irish Parliament and continued to receive funding from the Westminster Parliament following the Act of Union. A Board of Education in Ireland was established in 1806 to report on these schools and began to consider extending the provision of schooling for the lower classes through a national system of education.[3] Ireland however was a special case and a system of public elementary education was seen as one way of addressing the denominational divisions following the Union (1801), but progress floundered on the disagreements between Catholics and Protestants.

In Scotland something like a national system of elementary education existed on paper. In a series of Acts of the Scottish Privy Council and Parliament in the 17th century, local landowners were taxed in each parish to maintain a school and a suitably qualified master. The influence of the Kirk was also central. Local ministers and presbyteries monitored and inspected standards and ensured that the Bible and the church catechism were the basic texts in the curriculum. This system came under pressure after 1750 with a rising population and parishes often too large for one master to manage. This resulted in an expansion of private fee-paying schools. Full- time schooling even in the parish system was of short duration, with attendance usually starting at seven, lasting no more than a year or two for the poorer scholars and less than four or five for the majority. As in England and Wales attendance fluctuated in rural areas, with numbers falling off in the summer when children were needed for work at the harvest.[4] Where schools were established, the salaries of schoolmasters (who were often boys who had recently left school) were barely enough to live on and were generally less than the earnings of tradesmen and day labourers.[5] The records of

2   M.G. Jones, *The Charity School Movement* (Cambridge: Cambridge University Press, 1938), p. 327.
3   Fourteenth Report of the Commissioners of the Board of Education in Ireland, House of Commons Sessional Papers 1812, passim.
4   T. M. Devine, *The Scottish Nation –A Modern History* (London: Penguin Books 2012), pp. 92-7.
5   Jones, The Charity School Movement, pp. 166-191.

Scottish regiments during the Napoleonic Wars contain instances of schoolmasters who had abandoned their profession and had enlisted as private soldiers.[6]

Although some of the charity day schools in England and Wales had resisted an association with one particular denomination, by 1800 many were in effect Anglican parochial schools, whilst others were non–conformist foundations. The Sunday schools' taught children to read, but their main purpose was religious instruction and they were associated with the established Anglican Church or one of the dissenting denominations. Indeed, in the 1800s education without religion was an alien idea and would have been regarded as anathema in polite society. The purpose of education for the poor was primarily a matter of moral and religious instruction and its guiding spirit was to ensure class discipline and an acceptance of the social order. Schooling for the children of the labouring classes provided an elementary education that was limited to what was considered sufficient and suited to their future stations in life.[7] Reading and writing and even a little arithmetic could be taught, but religious texts formed an essential basis of the instruction, although there were differences of opinion between dissenters and Anglicans and Catholics, about the texts and catechism that should be used and this reinforced the case for denominational schools. There was little enthusiasm in Great Britain for the state becoming involved in the provision of elementary education and very persuasive reasons would be needed to justify abandoning 'the voluntary principal' and establish schools at the taxpayers' expense in the regiments and corps of the Army. Furthermore, any scheme that set up an official system of regimental schools for soldiers' children would have to address the religious basis of its schooling and the type of denominational instruction that should be provided.

The most important developments in provision of elementary education for the lower classes in Great Britain in the 1800s came through the work of Andrew Bell and Joseph Lancaster and their advocacy of schools that were based upon the monitorial system. Schools employing monitors in the classroom had existed in the Eighteenth century and this practice had been adopted at the Hibernian Society's School in Phoenix Park Dublin, but very little is known about the actual classroom teaching at that school. Bell and Lancaster each published detailed proposals for a system of schooling using monitors, which they argued made teaching more efficient and allowed a larger number of pupils to be taught simultaneously at a modest cost. They were both effective publicists and succeeded in attracting influential support for the reorganisation of existing charity schools and new schools were founded based upon their teaching methods. The work of Bell and Lancaster stimulated an interest in the

6   Kings Own Scottish Borderers Regimental Museum, Miscellaneous Returns Book of the 25th Foot, 1811-1817.
7   Jones, The Charity School Movement, pp. 166-91. Elementary Education should not be confused with primary education, which in its modern day usage means the instruction in the knowledge and skills required as a foundation for progression to secondary and higher education.

possibilities of elementary education for the lower classes and significantly influenced the development of schooling in the British Army.

Andrew Bell (1753-1832) was born in St. Andrews Scotland to a well-educated middle-class family and graduated from St Andrews University aged 21, with prizes and impressive testimonials. After working as a private tutor in Virginia and London, he decided to enter the Church of England, was ordained as a priest in 1785 and moved to be curate in charge of the small Episcopal chapel in Leith near Edinburgh. He was encouraged to seek more remunerative employment in India and sailed for Calcutta (Kolkata) in February 1787, but he landed instead at Madras (Chennai) where he stayed for ten years. Influential contacts in Great Britain and locally gained him highly paid chaplaincies to the King's regiments stationed at Fort St. George and the East India Company's 4th Regiment of European infantry.[8]

In 1789 the East India Company opened a Male Orphan Asylum at Egmore Redoubt, Madras for the orphaned, illegitimate, and abandoned sons of European soldiers and invited Andrew Bell to draw up governing regulations and become its superintendent. He accepted the post and set about constructing a system that involved every aspect of the children's welfare and was as much concerned with character development as with scholastic achievement. All pupils were instructed in the Anglican faith and, working from the Society for the Propagation of Christian Knowledge (SPCK) textbooks, were trained to leave the school literate, numerate, honest and prepared for apprenticeship to a trade. The hall mark of his method was what became known as the 'Madras system'. This he claimed was inspired by a chance encounter with some children who were teaching younger ones the alphabet by drawing in sand on the seashore. It however would appear that the pedagogical techniques observed by Bell had already been developed in Madras. Mrs Eliza Fay, in a letter to friends in England whilst she was living in Madras in April 1780, related that school boys were taught to write in sand and that this saved on writing materials and enabled a number of boys to be taught at the same time. Mrs Fay also recorded that pebbles were used for teaching arithmetic and that in every respect the schooling of boys in Madras was undertaken at very little cost.[9]

Whatever his inspiration, Andrew Bell used trays of sand at the Male Orphan Asylum and the brighter pupils in each class were designated as assistant teachers or monitors. They were placed in charge of instructing a small group of pupils, who learned more quickly from the monitors, than was the case in a much larger class under the direction of an adult teacher. The method was successfully applied using syllabic reading to learn simple words with the aid of spelling cards suspended from the classroom ceiling. Bell never claimed to have invented the monitorial system, but he built on the practice of using ushers (boys who supervised the conduct and preserved order amongst younger boys) in other British schools in India and in the larger charity

8   Jane Blackie <www.oxforddnb.com/view/article1995> (accessed 30 July 2007).
9   E. Fay, *Original Letters from India* (London: The Hogarth Press, 1986), p. 167.

schools in Great Britain. This solved Bell's immediate problem of securing sufficient able and well-motivated teachers for the Asylum in Madras and demonstrated that a school employing one or two teachers and mobilising its more proficient pupils as monitors could successfully educate several hundred pupils.

Over the next few years Bell refined the Madras system to include a structured hierarchy of monitors, with small payments being made to the older and senior monitors. Pupils were grouped by ability and not by age and each child moved in and out of different 'monitorial' classes according to their progress. Bell emphasised the importance of rewards rather than punishment and pupils were encouraged to emulate other scholars' achievements, whilst miscreants were dealt with by being required to complete extra work and by a withdrawal of privileges.[10]

Although Bell's methods were criticised, visitors to the Madras asylum were impressed and when he returned to England in 1796, he produced a report explaining his achievements at the asylum. This report published in 1797 was entitled: *An experiment in education made at the Male Asylum in Madras, suggesting a system by which a family may teach itself under the superintendence of the master or parent* and 1000 copies were printed and circulated at his own expense. The publication was a great success and in the following years the Madras System was introduced in a number of charity day schools and Sunday schools. In 1801 Bell accepted the position of rector of Swanage, Dorset and set to work training monitors in a local school. In 1805 he published a more detailed edition of his *An experiment in education* and sent 2000 copies to the Archbishop of Canterbury. In the following year Bell was granted a two year leave of absence to visit any Anglican Church of England parish which needed help in reforming its parochial schools.[11]

Andrew Bell (1753-1832) by; after Charles Turner; William Owen. (© National Portrait Gallery, London)

10   Jane Blackie <www.oxforddnb.com/view/article1995> (accessed 30 July 2007).
11   Jane Blackie <www.oxforddnb.com/view/article1995> (accessed 30 July 2007).

Joseph Lancaster (1778-1838) by John Hazlitt.
(© National Portrait Gallery, London)

Joseph Lancaster (1778-1838) was the son of a former soldier working as a cane sieve maker in Southwark, South London. His father was a zealous non-conformist and Joseph probably received an elementary education at a local dissenting charity school. As a young man he joined the Society of Friends (better known as the Quakers) and in around 1798 after working as an assistant in local schools, he set up a day school that charged modest fees. He secured financial help from local sympathisers and fellow Quakers including Elizabeth Fry, and around 1803 he established a free school in a large building near Borough Road Southwark, advertising free instruction to those who could not afford to pay fees.[12] Before long the number of children seeking admission became overwhelming and to deal with the cost of employing a large number of teaching assistants, he adopted the method whereby older boys, who he called 'monitors' and led by a monitor general, taught the younger children under the supervision of a schoolmaster. This enabled Lancaster to create an enormous free school at Borough Road consisting of 1,000 children, in which the whole system of tuition was almost entirely conducted by the boys. He also reduced expenses by using sand trays and slates instead of writing books and sheets of paper pasted on the walls to reduce the need for reading books. Groups of children, under the control of a monitor, learned the alphabet by repeating simple words and the basis of arithmetic by practising figures. The better monitors and pupils were awarded silver-plated badges worn on their caps or suspended by chains. An elaborate system of reward, including toys and small amounts of money, encouraged diligence. Whilst disruptive behaviour and failure were dealt with by humiliating penalties designed to expose the child to the ridicule of his fellows.[13]

In terms of pedagogy there was little of significant difference between the Madras and Lancastrians systems and both depended on mechanical and rigid regimentation

12   D. Salmon, *Joseph Lancaster* (London; Longmans & Co., 1904), pp.1-4.
13   Salmon, *Joseph Lancaster*, pp. 7-11; G.F. Bartle <www.oxforddnb.com/view/article 15963> (accessed 25 May 2011).

in the classroom. In each the essential was a large room, with desks around the walls for writing lessons and a floor space chalked out into squares, in which the children stood in classes for their lessons. In the Borough Road school eight to ten children formed a class that was placed in the charge of a monitor. Under the 'Madras Plan' the assistant teachers, whose age ranged from 11 to 14 years, were aided by younger boys whose ages might be anything between seven and eleven years to teach and discipline from 24 to 36 children. The teaching methods employed by Bell and Lancaster in the classroom showed little advance on those of the Eighteenth century schoolmaster except that the daily instruction was divided into a number of short lessons. The approach was based on memory and learning by rote. The content and meaning of a passage that was being read or written, or the concept of the numbers in arithmetical calculations, was not the concern of the monitors and teaching assistants. Both systems however were cheap and offered a solution to the difficulty of financing and staffing day schools for the poor.[14]

Lancaster set about proclaiming the cheapness and effectiveness of his system and in 1803 published the first edition of *Improvements in Education as it Respects the Industrious Classes of the Community*. The book was well subscribed, and the Borough Road School soon attracted eminent and influential visitors many of whom donated funds to support its work. The climax of this interest and support came in 1805 when Lancaster was given an audience by King George III, who congratulated him on his achievements and subscribed £100 and subscriptions followed from other members of the royal family. Lancaster was not known for his modesty and his growing fame and royal patronage encouraged him to envisage the founding of monitorial schools throughout the country based on what he now called the 'Royal Free School' in Borough Road. He also established a series of costly educational ventures associated with the Southwark school and embarked on a number of extravagant tours around the country to publicise the merits of his system. Lancaster soon found himself in debt and the financial position of his school in Borough Road became increasingly precarious.[15]

More worrying for Lancaster was that despite royal approbation, his scheme began to attract increasingly vocal opposition from members of the Anglican Church. He had opened his school on Borough Road to children of all religious denominations and although the bible was read diligently, no specific denominational religious instruction was given. At first members of the Anglican clergy made donations to the School, especially as it had received royal patronage. This support changed to opposition when Sarah Trimmer visited the Borough Road School and began a campaign to discredit Lancaster's work and advocate the adoption of Bell's scheme. She attacked Lancaster's methods of rewards and complained that awarding badges and medals gave the children ideas above their station in life. She also accused him of

14   Jones, *The Charity School Movement*, p. 336
15   G.F. Bartle <www.oxforddnb.com/view/article15963> (accessed 25 May 2011).

basing his monitorial scheme on Andrew Bell's Madras System, which was starting to gain support within the Anglican Church.

Lancaster in the first edition of *Improvements in Education as it Respects the Industrious Classes of the Community* had acknowledged the influence of Bell's work on his own system and in December 1804 he had a cordial meeting with Bell at Swanage. Bell however declined to subscribe to Lancaster's *Improvements in Education as it Respects the Industrious Classes of the Community*", possibly because it did not include the teaching of the Anglican catechism.[16] Sarah Trimmer's main objection was that she thought that Lancaster's non-denominational approach to religious instruction would weaken the position of the established Anglican Church. Although King George III had told Lancaster that: 'It is my wish that every poor child in my dominions is taught to read the Holy Scriptures' and this was displayed in large letters in the school room at Borough Road, there were many, especially amongst Tories in Parliament, who were suspicious of giving education to the labouring classes.[17] They feared it might encourage challenges to the existing social order and encourage children '...to read seditious pamphlets, vicious books and publications against Christianity; it would render them insolent to their superiors.'[18] At the very least to avoid these dangers an elementary education for the poor must include instruction in the Anglican catechism. Trimmer saw Bell's system as a way of combatting Lancaster's dangerous liberalism, which she thought of as inimical to the interests of the established church.[19]

Predictably this Anglican onslaught provoked a response from non-conformists and advocates of non-denominational education and support for Bell and Lancaster became increasingly polarised on denominational and party-political lines. The Whig Edinburgh Review publishing a powerful defence of Lancaster and his system, whilst the Tory Quarterly Review championed Bell. A catalyst for what was now becoming a feud between the supporters of Bell and Lancaster was Samuel Whitbread's unsuccessful motions in the House of Commons in February 1807 for the reform of the English poor laws, in which he advocated parochial schools based upon Lancaster's system. It has been suggested that Bell resented Lancaster's royal patronage and he became increasingly assertive, advocating his own the Madras System in opposition to Lancaster's schools. Bell was successful in securing the support of the senior bishops in the Church of England and Anglican day and Sunday schools based on the Madras System spread across England and Wales and Ireland.[20]

In 1808 a small committee was formed to raise money to pay off Lancaster's debts and put the finances of Borough Road on a sound basis. The most effective member of this group was William Allen, a wealthy manufacturing chemist and Quaker

---

16   G.F. Bartle <www.oxforddnb.com/view/article15963> (accessed 25 May 2011).
17   G.F. Bartle <www.oxforddnb.com/view/article15963> (accessed 25 May 2011).
18   David Giddy MP when opposing Samuel Whitbread's motions to reform the Poor Law in the House of Commons in February 1807. Hansard, 1st Series, Vol. IX, pp. 798-806.
19   Salmon, *Joseph Lancaster*, p. 25.
20   Jane Blackie <www.oxforddnb.com/view/article1995> (accessed 30 July 2007).

philanthropist, who became treasurer to the committee and had influential friends, including the Royal Dukes of Kent and Sussex - brothers to the C-in-C, the Duke of York.

The reputation of the Borough Road School and Lancaster's success in publicising his methods increased the need for funds to train teachers in his system at the School and in 1810 the committee was enlarged under the presidency of Field Marshall, Edward Duke of Kent and included enthusiasts for popular education such as James Mill, Henry Brougham and Samuel Whitbread. This enlarged committee called itself the *Royal Lancastrian Institution for the Education of the Poor of Every Religious Persuasion* and in 1814 was re-named the British and Foreign School Society.[21] Money soon flowed into the charity and 95 new schools were established on a non-denominational basis in two years.

The Church of England establishment responded by founding the *National Society for the Education of the Poor in the Principles of the Christian Church* in October 1811 to promote the teaching of the Anglican catechism through the Madras System in its affiliated schools. The Prince Regent, the Duke of York, and General Sir Harry Calvert [the Army's Adjutant General] were early subscribers and Andrew Bell was co-opted onto the Society's managing committee. The Society was very successful and new schools were established and many old charity schools, such as those in Marylebone and Whitechapel in London, changed their names and became 'National Schools'. By 1813 the National Society claimed some 40,484 children in 230 schools.[22]

The British and Foreign and the National Society both played an important part in the promoting elementary education for the lower classes during the Nineteenth century. The National Society was far the most successful of the voluntary bodies and by the time of Bell's death in 1832 involved over 12,000 schools and claimed 346,000 pupils in the United Kingdom and its colonies.[23]

It would have been surprising if Bell's and Lancaster's systems had not attracted the attention of those senior officers in the British Army who were considering establishing schools for young soldiers and soldiers' children. In 1801 the British Government decided to follow the example of the Hibernian Society for Soldier's children in Dublin and open a Royal Military Asylum (RMA) for soldiers' children based at Chelsea near London. It has been suggested that Lancaster's methods were first adopted at the Royal Military Asylum when it was opened in 1803.[24]

Lancaster had already published the first edition of his *Improvements in Education etc.*in that year and it is possible that there had been some contact between RMA

21 G.F. Bartle <www.oxforddnb.com/view/article15963> (accessed 25 May 2011).
22 *First Report of the National Society for the Education of the Poor etc.* (London, 1812), pp. 6, 13, 25; *Second Report of the National Society* (London, 1814), p. 7.
23 Jane Blackie <www.oxforddnb.com/view/article1995> (accessed 30 July 2007).
24 A.W. Cockerill, Sons of the Brave –The Story of Boy Soldiers (London: Secker and Warburg, 1984), p. 70; A.W. Cockerill, The Charity of Mars: a history of the Royal Military Asylum (Cobourg, Ontario: Black Cat Press 2002), p. 83.

and the Borough Road School, but there is no mention of this in the Commissioners' Minute or Letter Books.[25] King George III and the Duke of York had made a subscription to support the Borough Road School, but there is no mention by any of Joseph Lancaster's biographers that Duke of York had any further involvement in Lancaster's project.[26] It is the case that some of Lancaster's curious methods of punishing and shaming idlers and malcontents, such as putting a log around the boys' necks or legs and confining boys in a cage or basket suspended from the roof, were adopted at the Royal Military Asylum and were still in use when Professor Henry Mosley inspected the Asylum at the request of the War Office in 1846.[27] This does not mean that Lancaster's methods were adopted in their entirety in the early years at Chelsea. The Commissioners had been happy to cherry pick the regulations of the Hibernian Society's Dublin School and Christ's Hospital in England in designing the interior economy of the Asylum and they might have borrowed selectively from Lancaster's procedures at Borough Road. Christ's Hospital employed ushers to assist the schoolmaster and the Hibernian School operated its own variant of the monitorial system, with ushers and assistant ushers acting as monitors.[28] Furthermore, the regulations of the Royal Military Asylum and the charter establishing the Hibernian Society in Dublin School required their children to be instructed in the catechism of the Church of England and to attend Anglican worship on the Sabbath. This would have favoured the adoption of Bell's system.

Whatever the particular system of instruction that was used in the first years at the Military Asylum, the Commissioners' Minute Book records that Andrew Bell's system was well established at the institution in 1808.[29] Sarah Trimmer had commenced her attack on Joseph Lancaster's scheme in a pamphlet in 1805 and called on Anglicans to insist on the inclusion of teaching of the Church in any programme of elementary education. The Duke of York was a staunch supporter of the Anglican Church and would have been very sympathetic to this suggestion. Trimmer had entered into correspondence with Andrew Bell in 1805 and it has been suggested that she encouraged him to press for the adoption of the Madras System by all Anglican

25   The Royal Military Asylum was established by Royal Warrant and was governed by the Board of Commissioners appointed by the Crown. The Commissioners' Minute and Letter Books are preserved in the UK National Archines (TNA WO 143).

26   A.C.T. White in *The Story of Army Education*, states that the Duke of York joined 'Lancaster's committee', but he does not identify the purpose of this committee or cite a reference or source.

27   TNA WO 43/796: 'Chelsea Royal Military Asylum, Decision to upgrade following critical report by Privy Council', pp. 6-8.

28   TNA WO 143/6: Minutes of H M Commissioners of the RMA, 14 December1802; Clarke, *A New History Royal Hibernian Military School*, p. 124.

29   TNA WO 143/6: Minutes H M Commissioners of the RMA, 30 March 1808, 24 December 1808, 20 February 1809. See also: Andrew Bell, *An Analysis of the Experiment in Education, made at Egmore, near Madras*, Third Edition (London: Cadell and Davies, 1808).

Schools throughout the country.[30] The regulations at the Military Asylum required the Chaplain to instruct the children in the Anglican catechism and this was an integral part of the curriculum in Bell's Madras System. Moreover, the commissioners had decided to appoint one sergeant instructor for every fifty boys and after allowing for a number of monitors and teaching assistants selected from the older boys, this closely approximated to the staffing numbers recommended in Bell's system.

Royal Military Asylum, Chelsea c. 1860. From 1909 it was known as the Duke of York's Headquarters of the Territorial Army and now houses an art gallery. (Open Source)

J.M.D. Meiklejohn, who published a biography of Bell in 1881, states that Bell was invited to remodel the RMA in 1808 and in that year Bell first makes a reference to the RMA in his third edition of *An Analysis of the Experiment in Education.*[31] Robert Southey's 1844 biography of the Rev Andrew Bell gives more detail of the circumstances surrounding the introduction of the Madras System at the Military Asylum Early in 1807, Bell received a request from the Rev George Clark, the Chaplain and Superintendent of Morals at the RMA, to assist in re-modelling the pedagogy at the Asylum. Bell had previously visited the Asylum at the request of Dr Sutton,

30   Jane Blacke <www.oxforddnb.com/view/article1995> (accessed 30 July2007; G.F. Bartle <www.oxforddnb.com/view/article15963> (accessed 30 July 2007).
31   Bell, An Analysis of the Experiment in Education, p. 295; E.A. Smith, 'The Army Schoolmaster and the Development of Elementary Education in the Army,1812-1920', PhD Thesis: London Institute of Education, University of London, pp. 48-9.

the Archbishop of Canterbury, and in April 1807 made a further visit to Chelsea to evaluate the system then in place and to propose changes that would make the schooling 'more lenient' and 'more effectual.' Bell took up residence in Sloane Square from August 1807and with the full co-operation of the staff and the encouragement of the Commissioners he established the Madras System at the RMA. Towards the end of October 1807, the work was completed and Mathew Lewis, the Deputy under Secretary at War and an RMA Commissioner wrote to Bell expressing his satisfaction and his hope that the remodelled RMA would become a public exemplar of the benefits of the Madras System. Bell was about to return to his parish in Swanage, when he was recalled to show the Duke of York the method of instruction that he had established at Chelsea.[32]

The Duke was impressed with the operation of Bell's system at the RMA Chelsea and in due course would ensure that it was adopted in regimental schools throughout the Army.

Bell was certainly satisfied with his work at the RMA and he included some details of the system he had introduced at Chelsea in his third edition of the *Experiment in Education* and praised the Military Asylum as an innovative institution, which combined the features of a charity and an industrial school:

> But the grandest, most interesting and affecting spectacle of the perfect union of education and industry is the Royal Military Asylum at Chelsea. There tailors and the shoemakers are in their shops as well as in school, arranged into classes, and have their teachers on the Madras System.[33]

Bell soon suggested that any charity schools that were considering adopting the Madras System might be able to secure experienced boys from Chelsea to be employed as monitors. On 30 March 1808, the Commissioners agreed to a request from the Bishop of Durham for the services of a boy to accompany Dr Bell, who was leaving London in order to establish to large schools in the parishes of Sunderland and Bishop Wearmouth, County Durham. A similar request was considered from Lord Spencer on 24th December 1808 for a boy capable of teaching at a school that was being established on Bell's system near Northampton. A boy, Thomas Bunny, was selected and sent to lodge with the schoolmaster and his appointment was so successful, that the following February a request was received from the Rector of Lutterworth in Leicestershire for Bunny to teach at his parochial school.[34]

32   R. Southey, *The Life of the Rev. Andrew Bell* (London: John Murray, 1844), Vol. 2, pp. 180-190.

33   Bell, *An Analysis of the Experiment in Education*, p. 295.

34   TNA WO 143/6: Minutes of H M Commissioners of the RMA, 30th March 1808, 24th December 1808, 20th February 1809.

In 1811 two RMA boys were sent to Lisbon, Portugal to assist in forming a school that was being formed on Dr Bell's principles for children of soldiers of the British Army. This was probably the garrison school established in the same year by Wellington at Belem to educate soldiers' children who had become something of a nuisance in the encampments around Lisbon. The RMA commissioners' minutes however do not record any similar requests from commanding officers in the United Kingdom for boys to assist in their regimental schools.[35]

From about 1810, some interest was developing within the British Army about the possibilities of the Lancastrian Schools. We have seen that the Duke of Kent had become closely involved with the *Royal Lancastrian Institution* and he was instrumental in establishing a school for young soldiers and the children of soldiers in the 4th Battalion of the Royals (1st Regiment of Foot), of which he was Colonel. Kent arranged for one of the battalion's sergeants to spend some time at the Borough Road school to be trained in Lancaster's system and he was subsequently placed in charge of the regimental school that had been established whilst the battalion was stationed from July 1809 to July 1810 at Malden in Essex. The school remained with the battalion when it moved to Dunbar in Scotland. A letter written in 1849 by a retired officer of the regiment recalled that Joseph Lancaster came from London to examine the pupils and was perfectly satisfied with their progress.[36] This may refer to the occasion when 12 of the children with their schoolmaster travelled to Edinburgh and were examined by Lancaster before members of the university, the magistrates, and eighteen-hundred members of the public. Lancaster argued at that occasion that regimental schools were particularly useful for the education of existing and prospective Non–Commissioned Officers.[37] An inspection return dated 16th October 1810, whilst the battalion was stationed at Dunbar, recorded that the 77 boys in the battalion attended the school. The general officer conducting the half-yearly inspections in the military district wrote that: 'I cannot help stating my admiration of a school Lieutenant Colonel McLeod [the battalion's commanding officer] has established according to Mr Lancaster's Plan by which all his men and boys are instructed in reading, writing and arithmetic in a simple and easy manner and from which source had been drawn some of the best NCOs. It would be an excellent plan for all second battalions.'[38] When the

35   TNA WO 143/6: Minutes of H M Commissioners of the RMA, 20 November 1811; Wellington, 'General Orders, 25th February and 8 May 1812', quoted in St John Williams, *Tommy Atkin's Children*, p. 9.

36   M. Dickson, *Teacher Extraordinary: Joseph Lancaster 1178-1838* (Lewes Sussex: Privately Published 1986), p. 124; J.C. Leask and H.M Mcmance, *The Records of the Royal Scots* (Dublin: Alexander Thom & Co., 1915), p. 344; A.E. Watts, 'An Early Instance of Civilian Assistance to Army Education', *Journal of the Royal Army Educational Corps*, Vol. XXIV, No.3, September 1950, pp. 106-10.

37   Charles Dupin, *A View of the History and Actual State of the State of the Military Forces of Great Britain* (London: John Murray, 1822), pp. 50-51.

38   Leask and Mcmance, *The Records of the Royal Scots*, p. 344.

battalion moved to Stirling in February 1811 the school was at the request of the town magistrates quartered in the Guildhall of Stirling Castle and many of the town's children were also allowed to attend. The 4th Battalion of the Royals was serving as the regiment's depot battalion and Lancaster is recorded as claiming that nearly 800 youths were successfully educated at the regimental school in the two years to May 1811, with the Duke of Kent awarding silver medals to deserving pupils.[39] The regimental history records that the school attained such a high reputation that several other regiments applied for and obtained a number of its best scholars as teachers.[40]

Around the same time Joseph Lancaster visited Ireland in order to promote the Lancastrian system. In June 1810 he presented a memorial to the Duke of Richmond, the Lord Lieutenant in Ireland, seeking his patronage for establishing schools in the country on the Lancastrian plan and suggesting that an experimental school for soldiers' children should be established at the Royal Barracks in Dublin. In his memorial he quoted the success of the 4th Royal's school and explained that the system of instruction was so simple that young drummers could be quickly instructed as teachers and that when the battalion had moved from Essex to Dunbar its desks and equipment had been easily conveyed with its baggage.[41] The Lord Lieutenant asked for the views of the Commander of the Forces in Ireland, General the Earl of Harrington, on Lancaster's proposal. Harrington replied '…that it would be very desirable to extend the means of education to the children of soldiers, as well as to each of the men as would be willing to avail them of it.' He thought that the opening of a school at the Royal Barracks in Dublin would be the best way of giving Joseph Lancaster's system a fair trial.[42] Lancaster also received inquiries from the Royal Artillery's depot at Woolwich asking whether assistance could be provided to set up a school for young soldiers and soldiers' children and similar requests were received from the cavalry barracks at Maidstone and Chelmsford.[43]

By 1811 something of a groundswell was developing in the Army in favour of the Lancastrian system. The simple and mechanical nature of the model Lancastrian School was likely to appeal to the military mind. An article in the *Philanthropist* periodical in 1811 explained that: 'In the Royal Free School, at Borough Road, a little boy of twelve or thirteen years of age often commands the whole school, and that with the same ease to himself, and with equal obedience from the many hundred children of which the school is composed, as a military officer would experience with

---

39   Dupin, *A View of the History and Actual State of the State of the Military* Forces, pp. 50-51.
40   Leask and Mcmance, *The Records of the Royal Scots*, p. 344.
41   Dickson, *Teacher Extraordinary*, p. 124.
42   National Library of Ireland (NLI), The Kilmainham Papers, 'Letter from Harrington to Lancaster', MS1023, f442- 3. Harrington was a Commissioner of the RMA, but he had not attended any of the Board of Commissioners' meetings since April 1806.
43   Dickson, *Teacher Extraordinary*, p. 124. It is not certain whether this referred to a new school or a reorganisation of the school that had been established at the Woolwich depot in 1797.

a body of well-disciplined troops; the firmness, promptness and decision on military order are interwoven in the school discipline.[44] Furthermore Lancaster's insistence on a Christian education with the Bible as a text book, but without denominational bias, had a certain practical appeal for commanding officers in an army that enlisted Anglicans, Presbyterians, Non-conformists and an increasing number of Irish Catholics.

The C-in-C, the Duke of York, however, had other ideas and in 1811 he persuaded Spencer Perceval's Tory government to introduce a uniform system of regimental schools at public expense throughout the Army and a series of orders from the War Office and the Horse Guards soon followed making it clear that the instruction in these schools would be conducted according to Rev Dr Andrew Bell's system.

44   Anon. "On the Importance of Promoting the General Education of the Poor", *The Philanthropist* (London, 1811).

4

A School for Every Regiment and Corps

On 26th August 1811, the C-in-C, Frederick Duke of York wrote to Viscount Palmerston the Secretary at War, requesting him to submit a proposal to the Lord Commissioners of the Treasury for the establishment of regimental schools for 'the education of young soldiers and soldiers' children.'[1] He proposed the appointment of a schoolmaster sergeant in each battalion, at the rate of pay then attached to a paymaster's clerk, to instruct enlisted boys and soldiers' children free of charge. He thought that it would be necessary to appropriate a room in each barracks for the use of the school, with an amount of fuel in the winter months and to allow a sum for each regiment for stationery and books. The expense he argued would be trifling compared with the benefits that would follow for the service. The Duke concluded with a request that: 'as the future discipline of the service' was much involved 'in the importance of this subject', he would be glad to receive the Lord Commissioners decision, 'in order that in the event of their approval' he could 'take the earliest opportunity of carrying the necessary arrangements into execution.'[2]

In emphasising the important role that regimental schools could play in the 'future discipline of the service', York was most probably alluding to the provision of an elementary education for enlisted boys and the sons of soldiers that would qualify them to be future non-commissioned officers. The Duke's successive schemes for enlisting boys in a designated number of line regiments, starting in 1797, had envisaged that a proportion of these boys would be trained up as NCOs and he had encouraged commanding officers to establish regimental schools that would give boys and young soldiers an elementary education. In December 1804 the commanding officers of the second battalion of regiments of the line had been directed to add ten boys not exceeding sixteen of age to each company and were similarly exhorted to

1   The Prime Minister, Spencer Percival, was the First Lord Commissioner of the Treasury and therefore York was seeking the approval of the British Government for his proposals.
2   J.H, Lefroy, *Report on the Regimental and Garrison Schools of the Army* (London: War Office, 1859), Appendix I.

establish regimental schools (See Chapter 2). In November 1808, a letter was sent by the Adjutant General to the commanding offices of fourteen regiments of Foot suggesting the establishing of regimental schools 'for the instruction of boys in order to prepare them as future NCOs.'[3] The Duke of York however could only exhort the commanding officers to establish schools, which in the absence of a vote under the Army Estimates, had to be financed from regimental funds and donations from the officers and men. It was left to the commanding officer and his subordinates to decide on the curriculum, the methods of instruction and the general organisation of their schools and although there were similarities in the subsequent regimental standing orders establishing schools, there was no guarantee that a school established in particular regiment would survive and continue to provide effective instruction.

There was an increasing concern throughout the war about the quality of enlisted men and the difficulty of finding soldiers suitable for promotion and there were discussions within the military departments and amongst the general officers about how the Army might attract a better class of recruit. Much of the debate centred on the merits of short term as opposed to lifetime enlistment, but there was general agreement that the Army would benefit from enlisted men with an education that would make them useful non-commissioned officers.[4]

The Duke of York was an opponent of short-term service and strongly supported enlistment for life.[5] It may have been that York considered regimental schools for soldiers' children as one of a number of improvements that might encourage and support long term enlistment. However, in March 1809 he resigned as C-in-C because of the 'Mrs Clarke affair'. Mary Ann Clarke had been York's mistress since 1802, but in 1806 he became aware that she was taking bribes in exchange for securing the Duke's patronage for military and civil preferment. The Duke ended the affair, but the matter was raised in Parliament. Although, he was cleared of any wrong doing by a committee of inquiry, he was censured for his association with Mrs. Clarke and in 1809 resigned as C-in-C and did not resume the post until May 1811. It is significant that York approached the Government to establish regimental schools in August 1811, shortly after he had returned to the Horse Guards.

The annual inflow of boy soldiers into the regular Army had continued during the Duke of York's absence and it is estimated that from 1809 to September 1811, 5,713 boys enlisted, which was a little over 21percent of the total recruitment excluding

3   NAM, Records of the Royal Army Educational Corps, Army Education before 1846, Box 22125, 'Circular Letter to Commanding Officers November 1808'.
4   For the benefits of short term enlistment in securing a better class of recruits, with the best of them being promoted as NCOs see: BL, Windham Papers Add. MS37880 'Letter from John Gaspard Le Marchant to William Windham', 5 February1801,ff. 62-86. For the debate in 1804 amongst the generals on the merits of short term enlistment and a long service professional army. See TNA WO 1/ 628/902/209-39 and WO 1/ 902/9-139.
5   For York's opposition to short term enlistments. See: TNA WO 1/ 628/902/209/39.

volunteers from the militia.[6] A further 2,419 boys were enrolled in the English, Scottish and Irish Militias from May 1809 to October 1813.[7] There were also large numbers of soldiers' children accompanying the regular and militia regiments. A return compiled by the Adjutant General's Office, dated 12 January 1811, covering 27 line battalions and three infantry depots records that 14,427 NCOs and men were accompanied by 1,816 women and 1,595 children of which 787 were boys.[8] Embarkation Returns from three English Militia regiments returning from Ireland in October record that 1,419 officers and men were accompanied by 251 women and 274 children.[9]

The Royal Military Asylum at Chelsea had opened in 1803 and soon began to prove a useful source of recruits for the army. The first boys were discharged from Royal Military Asylum into the army in 1806 and the Commissioners ordered that, in conformity with a letter from the Deputy Secretary at War, the Commandant was to make a quarterly return of the boys volunteering for the army.[10] The Commissioners later placed on record that up to 16 September 1812, 219 boys had volunteered, and in the same year the Commissioners of Military Enquiry recorded that nearly half of the boys discharged since the Asylum was opened had volunteered for the army and that it was 'understood that many of those who go out to as apprentices afterwards enlist.' A comprehensive system of regimental schools might be expected to produce similar numbers of educated boys for the Army.[11]

As was the case at the Military Asylum, a proportion of the boys attending regimental schools might decide to follow their fathers and enlist. In short by giving an education both to enlisted boy soldiers and the sons of serving soldiers, a school in every regiment and corps could be expected to produce a steady supply of future NCOs, support long term enlistment, whilst also usefully occupying children who otherwise might be a nuisance around the barracks.

Spencer Perceval's government responded positively to York's request and the military departments began drawing arrangements for establishing and managing a uniform system of regimental schools. On 14th November 1811, the Adjutant General, Sir Harry Calvert, sent a circular letter to the Colonels, or Commanding Officers of Regiments of the Regular Army and the Militia stating that he had been ordered by the C-in-C to inform them, that the government was contemplating establishing regimental schools for the care and instruction of the children of Non-Commissioned

---

6   J.W. Fortescue, *The County Lieutenancies and the Army1803-1814*, Appendix 1 (East Sussex: Naval and Military Press, no date).

7   Fortescue, *The County Lieutenancies*, Appendix1.

8   TNA WO 25/1146, f.53, Embarkation Returns.

9   TNA HO 100/174/157/167/176: Militia Embarkation Returns.

10   TNA 143/6: Minutes of H M Commissioners of the Royal Military Asylum, 10 December, 1806.

11   XIX Report of the Commissioners of Military Inquiry, House of Commons Sessional Papers, 1812; TNA WO 143/9: Minutes of H M Commissioners of the Royal Military Asylum, 6 February 1826.

officers and soldiers. He explained that it was the C-in-C's intention that these schools should be conducted on the plan recommended by the Rev Dr Bell, which had been very successful at the RMA. The circular stated that the purpose of the schools was to implant in the children the 'habits of morality, obedience and industry, and to give them that portion of learning, which may qualify them as Non–Commissioned Officers.' The Colonels were asked to immediately select a suitable person to superintend the school, who would be placed on the strength of the regiment as a sergeant in addition to the current establishment. This prompted a letter from the Duke of Kent on 4 December 1811 urging that any regulations for the organisation of regimental schools should emulate those in place in the Royals' (the 1st Foot) school. Sir Harry Calvert replied that he had been directed by the C-in-C to inform the Duke of Kent that the general regulations that were being framed 'will enjoy the strictest conformity with the school already established in the Royal Regiment of Foot.'[12]

On 27 December, Lord Palmerston, the Secretary at War, sent a circular letter to the Colonels informing them that the Prince Regent, in the name of the King, ordered that a regimental school should be established immediately in every regiment and corps and that they should select an attested soldier as a schoolmaster sergeant to superintend the school, with the same pay and allowances as the paymaster sergeant of the corps. When the corps was in barracks, a room would be allocated together with an allowance of fuel during the winter months. A sum of £10 per annum, payable half yearly would be allowed to each corps for the stationery and other expenses of the school. Instructions for the plan of education to be adopted by the regimental school would subsequently be issued by the C-in-C.[13]

The piecemeal introduction of schools in the British Army during the Revolutionary and Napoleonic Wars was motivated in part by benevolence, but arguably to a greater degree by the perceived benefits that would follow for the military service. The focus had hitherto been on schooling for enlisted boys and young soldiers as well as for soldiers' children. However, when Palmerston presented a vote in the Army Estimates for the expenses of the regimental schools to the House of Commons on 22 February 1812, he omitted any reference to schooling for the boys and young soldiers and referred only to soldiers' children. He explained that:

> For some years, the schools for the instruction of soldiers' children had been supported by no established fund, but by the zeal, intelligence and liberality of the officers and by private contributions. The necessity of placing such schools on a regular and permanent establishment had been regularly felt by the C-in-C,

12   TNA WO 3/54: f. 471, 'Letter from the Adjutant General to Field Marshall the Duke of Kent', 8 December 1811.
13   TNA WO 44/647: 'Letters from Lt Colonel Rottinger to the Board of Ordnance 24 July 1812'; 'General Orders and Instructions for Establishing and Conducting Regimental Schools 1812'.

whose attention to the welfare of the Army is too well known to the House to require any comment from him. In consequence of this schools had been established in every battalion of the service.[14]

Palmerston proposed an addition of ten men to the Household regiments as sergeant schoolmasters at a cost of £1,700 and an expenditure of £20,000 for the pay of the sergeant schoolmaster in the line and militia regiments and for books and other contingencies. He argued that this expense would be neither 'useless nor lavish' when the benefits derived for the country and the advantages it offered to the Army were considered.[15] Palmerston's presentation was astute. By emphasising that the schools would only be for soldiers' children, whilst simply alluding to the broader benefits that they would bring to the Army, he avoided any opposition from MPs who might otherwise object to an attempt to establish what could be seen as military schools serving as nurseries for the regular Army. Hansard does not record any opposition in Parliament to the proposed expenditure, unlike in 1810, when the opposition in the House of Commons had forced a reduction in the Army Estimates in the case of a number of proposed staff appointments.[16] The scheme for regimental schools was not expensive and there was no expenditure on a staff of officers to superintend and manage the schools. In the following years the expense for the schoolmaster sergeants would be subsumed within the general expenditure for the Army's establishment and the only vote that could be directly attributable to the regimental schools would be the small amount for books and other contingencies. This would provide protection for the regimental schools after the War when there would likely be considerable political pressure to reduce the expenditure on the Army.

Meantime, the Horse Guards lost no time in proceeding with the arrangements for the organisation of the regimental schools. On 28 December 1811, Sir Harry Calvert issued a circular to the commanding officers of the regiments and corps in England ordering the soldier selected to fill the post of schoolmaster sergeant to proceed to the RMA where he would be given information about 'instructing children according to Dr Bell's system.'[17] This was followed on 1st January 1812 by General Orders from the C-in-C, the Duke of York, explaining the purposes of the regimental schools, together with a set of appended instructions for establishing and conducting the schools according to Dr Bell's system already in place at the RMA. The Duke of York emphasised the government's 'benevolent intention in favour of soldiers' children' in establishing the schools and impressed on all general officers, colonels of regiments

14   *Hansard*, First Series, Vol. XXI, 894.
15   *Hansard*, First Series, Vol. XXI, 894.
16   K. Bourne, *Palmerston: The early years 1784–1841* (London: Allen Lane 1982), p. 134.
17   TNA WO 44/647: Letters from Lt Colonel Rottinger to the Board of Ordnance; General Orders and Instructions for Establishing and Conducting Regimental Schools 1812.

and commanding officers the importance of their 'special superintendence' of the regimental schools under their command.

A special duty was assigned to chaplains and other clergymen engaged in clerical duties with the Army to help the military staff in making the schools a success, by frequently visiting the schools of their divisions and garrisons, diligently scrutinising the conduct of the sergeant schoolmasters, examining the progress and general behaviour of the children and reporting the results of their observations to commanding officers. With regard to the interior economy of the schools, the orders stated that, although it was for the children to choose their future occupation, it was essential that the children should at an early age learn order, regularity, and discipline derived from 'a well-grounded respect and veneration for the Established religion of the country and with this view, the schools were to be conducted on military principles, and as far as possible correspond to the organisation of a regiment.'

The orders explained that although the set of appended instructions mentioned only boys, it was intended that girls should also attend the schools, 'wherever the accommodations and other circumstance will permit.' The Duke of York concluded by emphasising that the main purposes for which the regimental schools were established were 'to give to the soldiers the comfort of being assured, that the education and welfare of their children are objects of their sovereign's paternal solicitude and attention; and to raise from their offspring a succession of loyal subjects, brave soldiers, and good Christians.'[18]

The Duke of York's orders establishing regimental schools had a wider circulation within the Army than his previous exhortations to establish schools and would have been brought to the attention of the rank and file. It is interesting that there was no mention of schooling for the enlisted boys and young soldiers and that the emphasis was now on the benevolent intentions of the military authorities towards soldiers' children, with only a suggestion that some of the boys might subsequently decide to volunteer. The affirmation in the orders that the main purposes of establishing the schools was to assure the rank and file that the government was anxious to promote the education and welfare of their children should be considered in the broader context of other reforms that the Duke of York was introducing in the Army.

The Duke of York had been adamant in his opposition to short term service, although it was forced on him when William Windham was Secretary for War in 1806. He continued with his opposition and life enlistment was restored alongside short-term service in 1808. Short term enlistment had been looked at as service until the end of the war and it was argued that it was totally inappropriate in the longer term, given particular circumstances of the United Kingdom as a country with extensive overseas possessions. Whilst the Army would never be a popular career, it could at least be

18   TNA WO 44/647: 'Letters from Lt Colonel Rottinger to the Board of Ordnance'; 'General Orders and instructions for Establishing and Conducting Regimental Schools 1812'.

made more attractive by showing that the soldier and his family's well-being were taken seriously by the government. It has been suggested that it was no coincidence that the Duke of York was introducing measures to improve the conditions of service and the welfare of the private soldier, whilst he was also arguing for lifetime enlistment and against short term service. These measures included the provision of hospitals, the reform of army chaplaincies and less reliance on corporal punishment for maintaining discipline, alongside proposals for more generous pensions and financial assistance for soldiers' families when a regiment embarked for overseas service. The introduction of a uniform system of schools in every regiment throughout the Army similarly demonstrated a commitment by the government to the welfare of soldiers' families, whilst also offering enlisted men the opportunity to improve their education and better qualify themselves for promotion.[19]

It can be argued that the system of regimental schools introduced by the Duke of York played an important part in the creation of the Victorian professional army. Permanent barracks had been constructed in the British Isles during the Revolutionary and Napoleonic Wars and as the Empire had grown the number of colonial stations had increased. Infantry battalions at home and abroad functioned as self-contained communities. Men enlisted for life with perhaps a pension for long service. They were increasingly conscious of their regimental identities; their ranks provided the non-commissioned officers who were responsible for the regiment's day-to-day management; the men were accompanied by their families at the barracks and depots and their children were educated in regimental schools, with their sons being encouraged to follow their fathers in a military career and their daughters often marrying into the regiment.[20]

Although there were good reasons why the Duke of York wished to establish a uniform system of regimental schools, it is less obvious why he was in such a hurry to establish a system in 1811. He may have been considering seeking the Government's support to establish a system of regimental school when he had been forced to resign as C-in-C in 1809. It also may be that the military departments were compelled to seek early parliamentary approval for the public funding for schools for boy soldiers and soldiers' children because of the legal judgements in 1811 in the case of Warden v. Bailey.

This case arose out of the decision of Samuel Whitbread, Colonel of a Bedfordshire militia regiment (and a supporter of public funding for elementary education) to issue a regimental order in November 1809 establishing an evening school at Bedford and ordering all sergeants and corporals to attend to learn to read and write. In order to finance the school, Whitbread required non–commissioned officers to make a weekly payment to pay for a schoolmaster and the expenses of a schoolroom. Some of the non–commissioned officers failed to attend the school and were tried by regimental

19 Cookson, *The British Armed Nation*, pp. 122-4.
20 Cookson, *The British Armed Nation*, pp. 124-5.

court martial and reprimanded for their conduct and they promised to attend more regularly. Shortly afterwards, following a regimental parade, Adjutant Bailey ordered Sergeant Warden to be imprisoned, because he alleged that Warden had encouraged another sergeant to disobey orders and not attend the school. It was alleged that Warden had declared that he would not abide by the decision of a regimental court martial and he demanded to be tried by a general court martial. Whitbread as the regiment's commanding officer confirmed the order to imprison Warden, who was confined in miserable conditions in Bedford Town Jail for over 50 days until a general court martial could be convened. Warden was subsequently acquitted at this court martial and released from custody. He then proceeded to sue Adjutant Bailey in a civil action for damages for illegal imprisonment. The judges' ruling on appeal in the Court of Common pleas was that the colonel of a regiment had no authority to order a soldier to attend at a school in order to learn to read and write or to order him to make payments towards the costs of a schoolmaster's salary or towards other expenses in for the running of a school.[21]

It may be no coincidence that the parliamentary votes and the orders from the military departments to establish regimental schools throughout the Army took place within a few months of the ruling in Warden v. Bailey in the Court of Common Pleas.[22] The point here is that it was imperative to formalise the position of regimental schools and provide for the payment for schoolmasters through a vote under the military estimates in order to ensure that army schools survived and would be established in every battalion, regiment, and corps throughout the Army.

We have seen that the Duke of York's letter of 26 August to Viscount Palmerston requesting him to submit a proposal to the Lord Commissioners of the Treasury for the establishment of regimental schools explained that these would be for 'the education of young soldiers and soldiers' children.' Palmerston, in his circular to the Colonels of Regiments on 27 December 1811 had explained that the schools would be 'for the instruction of young soldiers, and of the children of soldiers.'[23] The Adjutant General, Sir Harry Calvert in his circular to the Army on 14th November 1811 however explained that the government was contemplating establishing Regimental Schools, which would only be for 'for the care and instruction of the children of Non-Commissioned officers and soldiers.' The General Orders from the Horse Guards, dated 1st January 1812, similarly focused on the schools' provision for soldiers' children and made no mention of providing instruction for 'young soldiers.' Palmerston, when presenting the vote for the payment of schoolmaster-sergeants in the Army Estimates in February 1812, judiciously omitted any reference to schooling for the boys and young soldiers and referred only to soldiers' children. This change of

21   Taunton, W.P., Reports and Cases in the Court of Common Pleas 1781-1813 (London: I. Riley, 1816), pp. 67-8; White, *The Story of Army Education*, p. 21.
22   White, *The Story of Army Education*, p. 21.
23   St John Williams, *Tommy Atkin's Children*, p. 15.

focus by the military departments on the purpose of the schools was most probably calculated to neutralise any opposition ensure the broadest support in Parliament for the measure.

By emphasizing that the main purpose of the regimental schools was 'to give the soldiers the comfort of being assured that, the education and welfare of their children' was the overriding concern, the government avoided any involvement in the debate about whether attested soldiers should be ordered by their commanding officers to go to school. When in the following month Palmerston asked the House of Commons for the renewal of the annual Mutiny Act he made no attempt to introduce amendments that would have overridden the ruling of the Court of Common Pleas, by giving commanding officers legal powers to order attested soldiers to attend at the regimental schools. This caused Samuel Whitbread to protest in the House of Commons that this omission would encourage insubordination and endanger discipline in the Army. Whitbread was smarting from the ruling in Warden v. Bailey that he had no authority to compel soldiers to attend his regimental school and he feared that a civil action for illegal imprisonment would be brought against him by Warden. He argued that many schools had previously been established in the Army in order to qualify soldiers for promotion as non-commissioned officers and that the Duke of York had previously exhorted commanding officers to ensure that men attended in order to improve their education.

Palmerston replied that there would be no prohibition against soldiers attending the regimental schools that were being established throughout the Army, but attendance would be voluntary. He thought that any soldier who was otherwise qualified and ambitious for promotion 'would be happy to avail himself of the advantage held out by these schools, and therefore it was well to leave it optional for him to attend.'[24] This remained the position of successive governments and was for many years to bedevil attempts to promote and extend elementary education within the Army's rank and file.

Although there was an urgent need to provide official recognition and support to ensure the continuation of the existing regimental schools following the ruling in the Warden v. Bailey case, it is probable that the Duke of York was also concerned about the growing influence of Joseph Lancaster's ideas in the Army. The Duke of Kent was president of the Royal Lancastrian Institution for the Education of the Poor of Every Religious Persuasion and his advocacy of the successful regimental school of the 4/1st Royals might lead to the spread of non-denominational schools on the Lancastrian principle throughout the Army. York had firmly identified himself with the Anglican National Society for the Education of the Poor when it was formed in October1811. The introduction of regimental schools in the regular army and the militia based on Bell's Madras system, with instruction in the catechism of the established church, would neutralise the influence of the Lancastrian system, whilst also enhancing the

24 *Hansard*, First Series Vol. XXI, p. 1202.

prestige of the National Society and providing an impetus for the development of its school. This was acknowledged by the National Society in its report for 1814, which emphasised that the children at the Royal Military Asylum and in all the recently established regimental schools were instructed according to the Madras system, and that these institutions owed their existence to the Duke of York's 'paternal care for the welfare of the British Army.' Moreover, the introduction of a uniform system of regimental schools with a curriculum prescribed by the C-in-C based on the Madras System incorporating the teachings of the established church and teaching a respect for lawful authority, would counter any apprehension in the country that the schools might encourage soldiers and their children to the read seditious pamphlets and the foster radical political ideas.[25]

There was also one important political consideration that pointed to the avoidance of any delay in establishing an official system of regimental schools. King George III's illness had returned in the last months of 1810 and a Regency Act was passed in February 1811, with the Duke of York's brother the Prince of Wales being appointed regent, although for twelve months his powers were restricted. The Prince Regent had friends amongst the Whig opposition, but although initially he made no attempt to include them in the government, there was anxiety that when the restrictions on his powers came to an end on 18th February 1812, he might seek a 'broad bottomed' administration of Tories and Whigs.[26] It can be assumed that the Prince Regent had knowledge of and supported York's proposal for regimental schools. Whether the King recovered, and the Regency lapsed, or it was confirmed because of the King's

Frederick, Duke of York and Albany, (1763-1827), Commander-in-Chief of the Army 1795-1809 and 1811-27 by; after Thomas Hodgetts; Andrew Geddes. (© National Portrait Gallery, London)

25 *Second Report of the National Society 1814*, pp. 18-19.
26 J.S. Watson, *The Reign of George III* (Oxford: Clarendon Press 1960), pp. 489-92; *Second Report of the National Society* 1814, pp. 18-19.

continuing illness, it was prudent for York to move at the earliest opportunity and secure parliamentary approval for a uniform and publicly funded system of regimental schools throughout the Army.

Henry John Temple, 3rd Viscount Palmerston, (1784-1865), Minister at War 1809-27 by John Partridge. (© National Portrait Gallery, London)

5

Establishing and Staffing Regimental Schools, 1812-1816

During the winter of 1811-12, the Duke of York and his staff at the Horse Guards began to implement the plan to establish regimental schools throughout the Army. This required each regiment and corps to identify a soldier to be designated the schoolmaster-sergeant; providing written guidance for the instruction of the pupils according to the Madras System; training at the Royal Military Asylum for the sergeant schoolmasters in units within the United Kingdom; fitting out barracks with school rooms and instituting procedures for inspecting and reporting on the condition of the schools.

The parliamentary appropriation of £20,000 voted for schools in the line and militia regiments provided about £45 per unit to cover the annual salary of the schoolmaster-sergeant, stationery and other incidental expenses. This sum was more than sufficient to establish schools in the 31 regiments of cavalry, 183 battalions of infantry and the 41veteran, colonial, and foreign units, the 15 regiments of the Kings' German Legion and the Royal Wagon Corps of the regular army, and still leave enough for schools in the militias of Great Britain and Ireland.[1]

Some 40 percent of the regular Army was serving outside the United Kingdom and it was many months before the general orders and circular letters from the Horse Guards reached their stations. The pay roll of the 1/22 Regiment of Foot stationed on the Isle of Bourbon (now Reunion), for example, records that the General Order and Circular letter relating to regimental schools were only received in the summer of 1812. It was not until November 1812 that a regimental school was established, and Corporal John Joplin was appointed the schoolmaster sergeant.[2]

Nonetheless, the Adjutant–General's papers record that a schoolmaster-sergeant was added in December 1811 to the establishment of over 70 battalions of the infantry

---

1   *Hansard,* First Series, Vol. XXI, 894; Haythornthwaite, *The Armies of Wellington,* pp. 271-275; R. MacArthur, 'British Establishments during the Napoleonic *War', Journal of the Society for Army Historical Research,* Vol. 87, (Summer 2009*),* p. 155.
2   TNA WO 12/3883: General Muster Books and Pay lists 22nd Foot.

that were serving overseas.[3] Many of these units were stationed in colonial garrisons, but others were on active service in Spain, Portugal, and elsewhere in Europe. Whilst women and children accompanied regiments overseas, the particular circumstances and exigencies of active service meant that it was often difficult, and sometimes unnecessary, to establish a regimental school.

In cases where regimental schools had been established, the schoolmaster-sergeant often remained with the depot company when a regiment or battalion was sent on active service. In December 1811, James Watts was appointed schoolmaster-sergeant of the 10th (Prince of Wale's Own) Light Dragoons and Joseph Bullin of the 15th (King's) Own Light Dragoons. These men remained in charge of the schools at their respective depots whilst their regiments served in Spain from 1812 to 1814.[4] The Horse Guards recognized the wisdom of retaining schoolmaster-sergeants in the depots. In March 1813, the Adjutant-General wrote to the Duke of Kent, informing him that the C-in-C approved of Kent's decision to retain the schoolmaster of one of the battalions of the 1st Foot at the depot, because '...the schoolmaster can be of little use to a regiment on active service.'[5] Nevertheless, there were schoolmaster sergeants who saw active service and fought with their regiments in the Peninsular War. Schoolmaster-sergeant John Judson of the 1/39 was mortally wounded in the storming of the Heights of Garris, near Bayonne, in February 1814.[6]

Regimental schools were easier to establish and maintain in units permanently housed in barracks, provided that suitable rooms could be found. Classroom space was a problem for units stationed outside large barracks. Early in 1812, the Commander of the Forces at Kilmainham, Dublin rejected a request to hire a room for the regimental school at Killarney on the grounds that this was not sanctioned by existing regulations. Doing so might be taken as a precedent that would lead to further similar requests.[7] In July 1812, a Royal Warrant was issued authorising the Commissioners for Affairs of Barracks to furnish rooms for regimental schools and to supply coals and candles. It specified that in barracks constructed for at least a 1,000 men, but not more than 2,000, a room was to be marked 'the schoolroom' and furnished with desks and tables. In barracks built to accommodate 2,000 to 4,000 men, two rooms were to be provided. In barracks accommodating less than 1,000 men, a room was to be provided for occasional use without dismantling its regular furnishings. The

3   TNA WO 380/3: Establishments and Stations of Regiments1803-1881.
4   TNA WO 12/934 and WO 12/1202: General Muster Books and Pay lists, 10th and 15th Light Dragoons.
5   TNA WO 3/59: Commander- in- Chief Out-letters, 'Letter from Sir Harry Calvert to the Duke of Kent' March 1813, pp. 166-8.
6   E. O'Keefe, 'The Old Halberdier: From the Pyrennes to Plattsburgh with a Welshman of the 39th (Memoirs of the 39th Foot,1808-1814)', *Journal of the Society for Army Historical Research*, Vol. 95, No. 382 (Summer 2017), pp. 158-9.
7   NLI, Kilmainham Papers, MS 1028/20, 'Letter from Major Forbes at Killarney to the Commander of the Forces in Ireland'.

warrant specified that where there was pressure on accommodation, classes were to be split to teach some scholars in the morning and some in the afternoon.[8] This at least recognised that regimental schools required some minimal accommodation, but also tacitly admitted that the schooling offered would be limited by the space available. In barracks that accommodated two or more battalions, the warrant allowed for the sharing schoolroom space and this presaged the garrison schools that replaced the regimental schools later in the century.

The royal warrant did not address the accommodation difficulties for the officers in charge of smaller units. Lieutenant Gilbert, for example, left in charge of the depot of the 20th Foot at Fermoy in Ireland in 1813, requested a tent to use as the regimental school.[9] Whether this request was granted is not known, but the Lord Commissioners of the Treasury were reluctant to sanction what it considered to be unnecessary expenditure. In August 1813, the Lord Commissioners turned down requests for additional allowance for candles in regimental schools above that allocated in the royal warrant.[10]

The Adjutant–General's authorisation to appoint a sergeant schoolmaster in a particular unit did not mean that a schoolmaster was always appointed, and a regimental school opened. The pay rolls and order books of the infantry battalions, which made up the majority of the regular army, reveal an incoherent and sometimes confusing record of the appointment of schoolmasters both within and between different units. In part this is because printed pages on the pay rolls, with a space for the name and pay of the schoolmaster-sergeant, were not generally available until 1813. Before these printed documents were issued the paymaster or his sergeant had to make a manual entry on the roll to identify that a soldier was the designated as the schoolmaster. In many cases, especially in units stationed overseas, paymasters continued to use the old pay rolls for some time and individual soldiers were not consistently listed as the sergeant schoolmaster in successive musters.[11]

From 1803 second battalions had been raised in a number of regiments of infantry, initially for home service. They often functioned as recruiting units, whilst the first battalions served overseas.[12] In these cases it was a relatively straight forward matter to establish regimental schools in the second battalions. For example, the first battalion of the 36th Foot was in Portugal in 1811 and the regimental school was established in the second battalion (the 2/36) stationed at Horsham in Sussex. Private George

8   Lefroy, Report on the Garrison and Regimental Schools of the Army, Appendix No.3.
9   NLI, Kilmainham Papers, MS1031/58, 'Letter from Lieutenant Gilbert commanding depot, 20th Foot at Fermoy to Commander of the Forces 1813'.
10   NAM, Records of the Royal Army Educational Corps , Army Education before 1846, Box 22125, 'Letter from Lord Commissioners to Deputy Adjutant General, 26th August, 1813'.
11   Fortescue, The County Lieutenancies and the Army 1803-1814, Appendix XI; R. MacArthur, British Establishments during the Napoleonic War, p. 155.
12   Fortescue, The County Lieutenancies and the Army 1803-1814, p. 180.

Wilson was promoted schoolmaster-sergeant. He completed the training course at the RMA in February 1812 (See below).[13]

Over time both the first and second battalions of a number of regiments were posted overseas. The two battalions of the 48th Foot were in Spain from 1809 and suffered heavy casualties at the battle of Albuera on 16 May 1811. The first battalion remained in Spain and does not appear to have appointed a schoolmaster, although 23 boy soldiers are recorded on the pay and muster rolls. A section of the remains of the second battalion moved to England to recruit and a school was established in 1812, whilst it was stationed at Banbury, although it is not certain when it became operational. Richard Booth was promoted to sergeant from private during the quarter, December 1811 to March 1812. The payrolls and regimental accounts record that he attended for training at the RMA Chelsea. An unnamed schoolmaster-sergeant from the 48th regiment – presumably Booth – is recorded as having satisfactorily completed a training course in the Madras System at the RMA under the supervision of Dr Andrew Bell in February 1812. Sergeant Booth however was not described as schoolmaster until the December–March 1813 pay roll, but this may have been a clerical omission. He remained as the schoolmaster until discharged in October 1814.[14]

The infantry's second and any additional battalions, when not serving overseas, were regularly moved between the military districts in the British Isles and the schoolmasters accompanied the battalions to their successive stations.[15] The 4th battalion of the 1st Foot (Royals) had already demonstrated that it was possible to maintain a school whilst moving around the country. The school had been inspected by Major General Sir John Dalrymple, the general officer commanding the North Britain district on 15 June 1811, whilst the battalion was at Stirling. Dalrymple had reported that it had a good schoolmaster and was well attended with a roll of 21 boys and 18 girls.[16] The battalion received very substantial enlistments from the British and Irish Militias during 1812 and these included a significant number of boys. Lieutenant H. Miles, a newly joined officer wrote in October 1812 that the battalion had 'a school for soldiers' children on Dr Bells 'Plan' and he remarked that '...some of the boys are remarkably clever at writing and figures'.[17] Sir Hugh Dalrymple again inspected the school in October 1813, May 1814 and September 1814 after the battalion had moved to Musselburgh. He reported that it was well attended and 'most admirably managed'

13   TNA WO 12/ 5099: General Muster Books and Pay lists, 36th Foot.
14   TNA WO 12/6031: General Muster Books and Pay lists,48th Foot. NAM, Records of the Royal Army Educational Corps, Army Education before 1846, Box 22125, 'Letter from Colonel Williamson, Commandant RMA to Adjutant General 06/02/1812'.
15   MacArthur, 'British Establishments during the Napoleonic War', p. 155. By the end of the War the 14th, 27th and 56th Foot had three battalions, the 1st Foot four battalions and the 60th Foot eight battalions.
16   Leask and McCance, *Regimental Records of the Royal Scots*, p. 345.
17   Leask and McCance, *Regimental Records of the Royal Scots*, p. 346.

and he made special mention of the encouragement and support of the CO Major Nixon.[18] There were however a succession of three masters in charge of instruction at the regimental school during this period. In these cases, the inspecting general officers acknowledged that a great deal of a school's success was because of the interest taken by the senior regimental officers.

In the post-war reduction in the size of the army, the second battalions of the infantry were disbanded, and depots were established in Great Britain to receive and train recruits for the first battalion. During this period schools were regularly opened and then closed and NCOs who were designated as schoolmasters were often returned to other duties as and when they were needed.

The Adjutant-General's Department added a schoolmaster-sergeant to both battalions of the 30th Regiment in 1812. The first battalion was in the East Indies, where it established a school. The second battalion had been formed in 1803 and was rushed from Cork to Portugal in March 1809 following the evacuation of the army from Corunna. The 96 women and 209 children with the battalion were sent to their homes with a gratuity of £1-2-8d for each woman and 50d for each child. The Battalion was subsequently heavily involved in the Peninsula War and was present at Fuentes de Onoro, Salamanca, and the storming of Badajoz. It sailed home from Portugal in a much depleted state in June 1813 and was stationed in Jersey, where in December 1813 Luke Lyndon (a veteran of the siege of Badajoz) was designated schoolmaster-sergeant. Nothing is known about his qualifications for the post, but Lyndon remained as schoolmaster at the depot when the second battalion moved to Flanders. From June to December 1814 he appears as the schoolmaster-sergeant with the second battalion at the regimental school at Antwerp. In January 1815 he is listed on the rolls as a sergeant at the depot in England. Lyndon remained as a sergeant on the depot pay roll until March 1817, but neither he nor any other soldier was designated as schoolmaster and it is probable that the school remained closed. There is no record of a schoolmaster at the depot during 1817 or 1818, but a regimental school was maintained by the First Battalion at Fort George Madras India, where in December 1817, Sergeant John Franklin is listed as the schoolmaster-sergeant.[19]

The Household Cavalry and the Foot Guards always had a substantial presence in and around London and were well placed to establish regimental schools. There was a separate Parliamentary vote in the Army Estimates for schoolmasters in these regiments because of the higher rates of pay and allowances received by the household troops. This vote provided for ten additional men for appointment as schoolmasters: three as corporals of horse in the Royal Horse Guards and the 1st and 2nd Life Guards and seven as sergeants in the three battalions of the 1st Foot Guards and the

18   Leask and McCance, *Regimental Records of the Royal Scots*, p. 296.
19   N. Bannatyne, *History of the XXX Regiment 1689-1881* (Liverpool: Litlebury Bros, 1923), pp. 270-85; TNA WO 12/4582: 4646, 4647, General Muster Books and Pay Lists, 30th Foot.

two battalions of the Second and Third Guards.[20] Within London, detachments of the Foot Guards were stationed at the Tower of London and Somerset House and at the St George's, Portman Street, and Knightsbridge barracks.

It is difficult to establish from the pay rolls exactly when and where schools was established in the Foot Guards, partly because the existing printed pay rolls do not conform to the pattern in use in the line regiments, and also because non-commissioned officers and men are listed under the names of their company commanders. The pay roll of the First (Grenadier) Guards for 1812 do not show any designations to the rank of schoolmaster-sergeant, although there were three promotions to the rank of sergeant in individual companies during this year. Two unnamed sergeants however are known to have attended training courses at the RMA.[21] The Order Book of the Second (Coldstream) Guards records that, pursuant to the directions received from the Horse Guards, Corporal George Leyland of Lieutenant Colonel Macdonell's company was promoted sergeant on 17th February 1812 to superintend the school. Similarly, the Order Book of the Third (Scots) Guards records that on 7th March 1812 Sergeant Joseph Muscott was appointed regimental schoolmaster. Both these schoolmaster-sergeants subsequently attended training courses at the RMA Chelsea.

Some children from the Foot Guards, seemingly with the approval of the regiment's' colonels, attended the National Society's Free School at Westminster instead of their regimental schools. This school was established in 1812 and was enlarged in 1814 and became the largest of the Society's schools. It was designed to accommodate one thousand children. The Second Report of the National Society based upon the report of its General Committee for 1813 recorded that within the previous year 207 boys and 95 girls had been admitted. The Dukes of York, Cambridge and Gloucester, were the Colonels of the three regiments of Foot Guards and also patrons of the Westminster National school whose regulations gave preference to the admission of soldiers' and sailors' children. More than one third of the pupils at the school in that year were the children of soldiers. The Duke of York had inspected the school and expressed his approval of the way in which it was conducted. He considered that its teaching was very suitable for children who might subsequently be candidates for admission to the RMA.[22]

The King's German Legion was an integral part of the British Army formed initially from the disbanded Hanoverian Army after France overran the state in 1803. It was expanded with recruits from Germany and other nationalities during the War and some 28,000 served in its ranks. It expanded ultimately to 10 line and two light

20   *Hansard*, First Series, Vol. XXI , 8.
21   TNA WO 12/1589: General Muster Books and Pay Lists, First Foot Guards; NAM, Records of the Royal Army Educational Corps, Education before 1846, Box 22125, 'Letter from Colonel Williamson, Commandant RMA to Adjutant General 6/02/1812', Regimental Head Quarters, 1st (Grenadier), 2nd (Coldstream) and 3rd (Scots) Guards, Order Books, passim.
22   *Second Report of the National Society 1814*, pp. 31-3.

battalions and five cavalry regiments, and foot and horse artillery.[23] The orders and circulars from the Horse Guards establishing regimental schools had been sent to the commanding officers of the cavalry and infantry regiments of the Legion, but not to its artillery, which came under the Board of Ordnance. This prompted Lieutenant Colonel Augustus Rottinger, who commanded the Legion's artillery, to write to the Board of Ordnance asking for permission to appoint a supernumerary schoolmaster to take charge of a regimental school at Bexhill on Sea, East Sussex. Bexhill was the main station for the Legion's units in England and in 1813 became the home for a veteran battalion that was formed from soldiers who were unfit for active service but were capable of garrison duties. The augmented establishment for this unit as at 2nd February 1814 included a schoolmaster-sergeant.[24] Colonel Rottinger not only secured the agreement from the Ordnance to his request for a schoolmaster, but proceeded to also organise a combined school for the children of the artillery and infantry battalions at the Bexhill camp. The registers of this school for the week 22-27 February 1813 have survived and record the attendance of 15 boys and 12 girls from the artillery and 49 boys and 39 girls from the 1st and 2nd Light battalions and 1st, 2nd, 3rd, 7th Line battalions and at the Legion's depot. Colonel Rottinger's letter to the Ordnance requesting a schoolmaster for the King's German Legion Artillery prompted the Board to obtain details of the Horse Guards' scheme for establishing regimental schools in the Army. The Board then made a request to the Treasury for funding sufficient to appoint supernumerary sergeant schoolmasters in every battalion of the Royal Artillery. This request was granted and on 25 January 1813 a general order authorised the establishment of regimental schools conducted on Dr Bell's system throughout the Royal Artillery.[25]

In 1813 there was a regimental school for the Royal Artillery at Woolwich with one staff sergeant and a non-commissioned officer instructing 268 boys and a school room for girls was under construction, which when completed, would accommodate about 150 girls. It is unclear whether this garrison school with its combined roll of four hundred and eighteen pupils was a continuation of the school established at Woolwich in 1797 or a new school that had been established with the help and encouragement of Joseph Lancaster in around 1811. It was however the forerunner of the much larger garrison schools that operated for the Royal Artillery at Woolwich later in the Nineteenth century[26]

23 N. L. Beamish, *History of the King's German Legion*, (East Sussex: Naval and Military Press, 1997), Two volumes.

24 TNA WO 44/647: 'Correspondence between Lt Colonel Rottinger and the Board of Ordnance, 24th July1812'; Beamish, *History of the King's German Legion*, Vol. II, pp. 436-7.

25 *Bexhill Hanoverian Study Group* <info@bexhillhanoveriankgl.co.uk historishes.museum@ hannover-stadte.de> (accessed 11 December 2011).

26 TNA WO 44/647: 'Correspondence between Lt Colonel Rottinger and the Board of Ordnance, 24th July 1812'.

The circular letter that Adjutant General Sir Harry Calvert had issued on 14th November 1811, anticipating the Duke of York's General Order of 1st January 1812, instructed the commanding officers to proceed immediately in selecting a suitable person to superintend the regimental school and to be very careful in making their selection. Other than being informed that York's intention was that the schools should be conducted on the plan recommended by Dr Andrew Bell, which had been introduced successfully at the Royal Military Asylum, they were given no guidance about how to proceed.[27] Commanding officers would have looked for advice from their adjutant and probably also the sergeant major in making the selection. Generally, the recruits to the infantry had been manual workers, but some of these men would have been able to read and write and this would have come to the attention of their officers. In some regiments the task was relatively straight forward. In the case of the 2/25 Foot there were a number of obvious candidates who had worked as schoolmasters before enlisting. Joseph Smith, who was born at Closeburn, Dumfries, Scotland and enlisted aged 24 and gave his previous occupation as a civilian schoolmaster. He appears as the battalion's schoolmaster-sergeant in the pay rolls from March 1812 to December 1813.[28] This however was an unusual appointment, that reflected the particular pattern of civilian schooling in lowland Scotland.

The names of men who had previously worked as weavers appear frequently in the pay rolls of regiments and in the case of the 3rd Foot Guards provided the regiment's first schoolmasters. Joseph Muscott was born at Crick in Northamptonshire and attested in the regiment's 1st Battalion aged 24, from the Northampton militia in the March 1800, having worked previously as a weaver. He was promoted from corporal to sergeant in May 1810 and was designated schoolmaster in March 1812. He served in this capacity until April 1817 when he was discharged with a recommendation for a pension. He was succeeded as schoolmaster by Sergeant Thomas Dunwell, who had been born in the parish of Berwick Elmet, York. He also described his occupation as a weaver, when he had attested aged 22 in July 1804. He had been promoted from corporal to sergeant in April 1814 and he may have improved his education by attending at the regimental school.[29]

The post of schoolmaster-sergeant was treated as a staff appointment and the occupant was in the same privileged position with regard to the allocation of barracks accommodation as other staff sergeants specified in the Royal Warrant of 25 December 1807. This may have influenced some literate sergeants to volunteer for the post of schoolmaster. This may have been a consideration for Sergeant John Seaton of

27 *General Orders and Regulations for the Army* (London: Adjutant General Office Horse Guards 1811 and 1816, facsimile edition published by Frederick Muller Ltd., 1970), Circular 592, 14th November,1811, p. 331.
28 King's Own Scottish Borderers Museum, Miscellaneous Return's Book 25th Foot 1811-1817; TNA WO 12/4172: General Muster Books and Pay Lists, 25th Foot.
29 Regimental Head Quarters 3rd Foot Guards (Scots Guards), Regimental Order Book, List of Sergeants 1815.

the Royal Waggon Train, when he transferred from the post of armorer sergeant to that of schoolmaster-sergeant at Croydon barracks in the autumn of 1812.[30]

Literacy was routinely looked for in promoting a soldier to sergeant, but the definition of literacy could be wide and would not of itself confer the abilities to teach competently and effectively manage a school. Furthermore, sergeants were by no means always models of propriety or exemplars for the standards of behaviour that Andrew Bell's system aimed to instil in the Army's children. The pay rolls and records of service show that men were promoted and reduced with regularity for crimes mostly involving intoxication and conduct unbecoming of their rank. The Commissioners of the Board of Education in Ireland following their visit to the Hibernian School in Phoenix Park in 1809 had commented that the appointment of old soldiers as sergeants of instruction was helpful in maintaining order and discipline amongst the boys, but unless the selection was made with great care it could have adverse consequences for '…their religious and moral instruction.' In the opinion of the Commissioners the sergeants of instruction at the School, though competent to teach reading and writing, appeared to be '…totally ignorant in the simplest principles of the Christian Religion.'[31]

There were often good reasons for the commanding officers to look beyond the rank of sergeant and consider corporals or indeed privates for promotion as schoolmaster-sergeants. For example, Corporal Joseph Ashton was promoted sergeant and also designated schoolmaster in the 2nd battalion of the 3rd Foot Guards on 5 July 1814. He had been born at Alloa in Clackmannan and when he had attested, aged 18 in September 1808, he entered his occupation as a weaver. He was succeeded as schoolmaster by Corporal George Copeland in May 1817, although Copeland was not promoted sergeant until July of that year. Copeland had been born in the parish of St. George Bloomsbury London in 1789 and worked as a clerk before enlisting in May 1812.[32] In many units the commanding officers, if they were to follow orders and proceed immediately to establish regimental schools, had had little alternate but to promote a private soldier as the schoolmaster-sergeant. For example, James Bower of the 10th Light Dragoons and privates George Wilson (2/36 Foot), Charles Kent (2/43 Foot) and Richard Booth (2/48 Foot) were all promoted from private soldier to schoolmaster in 1812.[33] In some cases new recruits were rapidly promoted to the rank of schoolmaster-sergeants. Thomas Temple was enlisted in the 2/57 Foot at Durham on 30th October 1811 by Captain Charters' recruiting detachment, was quickly

30 TNA WO 12/1528: General Muster Books and Pay Lists, Royal Waggon Train.
31 Clarke, *A New History of the Royal Hibernian Military School*, p. 123.
32 Regimental Head Quarters 3rd Foot Guards (Scots Guards), Regimental Order Book, List of Sergeants 1815.
33 TNA WO 12/934: 12/ 5099; 12/5635;12/6031, General Muster Books and Pay Lists,10th Dragoons, 36th Foot, 43rd Foot, 48th Foot.

promoted, and is listed as the schoolmaster-sergeant in the battalion's pay rolls from December 1811 to March 1812.[34]

On 28 December 1811 a Circular letter was sent from the Horse Guards under the signature of Sir Harry Calvert, still Adjutant General, to the officers commanding regiments and corps in England, directing that when a soldier had been selected to fill the post of Schoolmaster-Sergeant, he was to travel to the Royal Military Asylum Chelsea to receive information explaining the methods adopted at that institution for instructing children according to Dr Bell's system. The commanding officer was to notify the name of the sergeant to the Horse Guards with the date of his probable arrival at Chelsea, where he was to report to Lieutenant Colonel Williamson, the Commandant of the Asylum.[35] Arrangements were made to billet the sergeants at taverns in Chelsea and the first group had completed their instruction by 6 February 1812. Calvert's circular was addressed to 31 regiments and Lieutenant Colonel Williamson informed Calvert that Dr Andrew Bell reported that 22 sergeants had conducted themselves in an orderly manner and were qualified to join their respective corps and discharge the duties of schoolmaster in their regimental schools. Calvert's circular was subsequently sent to other units and a further group of designated schoolmasters was instructed by Bell and together these two courses produced 82 qualified schoolmasters. Other courses followed, each lasting about four weeks and embracing regiments and corps stationed throughout the United Kingdom. The fifth group of 32 sergeants, who had been instructed by Rev. Clarke, the chaplain at the RMA, completed their course in July 1812.[36]

The soldiers receiving instruction at Chelsea came from a broad range of regular regiments and corps and from the British and Irish Militias. The first group of sergeants completing the course at Chelsea in February 1812 were from: the Royal Horse Guards and the first and second battalions of the 1st and 3rd Foot Guards; the 10th, 15th and 18th Light Dragoons; the Royal Waggon Train; the 36th, 43rd, 47th, 48th, 57th, 60th and 69th regiments of Foot; the North Gloucester, North York, Stafford, Sussex, Sligo and Tipperary Militias.[37] The audited Accounts of the Hibernian Society for Soldiers Children record that John Warren, who was one of the sergeants of instruction at the Hibernian School, also attended one of the courses at Chelsea and Bell's system remained the basis of the classroom instruction at Phoenix Park until the early 1840s.[38]

34   TNA WO 12/6708: General Muster Books and Pay Lists,57th Foot.
35   St John Williams, *Tommy Atkins' Children*, p.29.
36   St John Williams, *Tommy Atkins' Children*, p. 29.
37   NAM, Records of the Royal Army Educational Corps, Army Education before 1846, Box 22125, 'Letter from Colonel Williamson, Commandant RMA to Adjutant General 6/02/1812'.
38   Second Report of the Commissioners for Auditing Public Accounts in Ireland 1813, p. 150.

Many of the men attending the courses at Chelsea had to travel considerable distances from their regimental stations and their expenses were paid by their units after receiving authorisation from the Horse Guards. The pay roll for the 2/25 Foot for April to June 1812 includes a contingency, granted by the Horse Guards on 3rd June, for passage money (probably by sea) for schoolmaster sergeant Joseph Smith to travel from Berwick on Tweed to London. A soldier on the march received additional pay to cover his subsistence, but this does not always appear to have been sufficient to meet the cost of bread and meat in inns and taverns. Sergeant Robert Booth of the 2/48 Foot received an allowance to cover the extra cost of provisions during his journey from Banbury to the RMA. The pay roll of the 15th Light Dragoons contains an entry for Sergeant John Bullin for an allowance in lieu of meat and bread whilst on duty at the RMA '...learning Dr Bell's system of education.' Similarly, the regimental contingencies for Tipperary Militia, which was stationed at Chatham, show an allowance for its schoolmaster, Sergeant Ralph Reylance, whilst he was studying at Chelsea.[39]

There were no separate colleges for training elementary school teachers in Great Britain until the 1840s and the program of training courses at Chelsea in 1812 was a novel and ambitious undertaking. It unfortunately was not repeated and there were no more attempts to provide systematic training for regimental schoolmasters until 1846. In the intervening years, the soldiers who were appointed as sergeant schoolmasters had to refer to 'The Instructions for Establishing and conducting Regimental Schools', which had been circulated with the General Orders on regimental schools issued by the Horse Guards on 1 January 1812. The Orders emphasised that although the 'Instructions' only mentioned boys, the daughters of soldiers were also allowed to attend the schools, 'whenever the accommodations, and other circumstances will permit.'[40] The 'Instructions' also explained that there was an expectation that many of the sons of soldiers would follow their fathers and enlist in the Army.

A synopsis of the 'Instructions', which provided detailed guidance on the organisation of a regimental school and the methods of teaching reading writing and arithmetic is included in Appendix I. In common with most charity schools of the day, the regimental schools were ordered to commence the day with prayers and the lessons devoted to reading were to use selected religious texts. This was calculated to impress on the children 'from their earliest years, the principles of our Holy Religion, as Established in this Kingdom.' This did not cause any problems for the Scottish Regiments which simply interpreted this to mean the prayers and texts of the Established Presbyterian Church of Scotland, but in later years it would became a concern to the many Catholic (mainly Irish) soldiers in the Army, who with some

39   TNA WO 12/1202/4232/6031, 15th Light Dragoons,2/25,2/48 Foot; TNA WO
     13/3225/3226, Militia and Volunteers, Muster Rolls and Pay Lists, Tipperary Militia.
40   *General Orders and Regulations for the Army, 1816*, p. 333.

encouragement from their clergy, objected to their children being exposed to Anglican religious instruction.

Some of the early appointees as schoolmaster sergeants remained in post for many years. One notable example was Sergeant Thomas Rising of the 7th Dragoon Guards. He was born at Wymondham, near Norwich, Norfolk and attested in the regiment at Westminster on 12 August 1805. He served in Spain in 1808 and 1809 during Sir John Moore's campaign. He was appointed to schoolmaster sergeant on 25 December 1811 and remained in post for 22years until he was discharged having served 'in the most meritorious manner', on 12 November 1831, 'worn out' and with defective eyesight.[41] Long service as schoolmaster sergeants was probably more common in the Household regiments and the line cavalry, which typically spent most of the thirty years following the Napoleonic War at stations in Great Britain and Ireland. Infantry regiments of the line were rotated throughout the Empire and often spent many years at stations in the colonies. As we shall see in the following chapters, the manpower of these regiments suffered constant attrition, most commonly through disease, and this resulted in a high turnover of schoolmaster sergeants.

Others appointed during the War, including a few of those who had been instructed at the RMA, remained in post for relatively short periods of time and are recorded in the pay rolls as moving to other posts in their battalion, or as having been reduced to the ranks. Private George Wilson of 2/36 Foot had been promoted to schoolmaster sergeant whilst his battalion was stationed at Horsham, Sussex in December 1811 and he successfully completed Dr Andrew Bell's training course at Chelsea. He was the battalion's schoolmaster for some twelve months but is recorded as having transferred to serve as a 'hospital mate' at the York Military Hospital in March 1813. He was succeeded as schoolmaster-sergeant by Private John Jewry, who remained as the second battalion's schoolmaster until he transferred to the first battalion in October 1814.[42]

Some of the early appointees would have been found wanting during training at Chelsea, others may have been uncomfortable with their duties as schoolmasters. Soldiers who were literate and numerate, and of good a character, were widely sought after as staff sergeants in the paymaster's office or the orderly room and were able to transfer to these posts if they were unhappy with their duties at the regimental schoolmaster. George Frederick Munns was promoted to corporal in the 4/1 Foot on 25 December 1811 and to schoolmaster-sergeant on 25 January 1812. On 1 May 1812 he moved to the post of Quarter master sergeant and John McGowan was promoted from private as the schoolmaster in his place.[43] At least one of the early appointees as schoolmaster found time to combine his duties with that of paymaster clerk. The

41   TNA WO 100/106: Peninsular Medal Roll.
42   TNA WO 12/5009: General Muster Books and Pay Lists, 46th Foot.
43   TNA WO 12/2018/9: General Muster Books and Pay Lists, 1st Foot.

pay rolls of the 2/48 Foot record that Richard Booth drew pay for both posts from December 1812 until discharged in October 1814.

We have seen that Joseph Smith, the schoolmaster of the 2/25 Foot, attended one of the first training courses at the RMA. He is described as the schoolmaster in the battalion's pay rolls for 1812 and 1813, although confusingly he is listed and paid both as a sergeant and a private. The battalion formed part of the expedition to Stralsund in the summer of 1813, but Joseph Smith remained with the depot at Woodbridge. In the June to December 1813 musters he is listed as schoolmaster-sergeant but rated and paid only as a private. At the end of December, the battalion was in Holland and Smith joined it from the depot, but in the subsequent musters the post of schoolmaster-sergeant is unfilled and Smith is listed and paid as a private. A small number of women and children accompanied the battalion to Holland, but the regiment's inspection returns indicate that a school was not opened whilst the battalion was in that country. Smith was reduced to private on 20th December 1813, but in January 1814 he was promoted corporal and remained with that rank until the battalion returned from the continent. His education qualified him for useful employment during this time and he served variously as clerk to a brigade major and on other public duties in Antwerp and Brussels. Smith transferred to the 1/25 when the second battalion was disbanded at Cork in February 1816 and served with the regiment until he was discharged as a sergeant after 26 years' service in 1838. Interestingly, Smith did not serve again as the schoolmaster, but like many other non-commissioned officers of the day he was repeatedly reduced to private and subsequently again promoted to sergeant (in his case on three further occasions) during the remaining years of his enlistment.[44]

The case of the third battalion of 14th Foot (3/14) is particularly interesting. Sir Harry Calvert, the Army's Adjutant General was the Colonel of the regiment and exceptionally a third battalion was formed at Weedon barracks in 1813 with volunteers from the militia, many of whom were raw lads and farm boys from Buckinghamshire. James Bower is listed as a private in No.7 Company in the battalion's muster rolls from 25 December1813 to 24 February 1814. In the following month he was designated as the battalion's schoolmaster-sergeant. A number of older soldiers were attached to the battalion as sergeants, but the low average age of the unit meant that there would have been few children for pupils at the regimental school and the intention must have been to provide some elementary education for the boys and young soldiers. The choice of James Bower as schoolmaster, however, was unfortunate and in the March to June 1814 muster he is listed as having deserted from the battalion 'on consequence of having (previously) deserted from another corps.' In the autumn of 1814, it was intended to send the battalion to America, but on 24 December 1814 it was ordered to remain at Plymouth to await disbandment. The battalion however was reprieved and sent to Flanders in March 1815, but there is no record of a schoolmaster-sergeant,

---

44   King's Own Scottish Borderers Museum, Miscellaneous Return's Book 25th Foot 1811-1817; TNA WO 12/4232: General Muster Books and Pay Lists, 25th Foot.

neither during these months, nor in the months before the battalion was disbanded in December 1816. Confusingly, James Bower is listed on the Waterloo Medal Roll, as the 'Schoolmaster Sergeant' of the 3/14 Foot, but although the young soldiers of the 3/14th may have had little opportunity to attend school, they received a rather different education when on 18th June they served bravely, although in no great danger, on the right flank of the allied army at Waterloo.[45]

The importance of the senior NCOs in a battalion was recognized in 1813 by the decision to appoint a 'colour sergeant' to every company in the infantry. This probably increased the commanding officers' difficulties in selecting and retaining suitable men of good character as regimental schoolmasters. The pay for colour sergeants was above that earned by schoolmaster sergeants.[46] The colour sergeants were likely to proceed on active service with the possibility of a share of any prize money, whilst the schoolmaster might remain at the regiments' home station or depot. Furthermore, commanding officers would look to the establishment of colour sergeants when the post of sergeant major became vacant. The advantages of remaining as colour sergeants was still being cited in the early 1840s as one of the difficulties in persuading promising soldiers to accept the post of schoolmaster-sergeants. The experience of the 4th battalion of the 1st Foot (Royal Scots) is a case in point. John McGowan had been promoted schoolmaster-sergeant from private in May 1812 in the place of George Frederick Munns who had moved to become Quartermaster sergeant. In August 1813 when most of the battalion sailed to Stralsund, a very large depot remained at Musselburgh and included two boys' companies and a regimental School. The Horse Guards had decided that schoolmaster-sergeants should not accompany their battalions on active service and McGowan is listed sergeant in the August muster and was appointed a colour sergeant in September 1813.[47] There is some uncertainty about the superintendence of the regimental school at the depot from August 1813 to February 1814 and the pay rolls do not mention a schoolmaster until March 1814, when Henry F. Worthington was promoted as schoolmaster from private. The District Inspection return nevertheless confirms that there was a well conducted regimental school with 174 pupils when the depot had moved to Edinburgh in September 1814 and it may have been placed under the general superintendence of one of the battalion's officers with some of the boys acting as monitors.[48]

The general orders from the Horse Guards of 1st January 1812 emphasised the commanding officers' duty to ensure that the regimental schools were under proper guidance and management and were 'conducted on military principles.' This was

45 H.O'Donnell, *Historical Records of the 14th Regiment* (Devonport: A. H. Swiss 1892), pp. 102-18, 333; TNA WO 12/3227: General Muster Books and Pay Lists 14th Foot .

46 *General Regulations and Orders for the Army 1816*, General Order, Horse Guards, 6th July 1813. The pay amounted to 2s/4d for colour sergeants and 1s/10d for other sergeants.

47 TNA WO 12/2019: General Muster Books and Pay Lists,1st Foot; Leask and McCance, *Regimental Records of the Royal Scots*, pp. 295-6.

48 Leask and McCance, *Regimental Records of the Royal Scots*, pp. 295-6.

followed by a Circular Letter from the Adjutant General to the General Officers Commanding Districts at Home and Stations on 18 January 1812, instructing officers in command of brigades and districts '...to be minute in their confidential reports as to the regimental schools in the corps under their command.' They were required to receive and make returns of the schools, the number of scholars of each sex, and to include the opinions of the general officer and the chaplain, or officiating chaplain, as to the talents and the correctness of conduct of the sergeant schoolmaster, and of the progress of the children under his tuition.[49]

Commanding officers included an inspection of the condition of the regimental school in the list of duties for the orderly officer in their regimental standing orders. The officer was usually required to make a written report stating the time at which he had visited the school and record whether he had found the school to be clean and to list any complaints about its operation.[50] The regimental schoolmaster was required to keep a register and to make a weekly return to the commanding officer of the individual pupils' attendance at the school distinguishing between children and the men with their names and rank.[51] Some brigade and district commanders took steps to ensure that they were informed about the condition of the schools in the regiments in their respective commands, prior to the biannual district inspection by the Adjutant General's staff. In June 1812, Sir Henry Burnard, the commander of a brigade of the Foot Guards, issued an order requiring a return from the commanding officer of each battalion on the condition of its school and the number of scholars. This was followed in October by a brigade order, which required each battalion's quarter master to provide a weekly report for the commanding general on the condition of the schools.

Some regimental officers took a particular interest in their schools. In 1812, Major Peter Brown of the 23rd Regiment, who was the Commandant of the detachments at the depot at Belem (Lisbon) in Portugal, established a school for soldier's children on model of the RMA. Thirty years later he was appointed Commandant of the RMA and presided over its reorganization into a Normal school for training schoolmasters and a Model School for the Army.[52] Few officers took such a close interest in the progress of the pupils as Lieutenant George Peevor of the 17th Foot, who having been ordered to rest after the fighting in Nepal in 1816, volunteered to take charge of the regimental school at Ghazeepore (Ghazipur), which previously had been conducted by the army chaplain. During the next seven years until the regiment returned home, he spent his spare time instructing the children and young soldiers attending the school and gained regular commendation from the inspecting general. He also established the '17th Regimental School Reward of Merit', which was awarded annually from

49 *General Regulations and Orders for the Army 1816;* General Order, Horse Guards 1 January 1812; NAM, Circular letter Horse Guards, 18th January 1812.
50 Suffolk County Archives, Standing Orders of the 12th Regiment of Foot 1817.
51 King's Own Scottish Borderers Museum, Standing Orders of 25th Regiment of Foot 1834.
52 L. Rudd, *The Duke of York's Royal Military School* (Dover: St George's Press,1935), p. 95.

1816.[53] Most officers' contact with the regimental schools, however, was restricted to visiting the school and reporting on its general order and cleanliness as part of their duties as the orderly officer of the day.

The Horse Guards acknowledged from the outset that the regimental officers could not be expected to assess the progress and educational attainment of the pupils. The General Order of the 1st January 1812 stated that it was incumbent on the chaplains and other clergymen engaged in clerical duties in the army to assist the military officers in promoting the success of the schools, by frequently visiting those in their area and scrutinizing the conduct of the schoolmasters; examining the progress and general behaviour of the children and reporting their observations to the commanding officer. The Adjutant General's Circular of 18th January 1812 went further and expected the general officers and chaplains to report not only on the conduct, but also the talents of the schoolmaster.

In giving chaplains such a key role in supervising the performance of the schools the Horse Guards may have been drawing on the regulations of the RMA and the Hibernian School Phoenix Park, both of which designated the chaplain the 'Inspector of Education' for the institutions. Although the chaplains' posts at Chelsea and Phoenix Park were residential, supervision by the commandant and the oversight by the commissioners and governors were essential to ensure that a satisfactory standard of schooling was maintained.

During the eighteenth century the post of regimental chaplains came to be regarded as little more than a sinecure, and in 1796 they were replaced by garrison chaplains and a Chaplains' Department was established headed by a Chaplain General, responsible to the Secretary at War. This effort to revitalise the chaplain's service met with no great success and in 1809 a number of staff chaplains were appointed through the offices of the Archbishops of Canterbury and York and the Bishop of London.[54] The primary duty of military chaplains, whether attached to garrisons, brigades or regiments, was to perform divine service on Sunday for the various units in their division and to visit the sick in the hospitals in their areas at least twice in each week. Visiting and scrutinizing the regimental schools was an additional responsibility, which did not carry any extra pay and was not always welcomed by the incumbents. Although the pay and allowances for a chaplain was that of a major, there were never enough military chaplains to provide any meaningful supervision of the schools across all the regiments and corps in their various stations at home and overseas.

The half yearly confidential reports and returns for the military districts in the final years of the Napoleonic War contain little about the condition of the schools

53   E.H.B. Webb, *A History of the 17th (The Leicestershire Regiment)* (London: Vacherand and Son, 1912), pp. 121-2; White, *The Story of Army Education, p.* 28. White mistakenly places Lt. Peevor in the 18th Foot. Peevor subsequently transferred onto half-pay and was appointed a Captain of Invalids at the Royal Hospital Chelsea but maintained an interest in elementary education and was a subscriber to a number of educational charities.

54   TNA WO 4/347: 'Administrative History of the Chaplains' Department', p. 3.

and focus largely on noting failures to submit returns and recording that chaplains or officiating clergymen had visited the schoolroom. The Adjutant General admonished the commanding officers of districts for any omissions in their returns and ordered to them to ensure that in future this was remedied and that the chaplains visited all the schools. Letters from the Adjutant General to District commanding officers commenting on the December 1812 and June 1813 reports and returns relate mainly to the absence of numerical returns and chaplains' visits to militia regiments.[55] In 1814, in addition to the Chaplain General, the department contained only 36 other chaplains and recourse was often made to Anglican clergy in the locality where the troops were stationed, and who received an annual stipend to act as officiating clergymen and undertake 'the clerical duties of the Army.'[56] Although there were chaplains at the larger garrisons such as Gibraltar, in the West Indies, and at the Cape Colony, there was a particular difficulty in obtaining suitable clergymen willing to accompany the army on active service. In the post Napoleonic war years, a weakened army chaplaincy was no substitute for a properly constituted inspectorate to supervise the standard of education provided by the regimental schools.[57]

The system of regimental schools that was established in 1812 was to last, with very little change, until 1846, when a Normal School for selecting and training army schoolmasters was opened at the Royal Military Asylum, and arrangements were made for educational inspections army schools. The system of regimental schools established was far from ideal and commanding officers faced many difficulties in finding and retaining a suitable soldier in their regiment for promotion as schoolmaster sergeant. There were no long term arrangements for the training of schoolmasters and the general orders, including the *Instructions for Establishing and Conducting Regimental Schools* according to Dr Andrew Bell's system, remained the only guidance available for conducting the schools. Commanding Officers could not order soldiers to attend at the school and parents could not always be relied on to ensure that their children were regularly in class. Nevertheless, the regimental schools survived the retrenchment in the military expenditure in the years following the end of the Napoleonic War. In the absence any system of regular assessment of the pupils' progress or the systematic inspection of the regimental schools, we have no measure of the standards of literacy and numeracy achieved by the pupils and these would have varied greatly over time and between regiments. Doubtless the quality of the teaching provided by the schoolmaster sergeants left a great deal to be desired, but this was at a time when there was no formal system of teacher training and little control over the standards of teaching at the civilian schools.

55   TNA WO 3/59: Commander-in-Chief Out-letters 1813.
56   *General Regulations and Orders for the Army1816*, General Order, Horse Guards, 8 November 1811.
57   Haythornthwaite, *The Armies of Wellington*, pp. 123-5.

Establishing the regimental schools across the Army was nevertheless a considerable achievement and they were the first centrally organized and publicly funded elementary schools for children and adults in Great Britain. In the year ending January 1837 there were on average 46 boys, 47 girls and 14 adults in each of the schools of the cavalry regiments and an average of 47 boys, 41 girls and 44 adults at the regimental schools of the infantry. On 1st January 1841, the 171 regiments of the British Army were providing an elementary education for upwards of 15,000 adults, children and adults.[58]

It was not until 1833 that the first grants were made by the Westminster Parliament to support elementary education for children in the British and National Societies' schools in England and Wales, and it was 1870, before Parliament enacted legislation empowering elected local school boards to raise rates and establish schools for children who were not receiving an elementary education in 'charity schools'. It was much later still before there was any public provision for adult education.

The success of the Horse Guards in establishing regimental schools throughout the Army owed a great deal to the partnership of the Duke of York, the C-in-C, and the Adjutant General Sir Harry Calvert. They had worked together from 1799 and in the following decade had established the Royal Military Asylum and encouraged the COs who had been given permission to enlist boys to form regimental schools, before finally establishing a uniform system of regimental schools across the Army.[59] Frederick Duke of York has received most of the credit for these achievements and Sir Harry Calvert's influence is difficult to assess. In the words of a fellow officer, he may have been more than '...an able instrument in giving effect to many valuable improvements in the administration and discipline of the army'[60], or perhaps he was simply the 'faithful organ' of the Duke of York's 'benevolent intentions.'[61] Both men however came to believe that greater attention to the welfare of the rank and file would be of considerable benefit to the efficiency of the Army and York in particular has been called the 'soldiers' friend'.[62] The success in establishing the RMA and the system of regimental schools would not have been possible without political support at the highest level within successive governments that sanctioned the necessary public funding. With hindsight, the military departments appear to have been politically adept in shifting the emphasis of their advocacy in support of these innovations: at

58   NAM, Records of the Royal Army Educational Corps, Army Education before 1846, Box 22125, 'Letter from the Secretary at War to the Commissioners of the Royal Military Asylum showing the existing grants for teachers and the numbers of children attending schools in the regiments in the several varieties of the Service, February 1842'.
59   Calvert served as a Commissioner of the RMA until his death in 1826 and the Commissioners' Minute Books show that he rarely missed a Board meeting.
60   Oxford Dictionary of National Biography, First Edition (1885-1900), p. 725.
61   Memoir of General Sir Harry Calvert, The United Service Journal 1829, Part I, pp. 26-30.
62   Oxford Dictionary of National Biography, p. 25; Haythornthwaite, The Armies of Wellington, p. 16.

one time in the case of the Royal Military Asylum arguing that the nation had an obligation to make some provision for the orphans and children of soldiers, whilst later also to provide schooling for the children of serving soldiers in regimental schools. At other times, the emphasis was on the practical advantages to the Army that would flow from the provision of elementary education for soldier's children and particularly their sons, and from giving some education to enlisted boys and young soldiers.

An appeal to the obligations of a grateful nation to its soldiers could have been expected to strike a sympathetic chord with the public and in Parliament during the War, when enthusiasm for the Army was high, but sentiment might change rapidly once peace was declared. On 16 January 1815, the Duke of York issued a General Order to commanding officers in which he expressed satisfaction about the progress of the regimental schools in meeting their objectives, but he drew attention to the importance of the children being instructed in the '...means of making themselves useful and gaining their livelihood' This he argued could be cheaply effected by '... employing the best qualified and best behaved woman of each regiment in instructing the girls in plain work and knitting' and the regimental tailors and boot and shoe makers in instructing the boys in their respective trades. By these means the children at an early age would be 'rendered useful to the regiment and be enabled to gain their own subsistence.' The Horse Guards considered that by an economical application of the funds allocated for the regimental schools and for arranging for the sale of the children's work there would be no need for any additional expense.[63] None of these suggestions would have been regarded as reprehensible or out of place at a time when children helped out on farms and undertook household chores, and were sent out to work at an early age as domestic servants or in workshops, factories, and coal mines. Moreover, the Hibernian School in Phoenix Park and the Royal Military Asylum at Chelsea were already providing some instruction in trades for both the boys and the girls, but the timing of the Order nevertheless is significant.[64] The Horse Guards may have been anticipating that the end of the wars with France would be followed by reductions in the Army Estimates, and that it might unwise to rely upon the continuing benevolence of Parliament towards the Army or the sympathy and gratitude of a grateful nation to ensure the future of the regimental schools.

63   *General Regulations and Orders for the Army 1816*, p. 409.
64   The Inspection reports for the North Britain District for October 1813 and May 1814 noted that the Musselburgh depot school of the 4/1st Foot taught some of the girls needlework and that they were making shirts for the soldiers. This and similar reports may also have had some influence on the thinking at the Horse Guards. Leask and McCance, *Regimental Records of the Royal Scots*, p. 296.

6

Management of the Regimental Schools 1816-46

The structure and administration of the Army's regimental schools changed little in the thirty years following their introduction in 1812. During these years there was no staff of officers at either the Horse Guards or the War Office with responsibility for the supervision and inspection of the schools. The largest expense to the public was the salaries of the schoolmaster sergeants, one of whom had been added to the establishment of each regiment and corps. The first votes for these expenses were enumerated in the annual Army Estimates from 1812. The expenses were included in the total vote for the Army establishment - cavalry, infantry, and household troops. There was no specific reference in the vote to the costs of paying the schoolmaster sergeants and the only expense for the regimental schools that could be separately identified was a small amount to cover the costs of writing and learning materials.[1] When for reasons of economy, the line infantry battalions were reduced to eight companies in 1821, the schoolmaster sergeants remained part of the authorised establishment of each battalion. This simple piece of accounting protected the regimental schools from the attention of those in Parliament who wished to see further retrenchment in military expenditure and who were pressing for the abolition of any departments of the Army not deemed essential to its operations. The succession of orders that established the regimental schools issued from November 1811 to January 1815 were incorporated in the General Regulations and Orders for the Army, subsequently described as King's (or Queen's) Regulations as issued from time to time by the Adjutant General. The regulations for 1822 and 1837 contain identical instructions for the conduct of the regimental schools. They explained that the main purpose of the schools was to assure non-commissioned and private soldiers that the Crown wished to promote the education and welfare of their children so that they should be raised to become loyal subjects and good Christians. In the case of boys, it was expected that they would become soldiers with schooling sufficient to qualify them to be efficient NCOs.

---

1   There was a similar parliamentary procedure for the schools of the Royal Artillery and the Corps and Sappers and Miners that were part of the Estimates of the Board of Ordnance.

Throughout these years, the Army regarded the presence of soldiers' wives and their children in the regiments and corps as at best a necessary evil. It was recognised that inevitably in an army recruited through long-term enlistment, a proportion of the NCOs and men would marry. Regimental standing orders warned men against marriage and pointed to the inconvenience that arose and the evils that would follow when a regiment was 'encumbered with women.'[2] The standing orders of the Queen's Dragoons Guards in 1795 had warned that the regiment already had more women 'than could possibly be allowed to embark on Foreign Service.' Officers were ordered to explain the miseries that soldiers' wives were exposed to when there were too many accompanying the regiment.[3] Standing orders exhorted the regiment's officers to take every opportunity to dissuade their men from marriage and pointed to the poverty endured by some of their comrades who had wives and children. Similar injunctions were included in the Standing Orders issued by the 10th Light Dragoons in 1799.[4] This issue was recognised in a number of regiments by the formation of friendly societies to assist soldiers' widows and orphans and to alleviate distress to families that could follow when a married soldier became ill and was sent to the regimental hospital. Nevertheless, many men wished to marry, and the Army attempted to regulate the numbers.[5]

Standing orders warned that men were on no account to marry without the consent of their CO and that those who did marry without this consent would be punished. Specifically, where permission to marry had not been obtained, men were forbidden to bring their wives into their quarters or sleep out of the barracks.[6] The wives of men who married with the permission of their CO however were admitted to 'the strength of the regiment' and were allowed to live in the barracks and receive rations. Nevertheless, the regimental order books indicate that many men married 'off the strength' [meaning without permission] in sufficient numbers for COs to frequently

2   Firing Line: Museum of the Queen's Dragoon Guards and the Royal Welsh; *Standing Orders, King's Dragoon Guard 1840*, p. 63.

3   Firing Line, *Standing Orders, Queen's Dragoon Guards1795*, p.74. A General Order from the Horse Guards dated of 10[h] April 1813 specified that when a regiment embarked for garrison duty abroad the lawful wives of soldiers were permitted to embark in the proportion of twelve per company and rations were to be issued to them. See *General Regulations and Orders for the Army1816*, p. 255.

4   Firing Line, Standing Orders King's Dragoon Guards 1840, p. 63; Horse Power Museum, *Standing Orders 10th Light Dragoons 1797*, p. 70.

5   M. Cuncliffe, *The Royal Irish Fusiliers* (Oxford: Clarendon Press 1859), p. 164; TNA WO 27/298: 'Confidential inspection report the of 39th Regiment at Xante, Ionian Islands 1840'.

6   Royal Irish Fusiliers Museum, *Standing Orders of 87th Regiment*, p. 30; Firing Line, Regimental Standing Orders, King's Dragoon Guards, p. 63. King's Regulations 1816 specified that only men with wives, who had married with the consent of their commanding officer (if not married previous to enlistment), were allowed to sleep out of their quarters, p. 67.

warn against the practice.[7] Recruiting parties earned bounties for the number of men they enlisted, but they were warned against enlisting married men. There are instances however where recruiting parties led married men to believe that once they had enlisted, they would be allowed to bring their wives into barracks.[8]

Regimental standing orders and entries in the regimental order books emphasised that marriage with the permission of the CO was a strictly limited 'indulgence' that entailed specific obligations.[9] A regimental order of the 83rd Regiment in May 1832 allowed one women for every seventeen men (exclusive of the wives of sergeants) to be admitted on the strength of the regiment, whereas the 12th Regiment limited the number of women to between two and four per barrack's room, depending on it size. In return for the indulgence of being allowed to reside in the barracks the wives were expected to undertake certain domestic duties.[10] This included undertaking the men's washing for their husbands' company or troop. The King's Dragoon Guards admitted women on the strength of each troop to 'one for about every ten men', which appears to have been determined by the number of women needed to do undertake this work. The married women of the 87th regiment were also expected to do the men's washing and any woman (sergeants' wives excepted) who refused to do so without good reason would be refused assistance when ill or in confinement.[11] Similarly, wives in the 12th regiment were required do the washing and also to cook for the men when the orderly cooks were attending parade. The regiment's women were warned that they must be as clean in their persons and dress as their work would permit and that on '...the first irregularity, dirt, wanting sobriety or inattention to what is required of them, they will be deprived of the 'indulgence' of living in barracks.'[12]

The Army was candid about the behaviour that could be expected from soldiers' wives. The CO of the 87th regiment required men who wished to marry to produce a certificate of the woman's good conduct before giving his permission. The regiment's standing orders also stated that the CO was determined never to allow his men to risk their happiness 'by marrying women of improper character.'[13] The Standing Orders of the 25th Foot, a regiment that drew many of its recruits from the Scottish Lowlands and Boarders, was not at all sanguine about the likely behaviour of its soldiers' wives. The women and children of the regiment were told that they were subject to military regulations and that orders that applied to them must be obeyed. There was a warning to the women that:

7   Royal Ulster Rifles Museum, Regimental Order Book 83rd Regiment, 27 June 1832.
8   Royal Ulster Rifles Museum, Regimental Order Book 83rd Regiment, 10 January 1831.
9   King's Regulations 1837, p. 370.
10   Royal Ulster Rifles Museum, Regimental Order Book, 83rd Regiment, 5 May 1832; Suffolk County Archives, Regimental Standing Orders of 12th Regiment of Foot, 1817, p. 36.
11   Royal Irish Fusiliers Museum, Standing Orders of 87th Regiment, p. 31.
12   Suffolk County Archive, *Standing Orders of 12th Regiment of Foot 1817*, p. 36.
13   Royal Irish Fusiliers Museum, *Standing Orders of 87th Regiment 1827*, p. 31.

Those who conduct themselves in any manner to disgrace their husbands, or the corps, will be precluded from any participation whatever in the indulgences granted to those of regular and respectable habits.

There was a warning about the evils of drink and a caution that:

A woman who gets drunk is sure to be the ruin of her husband, sooner or later; she cannot pretend to the slightest regard for her own reputation, or the comfort of her family, and must be expected to be classed below those of notorious infamy.

Soldiers' wives were advised never to make 'an appearance above their station', because any 'extravagant behaviour' would invariably lead to 'vanity', which 'was sure to terminate in vice.' They were also told to set their children a good example by their sobriety, frugality and neatness.[14]

Standing orders of the 3rd, 25th, 30th and 47th regiments all required the wives on their establishments to make sure their children attended regularly at the regimental school. It was emphasised that this was a duty incumbent on the soldiers' wives who were allowed live in barracks and receive rations. Wives and children were also required to attend divine service according to their religious persuasion.[15]

There was no suggestion in Kings' Regulations that married soldiers had a duty to make sure that their children attended regularly at the regimental school, or at what age the children might first be expected to attend. By the1840s some regimental standing orders prohibited the removal of boys and girls from the school without the permission of the CO and specified that absences through illness were to be certified by the regimental surgeon after a medical examination.[16]

Wives were not always willing to follow the orders of the CO. When the 40th Regiment was stationed on convict guard duty in Tasmania in April 1826, the women were especially truculent. They objected to the charges ordered by the CO as payment for doing laundry by asking for what they considered fair remuneration. Lieutenant Colonel Balfour the CO observed that the wives were under the apprehension that they were not under military discipline and that they alone could determine the remuneration for their work. He issued an order reminding the regiment that it was 'solely an indulgence' that wives could accompany their husbands and receive rations for their families at public expense. In return, they were expected to make themselves useful to the soldiers and officers of the regiment. He reiterated that the rates for

14 King's Own Scottish Boarders Museum, Standing Orders of 25th Regiment 1834, pp. 150-1.
15 Royal Irish Fusiliers Museum, Standing Orders of 87th Regiment 1827, p. 5.
16 Royal Ulster Rifles Museum, Regimental Order Book, 83rd Regiment, Leeds 12th March 1845, Limerick 26th May 1846.

washing and making shirts were fixed and non-negotiable. A list of the women who were entitled to receive rations was included in the regimental orders and the names of women refusing to work upon the terms set down were to be recorded and their families deprived of the 'indulgence' of rations. The names of these women would be sent to the Lieutenant Governor with view to their being sent back to their homes in the United Kingdom.[17] This was probably an exceptional case. However, children's absences from the regimental school of the 40th Foot at Hobart were so numerous that on 28th May 1826 Colonel Balfour issued an order that parents were always to send their children to school unless they were sick.[18]

The attendance of the regiment's children at school was encouraged not only for the munificent reasons declared in the Orders issued by the Duke of York in 1812 and subsequently repeated in King's Regulations. Children not in school or without supervision could be a nuisance around the barracks. COs did not expect the Schoolmaster's duties to be limited to instructing children. He was expected to supervise their behaviour outside the classroom and to reprimand and chastise them if they misbehaved.[19] The standing orders of the 3rd Foot (Buffs) required the schoolmaster to attend to the general smartness of the boys and to instruct them in saluting and showing respect for their officers. The officers of 3rd Foot Guards, the 3rd, 54th and 88th foot organised subscriptions to provide uniforms for children in their regimental schools.[20] For the same reason, the 87th Regiment encouraged families to buy clothing from the Quartermaster's Store at a discount. The regiment established a school fund and awarded 'premiums' [prizes] to deserving pupils.[21] It was the practice in this and in other regiments for the Schoolmaster Sergeant (and, if engaged, a schoolmistress) to march the children at the rear of the battalion on Sunday church parade. All of this was calculated to contribute to a sense of discipline and ensure that the children behaved in an orderly manner.[22]

King's Regulations specified that the Schools were to be run along military lines and organised according to Dr Andrew Bell's system, which been instituted at the Royal Military Asylum. Instructions for conducting a school based on Bell's system were issued to every regiment and battalion in 1812 and although they only mentioned boys, they specified that where accommodation and other circumstances permitted

---

17   Lancashire Infantry Museum, Regimental Order Book, 40th Foot 1824-6, pp. 156-7.

18   Lancashire Infantry Museum, Regimental Order Book, 40th Foot 1824-6, p. 171.

19   NAM, The Royal Army Educational Corps Archives, Army Educational Policy and Regimental Schools, Box 22126, Extracts from the 'Standing Orders of the 3rd Regiment (The Buffs) 1848'; 'Letter from the commanding officer 6th Dragoons, Brighton 12 November 1857'.

20   Headquarters, 3rd (Scots Fusilier) Foot Guards, Order Book, 20 October 1836; TNA WO27/150 'Confidential inspection report for 54th Regiment October 1820'; 'Confidential inspection report on 88th Foot, October 1820'; NAM, 'Standing Orders of the 3rd (The Buffs) Regiment 1848'.

21   Royal Irish Fusiliers Museum, Standing Orders of 87th Regiment, 1827, p. 72.

22   Royal Irish Fusiliers Museum, Standing Orders of 87th Regiment 1827, pp. 5, 72, 73.

girls should be allowed to attend. King's Regulations continued to refer to Dr Bell's 'Instructions', but further copies of these do not appear to have been included in subsequent issues of Kings' Regulation. The archives of the Army Educational Corps contain a note that the 'Instructions' were revised in 1827, but it is uncertain how widely any such amended instructions were circulated across the Army.[23]

The 'Instructions' specified that children should be taught the Catechism of the Anglican Church and that following morning prayers this was to be the first lesson of the day. This had the potential to cause some friction in the regiment and was a particular difficulty for COs who wished to encourage their children to attend the schools, especially were there was a large number of Roman Catholics in the ranks.

King's Regulations required COs to arrange for the regular acts of divine service on Sundays. Wherever military chaplains had not been appointed, the men were to be marched to and from the parish churches nearest to their quarters. However, the same regulations cautioned COs that men must not be punished for not attending the divine worship of the Church of England and that every soldier was at liberty to attend Sunday worship according to his religious persuasion providing that this did not interfere with his military duties.[24] In practice the Scottish regiments, wherever possible, attended the services of the established Presbyterian Church in Scotland and the children at their schools said the prayers and read texts that were used in these services. There was generally no objection in the Scottish regiments to the children being taught the Catechism of the Church of England.

The regiments that were predominantly Roman Catholic, often secured a Catholic clergyman to conduct divine service, but the religious education of Catholic children according Dr Bell's 'Instructions' in the regimental schools was a different matter. The Catholic Church was strongly opposed to the laity reading the bible without the guidance of its clergy and there were no Roman Catholic military chaplains during this period. Catholic families might prevent their children from attending the regimental schools if this involved reading the authorised King James' Bible and learning the Anglican catechism. This danger was avoided by allowing Roman Catholic parents to withdraw their children from the first lesson of the day at the regimental schools. In 1839, there were 165 children in the regimental schools at Portsmouth and 82 of these children were Catholic, whilst at Devonport there 141 children at the schools of which 53 were Catholic. At both stations the Catholic children were not required to learn the catechism of the Church of England and their parents were allowed to withdraw them from the first lesson of the day.[25] These arrangements appear to have worked

23 When the historical records of the Royal Army Educational Corps were transferred to the National Army Museum Chelsea, a list of items relating the History of Army Education before 1846 was included in Box 22125. Copy of Dr Bell's 1812 instructions was included in the box and the list notes that these were amended in1827.
24 General Regulations and Orders for the Army 1816, pp. 83-4.
25 TNA WO 143/38: 'Royal Military Asylum, Correspondence, Reports and Memoranda 1832-1845'. This information was provided by the COs of regiments and depots at these

well until the 1850s when the attitude of the Catholic hierarchy hardened against the regimental schools. In part this was because some books with marked Protestant characteristics, such as those issued by the Anglican National Society, continued to be used in the regimental schools, but more the significantly it was because the Catholic hierarchy in Ireland under the leadership of Archbishop (subsequently Cardinal) Paul Cullen, opposed 'mixed schools' in which Protestant and Catholic children were taught together by teachers who were not Catholics.[26]

The reports of the half-yearly confidential inspection on the state of the regiments in each military district (see below) reveal very little about the day to day organisation of the schools and the inspecting officer, who was normally a general officer, or a senior field officer, simply confirmed that they were conducted according to the regulations. Dr Bell's 'Instructions' were not reprinted in the King's Regulations and there is no record of how many schoolmaster sergeants had sight of a copy of these instructions or indeed the use that they were able to make of them. The 'Instructions' were written in a language that demanded a good standard of literacy and would have presented some difficulty for a soldier who had only a basic elementary education. A newly appointed schoolmaster sergeant very probably looked to his predecessor, or perhaps to the adjutant or a sympathetic officer, for guidance.

Bell's *Instructions* explained that the children should be arranged in classes, with those who were making a similar level of progress and attaining a particular standard being placed together in the same class. Children whose progress placed them at the top of a particular class were then promoted to a higher class and they were demoted from a class whenever they failed to maintain the required standard. The allocation of a child to a particular class therefore was determined not by age, but by attainment. The number of classes required in a particular school depended on the number of children at the school, but also on their attainments.

The military departments did not publish reports on the general condition and organisation of the Army's school during this period, but at least two descriptions of how a regimental school was organised have been traced. The earliest example, which has been preserved in the archives of the Hanover City Museum, is a handwritten copy of the weekly timetable for the Depot School of the King's German Legion at the Bexhill on Sea in 1813. This timetable shows that the Bexhill School was modelled on Dr Bell's *Instructions*. There were 63 boys and 51 girls at the school and children who were organised in three classes, although it not clear whether the '1ste Klasse' (First Class) was the highest or the lowest in terms of the pupils' achievements.

stations, in reply to inquiries from the Commandant of the Royal Military Asylum, acting upon the instructions of the Commissioners. The information was requested following questions in Parliament about the Anglican exclusivity of the religious instruction given to the children at RMA Chelsea.

26   P. Cullen, *Two Letters to Lord St. Leonards on the Management of the Patriotic Fund and the Second Repot of the Lord Commissioners* (Dublin: James Duffy 1858), pp. 23-8.

The timetable shows that the school was in session from Monday to Saturday, starting at 8.00 and finishing at 17.00, with a three hour break during the middle of the day. In conformity with Bell's instructions the lessons were organised in half-hour sessions. The school day commenced with lessons on the Catechism (which in the case of the King's German Legion would have been Lutheran), before proceeding to reading and writing of the alphabet and the formation of simple words. There was more reading and writing followed by arithmetic in the afternoons.[27]

A later example of the timetable for a regimental school is that for the 5th Dragoon Guards inspected at Manchester Barracks on 9th September 1840. The boys and girls in this school were taught together in the same class under the direction of schoolmaster-sergeant James Foster. The small size of the schools at the typical regimental station meant that in most cases it was impractical to maintain separate classes for the boys and girls, or to establish an infants' school for the very young children.[28] The 5th Dragoon Guards' school had only 38 children but was organised into five classes with the 5th Class being the lowest and the 1st Class the highest as defined by the pupils' achievements. The curriculum for each class reflected the educational attainment and progress of the pupils: the 5th Class concentrated on learning the alphabet, the 4th Class on spelling, the 3rd Class had lessons in spelling, reading and writing, the 2nd Class in reading, writing and arithmetic, whilst the 1st and highest class continued with these subjects and in addition had lessons in grammar and geography.

It was not explained whether the classes met together in a single large room as Bell's System envisaged or whether the classes met at different times or in separate rooms, but in each case it would have been common practice for the highest class to provided monitors to assist in teaching the lower classes.[29]

27   *Bexhill Hanoverian Study Group* <info@bexhillhanoveriankgl.co.uk historishes.museum@ hannover-stadte.de> (accessed 11th December 2011).
28   TNA WO 27/298: 'Confidential Inspection Reports and Returns for Regiments 1840, 5th Dragoon Guards'.
29   It is unlikely that there was dedicated school room at the Manchester Cavalry Barracks in 1840. The accommodation blocks were rebuilt in 1829-30 forming 49 barracks room for the sergeants and men, providing a cubic space of 494 feet per man. The 1849 plans identified a large married soldier's block of around 175 x 25 feet and smaller block incorporating a workshop, school and library. R. Bonner, 'Hulme Cavalry Barracks, Manchester', *Journal of the Society for Army Historical Research* (Autumn 2013), pp. 206-25.

Table 1. Regimental School of 5th Dragoon Guards, 9th September 1840. (TNA WO 27/298)

	Boys	Girls	Total
1st Class	5	4	9
2ndClass	9	3	12
3rd Class	5	0	5
4th Class	0	5	5
5th Class	5	2	7
Total in School	24	14	38

It is interesting to compare the organisation of the 5th Dragoon Guards' school with that of a civilian school of the same period. At the Kildare Society's Model School for Girls at Kildare Place Dublin in 1838, a girl was allocated to one of eight classes in reading, writing and arithmetic according to her proficiency in these subjects and with regard to the particular class in which she could make the greatest progress. However, the 1st class in each of the three subjects was the beginners' class and girls moved upwards through the classes as they exhibited the required attainment in each discipline. For example when learning to read: the girls in the 1st class learnt the letters of the alphabet; those in the 2nd class learnt to read words of two letters; those in the 3rd words of three letters; those in fifth, by line and part sentence and so on until they reached the 8th or highest class, where they read passages of ordinary sentences in paragraphs. The monitors who would help the schoolmistress with the lower classes were selected from the girls in the 8th class.[30]

The Designation of the beginners' class as the 1st class, with the children progressing to the 2nd and 3rd classes etc., as in the Dublin school, became the standard practice in elementary schools throughout the British Isles and was adopted in primary schools in the 20th century, although progression was then usually by age rather than attainment. The British Army's schools appear to have continued for some years with the practice of designating the two classes containing the most advanced pupils as the 1st and 2nd Class, with the 3rd, 4th Classes etc. containing the children who were working to a lower standard of attainment. The school of the 1st Battalion of the Grenadier Guards at Beggar's Bush Barracks in Dublin in 1869 for example had six classes. The 6th class was designated as the class for the pupils with the lowest

---

30   Private Papers, Elizabeth Crowther, Description and Observation Book, 9th March to 14th July 1838, Model School Kildare Place, Dublin. (I am grateful for Colonel J.B. Crowther, US Army, for permission to quote from this document.)

attainment, who were taught the rudiments of reading writing and arithmetic and the1st was for the most advanced pupils who were taught, inter alia, algebra, grammar and to how write from dictation. Similarly, at the RHMS Phoenix Park in 1870, the boys with the highest standards of achievement were in the 1st and 2nd classes and those with lower attainments were placed in the 3rd and 4th.[31]

The regimental schools in the post war years were not able to extend the children's elementary education much beyond instruction in reading, writing and some simple arithmetic. The typical untrained schoolmaster-sergeant of the day probably would not have been able to offer the lessons in history or geography that would be taught in higher classes of the Army's schools in the 1860s. There were however those in the 1820s who considered that some of the more able boys might usefully be taught some more advanced mathematics, such as algebra and geometry. This had been attempted with some success at the Hibernian Military School in order to prepare boys for entry to surveying companies of the Corps of Sappers and Miners. In India there was some recognition that sons of soldiers in the European regiments might benefit from a more advanced education and from 1823 the Governor General of Bengal instituted an annual system of grants to support the Cawnpore (Kanpur) Free School. This school had been established to provide young soldiers with a superior education than was offered by the regimental schools and included instruction in trigonometry. A succession of divisional commanding officers at Cawnpore took an interest in the school and it was developed to provide instruction for boys and young soldiers in both the European and native regiments at the station.[32]

The General Orders and Regulations issued in 1816 made no reference to attendance by enlisted boys and young soldiers at the regimental schools. This was probably because of the legal ruling in the case of Warden v. Bailey in 1811 that soldiers could not be ordered, as part of their military duties, to attend a regimental school. Nevertheless, adult soldiers and enlisted boys regularly attended the schools, and commanding officers reminded men who aspired to become NCOs of the need to attend and improve their elementary education to qualify them for promotion. The Horse Guards was well aware of this and in the 1837 Regulations COs were ordered to make an annual return (see below) of the state of the regimental school and the number of boys, girls and also the adults who had attended during the year.[33]

31   St John Williams, *Tommy Atkins Children* pp. 95-99;'Second Report of the Royal Commission on Military Education 1870', pp. 179-80.
32   *Bengal Presidency and Asiatic Register* (Calcutta, 1835).
33   *King's Regulations 1837*, pp. 234-5.

STATE of the SCHOOLS of the Regiment, Dated at on 1 January

	Admitted during the last Year	Quitted During the last Year	Now attending the Schools
Male Children			
Female Children			
Adults			
Totals			

Questions   Answers

Are the schools conducted according to established regulation?
Is the sergeant- schoolmaster duly qualified for his situation?
Name and age of the sergeant-schoolmaster?
Are the Schools visited frequently by the officiating Clergyman?
Signature of Commanding Officer

Although the legal ruling in the case of Warden v. Bailey prevented a CO from ordering an enlisted soldier to attend for instruction at the regimental school, many COs were prepared to put considerable pressure on NCOs to attend so that they could be better qualified to discharge their duties. The regimental order book of the 3rd Foot Guards contains a 'Battalion memo' issued in September 1816, which states that: 'The Commanding Officer is surprised to learn that so very few of the NCOs who are incapable of doing their duty in regard to writing attend the School.' He warned that if this continued, he was 'determined to punish them for neglect of duty.' NCOs were ordered to provide the Adjutant with a sample of their handwriting so that he could determine who should attend the school. In addition, the schoolmaster -sergeant was ordered to report any of these NCOs who failed to attend school when they were 'off duty'.[34] This was little short of a direct order.

The CO of the 2nd Battalion of the 3rd Foot Guards went a step further and, on 24 June 1836, he issued a battalion order directing:

> [T]hat all sergeants of every class, who have not sufficient knowledge of accounts to qualify them for the due performance of every duty which they may be called on to perform, will place themselves under the tuition of the

34   Regimental Headquarters, 3rd (Scots) Foot Guards, Order Books 1813-1836.

schoolmaster-sergeant, who will report monthly with the progress they are making in this branch of knowledge so indispensably necessary to soldiers.[35]

Many regiments published standing orders that were based upon the Regulations and General Orders issued by the Horse Guards. These invariably contained a section on the regimental school. The Sanding Orders of the10th Hussars issued in 1833 specified the duties of the schoolmaster-sergeant in relation to the children and stressed the importance of their attendance at the regimental school.[36] The Standing Orders of the 12th (The Suffolk) Regiment, issued by its CO, Lieutenant Colonel W. H. Forssteen in January 1817, omitted to specify the duties of the schoolmaster-sergeant and was silent about the attendance of the soldiers' children at the regimental school. Enlisted Boys, however, were ordered to attend until dismissed by the Adjutant. NCOs 'deficient in accounts, writing and spelling' were also expected to attend. The standing orders made clear that attendance at the school was a prerequisite for promotion and stated that '...nothing will give the Commanding Officer so good an opinion as the young man who desires to improve himself and those who make the greatest proficiency will be the first for promotion.'[37]

The Standing Orders of the 87th (Prince of Wales Royal Irish Fusiliers) dated 1827 stated that 'the discipline and interest of the regiment' required that when selecting NCOs, preference would be given, ceteris paribus, to men who on joining the regiment had attended the school and had acquired a competent knowledge of reading, writing and arithmetic. The officers of the regiment were encouraged to impress upon men who showed promise that a few months attendance at the school would be to their advantage. Adult soldiers who attended the school were charged fees that varied according to rank, but the Standing Orders explained that it would be worth the 'mere trifle' of one day's pay per month that it would cost them for their tuition. There were quarterly examinations of the men's progress in school and a note was made of those whose educational and general conduct qualified them for promotion. The CO scrutinised a sample page of writing from each man being considered for promotion. Any NCO whose education was not up to the standard for the discharge of his duties would be ordered to attend the school.[38]

The Standing Orders of the 47th Regiment issued in 1834 stated that candidates for promotion must attend the school every month before quarterly examinations and that they should attend as long before that date as possible. Once again, all NCOs who were not proficient in accounts, writing and spelling were expected to attend.[39]

35   Regimental Headquarters, 3rd (Scots) Foot Guards Order Books, 1813-1836.
36   Horse Power Museum, 'Standing Orders of 10th Hussars, 1833'.
37   Suffolk County Records Office, Standing Orders of 12th Regiment of Foot 1817, p. 54.
38   Royal Irish Fusiliers Museum, Standing Orders of 87th Regiment 1827, pp. 71-72.
39   Lancashire Infantry Museum, Standing Orders 47th Regiment 1834, pp. 84-5.

During the 1830s some similarity began to appear in the content and the wording of these regimental standing orders: for example the regulations of the 25th Foot and the 47th Foot each specified that NCOs and men at the school were 'to attend as regularly as at any other parade or roll calling.'[40] By the 1840s, these similarities had become pronounced and there was invariably a reference to the expectations that all NCOs deficient in writing, spelling, and accounts would attend at the schools and that private soldiers should attend if they had any ambition for promotion. The standing orders of the King's Dragoon Guards was unequivocal in stating that unless men attended the school, '...however deserving they may be in other respects, they will never be promoted', because they would be unfit for the due performance of their duties.[41] Boys taken in as drummers were expected to attend school until dismissed by the adjutant and any absence by men who were on the school registers was to be reported by the orderly officer. Most standing orders included forms on which the names and attendance of the scholars were to be entered and which were to be returned to the CO or the adjutant at monthly or weekly intervals.

Some attention in regimental standing orders was given to the curriculum for the instruction of adult soldiers. In particular, orders mentioned that men must be instructed to copy reports, returns and passes; the names of the officers and NCOs of the regiment; the different ranks in the Army and military terms such as: patrols, reliefs, sentries, paroles and countersigns. Men were required to behave properly at the School and were reminded that any disturbance would be punished.[42] The 47th Foot went further and its CO, Lieutenant Colonel Dundas, ordered that a copy of 'A Military Manual of Light Infantry and other Duties', which had been compiled by the regiment's Adjutant John Sinnott, should be used in the regimental school.[43] Although there is no documentary evidence, it is possible that some informal guidance on the curriculum may have been given by the Horse Guards, but more probably officers of different regiments forming part of the same garrison simply had sight of copies of their various standing orders.

Until the middle years of the century there was no pool of trained army schoolmasters on which regiments could draw. The military authorities did not see the need to organise a programme of training for the soldiers who had been selected by their COs to fill the position of sergeant schoolmaster. There was no repetition of the centrally organised training courses that had been organised at the RMA Chelsea in 1812, although three regiments did manage to secure training in Bell's Monitorial System for their schoolmasters at the Asylum, These however were ad hoc arrangements and

40 Kings Own Scottish Borderers Museum, 'Standing Orders 25th Regiment 1834', p. 120; Lancashire Infantry Museum, 'Standing Orders 47th Regiment 1834', pp. 84-5.
41 Fireline: 'Standing Orders, King's Dragoon Guards 1840', p. 64
42 Lancashire Infantry Museum, 3rd (The Buffs) Regiment 1845; Lancashire Infantry Museum, 'Standing Orders 30th Regiment 1850', p. 47.
43 J, Sinnott, A Military Manual of Light Infantry and other Duties (Chester: privately published, 1845).

there is no mention in the minutes and correspondence of the RMA Commissioners of any further training after that undertaken by Sergeant Thomas Dragg of the 4th Dragoon Guards in April 1821.[44]

The standing orders of the 3rd Foot (the Buffs) summarised the qualities that there were required of the ideal schoolmaster: he was to be a good moral character, of temperate habits and of a kind and conciliating disposition; and he must be competent to instruct both children and adults.[45] Many COs no doubt had to settle for somewhat lower standards and appointed any soldier of good character who had an elementary education. This was particularly the case in the infantry where the majority of battalions were stationed overseas for long periods. The point was well made in 1820 by the officer who inspected the 53rd Regiment in India in the Madras Presidency, Bangalore. He reported that the schoolmaster-sergeant of the well-attended regimental school was 'a diligent, well-disposed man, but not very clever.'[46]

The COs of regiments in some of the more isolated garrisons had even less choice. The schoolmaster of the 9th Regiment in the island of Mauritius in 1835 was thought to be perfectly well qualified for his duties, but he had recently been reduced by sentence of a court martial to the rank of private for drunkenness. However, he was allowed to remain in charge of a school with 18 boys, 13 girls and 52 men on the register and after his court martial his conduct was reported to have been 'pretty steady.'[47] Drunkenness continued to be a major problem in the regiments in Mauritius and the inspection report for the 87th Royal Irish at Port Louis in 1840 recorded that the schoolmaster-sergeant had been reduced to the ranks for drunkenness since the last inspection, but no one in the regiment was better qualified to be the schoolmaster and he remained in charge of a school with 23 boys and 31 girls and 60 adult soldiers.[48]

The conduct of a regiment's school was placed under the immediate supervision of the adjutant. In the case of the King's Dragoon Guards the adjutant was ordered to visit the school at least once per week to see that the King's Regulations and Orders for the Army were being followed.[49] With the assistance of company commanders and the regimental sergeant major, the adjutant would also have been expected to identify suitable candidates for the post of schoolmaster-sergeant.[50]

44   TNA WO 143/30, Royal Military Asylum, 'Commandant's Letter Book 1818-1827'. The other schoolmasters were Sergeants William Daley and Henry Lear of the 80th Regiment and Corporal Martin of 3/1st Foot Guards.
45   NAM, 'Extracts from the Standing Orders of the 3rd Regiment (The Buffs) 1848'.
46   TNA WO 27/150B: 'Confidential Inspection Reports and Returns for Regiments 1820, 53rd Foot'.
47   TNA WO 27/246-7: 'Confidential Inspection Reports and Returns for Regiments 1835, 9th Foot'.
48   TNA WO 27/302: 'Confidential Inspection Reports and Returns for Regiments 1840, 87th Foot'.
49   Fireline: 'Standing Orders, King's Dragoon Guards 1840', p. 64.
50   Suffolk County Archives, 'Standing Orders of 12th Regiment, Article 7'.

The selection of a schoolmaster from the ranks was always an uncertain business. The rank of sergeant carried authority, but his possession of some elementary education was no guarantee of teaching ability. Some newly appointed schoolmasters were soon found to be either unsuitable or ill at ease with their duties. This was not simply a matter of coping with boys and girls in the classroom. Many COs looked to the schoolmaster to supervise and censure the behaviour of the children around the barracks. When combined with a duty to report the non-attendance of the children at lessons, this could lead to disputes with their parents. Adult soldiers were free to attend the school, but many attended only reluctantly and after pressure from their commanding officer. Schoolmasters were expected to report those who regularly failed to attend School. Regimental standing orders in consequence often warned that any NCO or soldier who behaved improperly or caused a disturbance at school would be punished.[51]

It is not surprising that after the experience of serving in the post for a short time some schoolmaster-sergeants requested a transfer to other duties or were removed or reduced in rank by their commanding officers. In November 1825, Private George Hamilton was promoted as the schoolmaster-sergeant of the 16th Lancers at Cawnpore in the Bengal when the previous occupant of the post became ill and had been sent as an invalid to Calcutta. Hamilton remained in charge of the school at Cawnpore whilst the regiment took part in the siege of Bharatpore (Bharatpur), but in August 1826 he resigned the post and continued to serve with the regiment in the ranks.[52]

The payrolls of many of the infantry battalions record a high turnover of schoolmasters and the experience of the 5th Foot in the 1830s was typical. There were three schoolmaster-sergeants from 1832-40, each of whom was appointed within five years of enlistment and each vacated the post and was reduced in rank after little more than two years in the post.[53]

The general orders establishing the regimental schools in 1812 had specified that the post of schoolmaster-sergeant was to be that of a staff sergeant with all the privileges that came with serving at the regiment's headquarters, including the provision of separate sleeping accommodation in the barracks. This was especially attractive for married men, whose wives would enjoy more privacy in the schoolmaster's accommodation, than was afforded in the shared barrack room, where the usual practice was to suspend blankets between the beds of married and unmarried soldiers.

As previously noted, from July 1813, one sergeant in each company of the infantry was designated 'Colour Sergeant', with a higher rate pay than that received by a staff sergeant.[54] The only way that a schoolmaster-sergeant could increase his income to

51   Lancashire Infantry Museum, 'Regulations of 82nd Regiment 1844'.
52   TNA WO 12/1261: 'General Muster Books and Pay lists,16th Lancers'.
53   Northumberland Fusiliers Museum: 'Records of Service of Officers, Sergeants and Corporals, 5th Regiment 1830-1854'.
54   *General Regulations and Orders 1816*, General Order, Horse Guards, 6 July 1813, pp. 386-8.

that of the colour sergeant was where the regimental standing orders enabled him to charge adult soldiers fees (referred to as 'pecuniary allowances') for their instruction. For example, the standing orders of the 82nd Regiment in 1844 required payment to the schoolmaster of one shilling a month by sergeants, six pence monthly by corporals and drummers, and three pence by private soldiers.[55] A survey of infantry regiments stationed in the British Isles in 1845 revealed that pecuniary allowances had not been sanctioned for schoolmaster-sergeants in a sizeable minority of units. The schoolmaster-sergeants who did not receive fees were not only at a financial disadvantage compared with colour sergeants, they also had little chance of promotion from this position to a higher rank. The colour sergeant was the senior NCO in his company, and it was from the colour sergeants that the Regimental Sergeant Major was appointed. Some soldiers might have decided that accepting the post of regimental schoolmaster would limit their career prospects. It might be thought to be an advantage to remain as a junior NCOs in the hope of future promotion to company sergeant and then to Colour Sergeant. Others who initially were happy to be promoted from to schoolmaster-sergeant may subsequently have decided that they were better served by requesting a sideways move to the rank of sergeant. This did not involve any loss pay and although there was a potential loss of fee income in some units, the move kept open the possibility of promotion to colour sergeant. These considerations were cited by COs in the early 1840s as a reason for their difficulty in appointing sergeant schoolmasters and were one reason why the War Office in 1846 decided to recruit and train its own schoolmasters to take charge of the regimental schools.[56]

The Household Cavalry (1st and 2nd Life Guards and Royal Horse Guards) and the regiments of Foot Guards had little difficulty in retaining their schoolmasters, probably because these units were mainly stationed in the barracks in London and Windsor. In 1837, the 2nd (Coldstream) Guards had a flourishing school at St. George's Barracks Charing Cross in which 33 boys and 32 girls were taught reading, writing, and arithmetic for five hours each day. In addition, the school was teaching 16 private soldiers to read and write, and 34 corporals attended classes to improve their grammar and arithmetic. The schoolmaster-sergeant was assisted by a corporal who was exempt from other military duties.[57]

One battalion of Foot Guards was regularly rotated each year to form part of the Portsmouth garrison and every summer from 1823 one battalion of Foot Guards was rotated to relieve another at Dublin. In these instances, the women and children accompanied the men and the battalion's school was closed for the duration of the movement between stations. From time to time, detachments were sent from London to support the civil authorities when there were disturbances in the industrial towns

55   Lancashire Infantry Museum, Regulations of 82nd Regiment 1844.
56   TNA WO 43/361: 'Adult Pupils to Pay Charges', passim.
57   First Report of the Statistical Society of London on the Condition of Education in the London District of Westminster in 1837 (London: Royal Statistical Society, 1838).

in the midlands and north of England, but on these occasions the women and children and the schools remained in barracks in and around the capital and it was possible to operate a school. Exceptionally, two battalions of Guards were part of the expedition dispatched to Portugal in 1826 and battalions were despatched to Canada during the 1837/8 Rebellions. When detachments of the 2nd Foot Guards were sent to Canada in 1841, the wives and children remained in England.[58] The Foot Guards for the most part avoided the long periods of overseas service that was the fate of the line infantry battalions.

The schoolmaster-sergeants in the Foot Guards who were content with their duties and conditions of service remained in posts for a good number of years. Joseph Muscot, the first schoolmaster of the 1/3rd Guards in 1812, served until he was discharged with a recommendation for a pension in April 1817. Thomas Dunwell succeeded him and served until his death in February 1827 at age 47. Joseph Ashton was made sergeant schoolmaster in the 2/3rd Foot Guards in July 1814 and died in post in February 1823 at age 33. It was death or discharge from the service through incapacity that created a succession of four schoolmasters in the 1/3rd Foot Guards from 1825-35.[59]

The cavalry regiments appear to have had less difficulty than the infantry battalions in selecting and retaining their schoolmasters even though they had a compliment of Troop Sergeant Majors, which was the equivalent rank to Colour Sergeant in the infantry. Perhaps this was because most of the cavalry was retained in the United Kingdom. The 1st Kings Dragoon Guards was in Canada during the 1837/8 Rebellions and the 7th Dragoon Guards served in Cape Colony from July 1843 - April 1847, but otherwise the seven regiments of the Dragoon Guards remained at home and were occupied in garrison duties, deploying in support of the civil powers in Great Britain and Ireland. The 1st Royal Dragoons, the 2nd (North British) Dragoons and the 6th (Inniskillings) Dragoons also remained in the British Isles throughout this period.

Sergeant John Bibby was the schoolmaster-sergeant for the 6th Dragoons in December 1815. Born at in Kilkenny in Ireland he had enlisted on 7th July 1810. He is not described in the   regimental payrolls as a 'Waterloo Man' and therefore may have remained in charge of the regiment's school when the 6th Dragoons were sent to Flanders in 1814.[60] In the post war years, the regiment moved between cavalry barracks in England, Scotland and Ireland. John Bibby served as the schoolmaster until 3rd August 1827, when he was admitted to the hospital at Nottingham Barracks. The regiment was without a schoolmaster until 14th February 1828, when Private James Emerson was promoted to the post whilst the regiment was at Ipswich. In the meantime, John Bibby had recovered from his illness and was appointed staff sergeant

---

58   TNA WO 379/6: 'Disposition and Movement of Regiment 1803-1827'; Regimental Headquarters, 2nd (Coldstream) Guards, Order Books.

59   TNA WO 379/6: 'Disposition and Movement of Regiment 1803-1827'; Regimental Headquarters, 3rd (Scots) Regiment of Foot Guards, Order Books.

60   TNA WO 12/717, 724: 'General Muster Books and Pay lists, 6th Dragoons'.

in charge of the regiment's hospital. This did not involve any diminution of pay, which remained at 2s/2d per day and periodically as the hospital sergeant he received the bonus of a beer ration.[61]

Men who were sufficiently literate and numerate to be schoolmasters were qualified to discharge a number of duties at the regiment's HQ. On 24th February 1830 James Emerson moved to the post of Paymaster Sergeant in the 6th Dragoons after two years as schoolmaster and was replaced by Private James McCarter. Promoted sergeant, McCarter remained charge of the 6th Dragoon's school until September 1837, when he exchanged positions with John Bibby, who resumed his old post of schoolmaster-sergeant. Bibby oversaw the school until March 31st, 1838, when he obtained his discharge from the Army after 28 years' service. The following day Sergeant James McCarter resumed the duties of schoolmaster-sergeant. The careers of Sergeants Bibby, McCarter and Emerson demonstrate that a small number of experienced, reliable and educated NCOs were essential in a regiment's HQ. There was a limited supply of such men and when filing the post of schoolmaster, the COs had to consider the need to make other staff sergeant appointments.[62] Where a regiment remained at home for long periods and as in the previously noted case of Thomas Rising of the 7th Dragoons, the schoolmaster was content with his duties and the CO valued his work at the school, he might remain in post for many years.[63]

Many schoolmaster-sergeants had a very a heavy workload, teaching classes of boys and girls of varying ages, alongside classes for new recruits and older soldiers ambitious for promotion. Sometimes a corporal might be appointed to assist in the classroom, but more commonly the women of the regiment, especially the wives and daughters of the schoolmaster, assisted him in teaching the girls and young children. A schoolmaster-sergeant was not always the best person to oversee the younger children and the employment of female assistants, effectively as schoolmistresses, anticipated the infant schools that were established by the War Office later in century.

In 1825, the Royal Barracks in Dublin accommodated one regiment of cavalry and three battalions of infantry. Each unit had its own school and the sergeant schoolmasters were assisted by women from the regiment. Sergeant Thomas Bright of the 1st Battalion, of the 3rd Foot Guards, oversaw 14 boys and the adult scholars and his wife helped with teaching the 18 girls. Sergeant Thomas Dragg of the 4th Royal Irish Dragoon Guards had a large school with 84 children and his wife received an annual salary of £7-14-0 (paid for out of regimental funds) for assisting in teaching 39 girls. The school of the 88th Regiment was something of a family affair for some years and in 1820 Sergeant George Beck was assisted by his wife and daughter in managing a school of 90 children at Chester. In 1825, when the regiment was at the Royal

61   TNA WO 12/719-722: 'General Muster Books and Pay lists, 6th Dragoons'.
62   TNA WO 12 /722-24: 'General Muster Books and Pay lists', 6th Dragoons.
63   TNA WO 97/114/27: 'Royal Hospital Chelsea, Soldiers' Service Documents, Thomas Rising, 7th Dragoons'.

Barracks in Dublin, Beck had a large school of 69 children and his daughter was paid 14 shillings each month that the school was open in order to assist her father in teaching 32 girls. A schoolmaster could sometimes look beyond his wife or daughter for assistance. Sergeant Lachlan McKenzie oversaw the 78th Highland Regiment's school with 70 children at the Royal Barracks and a Mrs Stewart was paid 10 shillings per month for assisting him with teaching the 33girls on the register.[64]

The wives and daughters of the schoolmasters and other women of the regiment who assisted in the school probably spent much of their time teaching the girls to sew and knit (see below), but their assistance in teaching reading and writing would have been welcome especially in the larger schools. This assistance was ad hoc and was not officially recognised by the military departments, but the presence of female assistants where it existed, probably encouraged soldiers' families to send their daughters to the regimental school. Many of the regimental schools were much smaller than those at the barracks in Dublin and it was often impractical to run separate classes for the boys and the girls.

There is evidence that some parents were unhappy sending their daughters to co-educational schools when there was no schoolmistress or female assistant. The 68th Regiment stationed at Fermoy, Ireland in May 1830 had 92 women and 78 boys and 92 girls on its strength and 28 boys, but only 13 of the girls, attended the regiment's school. The officer conducting the half-yearly inspection commented on the small number of girls attending the school and observed that many parents refused to allow their daughters to attend because there was no schoolmistress and that instead they were encouraged by 'a pious captain's wife' to send the girls to a civilian school in the town. It would be a further ten years before the War Office recognised the need to employ salaried schoolmistresses in the regimental schools.[65]

COs had been instructed by the General Order of 16th January 1815 to make sure children were taught in practical ways that would help them to secure employment. In the case of girls, COs were ordered to select 'the best qualified and behaved woman' in each regiment to instruct the children in 'plain work and knitting'. The confidential inspection reports throughout this period frequently mention that the girls were being taught sewing and knitting by the women of the regiment. This was easy to organise and would not have required additional specialist accommodation in the barracks. In many cases, especially where it was difficult to obtain a women or girl Capable of assisting the schoolmaster-sergeant in the classroom, the education for soldiers' daughters was restricted to instruction in sewing and knitting. This nevertheless was

---

64   NLI, 'Second Report from the Commissioners of Irish Education Inquiry', Appendix No.7 (Parochial Returns), p. 560; TNA WO 27/150, 'Confidential Inspection Reports and Returns for Regiments 1828, 78th Foot'.

65   TNA WO 27/200: 'Confidential Inspection Reports and Returns for Regiments 1830, 68th Foot'.

useful to the Army, because many of the girls subsequently married soldiers often at a very early age.

The marriage register of the 14th Regiment records that Mary Ann Brown, the daughter of Private Samuel and Eleanor Brown, married the apothecary sergeant of the 11th Dragoons on 21 April 1822, when the regiment was in Bengal. Mary had been born in Bengal, on 21 February 1808 and was a little over 14 years of age when she married.[66] The official records for the Bengal Presidency list the marriages of many soldiers serving with the King's regiments, but often without specifying the age of their spouses. When schoolmaster-sergeant Thomas Hyder of the 49th Foot) married Jane Bateman, at Hazareebaugh(Hazaribagh) in November 1835 her age was not recorded, but subsequent research into the history of the Hyder family suggests that Jane was between 14 and 16 years of age.[67] In 1835 William Musgrave, the schoolmaster-sergeant of the 16th Lancers married Esther Avery aged fourteen, the daughter of Troop Sergeant James Avery. Esther may have been one of his pupils[68].

The General Order of 16 January 1815 also instructed COs to make arrangements for regimental tailors and shoemakers to instruct boys in their trades. This order was repeated in the 1822 and 1837 regulations. The 1837 Regulations suggested that the parents should be consulted about the trades in which their children would be taught. Older boys in cavalry regiments should be permitted to attend during 'stable hours' for the chance to be employed as grooms. The intention to instruct the boys in a useful trade however was probably the least successful feature of the scheme for regimental schools in the post war years.

The printed confidential report forms asked the inspecting officer to indicate if the children were instructed in trades and in case of the boys this was largely answered in the negative. The inspecting officers commented that the boys were often too young to learn trades (most were under ten years of age) and that it was not practical for the corps to give any instruction. At the Royal Military Asylum and the Hibernian Military School, additional sergeants of instruction were employed specifically to teach the boys tailoring and from time to time shoemaking, and specialist workshops for these purposes were established at each of these institutions. The regiments in their various stations could not spare the manpower to provide regular instruction in these trades to any significant number of boys and the specialist workshops at Chelsea and Phoenix Park could hardly have been replicated across the large numbers of garrisons at home and abroad. The confidential reports do contain the occasional reference to a boy learning the trade of tailoring or sometimes training as an armourer

---

66   It was not until 1929 that the law was changed to raise the age of marriage to 16 with parental consent.

67   York Army Museum, Register of Marriages of 14th Regiment 1807-1831, Historical Record NO.20, 1-308;BL: IOR, Marriage Records of the Bengal Presidency, N/1/24f.147.

68   John. H. Rumsby, *Discipline, System and Style: The Sixteenth Lancers and British Soldering in India 1822-1846* (Solihull: Helion & Co., 2015), p. 93.

or a regimental clerk, although much more mention is made, in the case of regiments in India, of the boys training as drummers and musicians.[69]

When a soldier's son, who was living with his father at a station overseas was old enough to enter employment, he often had little alternative but to enlist in the Army. The quarterly pay rolls of regiments frequently record the names of one or two boys who had enlisted with 'the permission' or 'on the authority' of the C-in-C or the local commander of the forces in a military district. In 1828 the 49th Regiment at the Cape of Good Hope enlisted two boys: James Pettigrew and Bernard Kelly on the authority of the Commander of the Forces in the colony. James was most probably the son of Sergeant James Pettigrew and Bernard the son of Private Timothy Kelly, both serving with the regiment at the Cape. In April 1835, when the regiment was in Bengal, the pay roll records that six boys enlisted by authority of the C-in-C and at least three of these had fathers in the regiment.[70]

It is not surprising that a regiment that was stationed overseas for many years made an effort to prepare its boys at an early age for their subsequent enlistment as boy soldiers. The confidential report on the 49th Regiment at Hazareebaugh in 1835 records that: 'boys being destined for soldiers are instructed in the drum, fife and bugle.'[71] The 16th Lancers was stationed at Meerut in 1830 and at Cawnpore in 1835 and returned to Meerut in 1840.The inspection reports for each of these years explain that the boys were not taught trades, but were taught to be soldiers and that invariably when they reached a proper age were enlisted into the regiment.

The Ceylon Rifles was one of the locally recruited 'colonial' corps on the Army List that was part of the British Army during this period.[72] These corps were governed by King's Regulations, served alongside the King's regiments, and the confidential inspection reports confirm that they maintained regimental schools. The Ceylon Rifles had been formed in 1820 from a number of earlier units that had been recruited to garrison the island when it became a British possession after its capture from the Dutch in 1796. In 1820 the regiment was chiefly Malay, with some Sinhalese and with European officers. It was formed into 11 companies with around 1,800 NCOs and men.[73] The men were encouraged to marry, and the soldiers' families were a nursery for the regiment. When it was inspected in 1830, there were 1,052 legally married 'native' women on its strength and there were also 743 'native' children (360 boys and

69   TNA WO 27/247: 'Confidential Inspection Reports and Returns for Regiments1835, 8th King's Regiment'; WO 27/297: 'Confidential Inspection Reports and Returns for Regiments1840, 3rd King's Light Dragoons'.
70   TNA WO 12/6052/6059: 'General Muster Books and Pay lists', 49th Foot.
71   TNA WO 27/247: 'Confidential Inspection Reports and Returns for Regiments 1835, 49th Foot'.
72   In addition to the Ceylon Rifles, there were the two battalions of the West India regiment, the Royal Malta Fencibles, the Sierra Leone Corps and the Cape Mounted Rifles on the Army List.
73   R.K. Silva , Early Prints of Ceylon (London: Serendibm Publications, 1985), pp. 78-9

383 girls).[74] Similar numbers of local women and children were recorded when the corps was inspected in 1835, 1836-37 and again in 1840. The regimental schools of the Ceylon Rifles did not admit any girls and concentrated on educating its boys and training them to be soldiers. There were some 170 to 200 boys in the school and who were taught to read and write in English and their own language. In the 1830s the commander of the forces in the island, who was also the inspecting officer, established a 'Board of Examination' to ensure improvements and the efficiency of the school. The confidential reports on the regiment were very favourable and the 1836 report judged the schoolmaster-sergeant to be diligent and attentive and 'as well qualified as any European NCO we can get here in Ceylon.' The school was very successful in meeting its objectives and the inspections returns recorded a large number of boy soldiers on its establishment and that there were no difficulties in providing recruits for the regiment during this period. The Royal Malta Fencibles also permitted a large number of married women. In 1836 there were 356 women, 257 boys and 279 girls with the regiment. This school for some reason the regimental school did not admit girls and only had 28 boys and 64 adults on its registers.[75]

In order to establish a functioning regimental school, the schoolmaster had to be provided with suitable accommodation for a school room. This was a recurring problem especially in the infantry, which was constantly moving between stations. The Horse Guards had addressed the issue of accommodation in 1812, but the arrangements were focused on units occupying the larger barracks in the British Isles. The Commissioners of Barracks had been authorised by the royal warrant issued in July 1812 to appropriate and fit up barrack rooms for use by the regimental schools, but this does not appear to have been a priority, either in the British Isles or abroad in the post Napoleonic war years. The 1812 warrant required that schoolrooms were to be provided only in the barracks that accommodated one thousand or more soldiers. Where there were fewer than one thousand soldiers, the warrant did not prohibit the use of a space in barracks for the school, but specified that room used for the school was not be 'dismantled' and might have to be given up if there was a more pressing need for the accommodation. In all cases where a room for the pupils could not be provided without infringing the spaces required to accommodate the regiment, a proportion attended the school in the forenoon and the remainder in the afternoon.[76]

Very few army barracks had been constructed in the British Isles during the 18th century and the older accommodation, such as that for the Foot Guards at the Tower of London, was particularly insanitary and poorly ventilated. A large number of

---

74　TNA WO 27/200: Confidential Inspection Reports and Returns for Regiments 1830, Ceylon Rifles'. There were also 14 legally married European women and 14 European children on the establishment.

75　TNA WO 27/200/247/263/298: 'Confidential Inspection Reports and Returns for Regiments 1830-1840, Ceylon Rifles', passim.

76　Royal Warrant Authorising the Commissioners of Affairs of Barracks to appropriate and fit up Barracks Rooms for Regimental Schools, (London: War Office, 1812).

barracks had been constructed during the Revolutionary and Napoleonic Wars, but these had become overcrowded and were unhealthy places. A Parliamentary Return on the condition of the Army barracks in 1847 listed some appalling facilities: 63 percent of the barracks only had water pumped from a well and some were dependent on rainwater collected in cisterns. WCs were rare and the rank and file used communal lavatories, over rarely emptied cesspits.[77] There were few separate married quarters outside the common barrack rooms and where there was pressure on accommodation for the troops, the provision of a schoolroom had a low priority. The Royal Barracks in Dublin however was exceptional. In 1826, all four of the regiments stationed there were allocated space to establish their schools. This was sufficient to accommodate the 14 boys and 18 girls of the first battalion of the 3rd Foot Guards, 45 boys and 39 girls of the 4th Royal Irish Dragoon Guards, 37 boys and 32 girls of the 88th (Connaught) Regiment and 37 boys and 33 girls of the 78th Highlanders. The schoolmaster-sergeants of each of the regiments in the barracks were assisted by one of the regiment's women who as acted as a schoolmistress for the girls.

It is possible that the accommodation at the Royal Barracks was sufficient for each corps to operate separate schools for the boys and girls. This was certainly the case in 1826 at the Barracks of the Royal Artillery at Island Bridge Dublin. In 1826 there were separate school rooms, each measuring 60 x 24 feet for the 50 boys and 40 girls, but the newer Richmond Barracks in Dublin City provided a dedicated room measuring 39 x 32 feet that was shared by the 27 boys and 32 girls who attended the school.[78]

The typical regimental school elsewhere in the British Isles had to make do with whatever accommodation could be spared in the barracks. The 40th Regiment was at Rochdale in 1820 and the schoolmaster-sergeant was reported as intelligent and attentive to his duties, but he did not have a dedicated school room and the CO's application for one had been rejected. The general officer inspecting the regiment concluded that the children and soldiers would make good progress with the tuition given by the schoolmaster 'so long as the school could be kept up.'[79] When a regiment moved into a particular military district, its headquarters was based in the local barracks, whilst detachments often were posted elsewhere, sometimes in a number of different locations in support of the civil authorities. This disrupted the children's and soldiers' schooling. Sometimes alternative arrangements could be made: for example in 1830 the 50th regiment was stationed at Blackburn where it established a school and some of the children and soldiers on detachment were able to attend the schools of other regiments' schools at Bolton and Oldham.[80]

77   J. Douet, *British Barracks 1800–1914* (London: English Heritage, 1998), pp. 117-18.
78   NLI, Second Report from the Commissioners of Irish Education Inquiry, Appendix No.7, *Parochial Returns of Schools*, House of Commons Sessional Papers, pp. 542, 560-564.
79   TNA WO 27/50: 'Confidential Inspection Reports and Returns for Regiments 1820, 40th Foot'.
80   TNA WO 27/200: 'Confidential Inspection Reports and Returns for Regiments 1830, 81st Foot'. In total, 30 boys, 23 girls and 81 men of the 50th regiment attended the three

There does not appear to have been any purpose built school accommodation in Great Britain until chapels with attached schoolrooms were built in the 1850s. The large 'Napier Barracks' constructed at Bury, Ashton under Lyne, Preston, and Sheffield in the 1840s did not contain any dedicated facilities for the resident regiment's schools.[81]

The lack of suitable accommodation was often a greater difficulty for units serving overseas, especially in some of the smaller colonial stations. In 1835 the school of 76th Regiment at St Lucia in the West Indies had 24 children and 17 adults on its school's registers but was reported as being handicapped by the lack of a dedicated school room. The officer inspecting the 81st Regiment at St George, Bermuda in 1830 reported that schoolmaster-sergeant had only recently resumed his duties after illness. The local army chaplain had visited the school but was of the opinion that the 50 children and 46 soldiers on the register could make little progress because of the restricted and suffocating accommodation allocated for the school room. The commanding officer had asked for larger accommodation but had been told that under the terms of the 1812 Barracks Room Warrant there was no entitlement to a schoolroom, where there were fewer than 1,000 men in the barracks.[82]

Gibraltar was a long established colonial station and its garrison normally contained a number of infantry regiments. In November 1828, the garrison contained six regiments of infantry and also detachments of engineers and artillery. There were army schools at Gibraltar during the Napoleonic Wars, and these appear to have served the children of the various corps forming the garrison.[83] The garrison would have been entitled to at least two dedicated schoolrooms under the terms of the Barracks Room Warrant. In 1820, the inspection reports for the 26th and 27th regiments talk of the children regularly attending the 'garrison school' and the report for the 64th regiment in the same year stated that its children attended 'one of the garrison schools.' In 1843 there were six regimental schools each under its own sergeant schoolmaster.[84]

regimental schools.

81   St John Williams, *Tommy Atkins' Children*, p. 47 & J.Douet, *British Barrack*, p. 119. The Napier Barracks were named after Major General Sir Charles Napier, the author of a report into the barrack situation in northern textile towns in 1840. They did not refer to a particular type of barrack style and should not be confused with the Napier Cantonment system of barrack construction in India. The latter was named for and designed by the future Field Marshal Robert Napier.

82   TNA WO 27/200/247: 'Confidential Inspection Reports and Returns for Regiments 1830-1840', passim.

83   TNA WO 143/28: 'Royal Military Asylum Commissioners' Letter Book 1801-1827'. On 17th June 1818, the Commissioners of the Royal Military Asylum approved the request for two boys from the Asylum to be enlisted in the 11th and 26th regiments in order to assist as monitors in the garrison schools at Gibraltar.

84   A. H. Webb, *History of the 12th (Suffolk Regiment) 1683-1913* (London: Spottiswoode Co., 1914), p. 247; TNA WO 27/50: 'Inspection Reports and Returns for Regiments 1820'; Williams, *Tommy Atkin's Children*, p. 7.

When the Army established new stations at the extremities of the Empire the provision of a school room was not a high priority. In 1858 there was criticism of the colonial government for failing to provide accommodation for the 40th Regiment at Fort Melbourne and as a consequence the headquarters school was obliged to operate in a tent.[85]

In practice, whether at home or overseas, the arrangements for the school had to be adapted to the local circumstances at wherever the particular regiment or corps was stationed. Andrew Bell's original scheme of instruction envisaged that the children would be allocated to classes on the basis of their attainment and progress at school but could be educated together in large classrooms with the schoolmasters delegating the routine instruction to monitors. Although the typical regimental school contained many fewer children than at the RMA Chelsea or the Hibernian School Phoenix Park, the accommodation available as a schoolroom was often too small to effectively teach all the children. In these circumstances the children would have been taught in shifts across the day, as in some civilian schools. Regimental standing orders often specified the time that was set aside for the adult school, often in the late afternoon or earlier evening, after the end of the children's school and when men had completed their daily duties.[86]

The regiments stationed in Jamaica and India occupied barracks that had housed British regiments for many years and usually there was sufficient accommodation for a school. Some of the cantonments in India such as those at Fort George Madras, Poona (Pune) and Meerut were able to accommodate a number of King's regiments. There was very little mention of insufficient or unsuitable school rooms in the half -yearly inspection reports of the regiments at these large   stations in India. It was however difficult to keep the school open during the hot and rainy season, particularly when the roofing of the schoolroom, which was often thatched, had not been kept in good repair. When alterations were made to a barracks, as in 1830 at Belgaum in the Bombay Presidency the school had to be 'broken up' until the work was completed.[87]

A regiment could on occasions be suddenly deprived its schoolroom. On 2nd February 1843, between 11.00 and 12.00 in the morning, there was a destructive earthquake at Antigua in the West Indies that destroyed the barracks of the headquarters company and the school room of the 81st Regiment. The children's school was in session at the time and the building was hastily evacuated, but fortunately no lives were lost. An account of the evacuation was later recorded in the regimental history:

> When the first shock was felt, the schoolmaster-sergeant was in the school with the children of the regiment. He rushed from the building with the children

---

85 Lefroy, *Report on the Garrison and Regimental Schools of the Army*, p. 32.
86 Fireline, Standing Orders, King's Dragoon Guards1840, p. 64; TNA WO 27/50: 'Confidential Inspection Reports and Returns for Regiments1820,17th Light Dragoons'.
87 TNA WO 27/200: 'Inspection Reports and Returns for Regiments1830', passim.

after him; the first one caught him by the coat tail, another caught hold of the first child, and soon a string of children holding on, one to another, the first to the master's coat tail, all running frantically along the road away from the school. The sergeant did not stop until very nearly a mile and he subsequently declared that until he had accomplished this distance, he was not aware that he was dragging a string of children behind him.[88]

Selection of an educated and conscientious soldier as the schoolmaster-sergeant, who was an effective teacher capable of managing a regimental school and the availability of suitable accommodation for the schoolroom did not guarantee that the children and young soldiers would receive much more than rudiments of an elementary education.

The plan for the introduction of regimental schools in 1812 envisaged that Army chaplains, by virtue of their own education, would be able to function as educational inspectors. Their duties would include 'frequently visiting' the schools, scrutinising the conduct of the sergeant schoolmasters and examining the progress and general behaviour of the children. They would then report their observations to the CO of the regiment.[89] These expectations were reiterated in King's Regulations, which stated that 'the Commander-in Chief considers it particularly incumbent on chaplains, and other clergymen engaged in the spiritual duties of the Army, to give their assistance to the military officers, in promoting the success of the regimental school'[90]

Army Chaplains appointed for foreign and domestic garrisons were paid at 10 shillings per day, but it was always difficult to find clergymen willing to accompany troops overseas. In order to serve units in the British Isles and stations in India civilian clergymen were contracted to act as 'the officiating clergyman' and paid £25 a year.[91] King's Regulations specified their duties including taking divine service and required them to visit hospitals at least twice weekly, and to make regular visits to the regimental school. They were to report their observations to the unit's commanding officer.[92] The annual returns on the state of each regiment's schools that COs were required to end to the Hose Guards asked whether 'the officiating clergyman' frequently visited the schools.[93] The half yearly confidential inspections reports in the immediate post war years do not identify whether there was a military chaplain attached to the regiment or whether it relied upon the services of a civilian officiating clergyman. Reports for many of regiments of heavy cavalry, all of which were in home garrisons, simply recorded that a chaplain had visited the school. In the case of the infantry and cavalry units at Windsor, Chester Castle, and Manchester the reports included some

88   S. Rogers, *Historical Record of the 81st Regiment* (Gibraltar: The Twenty-Eighth Regimental Press, 1872), p. 167.
89   'General Regulations and Orders,1816', General Orders Horse Guards, 1st January 1812,
90   *King's Regulations 1822*, p. 196.
91   Haythornethwaite, *The Armies of Wellington*, pp. 123-5.
92   *General Regulations and Orders 1816*, pp. 181, 333.
93   *King's Regulations 1837*, p. 235.

favourable comments by the chaplain about the schoolmasters and their conduct of the schools. The majority of the reports in 1820 for the units stationed both in the British Isles and overseas however do not refer to any chaplains or clergymen visiting the schools.[94] The reports for the regiments stationed in Barbados recorded that that their schools were regularly visited by a chaplain, whilst the reports on those stationed in India record that the chaplains generally appeared at regimental schools, but rarely during the hot and rainy summer season.[95]

When the War Office introduced printed sheets for the confidential inspection report in the 1820s, there was a section for the duties of the chaplain. Drawing on King's Regulations, it queried:

> Whether he frequently visited the regimental school, examined the Children, and reported his observations to the commanding officer as to the talents and correctness of conduct of the Sergeant Schoolmaster, and of the progress and general behaviour of the children.

Most of the half-yearly inspection reports for 1830, 1835 and 1840 contain brief answers in the affirmative, but very few offered any additional comments. In some cases, the diligence of the chaplain was commended and his positive comments about the work and conduct of the schoolmaster were noted. On occasions the inspecting officer's observations differed from those of the chaplain. In 1830 the report of school of the 69th Foot at Athlone in Ireland recorded that the CO had commented favourably on the schoolmaster's diligence and propriety and this was confirmed by the chaplain, who was satisfied with the progress of the children. The inspecting officer nevertheless reported that in his opinion the sergeant was not a very good schoolmaster.[96]

In a few cases the inspecting officer had been told that the chaplain had visited the school, but that he had not reported to the CO, or more ambiguously, '…he had not reported favourably on the talent of the schoolmaster and the progress of the children.'[97] In other cases it was noted that the chaplain visited the school, but only infrequently. In 1830, the absence of a chaplain was noted in the case of the 50th regiment.[98] The schools of the regiments stationed in India during the 1830s were

94 TNA WO 27/150: 'Confidential Inspection Reports and Returns for Regiments 1820', Royal Horse Guards at Windsor; 54th Regiment at Manchester; 88th Regiment at Chester; 3rd Dragoon Guards at Hamilton; 10th Royal Hussars at Hounslow.
95 TNA WO 27/150: 'Confidential Inspection Reports and Returns for Regiments 1820, 4th Kings Own and 21st Foot at Barbados, 14th Regiment and 8th Kings Royal Irish Light Dragoons at Meerut'.
96 TNA WO 27/200: 'Confidential Inspection Reports and Returns for Regiments 1830, 69th Foot'.
97 TNA WO 27/204: 'Confidential Inspection Reports and Returns for Regiments 1830, 1st King's Dragoon Guards; 6th Dragoon Guards'.
98 TNA WO 27/200: 'Confidential Inspection Reports and Returns for Regiments 1830, 21st and 50th Foot'.

regularly visited and reported on by the local Anglican clergyman, at least during the winter season. In the case of the 20th and 40th regiments stationed in the Bombay Presidency and the 2nd Royals at Bangalore (Bengaluru) in the 1830, the attention given by the clergymen to the schools merited additional written commendations by the inspecting officers.

The reports on the 34 depot units in the British Isles in 1827 that operated schools show the limitations of relying upon chaplains and officiating clergymen to assist the COs or to provide the Horse Guards with assurances that teaching in the regimental schools was satisfactory. Thirteen of the schools had been visited regularly by a member of the clergy and all had reported positively on the work of the schoolmaster. The 10th Regiment at Cork was without a chaplain and in the case of twenty depots, there was no mention of a chaplain or clergyman having visited or reported on their schools.[99]

The problem was that the majority of regiments at home and abroad had not been provided with an army chaplain and in these cases King's Regulations specified that commanding officers were to secure 'proper persons' from the local clergy to officiate as chaplains in return for the payment of an annual stipend.[100] The majority of these officiating clergymen interpreted their obligations narrowly, and restricted their activities to performing divine service on Sundays, occasionally visiting the sick in the regiment's hospital, and only infrequently observing the work of the schoolmaster-sergeant and reporting on the condition of the regimental school. Indeed, by 1840 a growing number of the officiating clergymen were refusing to visit the regimental hospitals and schools.[101]

The demands placed on the Army to provide garrisons at home and across the Empire and the need for more regular relief for regiments serving overseas forced Viscount Palmerston, the Secretary at War, to introduce a plan in 1825 for the augmentation of the infantry. The Army was increased by 8,000 men and the battalions of infantry were increased from eight to ten companies and from five hundred and seventy-six to seven hundred and forty rank and file. Six companies each eighty-six strong were designated service companies and four companies each fifty–six strong formed the reserve or depot companies. At home the entire ten companies were treated as a single battalion. When ordered on service overseas, the six companies (reinforced when the station was in India) would go abroad, leaving the four reserve companies at home as a depot to obtain recruits and provided drafts.[102]

There were married men women and children with the reserve companies at the depots and many, and perhaps most of the boys and young men, who were brought in by the recruiting parties would have had little elementary education. The original scheme

99   TNA WO27/177: 'Confidential Inspection Reports and Returns for Regiments 1827, 10th Foot'.
100 *General Regulations and Orders for the Army 1816*, p. 83-4.
101 TNA WO 27/300: 'Confidential Inspection Reports and Returns for Regiments 1840, 10th and 27th Foot'.
102 Fortescue, *A History of the British Army*, Vol. XI, pp. 87-8.

for the introduction of regimental schools in 1812 added one post of schoolmaster-sergeant to the establishment of each regiment or corps, but there was no provision in the 1825 plan for the augmentation of the Army to provide an additional schoolmaster and purchase teaching materials for a school for the reserve companies at the depot.

In the case of infantry regiments serving in India and New South Wales, the depots were concentrated at Chatham and formed the Provisional Battalion, and the Army Estimates provided for a schoolmaster-sergeant and a schoolroom specifically for the children and young soldiers of this depot.[103] Similar arrangements were made at the Albany Barracks in the Isle of Wight, which that operated as a holding depot for corps in transit between stations.[104] The Provisional Battalion was sometimes referred to in army parlance as 'the pongo battalion'. A *'pongo'* meant a mischievous monkey and the term alluded to the boisterous behaviour of the young recruits at the depots. The young barrack boys of the *Provisional Battalion* were certainly mischievous and were famous for getting into scraps with the Chatham boys during their forays into the town.[105]

Regimental depots stationed in other parts of the Empire were distributed in barracks throughout the British Isles. It was especially difficult to find suitable men for appointment as schoolmasters for the depot companies. The pool of men at these depots from which a schoolmaster could be selected rarely exceeded 250 and this included many young soldiers who themselves had little education. For example, the depot of the 74th Highlanders at Perth in Scotland contained 104 soldiers who were under 20 years of age. The records of the half- yearly inspections for 1827 show that of the 42 regimental depots that were inspected that year only eight were unable to establish schools. The 34 depots that operated schools were catering for a total of 900 children (486 boys and 414 girls) and781one boy and adult soldiers.[106] The depot of the 74th Regiment had 40 adults on its school register, in addition to 27children, whilst the very large depot of the 22nd Regiment at Kinsale had 114 women and 146 children in the barracks with 58 children and 59 soldiers attending the school.[107]

103 The Light Cavalry regiments stationed in India shared a depot at Maidstone. See Rumsby, *Discipline, System and Style*, p. 118.

104 Army Estimates 1828; House of Commons Sessional Papers 1845, Account of finally Audited Receipt and Expenditure for Army and Militia Services: 1843-44, p. 7.

105 T.B. Strange, *Gunner Jingo's Jubilee* (London: Remington & Co., 1896), p. 6. The Shorter Oxford English Dictionary states that the word is derived from the Congolese *mpongo*, in use from the 17th century to describe a large ape. The term was later in use in Australian slang to refer to a soldier or marine. There is also the comic version, used predominantly by the Royal Navy, that suggest the term 'Pongo' derives from the fact that wherever the Army goes, 'the pong goes with them!'.

106 TNA WO 27/177: 'Confidential Inspection Reports and Returns for Regiments 1827', passim.

107 TNA WO 27/177: 'Confidential Inspection Reports and Returns for Regiments 1827', passim.

The teaching at these depot schools was undertaken by soldiers without the substantive rank and pay of schoolmaster-sergeants, although COs were probably able to offer them some of the privileges of the depot's headquarters' staff. A number of the depots had difficulty in identifying a sergeant who was suitably qualified for appointment as the schoolmaster and selected corporals and privates to serve in an acting capacity, in some cases for a trial period, until they had demonstrated their competencies. The reserve companies of the 22nd Regiment supplied regular drafts to reinforce the service companies in Jamaica during the early 1830s and only operated its school in Great Britain when there were sufficient numbers remaining at the depot. There was no schoolmaster at the 22nd Regiment's depot in 1834 and1835, but by January 1836 the strength had risen to 200 NCOs and men and Corporal Alexander Casey was appointed acting schoolmaster. He remained in charge of the depot school in Ireland in 1836 and 1837 until the service companies returned from Jamaica and schoolmaster-sergeant John Campbell opened a school for the entire regiment.[108]

In the case of the depot of the 86th Regiment at Armagh in 1827, the half-yearly inspection reported that, although the school was not conducted according to Army Regulations, it nevertheless was operated very creditably by the soldier placed in charge of it. The inspecting officer of the depot of the 64th Regiment in Jersey simply reported the testimony of its commanding officer that the school with 17 children and 29 soldiers had been conducted according to regulations prior 'to the desertion of the sergeant schoolmaster'.[109]

The 1827 records for the inspection of infantry suggest that many officers commanding depots were well aware of the limitations of their acting schoolmasters. The acting schoolmaster of the 77th Regiment's depot at Belfast had other staff duties in addition to managing the depot's school. It was decided that his duties as schoolmaster should be restricted to teaching 29 soldiers and the children were sent to a civilian school in the town. The officer commanding the depot of the 94th at Devonport also sent the children to a school in the neighbourhood of the barracks and because of a shortage of accommodation, attendance at the school was restricted to the twenty-five most promising young men of the regiment. The 95th Regiment at Portsmouth was unable to operate its depot school until a room became available when the 56th Regiment vacated the barracks, whilst the depots of the 27th Regiment also at Portsmouth and the 81st at Guernsey were unable to establish their schools because a lack of any suitable accommodation.[110] Sometimes the CO of the depot might persuade another unit with a functioning school to accept its depot children. In

108 TNA WO 12/3896-3900: 'Confidential Inspection Reports and Returns for Regiments1834-1837', passim.
109 TNA WO 27/177: 'Confidential Inspection Reports and Returns for Regiments 1827, 64th and 86th Foot'.
110   TNA WO 27/177: 'Confidential Inspection Reports and Returns for Regiments 1827', passim.

1835, the Depot of the 66th Regiment was in Portsmouth and seven of its boys and 18 of its girls were allowed to attend the excellently rated school of the 75th Regiment.[111]

There is little evidence that the COs of regiments in the British Isles could look beyond the small annual allocation for materials in Army Estimates for support in managing their schools. The exception however was in Ireland, where the Society for promoting the Education of the Poor aimed to provide an elementary education to all classes of professing Christians, but without any attempt to interfere with their religious convictions. It contended that the best way to do this in Ireland was to ensure that children should read the scripture, without notes or comments, and also to exclude denominational catechisms and all texts that might engender religious controversy. The funds of the Society were used to provide gratuities in support of the schools whose eligibility had been established by a visit from one of the Society's inspectors. In some cases, a school might not strictly conform to Society's regulations, but had been assessed creditably and was considered worthy of encouragement and deserving of support with grants of books for its library.[112]

The reports of the Society for promoting the Education of the Poor in the 1820s list a number of regimental schools that had connections with the Society. The Society's report for 1829 identified the following regimental schools and recorded the number of scholars in attendance:

Table 2. Attendance at regimental schools in Ireland, 1829

	Number of Scholars In attendance
37th Foot	84
29th Foot (Depot)	75
58th Foot (Depot)	68
86th Foot (Depot)	58
91th Foot	16
97th Foot	27
98th Foot (Depot)	60

111 TNA WO 27/247: 'Confidential Inspection Reports and Returns for Regiments 1835', passim.
112 Anon., 12th Report of the Society for Promoting the Education of the Poor in Ireland (Dublin, 1826), p. 175.

Although the Society's Report does not specify the particular nature of its connection with all these units, it does state that in 1826 and 1827 gratuities were paid to 86th and 98th Regiments. The report for 1827 records that although the regimental school at the Royal Barracks in Dublin was not conducted in conformity with the Society's regulations (presumably because of its was teaching the Anglican Catechism), it was nevertheless provided with cheap books for its library. Similarly the Society's Report for 1829 records that the 17th Foot at Tipperary, the 19th Foot at Kinsale, the 69th Foot at Westmeath and the 1st and 3rd Battalions of the 1st (Grenadier) Foot Guards at Dublin, all received grants of books during the year, although these units are not listed as having a particular connection with the Society.[113]

The Society had established a model school in Dublin, which was intended to exemplify the system of education recommended by the Society, and also to serve as a seminary for training schoolmasters and mistresses. In 1826 the Society's reported that a Protestant teacher aged 23 years started teaching at the school of the 86th regiment at Buttevant Barracks in Cork, but there is no indication whether this was a military or civilian appointment. The Reports for 1825 list gratuities paid to Arthur Marques and Elizabeth Grey, who were in charge of the boys' and girls' schools of the Royal Artillery at Island Bridge Barracks Dublin. There were a total of 91 children on the registers of these schools and the teachers may have received training at the Society's model school in Dublin.[114]

Regiments stationed in India and the colonies had to rely on their own resources. Canteens selling food, tobacco, and alcohol were common in barracks life in the early 19th century and were introduced in India from 1828.[115] The disposal of profits made on the sales was regulated to provide benefits for the men and their families with expenditure allocated at the discretion of the CO. In case of the 4th Light Dragoons which was in India from 1822-1841, the canteen profits were used to buy clothing for the children and books for the regimental school.[116]

From time to time some local support was available to King's/Queen's regiments in India. A General Order had been issued by the Governor General in Calcutta in 1814 establishing schools in all the East India Company's European Regiments. In 1820 the Governor of the Bombay Presidency instituted a system of allowances for these schools and these were extended to the King's regiments in its Army. These took the form of monthly payments that could be used by COs to pay the salary of a 'head master', purchase books, present small prizes to deserving scholars and assist parents in purchasing clothing for their children. COs had to provide the Bombay Government with an annual return of the numbers on the school registers

113 Anon., *12-14th Reports of the Society for Promoting the Education of the Poor in Ireland* (Dublin, 1827).
114 Anon., *12-14th Reports of the Society for Promoting the Education of the Poor in Ireland* (Dublin, 1827).
115 BL: IOR, Records of the Military Department, L/MIL17/1/1968, p. 103.
116 Rumsby, *Discipline, System and Style*, p. 144.

and a report on the condition of their school with an account of the disbursement of the allowances. This was incorporated into the Military Regulations for the Bombay Army, but it was emphasised that attendance of the men at the regimental schools was entirely voluntary, although young soldiers were strongly encouraged to attend.[117]

The Bombay Army regulations also referred to the 'Military Asylum' in Bombay that was maintained by the Bombay Education Society (The Society for Promoting the Education of the Poor within the Government of Bombay).This philanthropic Society had been was formed in 1815 to address the miserable condition of the destitute children of European soldiers in Bombay. From 1818 the Court of Directors of the East India Company made an annual contribution to the finances of the Society, but most of its income came from voluntary donations and subscriptions. It subsequently established two central schools for boarders and day pupils at Byculla on the island of Bombay, one for boys and one for girls, on land provided by the government.[118] Preference was given to the admission of the orphaned children of Europeans who had been killed or died in the service of their country, but its regulations also permitted the admission of serving soldiers' children from large families.

In 1821 the Society agreed under a guarantee from the Bombay Government to take the children of soldiers into the two central schools, provided that the soldiers had made a financial payment that was graduated according to their rank. The 'Military Asylum' referred to in the Bombay Army Regulations was not a separate institution but was simply a statement of the conditions on which soldiers' children became eligible for admission to one of the Society's two central schools. The hope was that all ranks in the European Regiments would subscribe and that the cost of maintaining soldiers' children would be met from these subscriptions and would not be a charge on the general income of the Society, which could therefore be used to provide for other needy children. In short, the 'Military Asylum' was a mutual benevolent society for the European Soldiers in the Bombay Army, which would care for and educate their children on their death or after their father's departure for England. This was initially very popular with the Army, but subscriptions declined in the early 1830s. In 1838 the number of subscriptions from some Queen's regiments increased, probably because these regiments were engaged on active service in Sindh and Afghanistan. In 1839, around one third of the children of the 4th Light Dragoons and approaching 60 percent of the children of the 17th Regiment were eligible to attend.[119] The history of

---

117 J.W. Aitchison, *A General Code of the Military Regulations in Force under the Presidency of Bombay* (Calcutta: Adjutant General Bombay Army1824), pp. 554-62.

118 Bombay was originally made up of a number of islands before 1845 when the British authorities undertook a series of land reclamation uniting many of the islands.

119 'The Twenty-Fourth and Twenty-Fifth Reports of the Society for Promoting the Education of the Poor within the Government of Bombay' (Bombay: Bombay Summacher Press, 1839, 1840). The reference to the Military Asylum maintaining the children of soldiers after their fathers had departed for England alluded to the fact that many European soldiers at this time had Indian wives.

the 22nd Regiment records that Private Daniel Brennan, who died had at the Battle of Miani (Meeanee) in the Sindh Campaign in 1843, had made financial provision for his son who was a pupil at the 'Byculla School'.[120]

The Bombay Society's Twenty-Fourth report explains that it also gave '…valuable assistance to the regimental schools in the training of masters and supplying books.' The Society had close connections with the National Society in England and its children were instructed in the Protestant religion according to the teachings of the Church of England in conformity with Dr Bell's system, in addition to being taught reading, writing and arithmetic. The girls were also instructed in sewing and household duties. In 1838 the Bombay Society, on recommendation of the National Society in England, decided to appoint a qualified master and mistress to take charge of the Central Schools. It was also decided to establish a 'normal class' for training schoolmasters. In 1840 one of its trained boys had been sent to assist at the school of the East India Company's European Battalion at Nuggur (Nugar). There is no evidence that, other than providing National Society books currently utilised in Great Britain, the Bombay Society provided any assistance in training masters for the schools of the Queen's regiments in the Presidency during the 1840s. When in 1852 Lord Frederick FitzClarence,[121] was appointed C-in-C of the Bombay Army most of the schoolmaster-sergeants of the Queen's regiments were judged to be incompetent teachers, with some also considered incapable of maintaining order in the schoolroom.[122]

120 Rigby, *Ever Glorious*, Vol. I, p. 191.
121 Lt General Lord Frederick Fitzclarence (1799-1854) was the third illegitimate son of the Duke of Clarence (the future King William IV) and his mistress Dorothea Jordan.
122 Lefroy, Report on the Garrison and Regimental Schools of the Army, pp. 100-10.

7

Regimental Schools Across the Empire

Throughout the 19th century the British Army was a peripatetic force and the regular movement of regiments and battalions between stations at home and across the Empire affected the continuity of teaching and the effectiveness of regimental schools.

From the 1790s, governments recognised that it was necessary to have Regular Army units present in the industrial areas of Great Britain, in places where troops could quickly move to deal with civil disorder. This resulted in a construction of barracks in the manufacturing towns in the midlands and north of England and with specialist cavalry barracks built at Manchester, Sheffield, Nottingham and Birmingham. There was a great deal of civil discontent in the three decades following the Napoleonic Wars. Industry was depressed in the immediate post war years and there was structural unemployment as hand loom weavers and other domestic workers in the textile industries were replaced by more productive machinery. This intermittent civil disorder in the manufacturing districts was accompanied by radical political agitation for parliamentary reform, culminating in the Chartist disturbances of the 1830s and 1840s, which resulted in numerous clashes with authority.[1] The headquarters of regiments of cavalry and infantry were generally located in the largest centres of populations, but detachments of troops were often dispersed to smaller urban areas where local magistrates feared disorders.

The Regular Army continued to play a vital role in law enforcement in Ireland with between 15,000 and 30,000 troops regularly stationed in that country. As in Great Britain a regiment's headquarters would be established in one of the larger barracks, but where regular disturbances were expected, such as at fairs, political meetings and parliamentary elections, or at times of rural unrest such as the 'White Boy' disturbances in the 1820s and 'Tithe Wars' of the 1830s, detachments of both cavalry and infantry were required to be on hand to support the civil powers.[2]

---

1   J. Douet, *British Barracks*, p. 11.
2   V. Crossman, 'The Army and Law and Order in the 19th century', in T. Bartlett and K. Jeffrey, *A Military History of Ireland* (Cambridge: Cambridge University Press 1997), pp. 358-9.

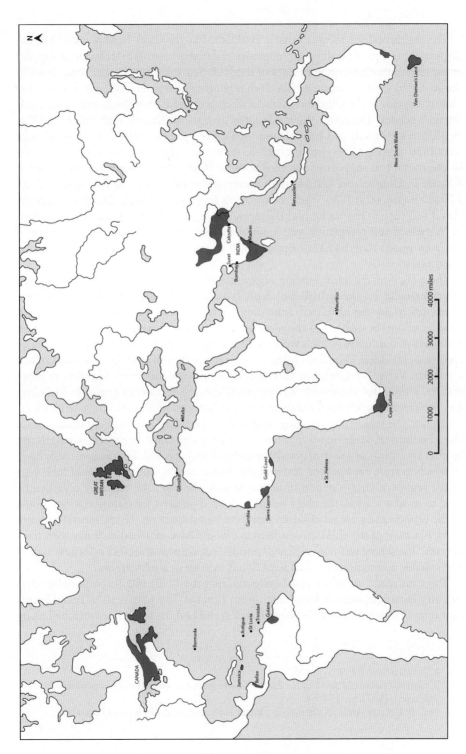

British Empire, 1815.

The regimental school was usually established at the unit's headquarters, but the dispersal of troops of cavalry and companies of infantry in small detachment in support of the civil authorities, on both sides of the Irish Sea, inevitably limited attendance at the school by the enlisted men.[3] The 26th regiment disembarked at Cork in 1822 after almost six years in the Gibraltar garrison where men would have been able to regularly attend a school. Thereafter the headquarters moved to Kinsale and Tralee in 1824. In 1825 it was briefly in Limerick and then moved to Naas, where it remained until May 1826. During these years most of the men were detached to form small garrisons in the country in support of the civil powers. When the regiment was inspected at Kinsale in October 1824, there were barely one hundred men at the headquarters. Matters improved in 1826, when the regiment was concentrated in Dublin, first at the Royal and then at the Richmond Barracks, but in July 1827 the headquarters moved to Waterford and companies were again dispersed onto small detachments. Most of the men would have had little opportunity to attend the regimental school during these years.[4]

The policy of regularly moving regiments of cavalry and infantry between the major barracks on the British and Irish commands inevitably resulted in frequent interruptions in the children's schooling. A network of turnpike roads was well established by the 1820s and the movement of regiments were usually scheduled on Mondays to Saturdays in each week, with a measured distance marched each day by the troops and their wives and children. Sunday, apart from attendance at church, was a rest day. When a regiment or battalion in the British Isles received orders to move station, a route for the march was prepared and the regiment's baggage, including the books and teaching apparatus of the regimental school would be assembled for transport. The regimental standing orders of the 12th Regiment of Foot explains that the schoolmaster-sergeant was provided with a wooden chest, one metre in length and around two thirds of a metre in width and depth and denoted '12th Regiment School' in which to store his teaching material during the march. The chest would form part of the regiment's baggage and if, as was usually the case, the regiment marched by road to its new station, the chest would be loaded on carts for transportation.[5] Some of the women and younger children may have found space on the regimental baggage carts, but most of the children of school age would have marched each day with their parents. The school was not reopened until the regiment was settled in its new station and suitable accommodation had been found to serve as a schoolroom.

The army made use of the canal system during the 1820s and 30s, especially when infantry battalions were ordered north from London. The battalions of Foot Guards that rotated in July each year between London and Dublin, sometimes marched along

3   J,Douet, *British Barracks*, p. 116.
4   T. Carter, *Historical Records of the 26th or Cameronian Regiment* (London: privately published, 1867), pp. 154-64.
5   Suffolk County Archives: 'Standing Orders 12th Regiment of Foot 1817', p. 41.

the Great West Road to Bristol, but more often embarked at the Paddington Basin of the Grand Union Canal and travelled on barges to Liverpool, where transports were waiting to convey them across the Irish Sea.[6] The 87th Regiment embarked from Paddington on 17 barges on 23 July 1827 and reached Chester on the 29th July, but there would have been very little opportunity during this time for the schoolmaster-sergeant to teach the children.[7]

The introduction of coastal steamships and the development of the railways speeded up the movement between stations and the reduced length of time that the regimental schools remained closed. The service companies of the 22nd Regiment returned to Ireland from Jamaica in 1837 and during the next three years the Regiment moved between barracks in Cork, Dublin, and Belfast and the use of steamers to convey the troops reduced the number of days on which the regiment's school was closed.[8]

On 29th November 1840, the regiment was ordered to proceed to the Bombay Presidency in India. The men and their families sailed from Dublin by steamer on 19 December 1840 and on the 21 moved for the first time by rail on the Liverpool and Manchester Railway to Warrington, and thence to Birmingham, where they were billeted for the night. On 22nd December, the regiment changed to the London to Birmingham Railway and de-trained in London on the same day. The rank and file and the women and children would have travelled, probably without seating with the baggage in open wagons. On the 22 December they marched to Greenwich, where they were billeted overnight, before marching the following day via Dartford to Chatham.[9] This journey from Dublin to Chatham had taken the 22nd Regiment four days, whereas in 1823, the same journey from Liverpool to Chatham had taken the 40th Regiment 30 days, with a 28 day march including three Sundays.[10]

The majority of the infantry was stationed outside the British Isles, with units often remaining abroad for many years. J.W. Fortescue in his *History of the British Army* observed that although the Government had fixed the proportion of service abroad at ten years to every five years in the British Isles this was impossible for the infantry, because the majority of battalions were stationed abroad and very few remained in the United Kingdom.[11]

---

6   Headquarters 2nd Foot (Coldstream) Guards, Order Book, July 1823.
7   M. Cuncliffe, *The Royal Irish Fusiliers*, p. 187.
8   B. Rigby, *Ever Glorious*, p. 144.
9   B. Rigby, *Ever Glorious*, pp. 145-6.
10 R.H.R. Smypthies, *Historical Records of 40th (2nd Somersetshire) Regiment* (Devonport: privately published, 1896), p. 216.
11 Fortescue, *A History of the British Army*, Vol. XI, pp. 19, 510.

Baggage train of the King's Dragoon Guards in the 1820s. (Reproduced by kind permission of the Trustees of the Queen's Dragoon Guards Museum, Cardiff Castle, Cardiff)

Table 3. Disposition of the Infantry Regiments 1820-40

	1820	1827	1830	1837	1840
Abroad all year	55	71	74	72	75
Sent out	3	5	8	6	6
At home all year	38	20	18	18	14
Sent home	1	7	3	7	8
Total	97	103	103	103	103

Source: TNA WO 379/2: Stations of Regiments 1818-59

Many regiments, especially those stationed in India, and the Australian penal settlements, remained abroad for upwards of 20 years. Regiments, such as the 49th that were sent to Cape Colony in 1819, moved after a few years to one of the stations in India. Regiments sent on convict escort duty to New South Wales, as were the 40th Foot in the 1824, might serve there for upwards of five years before then moving to India and only returning to the British Isles ten or more years later. (Table 2) A General Order issued to the Army in India on 19 October 1844 commended the service overseas of the 2nd, 3rd ,13th and 40th Regiments, which had been away from home for 20, 21,22 and 23 years, respectively.[12] Long periods of service overseas and the frequent movement between stations across the Empire had important consequences for the organisation and effectiveness of many of the Army's schools.

Table 4. The dispositions of four regiments: 22nd, 26th, 40th and 49th Foot, c.1815-1853

22nd	East Indies	Home	Jamaica	Home	East Indies
Reg.	1803-1819	1819-1827	1827-1837	1837-1841	1841-1854
26th	Gibraltar	Home	East Indies &China		Home
Reg.	1814 -1822	1822-1828	1828-1843		1843-1853
40th	Home	New South Wales	East Indies		Home
Reg.	1817-1823	1824-1829	1830-1845		1846-1852
49th	Home	Cape Colony	East Indies & China		Home
Reg.	1816-1821	1822-1828	1828-1843		1843-1854

Source: TNA WO 379/6, Disposition and Movement of Regiments1803-1827

The Army's stations across the Empire varied greatly in healthiness: those in Canada, Australia and Cape Colony being the best and the East Indies (India and Ceylon), the West Indies and Sierra Leone the least healthy. Mortality rates amongst soldiers from 1816 to 1836 varied from 13 in the 1000 at Cape Colony and 15 in the 1000 in the British Isles, to 71 in the 1000 in the Windward Isles, and 120 in the 1000 in Jamaica where yellow fever was endemic.[13] Regiments that were stationed in disease prone stations for many years had particular difficulties in appointing schoolmasters. There was often was a succession of men occupying the post, some of whom served for very short periods and in consequence COs had difficulty in keeping open their regiment's schools, let alone in providing any continuity in the teaching.

This is illustrated by the experiences of the 22nd (Cheshire) Regiment during its service in the British Isles and the West Indies from 1819 to 1837 and the 49th Regiment after it moved from Cape Colony to India in 1829 where it remained until 1843. The 22nd (Cheshire) Regiment had been part of the garrison at the Isle of Bourbon (Reunion), when it received the War Office Circular ordering the formation of a regimental school. Corporal John Joplin was appointed schoolmaster-sergeant

12   Smythies, *Historical Records of 40th Regiment*, p. 333.
13   J. W. Fortescue, *A History of the British Army*, Vol. XI, p. 20.

and he was in charge of the school when the regiment moved to England in 1819. He was the schoolmaster whilst the battalion's HQ was at Newcastle-upon-Tyne from April 1820 until January 1821, when he was sent as an invalid to Chatham prior to his discharge from the service.[14] Joplin was succeeded by Sergeant Edward Church, another soldier with long service overseas. He ran the School whilst the regiment was in Ireland from1821 to 1826. In December 1826, shortly before the regimental headquarters and the service companies sailed from Cork to Jamaica, Sergeant Church obtained his discharge from the Army with a pension and he was replaced by Private William Adderley.[15]

The 22nd Foot had recruited in Ireland before embarkation and when the regiment disembarked in Jamaica its establishment included three boy soldiers and 379 young adult soldiers each with less than 7 years' service. There were also an unrecorded number of women and children. Sergeant Adderley should have had little difficulty in maintaining a respectably sized regimental school. However, in September 1827 there was an outbreak of yellow fever on the island that decimated the regiment. By the end of the year the disease had carried away the commanding officer and 144 officers and men and an unknown number of women and children. Schoolmaster Sergeant Adderley was amongst the fatalities and he died at Stony Hill barracks on the 14th November 1827.[16]

The pay rolls show that Sergeant Adderley was not immediately replaced, and the school probably remained closed during the winter of 1827-28. A change of quarters was thought advisable and the headquarters of the regiment moved from Stony Hill barracks to Up-Park Camp to help the sick to convalesce. The buildings at the camp were in a poor state and re-establishing a school would not have been a high priority until the fever had abated. The health of the troops improved during 1828 and on 24th March, Corporal William Dunn was appointed as the schoolmaster-sergeant and set about re-establishing the school. In the following year, however, Dunn (now promoted sergeant) was reported sick and on 24 February 1829 he gave up the post of schoolmaster and on the same day Private Thomas Ellis Ward was appointed in his place.[17]

In 1830, the headquarters of the regiment in Jamaica moved to Falmouth Trelawney. It included 39 women and 47 children, although almost all the children were below ten years of age. Eleven of the children were enrolled at the regimental school and schoolmaster-sergeant Ward also provided classes for 13 young soldiers. The relatively

14   TNA WO 12/3887, 'General Muster books and Pay lists 22nd Foot'; Cheshire Military Museum, 'Digest of Service 22nd Regiment 1810-1820'.
15   Rigby, *Ever Glorious*, pp. 137-8; TNA WO 12/3888-3889: 'General Muster books and Pay lists 22nd Foot'.
16   TNA WO 12/3890, 'General Muster books and Pay lists 22nd Foot'; Rigby, *Ever Glorious*, p.139.
17   TNA WO 12/3891-2, 'General Muster books and Pay lists'; Rigby, *Ever Glorious*, pp. 139, 142-3.

small number of children and soldiers on the school's register was the consequence of a recurrence of yellow fever in the island. By comparison, in the same year the depot of the 22nd Foot at Fermoy in Ireland had an establishment of 84 women and 68 children. Sixty of the children and 17 young soldiers attended the depot's school.[18]

Sergeant Ward had been born in Calcutta and had enlisted on 25th April 1811 when the regiment was in India. On 31st January 1831, Ward's period of enlisted service expired and he was discharged. He was replaced by Corporal John McNiff, but the new schoolmaster was admitted to hospital with yellow fever on 11th November 1831 and died four days later. During October, November and December 1831 a recurrence of the disease killed 45 of the rank and file and an unknown number of women and children.[19]

In December 1831, the regiment was involved in suppressing the large scale slave rebellion that had broken out in the island. Detachments of the regiment were dispersed to deal with the uprising and this, together with the outbreak of fever, prevented the opening of the school.[20] The school remained closed until 1st July 1834, when Sergeant John Campbell was appointed schoolmaster. Campbell had joined the regiment in Jamaica on 14 March 1834 from the reserve companies at the 22nd's depot in the United Kingdom and remained as schoolmaster until he was appointed the regiment's Quarter–Master Sergeant on 31 July 1843.[21] He was one of the many drafts sent from the depot to Jamaica to make up the strength of the service companies, which altogether had lost 562 officers and men mostly from yellow fever in the island from December 1826 to March 1837. The regiment's school was probably closed for at least four of these years and was managed by a succession of five schoolmasters.[22]

In comparison to the West Indies, the Cape of Good Hope was regarded as a particularly healthy station and there had been only two masters in charge of the 49th Regiment's school whilst it was stationed in the colony from 1822-28. Schoolmaster William Thompson had been appointed in 1818, when the regiment was in Ireland and his enlisted period of service had expired in January 1825. He was succeeded by Private George D'Arcy who was the schoolmaster when the regiment moved to Bengal in December 1828.[23]

The regiment disembarked at Calcutta and moved by boat to the cantonment at Berhampoor (Berhampore) around 118 miles upstream, a little south of Murshidabad,

---

18 TNA WO 12/3892: 'General Muster books and Pay lists 22nd Foot'; TNA WO 27/200, 'Confidential Inspection Reports and Returns for Regiments1830'.
19 TNA WO 12/3894: 'General Muster books and Pay lists 22ndFoot'.
20 G. Heuman, 'The British West Indies' in A. Porter (ed.), *The Oxford History of the British Empire*, (Oxford: Oxford University Press,1999), Vol.III, pp. 475-6.
21 TNA WO 12/3898-3903: 'General Muster books and Pay lists 22nd Foot', passim.
22 TNA WO 12/ 3893-3897: 'General Muster books and Pay lists 22nd Foot', passim.
23 The succession of schoolmaster-sergeants during regiment's service in Bengal1828-1843 is taken from the regiment's payrolls, TNA WO 12/6045-60, 65: 'General Muster books and Pay lists 49th Foot'.

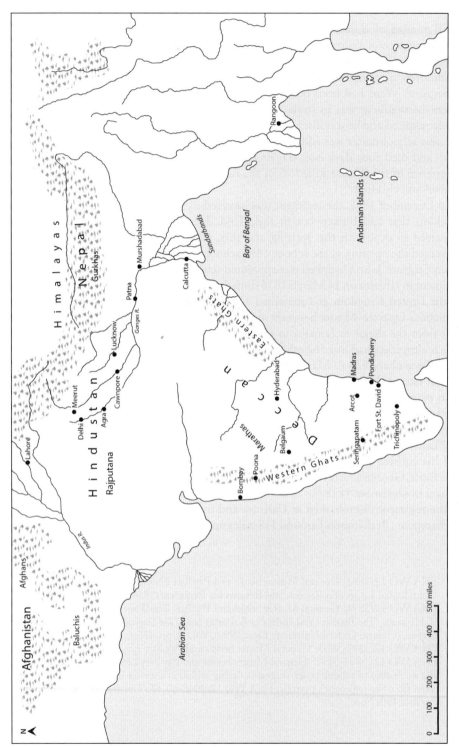

India in the 1830s.

on the Hooghly River. The soldiers and their families were housed in a large brick barracks built in 1767, which included a hospital and a regimental school for the soldiers' children. This station was regarded as particularly unhealthy for European troops and in March 1829 there was a serious outbreak of cholera causing a number of fatalities amongst the soldiers and their families. The disease abated in the following year and schoolmaster-sergeant George D'Arcy maintained a flourishing school. The records show that in May 1830 there were 89 legally married women, three widows, and 160 children with the regiment at Berhampoor. The school registers lists 39 boys and 52 girls attending the school, which was also providing tuition for 113 soldiers. The regiment's half- yearly inspection report judged the school to be satisfactory in every respect.[24]

The regiment had only just moved back to Fort William Calcutta when, in April 1833, Sergeant D'Arcy died, and Corporal Isaac Marshall was appointed schoolmaster-sergeant in his place. Isaac Marshall oversaw the school until August 1834 when for some unspecified reason he was reduced to the ranks. The CO managed to persuade Colour Sergeant Thomas Hyder to act as the regiment's schoolmaster.[25] Thomas Hyder had been educated at the Hibernian School Phoenix Park and was probably as qualified as any other soldier in the regiment for the position of schoolmaster. His move to schoolmaster-sergeant involved a reduction in pay, but there were compensating advantages. Thomas Hyder was married and as the schoolmaster-sergeant he was entitled to separate accommodation outside the main barrack rooms, which housed the company sergeants, the corporals, and the rank and file and their families. Furthermore, he was entitled to fees for teaching the adult soldiers and this provided some compensation for the reduction in his pay.

In May 1835 Hyder's wife died at Hazareebaugh, but he quickly remarried and remained in charge of the school for the next two years. In May 1837, the regimental payroll records that he transferred to the rank of company sergeant. We can only speculate about this move. Perhaps he no longer enjoyed his duties, or maybe he had ambitions for promotion to sergeant major, and thereafter if he was very lucky, to the commissioned rank of Ensign. The move was most unlikely to have been because of any serious breach of military discipline, because in October 1837, Thomas was again promoted, to the rank of colour sergeant.

Thomas Hyder was succeeded as the schoolmaster by Sergeant John Smith, who like many of the men in the Army in the early 19th century had been a weaver before enlisting. In 1838 the regiment moved to the divisional headquarters at Dinapoor (Danapur) a large cantonment with quarters adapted for European troops on the

---

24   TNA WO 27/200: 'Confidential Inspection Reports and Returns for Regiments 1830', 49th Foot.

25   Thomas Hyder's military career in the 49th Foot had flourished since he joined the regiment from the Hibernian Military School in July 1816, at the age of 13 years and three months.

south bank of the River Ganges, some eight miles west of Patna. Sergeant Smith chose to transfer back to company sergeant in February 1839 and in the following ten months the payrolls record a succession of four schoolmaster-sergeants. All these men had previously been company sergeants, but one died and two chose or were returned to this rank after a few months in the post.

Sergeant Warren took charge of the school in the autumn of 1839 and early in 1840 the regiment sailed downstream on the Ganges to Berhampoor. On 16th March 1840 most of the men sailed to Calcutta to join the expeditionary force that was being dispatched to China. The wives and children were in barracks at Berhampoor during the time that the men were on active service in the First Anglo-China (Opium) War 1839-42. Sergeant Warren continued as the regimental schoolmaster until he was drowned at Berhampoor on 24th March 1843. The post of schoolmaster-sergeant was vacant for the next twelve months and it is not known what, if any, arrangements were made for the schooling of the children. However, on March 1843 Robert Patton was appointed to the post as the regiment moved to Calcutta in preparation for its departure for England. He was the eleventh schoolmaster-sergeant since the 49th Regiment had sailed from England for Cape Colony in 1819 and the ninth during the 14 years (1829-1843) that the regiment was stationed in Bengal. None of these men had any formal training and they could look only to assistance from some of the regiment's women in running the school.[26]

The long years overseas sapped the strength of regiments and required the regular reinforcements to make good the losses. Between 1817-55 there were 815,634 British soldiers in India and 56,782 died on service (a mortality rate of 6.9 percent) in the three presidencies.[27] The 40th Regiment lost 51 NCOs and 775 men during the 15 years from 1830 that it was stationed in the Bombay Presidency. In the case of regiments stationed in the East Indies, the military authorities devised a cost effective method of replacing some of these casualties. When a regiment was ordered home from India, the men were given permission to volunteer to other designated King's/Queen's regiments that were remaining in the country and were below establishment. This had the advantage of reducing cost to the Government of transporting the regiment back to the British Isles and bounties were regularly offered to encourage men to volunteer. The success of this policy can be shown when the 40th Regiment was preparing to embark home in late 1844. Permission was given to volunteer and 421 rank and file chose to remain in India and transfer to other regiments. The 40th Regiment's strength was reduced to 347 men and 25 women and 20 children. Three ships were required to transport these men and their families to England, but without the large number of soldiers volunteering to transfer to other regiments, the Government would have incurred the cost of chartering three or four additional transports.[28]

26   TNA WO 12/ 6045-6065: 'General Muster books and Pay lists 49th Foot'.
27   Wiltshire and Swindon History Centre: 'Sydney Herbert Papers', 2057/F8/V/B/3696,
28   Smythies, *Historical Records of 40th*, p. 333.

The situation was by no means uncommon. When the 20th regiment was about to leave Bombay for Great Britain in September 1836, upwards of 400 men volunteered to remain in India and were transferred to other corps. In October 1826, the 87th Regiment received orders to move from Bengal to England and 123 men immediately volunteered for the 45th Regiment. When the 87th had reached Calcutta to embark, a further 259 men volunteered for other regiments, leaving only 280 men and their families to sail home.[29] These transfers increased the pressure on the schools of regiments that remained in India.

The inducement of a cash bounty was not the only, or indeed the main reason, why men volunteered for other regiments and chose to remain in India. Large numbers wished to remain because they had Indian wives and children and others had long term mistresses. Moreover, in these years commanding officers regularly gave their consent to men marrying local women and bring them onto the strength of the regiment. This was a sensible decision, the justification for which had been made by Lieutenant Colonel A. Wellesley – the future Duke of Wellington – in his standing orders issued to the 33rd Foot, when commanding the regiment at Calcutta in 1798:

> The soldiers are not to bring into Barracks any Common Prostitute, if they do the Sergeant must turn them out and confine the man; however if any man wishes to keep a native woman and obtains his Captain's consent, there is no objection to her being in the Barracks, and the Officer will be cautious not to give permission to any but well-behaved men.[30]

The military orphan's schools in the three presidencies admitted many 'half-caste' girls and their subsequent marriage to soldiers in the Kings/Queens and the Company's European regiments were legal and received a degree of official encouragement. Marriages entered into with the approval of COs tend 'usually to steady the soldier and induce in him the habits of sobriety.' Such marriages were far preferable to '…a system of concubinage and still more to a promiscuous and hazardous intercourse with the profligate women of a bazar.'[31]

In 1830, the 20th regiment, which had a school with 116 children, listed 102 legally married women and 26 of these, were identified as 'half caste and native.' Similarly the 26th Regiment at Fort George Madras in the same year recorded 94 legally married women of whom 80 were described as European, whilst the 2nd Battalion of the Royals (1st Regiment of Foot) at Bangalore, which had a very large school of 140 children,

---

29   TNA WO 27/200: 'Confidential Inspection Reports and Returns for Regiments 1830', 40th Foot; R. Cannon, *Historical Record of the 20th or East Devonshire Regiment* (London: Parker, Furnival & Parker, 1848), p. 50; M.Cuncliffe, *The Royal Irish Fusiliers*, p. 183.

30   'Colonel Wellesley's Standing Orders to the Thirty-Third Regiment 1798', ed. B. W. Webb-Carter, *Journal of the Society for Army Historical Research*, Vol.50 (Summer 1972), pp. 65-77.

31   BL: IOR, Records of the Military Department, L/ML5/376, pp. 132-3.

recorded 80 European and 85 native women legally married on its establishment.[32] The regular transfer of soldiers and their families from regiments leaving India to regiments remaining in the country ensured that there was no shortage of children wishing to attend the schools of Kings/Queens regiments.

During these years it was the practice to station four regiments of the light cavalry with the East India Company's Armies in the Bengal, Madras or Bombay Presidencies.[33] Ten of the thirteen regiments of light cavalry on the Army's establishment spent at least one period of between 10 and 24 four years in India during this period. For example, the 4th Light Dragoons (Hussars) was in the Bombay Presidency from 1821-1843, the 11th Light Dragoons served in the Bengal Presidency from 1819 to 1838, the 13th Light Dragoons in the Madras Presidency from 1839-1840 and the 16th Lancers in the Bengal Presidency from 1822-46.[34] These regiments were stationed in one of the larger cantonments that housed a number of European regiment in relatively healthy conditions. In Bengal, the two regiments of light cavalry were rotated between Cawnpore and Meerut. Cawnpore was some 628 miles by road and 1000miles by river west of Calcutta and in 1843 housed one Queen's and one native cavalry regiment and one Queen's and two native infantry regiments together with several European artillery batteries. Meerut was 42 two miles north-east of Delhi and housed the same number of Queen's regiments, but with three native infantry regiments. Meerut was considered to be a better location for European troops, and the barracks at both stations were reckoned to be more comfortable for families than those in Great Britain. From 1835 there was a standard specification and plan for the barracks including verandas the ends of which were partitioned off for the use of the sergeants and their families.[35]

Although the King's/Queen's cavalry regiments were involved in a number of military expeditions in the sub-continent, whenever detachments were sent on active service the schoolmaster-sergeant remained with the women and children at their cantonment. Illness and accidents apart, these factors helped to provide some continuity of service for schoolmasters in these regiments.

Schoolmaster-sergeant James Watts of the 11th Light Dragoons had completed his teaching training course at Chelsea in February 1812 and is shown on the pay roll as the schoolmaster in January 1815. He was succeeded by Sergeant William Jones, who remained as the schoolmaster until January 1819, when he purchased his discharge from the Army. Soon afterwards the regiment was ordered to the East Indies. Jones

---

32 TNA WO 27/200: 'Inspection Reports and Returns for Regiments 1830',20th, 26th, 2/1st Foot'.

33 The King's/Queen's Regiments when they arrived in India became part of one of the three Presidencies' armies alongside the Honourable East India Company's own regiments of European and native infantry, but their expenses were paid by the Company whilst they were stationed in India.

34 TNA WO 379/7: 'Disposition of the Army 1828-1856'.

35 Rumsby, *Discipline, System and Style*, pp. 129-30.

perhaps did not welcome the prospect of a long period of service India, which for many men was effectively a life sentence overseas and convinced them to leave the Army. It is probable that the fees that Jones' fellow soldiers paid him for teaching them to read and write contributed to the £20 he paid for his discharge. It is possible that his teaching experience in the Army helped him to find work as a schoolmaster in one of the many civilian charity schools.[36]

Private Tamerlane M. Goose succeeded Jones as the schoolmaster-sergeant and sailed with the regiment to the Bengal Presidency in India in 1819. He was in charge of the school, initially at Cawnpore in 1820, and in the following year at Meerut. Sergeant Goose remained in charge of the school when the regiment moved by river to replace 16th Lancers at Cawnpore in March 1826, but he died there on 15th March 1828 after serving for nine years as schoolmaster. He was succeeded by Corporal William Ritchley who was in charge of the school when the regiment moved back to Meerut in 1832.[37]

Table 5. Disposition of the Infantry 1827-40

Battalions	1827	1830	1837	1840
Abroad All Year	71	74	72	75
Sailing Out	5	8	6	6
At Home All Year	20	18	18	14
Sailing Home	7	3	7	8
Total	103	103	103	103

Source: TNA WO 379/2: 'Stations of Regiments 1818-59'.

Each year in the 1820s, 30s and 40s more than one tenth of the infantry battalions would be on the high seas sailing between the British Isles and India and the other colonial stations. The rank and file of a battalion together with the families that had been allowed to accompany the men were organised into divisions for embarkation and sailed in a number of chartered transports. It took the transports about 100 days to make the outward voyage from Gravesend to Bombay. Voyages further east took even longer; six months or more in the case of battalions moving to and from Bengal and the colonies in Australia.

The regimental school was closed for the duration of the voyage and was unlikely that the conditions on board the schoolmaster-sergeant's transport allowed him

36   TNA WO 12/989: 'General Muster Books and Pay Lists, 11th Light Dragoons'.
37   TNA WO 12/989-992: 'General Muster Books and Pay Lists, 11th Light Dragoons'.

to give any lessons to the children and soldiers on his ship. The movement of two regiments from Great Britain to Eastern stations in the 1840s illustrate the difficulties in keeping open a school and maintaining any continuity in the teaching.

Six chartered vessels were required to transport the 22nd Regiment to Bombay in the 1841. The officers and men and their families were carefully divided into six divisions for the march from Chatham barracks to Gravesend.

Table 6. Movement of 22nd Regiment of Foot from Chatham to Bombay, 1841

Division and date of march from Chatham	Officers	NCOs and men	Women	Children	Name of Transport	Date sailed
First: 8th Jan 1841	3	118	15	14	Guisichan	10 Jan 1841
Second: 9th Jan 1841	5	138	11	15	Tory	-ditto-
Third: 9th Jan 1841	4	160	11	19	Margaret	-ditto-
Fourth: 11th Jan 1841	7	190	26	29	Anne	12 Jan 1841
Headquarters: 26th Jan 1841	12	325	49	53	Inglis	27 Jan 1841
Sixth: 1st Feb 1841	4	100	9	12	Lady Feversham	2 Feb 1841
		1031	120	142		

(Source: Digest of Service of the 22nd Regiment)

Troops and their families were accommodated in crowded conditions on the chartered merchant vessels. Sergeant John Campbell was the schoolmaster of the regiment when it was ordered to Bombay and he sailed on 26th January 1841 with the regiment's Headquarters in the transport *Inglis*. There were 325 rank and file and 53 children on board the transport, but not all of the children would have been of school age. Sergeant Campbell might have been able to provide a little schooling for some of these children if a space could be found. An account of the voyage on the Inglis has survived and describes conditions aboard the transport would have made it very difficult for Sergeant Campbell operate a school during the voyage, or indeed to open one until the regiment reached its intended station in India.

Private George Rooks had volunteered from the 6th to the 22nd Regiment before it embarked from Gravesend and travelled with the headquarters division on the *Inglis*. In his diary he described the appalling weather encountered during the ships passage through the Bay of Biscay, which confined the troops and their families into cramped conditions in the lower decks. The *Inglis* lost its top mast and the terrified women and children were drenched as large waves broke over the vessel and cascaded into the lower decks.

The weather improved during the voyage south of Gibraltar and unusually there was no sickness aboard the ship. When the vessel approached the equator, a large awning was erected to give some protection from the sun and the men and their families were able to relax on the upper decks. Some schooling may have been possible in this part of the voyage, but after the ship had rounded the Cape of Good Hope, it again encountered some very rough weather on the passage across the Indian Ocean. The *Inglis* arrived at Bombay on 24 May 1841 and the regiment was immediately ordered inland to Poona in the Western Ghats.

When each of the six divisions of the regiments disembarked at Bombay, they were transferred onto small-rigged sailing vessels and sailed for the cantonment at Panwell on the Arabian Sea, a staging post on the regiments' march to Poona. By 13 June most of the regiment had been assembled at Panwell (Panvel) and the troops commenced the march. Private George Rooks considered that the conditions on the march were in many ways far worse than those on the sea passage to India. Small carts each drawn by two buffalos were provided to carry the regiment's light barrage and also any men and members of their families who were sick. Unless some space could be found, the women and children marched with the troops, and the very young children were carried by their parents. The regiment marched by night to avoid the heat of the day, striking camp around midnight, and halting to form a new camp at day breaks. The men and their families were housed in tents, but there were no beds or hammocks and they slept on the rough and cloddy ground. Each night's march covered around 12 miles on difficult roads, especially on the ascent up the Ghats to Poona. It was 1 July 1841 before the regiment moved into the cantonment at Poona and it was almost three months after leaving England before Sergeant Campbell was able to re-open his school.[38]

The schools of the regiments ordered to New South Wales were closed for even longer periods than those sailing to India. The 40th Regiment left Dublin for Liverpool on 30 March 1823 in eight small vessels. After disembarking in Liverpool, the regiment marched south to Chatham. During the next year the men were sent out in small detachments as guards on board convict transports sailing to New South Wales. The troops and their families embarked in twelve ships from April 1823 to June 1824. Corporal Hugh McLachlan had been appointed the 40th regiment's

---

38   R. Cannon, *Historical Records of the 22nd Regiment of Foot* (London: Parker, Furnival, and Parker, 1849), pp. 147-54.

schoolmaster-sergeant in September 1821. He would have been able to maintain a regimental school at Chatham from early May 1823 to December 1823, when he sailed with a small detachment of 36 rank and file and their women and children for New South Wales. Sergeant McLachlan arrived at the colony in June 1824 but would only have been able to open a small school, because on arrival the troops and their families were dispersed in detachments throughout the colony.[39] In 1825 the regiment started to move in detachments to the convict settlements in Van Diemen's Land (Tasmania) and the HQ was established at Hobart in February 1826. Once again there were difficulties in opening the school because the troops were dispersed at various stations across the colony. Fortunately, Sergeant McLachlan was well supported by the acting CO, Major Kirkwood, and a school was maintained with some success during 1827-28.

In July 1828, orders were received for the regiment to embark in detachments for Bombay. The first division of two companies comprising 192 officers and men and some 20 women and 38 children sailed in the transport *Phoenix* from Tasmania in September 1828. Following a long and unpleasant voyage, the vessel finally reached Bombay in January 1829. After a short time in barracks there, the division re-embarked on 13th February 1829 and sailed south for two days to Vingorla on the coast of the Arabian Sea. From there the troops and their families marched across the Western Ghats until they reached Belgaum(Belagavi) on 22nd March 1829, where they were quartered in the European barracks.[40]

Successive detachments of the regiment sailed from Bombay during 1829 and together with reinforcements from the depot in England the regiment completed at Belgaum in May 1830. The pay rolls of the 40th Regiment record that schoolmaster-sergeant McLachlan was in Tasmania in February 1829 and that he did not reached Belgaum until February 1830. Many of the children at Belgaum would probably have been without schooling since September 1828. Sergeant McLachlan quickly re-opened the school and when the regiment was inspected by Brigadier General Leighton on 17th February 1830, there were 40 boys, 44 girls and 51 soldiers on the register. The General reported that Sergeant McLachlan was very well qualified and that the school was very ably conducted.[41] It was not until the 1850s that the government purchased a number of vessels specifically to transport the Army across the Empire. Some of these iron ships had three decks and sufficient space to accommodate a school.[42]

39   Some soldiers and children of the 40th regiment, who remained in England when Sergeant McLachlan sailed from Gravesend, may have attended the Chatham depot school.
40   R.H. Smythies, *Historical of the 40th Regiment*, pp. 231-3.
41   Sergeant Hugh McLachlan was in charge of school at Belgaum throughout 1830, but in the following summer there was a great deal of sickness in the 40th Foot and he died in regimental hospital on 12th September 1831.
42   H.C.B. Rogers, *Troopships and their History* (London: Seeley Service,1963), pp. 105-10. These included the screw propelled iron ex-frigates, the *Megara* and *Simoom* and the ex-P&O ship the *Himalaya*.

The twenty or more battalions of infantry that were stationed in India moved regularly between cantonments within the three Presidencies. For the units in the Bengal Presidency this entailed long marches and slow river voyages and their schools were often closed for many weeks. The battalions arriving in Bengal normally disembarked at Calcutta and moved to barracks at Fort William or some 15 miles up the Hooghly River to the large cantonment at Barrackpore, before moving inland to their eventual stations. A typical infantry battalion consisted of 800 to 1000 men who were accompanied by 200-300 women and children. There was a large amount of regimental and personal baggage and the troops and their families soon acquired a complement of native servants. The movement of an infantry battalion therefore, whether by river boat or road, was a major logistical exercise and one that was managed by the Honourable East India Company always with an eye to the cost.

Depending on the destination, and the time of year, a battalion might sail up the Hooghly and into the River Ganges, or march west along the Grand Trunk (Military) Road, which ran from Calcutta via Benares (Varanasi) and Allahabad to Delhi. The cold season from November to February was generally favoured for movements by road, whereas transport by river boat depended upon the level of water in the Ganges river system and normally took place only during and in the months immediately following the summer monsoons.

When on 27th November 1831, a detachment reinforcing 49th Regiment moved upstream on the Hooghly River bound for the regiment's HQs at Berhampoor (a distance of 118 miles), the troops and their families sailed in a number of small thatched roofed sailing boats. The boats sailed during the daytime and were moored together each evening on the banks of the river. Progress was slow against a strong current and when the wind was not favourable, the boats were drawn up stream by ropes pulled by labourers walking along the banks of the river. The men and their families were disembarked from the boats and then marched by road for three days before reaching Berhampoor on 12 December.[43]

The children and soldiers of units sailing further upstream to Dinapoor (the military cantonment outside Patna), some 400miles up the Ganges, or on to stations further West, such as Benares (Varanasi), Cawnpore, and Meerut were not be able to attend school for many weeks. In July 1827 during the monsoon season the 87th regiment set out from Calcutta by river boat for Dinapoor. One division of the regiment left on 11 July and had rough sailing and some boats sank and three men five women and four children were drowned. The school was re-opened when the 87th reached Dinapoor on the 19 August. In October 1827, the school was broken up when the regiment was

---

43   Rifles Museum, *Diary of William Comerford*, pp. 12-14. William Comerford was born in Limerick and volunteered for the 1st Regiment of Foot (the Royals) aged 15 years in 1826. He volunteered to transfer to 49th Regiment in September 1831. His family later transcribed his journal and called it a 'diary'. A copy of the transcript is in the Salisbury Museum.

ordered to move to Ghazapore, upstream on the Ganges, near Benares. The conditions however were unsuitable for river transport and the men and their families were forced to march some 210 miles to their new station.[44]

Cantonment at Ghazipur. (© British Library Board)

Early in 1826 it was decided to move the 31st Regiment by water from Calcutta to Dinapoor on the Ganges. This was the dry season and the river levels were low. At that time of year the direct water route to the Ganges from the Hooghly River was impassable to boats of any size and the regiment had to proceed south towards the Bay of Bengal, before passing into the Ganges proper by way of the Sunderbans waterways, through swamps surrounded by tiger infested jungle. It took a whole month for suitable boats and their crews to be secured and when assembled the flotilla numbered some three hundred vessels of all sizes. The flotilla sailed on 13 February and took thirteen days to reach the Ganges and did not arrive at Dinapoor until 2nd May. The boats conveyed the troops and their families by companies in very crowded conditions and many men, women and children succumbed to cholera during the voyage. At the rear of the flotilla there was a hospital boat to carry the sick, but there is no record of any provision on the boats for the regimental school.[45]

44   Cuncliffe, *The Royal Irish Fusiliers*, p. 166.
45   R. Cannon, *Historical Records of the 31st, or the Huntingdonshire Regiment* (London: Parker, Furnival & Parker, 1850), pp. 93-4.

Contemporary prints of the type of boats employed to convey soldiers and their families along the Ganges and Hooghly rivers.

Small Hindu temple along the Ganges. (© British Library Board)

Lord Hastings' flotilla on the river Ganges with many pinnace budgerows. (© British Library Board)

Road travel was generally regarded as healthier than by river, but it involved a succession of long and arduous marches with the men, women and children sleeping under canvas, and with little or no opportunity for the schoolmaster-sergeant to open a school.[46]

In January 1835, the 49th Regiment was ordered to move from Fort William, Calcutta to Hazareebaugh by road, and a large convoy of transport was assembled to convey the regiment. This included 700 hackerys, heavily loaded with the regiment's women and children and their baggage.[47] Twice as many bullocks as usual were needed to pull the hackerys, and there were also a number of camels, dromedaries and elephants to transport the baggage. The convoy was delayed at Barrackpore for three days until boats could be assembled to ferry the regiment across the Hooghly River. The route took the regiment along the Military Trunk Road, but progress was slow and the convoy had to ford a number of rivers, before ascending from the plains and passing through the heavily forested Ranghur Hills, reaching altitudes of up to 3,000 feet above sea level. The regiment reached Hazareebaugh on 5th February but remained under canvas until quarters were made ready. Schoolmaster-sergeant Thomas Hyder would have had difficulty re-opening the school much prior to 4th March 1835, when the troops moved into the European barracks in the cantonment. Nevertheless, by the date of the first half yearly inspection later in 1835, there were 52 boys, 63 girls and 52 soldiers on the register, and both the garrison chaplain and the inspecting officer were pleased with Sergeant Hyder's superintendence of the school.[48]

Although the movements of regiments across Bengal involved the temporary closure of their schools, once they had reached their new stations regiments often remained at the same cantonment for a number of years. This enabled the children's schools to be kept open, although with frequent interruptions to lessons during the hot and rainy seasons. There was also the opportunity for the men to attend, unless they were sent on detached duty away from the HQs.

When a regiment embarked on active service in the field regulations prohibited soldiers' wives from accompanying their husbands.[49] In these circumstances the men's families in India would remain at their stations until the troops returned and the children would continue to attend the regimental school. When in December 1825 detachments of the 11th Light Dragoons and the 16th Lancers moved from their stations at Cawnpore and joined the forces investing the fortress at Bharatpur,

46   Cannon, *Historical Records of the 31st*, pp. 93-4.
47   A hackery was a two-wheeled bullock-drawn vehicle employed throughout India but synonymous with Bengal.
48   TNA WO 27/247: 'Confidential Inspection Reports and Returns for Regiments 1835', 49th Regiment; Rifles Museum, *Diary of William Comerford*, p. 28.
49   *King's Regulations*, 1822.

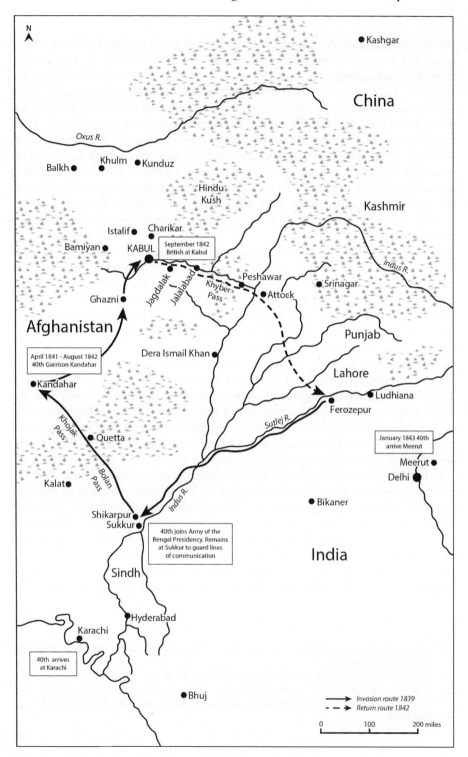

Invasion of Afghanistan, 1839-42.

schoolmaster-sergeants Goose and Hamilton remained in charge of their regiments' school at Cawnpore throughout the campaign.[50]

In 1838 the Government in Calcutta decide on military intervention in Afghanistan in order to place a friendly power in the eastern province of the country and establish a permanent barrier against possible aggression on the North-West Frontier. It was decided that a division of the Bombay Presidency Army would proceed up the River Indus through Lower Sindh to Sukkur, where it would be joined by a division from the Army of the Bengal Presidency. The combined force would then move through the Bolan Pass to Quetta and then to Kandahar in Helmand Province, from where it could march east to Kabul. The Amirs of Sindh however were resentful of British intrusion and it was decided to send further troops as a reserve force to guard the Bombay division's base on the Arabian Sea and the lines of communication through Sindh to Afghanistan.[51]

In December 1838, the 40th Regiment was at Deesa in the Northern Military District of the Bombay Presidency when it was ordered to proceed fully equipped for service with the reserve force at Karachi in Lower Sindh. The reserve force occupied the port of Karachi in February 1839, but a detachment of the regiment together with the women and children remained at Deesa.[52] On 11 November 1839 this detachment together with the women and children moved to Karachi. Sergeant Robert Mole was the regiment's schoolmaster at Karachi and opened a very successful school. The officer conducting the initial half-yearly inspection in 1840 reported that 22 boys and 21 girls attended the school and there were also ten non-commissioned officers and 22 private soldiers on the register. The inspecting officer was very impressed with the school and commented that the reading and writing and general proficiency of some of the boys 'would do credit to any academy in England.' This success he thought owed much to the efforts of Lieutenant S.K. Nelson, one of the regiment's officers who devoted some time each day to superintending the school.[53]

In July 1840, the 40th regiment started to send detachments into Upper Sindh in order to protect the lines of communication to Afghanistan. The bulk of regiment moved on from there to Quetta in April 1841 and then joined the British garrison at Kandahar in October of that year. It remained there until August 1842 and when it formed part of the 'Army of Retribution' that fought its way to Kabul an attempt to restore British prestige after the military disasters in Afghanistan earlier in the year.

During these months the school remained under the direction of schoolmaster-sergeant Mole at the regimental depot at Karachi and was described by the

---

50   TNA WO 12/ 992 and 1261: 'General Muster Books and Pay Lists, 11th Light Dragoons and the 16th Lancers'.
51   Fortescue, *A History of the British Army*, Vol. XII, pp. 30-49.
52   Smythies, *Historical Records of the 40th Regiment*, p. 253.
53   TNA WO 27/295: 'Confidential Inspection Reports and Returns for Regiments1840', 40th Foot.

inspecting officer in his May 1841 report as being well attended and managed.[54] The accommodation for the school at Karachi however was makeshift. Initially, the regiment was housed in tents, but later some wooden huts were constructed as temporary accommodation, but these were soon in a poor condition.[55]

Schoolmaster-sergeant Mole died at Karachi in March 1842 and there was no school for the children whilst the families of the 40th Regiment remained in Sindh. There had been some 40 children at the time of schoolmaster-sergeant Mole's death, but it was a decided not to appoint a successor until the men's families were able to re-join the main body of the regiment. The 22nd Regiment was also at Karachi until the autumn of 1842 and perhaps some the 40th Regiment's children were allowed to attend classes at its school.[56]

The British Army withdrew from Afghanistan through the Khyber Pass in November 1842 and the men of the 40th Regiment arrived at Meerut in the Bengal Presidency in January 1843 and remained there until September 1844. The regiment's women and children made the long journey from Karachi via Bombay to Meerut to join the men, but regiment's payrolls show that the regiment was without a schoolmaster-sergeant until March 1844, when Corporal Charles Smart was promoted to re-establish the school. The regiment's children may have joined the schools of other regiments when they reached Meerut, but they probably received very little schooling between March 1842 and March 1844.[57]

By one account, however, some classes were provided for the troops during these months. The Rev I.N. Allen, who was a military chaplain with the Bombay Army, recorded in his diary that despite the difficult conditions of service in the field in Upper Sindh and Afghanistan when the troops were under canvas, the 40th Regiment's school was as efficiently maintained as it could have been in barracks at Bombay or Poona. He observed that the regiment had a policy of requiring junior NCOs to pass examinations in 'some higher branch of mathematics' before they could obtain promotion. He thought that this kept the school well filled with adults and provided the regiment with responsible and educated NCOs. This would suggest that some schooling was provided whilst the 40th Regiment was on active service, but this could not have been provided by the schoolmaster-sergeant Mole who remained with the depot at Karachi until his death in March 1842. Allen commented that regiment's

---

54   TNA WO 27/301: 'Confidential Inspection Reports and Returns for Regiments 1840',40th Foot.

55   When the 22nd Regiment, with its women and children in tow, arrived at Karachi in April 1842, the barracks were described as a row of temporary huts, deep in sand, and infested with fleas and bugs. Rigby, *Ever Glorious,* Vol. I, p. 152.

56   TNA WO 12/5353: 'General Muster Boks and Pay Lists', 40th Foot; TNA WO 27/320, 'Confidential Inspection Reports and Returns for Regiments1842', 40th Foot.

57   TNA WO 12/5352-5355: 'General Muster Books and Pay Lists,40th Foot'.

officers attended to the 'comfort and real interests of the men', but he does not mention any details of their involvement in running a school.[58]

In August 1844 orders were received for the 40th Regiment to prepare to return to England and following the usual practice, men who wished to remain in India were allowed to volunteer for other regiments. Around 300 NCOs and men volunteered and in September the school was closed. Schoolmaster Charles Smart was promoted to colour sergeant when the battalion moved down the Ganges on route to Calcutta before it returned to England. There was further volunteering to other regiments when the 40th Foot reached Calcutta and only 25 women and 23 children embarked for home on three vessels in September and October 1845. There is no record of a schoolmaster-sergeant on the strength of the regiment until after it had reached England in February 1846.[59]

The 40th Regiment had been abroad for 23 years; had travelled enormous distances by sailing vessel across the Empire and had marched many miles between stations in India. During these movements there were long periods when the schools were closed and the frequent interruption in the children's and young soldiers' schooling meant that many would have gained little beyond the rudiments of an elementary education.

58 Smythies, *Historical Records of the 40th*, p. 296.
59 Smythies, *Historical Records of the 40th*, pp. 332-5; TNA WO 12/5355: 'General Muster Books and Pay Lists, 40th Foot'.

8

Praiseworthy but Flawed: The Record of Regimental Schools 1816-46

The military departments did not establish a school inspectorate to report on the condition of the regimental schools nor did they regularly publish details of the numbers of children and soldiers attending. King's Regulations in the 1830s did require the COs to provide an annual return of the numbers attending their schools and to confirm that they were conducted according to regulations and that the schoolmaster was 'duly qualified'.[1] The Adjutant General's Circular of 18 January 1812 instructed officers in command of brigades and districts '…to be minute in their confidential reports as to the regimental schools in the corps under their command.' The Half-yearly Inspection reports for the military districts were to record the number of scholars of each sex on the school registers at each regimental school and the opinion of the inspecting officers as to the talents and conduct of the sergeant schoolmaster and also the progress of the children under his tuition.[2] A succession of General Orders and Regulations emphasised that it was expected that all General Officers, Colonels, and COs would give their special care and attention to the regimental schools under their commands.[3]

Subsequent Regulations required the general officers conducting the half-yearly inspections to include a statement in their confidential reports confirming that the regimental schools were being run as directed.[4] Specifically the confidential reports were to include a reference to the schoolmaster-sergeant's 'qualifications' [his competency] for the post and whether he discharged his duties with correctness and

---

1 *King's Regulations 1837*, p. 235.
2 NAM, Circular letter Horse Guards, 18th January 1812, General Regulations and Orders for the Army 1816.
3 *King's Regulations 1822*, pp. 191,195.
4 The Inspecting Officer was directed to forward the reports to the Commanding General Officer of the Military District in the British Isles or the station overseas in which the regiment was serving. It was the responsibility of this officer to forward the reports on the regiments under his command to the Adjutant General's Department at the Horse Guards.

diligence.[5] The Inspection reports for 1820 were invariably brief and the wording suggests the inspecting officer had not always personally visited the school or spoken to the schoolmaster, but had relied on information provided by the regiment's CO. A report on the 4th King's Own stationed at Barbados in 1820 noted only that the school was run as required and 'was regularly attended and with great advantage to the young soldiers and children.' The schoolmaster was '...reported to be competent to the duty and zealous and kind in the discharge of it.' The inspection of the 20th Regiment in the same year at St Helena simply observed that its school was 'well attended and the children clean and healthy.'[6]

Although most reports completed in 1820 simply confirmed that the schoolmaster was competent and conscientiously did his duty, others commented on the state of the school and attempted to assess the progress of the pupils. The reports on the 8th King's Royal Irish Light Dragoons and the 14th Regiment of Foot, both stationed at Meerut in India, reported that the soldiers and children had 'made evident progress' since the previous inspection. In contrast, a report of the 2nd Queen's Regiment school in Demerara, British Guiana, commented that even though every effort was being made to improve the men's education, it was '...attended apparently with but very little success.'[7]

In general, inspection reports of units stationed in India in 1820 included some account of the condition of the school. The school of the 17th Light Dragoons at Kutch in the Bombay Presidency provided an evening school for soldiers. The children at the day school were reported as having made as much progress as could be expected in the circumstances of that station. The report on the 73rd Regiment at Trichinopoly (Tiruchirappalli) in the Madras Presidency observed that all of the children who were old enough attended the school, together with some boy drummers and many NCOs and private soldiers. Similarly, the report on the 34th Regiment at Fort George, Madras, recorded that all children old enough to attend school did so and progressed well in their studies. The school was well supplied with books and the sergeant and woman in charge of the 'female branch' were both competent and of good character.[8]

Throughout the 1820s, the Horse Guards provided the inspecting officers with pre- printed forms containing a number of questions, the answers to which formed the basis of confidential reports. In relation to the regimental school, the inspecting officer was directed to answer:

5   *General Regulations and Orders for the Army 1816*, pp. 279, 287, 338; *King's Regulations 1837*, pp. 493-4.
6   TNA WO 27/150: 'Confidential Inspection Reports and Returns for Regiments 1820', 4th and 20th Foot.
7   TNA WO 27/150: 'Confidential Inspection Reports and Returns for Regiments 1820', 8th King's Royal Irish Light Dragoons and the 14th Regiment of Foot, 2nd Queen's Regiment.
8   TNA WO 27/150: 'Confidential Inspection Reports and Returns for Regiments 1820', 17th Light Dragoons, 73rd Foot, 34th Foot.

Whether the school is conducted according to established regulations; and whether the schoolmaster is duly qualified for his situation and discharges his duties with diligence and propriety.

The introduction of the printed form and standardised questions no doubt assisted the Adjutant General's Department at the Horse Guards in evaluating and collating the reports, but they also encouraged the inspecting officers to be economical with their observations. Most were completed simply in the affirmative, or with little more than a brief statement recording that the schoolmaster-sergeant was diligent and that the CO's supported the school.

Some schools did receive particular praise. The school of the 37th Regiment at Enniskillen in Ireland in 1830 was reported to be admirably conducted and the children well instructed. The 31st Regiment at Meerut, India, got a good rating with a commendation for the schoolmaster for maintaining discipline as well as for his teaching.[9] A report of the school of the 14th Light Dragoons at Birmingham judged that scholars' reading and writing was 'carried to perfection beyond that seen in any regiment', whilst 16th Lancers' School at Meerut was reported as one of the best the inspecting officer had ever seen. In the case of the 78th Highlanders inspected at Colombo, Ceylon in February 1835 the report concluded that the school reflected 'the greatest credit' on a Lt MacAlpine, the officer who 'kindly and zealously devoted much time and attention to it.'[10]

The inspection reports invariably emphasised that the success of a regiment's school owed a great deal to the attention of its CO and his fellow officers. The 88th Regiment at Chester in October 1820 included 215 women and 205 children. Ninety boys and girls of this regiment attended the school and were uniformly clothed at the regiment's expense. The inspecting officer commented that the school was 'remarkably well conducted' and that this reflected the 'highest credit on Lt. Colonel Fergusson and his officers'.[11] The success of a regiment's school depended even more on the CO's commitment when on overseas service. Lieutenant Colonel Duffy, CO of the 8th Foot at Corfu, in the Ionian Isles, was commended in 1820 for his attention to the school, which was attended not only by the unit's drummers, young soldiers and children, but by some children 'of respectable natives' in the island. In the same year the state of the school of the 65th regiment in Barbados was commended and the inspecting officer recorded that this reflected favourably on the CO and his predecessor, who had both maintained the school in the face of difficult although unspecified circumstances in the colony. The 'difficult' circumstances may refer to

9   TNA WO 27/200: 'Confidential Inspection Reports and Returns for Regiments 1830',
      37th Foot, 31st Foot.
10   TNA WO 27/247: 'Confidential Inspection Reports and Returns for Regiments 1835',
      14th Light Dragoons, 16th Lancers, 78th Highlanders.
11   TNA WO 27/150: 'Confidential Inspection Reports and Returns for Regiments 1820',
      88th Foot.

outbreaks of yellow fever which were frequent across the islands in the West Indies. The 2nd (Queens) Regiment, when it was stationed in Barbados in October 1815, lost eleven officers and more than two hundred men and half its woman and children to yellow fever.[12]

The experience of the 40th Regiment in the Tasmanian penal settlement illustrates how a change of CO could have a significant impact on the temper of the regiment and demeanour of the men and their families. In the 1820s Tasmania was one of the Empire's frontier settlements and service was especially arduous for the troops and their families. The men were dispersed in small detachments guarding the convicts and faced hostility from the native population. Periodically, men were called on to undertake 'bush ranging' in the interior to deal with the outrages committed by runaway convicts. The regiment had been on the move for several years and unsurprisingly morale was low and there was some ill-discipline in the ranks. The regimental records for 1826 describe the truculent behaviour of some of the wives and their general reluctance to send their children to school. Brevet Lieutenant Colonel Balfour responded to what he considered to be insubordination with a succession of regimental orders accompanied with threats. Fortunately, Lieutenant Colonel Balfour embarked for England in December 1826 and command of the regiment passed to Major Kirkwood, who immediately set about improving the regiment's morale.[13]

Major Kirkwood instructed the Orderly Officers to give their personal attention to the school, keeping records of attendance and reporting on whether the schoolroom was being maintained in a clean condition. In July 1827 he issued a regimental order stating that he was 'desirous of giving every encouragement to soldiers of the regiment, who are inclined to attend at the regimental school' and that any man so disposed would be given leave of absence from evening parade for that purpose. However, he expected that this indulgence would not be abused.[14] The confidential report for the half-yearly inspection of regiment in October 1827 highly commended Major Kirkwood and his fellow officers for their zeal and attention to the men in the particularly difficult circumstances in Tasmania and judged that the regiment was in a creditable state of order and discipline.[15] The following inspection report in June 1828 commented favourably on the admirable appearance, discipline and order of the 40th Regiment and made particular reference to the regiment's school:

> The greatest credit is due to Major Kirkwood for his unremitting and successful
> education of the children; their improvement is striking and the system he has

---

12 TNA WO 27/150: 'Confidential Inspection Reports and Returns for Regiments1820', 8th and 65th Foot; R. Cannon, *Historical Records of the 2nd or Queen's Royal Regiment* (London: Clowes and Sons 1836), p. 67.

13 Smythies, *Historical Records of 40th Regiment*, p. 228.

14 Lancashre Infantry Museum, Regimental Order Book of 40th Foot,1824-26, pp. 181,201.

15 Smythies, *Historical Records of 40th Regiment*, p. 224.

adopted cannot fail to lay a foundation for forming excellent non-commissioned officers, whose character and abilities will at no very distant period be useful to His Majesty's service.[16]

The regiment was next inspected in February 1830 following the regiment's move to Belgaum in the Bombay Presidency. There were 40 boys, 44 girls and 51 soldiers on the school's register and the inspection report again commended Major Smallwood and judged that schoolmaster-sergeant McLachlan was well qualified and that he ably conducted the school.[17]

COs understandably put effort into preparing for the half–yearly inspections and ensured that the regiment's interior economy was in good order, but nevertheless the reports were not always favourable. The officer inspecting the 21st Regiment at Hobart Tasmania in 1835 reported that the school would benefit from 'a better qualified person' as schoolmaster.[18] The children in the 1st Royal Dragoons' school at Norwich in 1830 were thought to be 'backward in arithmetic' and the schoolmaster only 'tolerably qualified'.[19] Although the schoolmaster of the 2nd North British Dragoons (Scots Greys) at Dorchester in England 1830 was rated suitably qualified, the CO was told that the children did not seem to be making satisfactory progress. Matters were little improved when the regiment was inspected in September 1840, and school was again considered to be not well conducted. The inspecting officer reported that the schoolmaster did his best but concluded that a better master might be found.[20] The officer inspecting the 9th Lancers at Hounslow in Middlesex in 1830 was not satisfied with the state of the regimental school and unusually was prepared to offer some advice. The school recently had been placed in the hands of a newly promoted soldier and the CO was advised that he should be sent to the Brighton Cavalry Depot to get some instruction from the schoolmaster of the 14th Light Dragoons, whose school in the opinion of the inspecting officer was the best school he had ever seen.[21]

The Horse Guards required the half yearly Inspection Reports to be accompanied by a return showing the regiment or battalion's effective strength and authorised establishment and the number of women who were legally married and on the

16   Smythies, *Historical Records of 40th Regiment*, p. 226.
17   TNA WO 27/200: 'Confidential Inspection Reports and Returns for Regiments1830', 40th Foot.
18   TNA WO 27/247: 'Confidential Inspection Reports and Returns for Regiments1835', 21st Foot.
19   TNA WO 27/204: 'Confidential Inspection Reports and Returns for Regiments 1830', 1st Royal Dragoons.
20   TNA WO 27/204: 'Confidential Inspection Reports and Returns for Regiments1830', 2nd North British Dragoons (Scots Greys); TNA WO 27/298 'Confidential Inspection Reports and Returns for Regiments 1840', 2nd North British Dragoons (Scots Greys).
21   TNA WO 27/199: 'Confidential Inspection Reports and Returns for Regiments1830', 9th Lancers, 14th Light Dragoons.

strength of the unit. The return also recorded the number of male and female children and the numbers of each who were below 10 years of age.[22] A sample of the Returns for six regiments of cavalry and 16 battalions of infantry at the half-yearly inspections in May and October 1820 show that there were 1,996 boys and girls, but 1,171 of these children were below ten years of age.[23] The Royal Horse Guards at Windsor had 118 children, but only 18 of these were above ten years of age, whilst the 14th Foot at Meerut in India recorded 61 children, 49 of who were under ten years of age. Similarly, the 88th Foot at Manchester had 205 children of who 191 were under ten years and the 9th Foot at St Vincent in the West Indies had 72 boys and girls of which number only 4 were over ten years of age.[24]

There is no indication in the reports of the minimum age at which children were admitted to the regimental schools. The great majority of the children accompanying the regiments were below ten years of age and large numbers would have been infants who many were too young to attend school. There was no specific provision for infants at the regimental schools until later in the century, but it is reasonable to assume that most of the children would have been around five years of age before they were sent to school.[25]

The January 1812 Circular and the subsequent Regulations also required the return filed with the inspection reports to state the numbers of pupils of each sex attending the schools.[26] This instruction was not systematically followed by the inspecting officers during the early post Napoleonic war period. The 1820 confidential reports and inspection returns for the majority of units do not contain the numbers of pupils at the schools and data was recorded only for five regiments of cavalry and four battalions of infantry. In some instances, the numbers attending were inserted into the reports, probably by the Adjutant, alongside the number of children accompanying the regiment.[27]

During the early 1820s revised forms issued by the Horse Guard for the Inspection Returns included a section that specifically asked for the number of boys, girls and

22   *General Regulations and Orders for the Army 1816*, p. 288.
23   TNA WO 27/150: 'Confidential Inspection Reports and Returns for Regiments1820'. Returns for: 7thHussars; 10th, 11th, 12th, 14th, 19th Light dragoons; 9th, 10th, 13th, 14th, 16th, 19th, 21st, 22nd, 34th, 36th, 40th, 56th, 59th, 67th, 69th and 88th regiments of foot.
24   TNA WO 27/150: 'Confidential Inspection Reports and Returns for Regiments 1820', Royal Horse Guards, 14th Foot, 88th Foot, 9th Foot.
25   The Hibernian Military School did not normally admit children below seven years of age and the RMA below five years of age.
26   *General Regulations and Orders for the Army1816*, p. 338.
27   TNA WO 27/150: 'Confidential Inspection Reports and Returns for Regiments1820', passim. There was an average of 55 children on the school registers for the five regiments of cavalry and an average of 44 children for the 4 battalions of infantry. However, these averages are distorted because of the large numbers at the schools of the 11th and 12th Light Dragoons and the 88th Regiment.

adults who were attending the school. The inspection returns for 1830 for the seven regiments of dragoon guards and the three regiments of dragoons on the Army List, all of which were stationed in Great Britain or Ireland, record that there were a total of 282 boys and 235 girls on the registers of the schools. This gave an average of 52 children and an average of 28 boys and 24 in the schools of these ten cavalry regiments.

There were twelve regiments of light cavalry in the 1830 inspection returns four of which were stationed in India. There were 201 boys and 116 girls at the schools of the eight light cavalry regiments in the British Isles, but the four regiments in India had a total of 141boys and 127 girls on their registers. This gives an average of 40 children and an average of 25 boys and 15 girls for the regiments in Great Britain compared with an average of 67 children and 35 boys and 32 girls for the four regiments in India. The significantly larger number of children at the schools in India can be explained by the much larger size of the cavalry regiments when serving overseas. The typical establishment of a regiment of light cavalry in the British Isles was around 300 non-commissioned officers and men, whereas the 11th Light Dragoons at Cawnpore, the 13th Light Dragoons at Bangalore and the 16th Lancers at Meerut each had strength of some 640 men.[28]

The inspection returns for the infantry in the first half year 1830 (Table7) for 1st to 68th regiments of Foot, contain the records for the service companies of nineteen battalions and also the depot companies of the 22nd Foot.[29] Thirteen battalions were stationed overseas, although there are no entries with the numbers for the school of the 31st Regiment at Meerut in the Bengal Presidency. Nine of the thirteen battalions serving abroad were in India and the 12th and 23rd Foot were at Gibraltar, the 10th in the Ionian Isles at Corfu and the 22nd in Jamaica.[30]

28 TNA WO 27/200: 'Confidential Inspection Reports and Returns for Regiments1830', 11th Light Dragoons, 13th Light Dragoons,16th Lancers.
29 TNA WO 27/200: 'Confidential Inspection Reports and Returns for Regiments1830', passim.
30 TNA WO 27/200: 'Confidential Inspection Reports and Returns for Regiments1830', passim.

Table 7. Inspection Returns First Half Year 1830, School Registers: 1st-68th Regiments at Home and Abroad

Regiments at Home

Regiment	Boys	Girls	All Children	Adults	Total pupils
1st/1st(Royals) Scotland	17	20	37	30	67
9th Ireland	11	12	23	67	99
21st Ireland	19	6	25	52	77
22nd Depot Ireland	32	28	60	17	77
37th Ireland	52	22	74	----	74
50th England	23	31	54	81	135
68th Ireland	28	15	43	36	109
Totals	182	134	316	283	599
Average at home	26	19	45	40	

Regiments Abroad

Regiment	Boys	Girls	All Children	Adults	Total Pupils
2nd/1st(Royals) India	73	67	140	67	207
2nd India	35	30	65	106	171
3rd India	47	34	81	18	99
10th Corfu	16	14	30	30	60
12th Gibraltar	29	33	62	----	62
14th India	35	47	82	8	90
20th India	71	45	116	126	242
22nd Jamaica	7	4	11	13	24
23rd Gibraltar	28	8	36	----	36
26th India	25	29	54	20	74
40th India	40	44	84	51	135
49th India	39	52	91	113	204
31st India	NA	NA	NA	NA	NA
Totals	445	407	852	552	
Average abroad	37	34	71	46	
Average in India	46	44	89	64	

In 1830 the schools of the seven infantry battalions serving in the British Isles had an average of 45 children and an average of 26 boys and 19 girls on their registers. This compares with an average of 71 children and an average 37 boys and 34 girls for the twelve battalions stationed overseas for which data is available.[31] The schools in India were typically much larger. The schools of the eight infantry battalions in India in 1830, for which data is available, had an average of 89 children and 46 boys and 44 girls on their registers. Much of the difference between the size of the schools of regiments serving in the British Isles and abroad can be explained by differences in the authorised establishments and actual strengths of units serving in the United Kingdom and overseas.

When regiments returned home from long periods of service abroad their actual strength was often below their authorised establishments, especially in the case of units returning from India, where a substantial number of the rank and file had volunteered for other regiments so that they could remain in the country. Once the regiment was in the British Isles the service and depot companies would be combined and recruiting parties would make every effort to bring the regiment up to its authorised establishment before it embarked once again for service overseas. The new recruits would be unmarried men and those subsequently given permission to marry and bring their wives onto the strength the regiment would only have had very young children who were not of an age to attend school.

Soldiers in the British Isles who wished their children to learn to read and write would sometimes look outside the regimental school and send their children to a local charity school. The CO would not have been in the position to challenge this unless it in some way interfered with the discipline and good order of the regiment. When a regiment was abroad generally families had no option but to send their children to the regiment's school.

A soldier at this time had no legal duty to ensure that his children attended school and COs could not charge a soldier with a breach of military discipline for failing to send his children to the regimental school. The COs therefore resorted to persuasion and this was directed mainly at the soldiers' wives whose presence with their husbands on the strength of the regiment, they were reminded, was an indulgence. The line between persuasion and coercion was a fine one, and there were occasions when the military authorities had to reassure the troops they were free to decide for themselves whether their children went to school. For example, in 1828 the C-in-C in the Madras Presidency felt the need to issue a statement to the troops correcting 'an erroneous opinion' that the men might be compelled to send their children to the regimental schools. The statement emphasised that, whilst it was always proper for the military authorities to stress the benefits that the schools offered to the men and their families,

---

31   There is data for seven units stationed in Great Britain, but for only 11 of the 12 battalions overseas. There is no data for the 31st regiment at Meerut.

there were no circumstances in which persuasion would be replaced by coercion.[32] Nevertheless, the evidence suggests that COs of units stationed abroad, especially those in India, were on the whole successful in 'persuading' soldiers to enrol their children at the regimental school.

Table 8. Extracts from a tabular statement of children and adults attending schools in the regiments of Cavalry and Infantry in 1837 and 1841[33]

| | | Rank & File | 1837 | | 1841 | | 1837 girls | 1841 girls |
			boys	adults	boys	adults		
Cavalry at home	6 Troops	304	24	8	21	7	21	17
Cavalry in India	9 Troops	675	46	14	29	3	47	30
Infantry at Home	10 companies	800	23	38	29	82	19	30
Reserve at home	4 companies	200	18	27	11	31	16	11
Infantry in India	10 companies	970	47	44	63	106	41	39
Service Overseas	6 companies	600	2 1	35	20	47	18	17

Enrolment however did not ensure that the children on the registers would attend regularly at school. This was especially the case in India, where schooling was difficult during the hot summer months and attendance was affected by outbreaks of disease, which often as in the case of cholera, resulted in the periodic closure of the schools.

32   *Asiatic Journal (Asiatic Interchange)*, Madras 1828-29, p. 613.
33   NAM, Army Education before 1846, Box 22125, 'Letter from the Secretary at War to the Commissioners of the Royal Military Asylum showing the existing grants for teachers and the numbers of children attending schools in the regiments in the several varieties of the Service, February 1842'. The letter does not specify whether the numbers are actual averages or represent typical school sizes whenever regiments were at home, in colonial garrisons or in India.

The reports of army school inspectors well into the second half of the century consistently identified irregular attendance as the main obstacle to the educational progress of soldiers enrolled at the Army's schools at home and abroad. King's Regulations and military law during the post war years did not require enlisted soldiers to go to school, but in many regiments strong pressure was placed on young soldiers to attend. COs had no hesitation in ordering enlisted boys to go to school and the regimental standing orders were periodically reinforced by specific orders, emphasising that men seeking promotion to the rank of NCO should ensure that they possessed a good elementary education and that it would be wise for them to attend at school whenever circumstances permitted. Attendance however could not be guaranteed, and regimental duties and other exigencies frequently interfered with attendance.

The cavalry inspections returns for May 1830 paint an uneven picture of attendance at the adult schools. The returns for the seven regiments of Dragoon Guards, and for the 1st Royal Dragoons and the 2nd North British (Scots Greys) Dragoons, do not show any adults on their school registers, although 10 troopers of the 6th (Inniskilling) Dragoons attended school when the regiment was in Dublin. All of the cavalry regiments stationed in the British Isles had strength of only around 350 men. There would have been a slow turnover of the NCOs in these regiments and in consequence there may have been less incentive for the troopers to attend school.

Conversely, five of the eight regiments of Light Dragoons, Hussars and Lancers that were at home had an average of 20 men on their school register. In the case of the cavalry in India, there were 65 men on the register of the 4th Light Dragoons at Poona and 30 at the school of the 11th Light Dragoons at Cawnpore. Surprisingly, there were no adult soldiers on the returns for the 13th Light Dragoons and 16th Lancers, even though both regiments received very favourable confidential inspection reports. The inspecting officer recorded that the school of the 16th Lancers in 1830 was one of the best conducted that he had ever seen. This regiment however had a policy of educating and training the sons of its rank and file for enlistment in the regiment and this probably had the effect of reducing the number of its young-attested soldiers who required an elementary education.[34]

The average number of soldiers on the registers of the schools of the infantry abroad in 1830 (Table 5) was greater than the average for the units serving the British Isles, but schools of the battalions stationed in India were significantly larger. There were however considerable differences between the regiments in this sample that were stationed in India. The 14th and the 3rd Foot, both at stations in Bengal, had only eight and 18 adult soldiers respectively on their registers, whereas the 2nd Battalion of

---

34   TNA WO 27/199: 'Confidential Inspection Reports and Returns for Regiments1830', passim. There is some evidence that the 16th Lancers and other cavalry regiments had a greater level of literacy amongst their men than the Army as a whole. Rumsby, *Discipline, System and Style*, pp. 77-80.

the Royals (1st Regiment of Foot) at Bangalore recorded 67, whilst the 2nd (Queens) Regiment at Poona and the 20th Regiment at Bombay, the 26th at Madras and the 49th in Bengal each registered over 100 soldiers at their respective schools.[35] The difference in the adult attendance at these schools owed something to the particular circumstances of each regiment and probably also significantly to the commitment of their commanding officers.

The 14th regiment had been in the East Indies since 1807, and when it was inspected at Berhampoor in Bengal early in 1830, it was about to return to Great Britain. The 2nd Battalion of the Royals had also served in the East Indies from 1807 and would leave the Madras Presidency for Great Britain in 1831. This was a regiment that had been something of a pioneer in army education, and the 1830 inspection report commented very favourably on the qualities of the schoolmaster and the work of the chaplain in supporting the school.

The 2nd (Queen's) Regiment had arrived in the Bombay Presidency from England in 1825 and the 49th Regiment in the Bengal Presidency from the Cape Colony in 1828.The 20th (East Devonshire) Regiment had arrived in Bombay from St Helena in 1822 and the 26th (Cameronians) from England in 1828. These regiments faced a long stay in India, and it was sensible to encourage soldiers to attend school and qualify themselves for promotion as NCOs.

The return, which provided by the War Office for the Treasury in 1842 (Table 6), records a fall in the average number of adult soldiers at the schools of the infantry both at home and in India in 1837, in comparison with the sample taken from the May 1830 Inspection returns. However, by 1841 there had been a significant increase in the average numbers attending the schools both at home and in India. (Table 9)

Table 9. Average Number of soldiers at the regimental schools of the infantry in Great Britain and India, 1830, 1837 and 1841

	GB	India
1830 * (Table7)	40	64
1837 (Table 8)	38	44
1841 (Table 8)	82	106

*Sample of 19 infantry regiments and one depot in the British Isles.

Most of the difference between the numbers on the registers of the schools in Great Britain and India at each of the three dates can be explained by the greater number

35   TNA WO 27/200: 'Confidential Inspection Reports and Returns for Regiments1830', passim.

of men, approximately twenty per cent, on the strength of a ten company infantry battalion in India. The numbers at the schools in India in 1830 may have been distorted by the numbers and identity of the regiments in the sample, but the relative difference between the average numbers at the schools in Great Britain and India in 1837 and 1841 corresponds to the relative strengths of the infantry battalions at home and in the sub-continent. The significant increase in the average numbers at the schools both at home and India in 1841 suggests that there may have been some effort by the military authorities during the late 1830s to persuade soldiers to attend at the schools.

During the 1830s there was a growing recognition that soldiers in barracks and cantonments had little to occupy their time when not on duty and that the men frequently resorted to drink to alleviate boredom. In consequence drunkenness was a serious problem throughout the Army. The situation was exacerbated in India and elsewhere in the East Indies where local sprits, such as arak and toddy, could be purchased very cheaply and a high incidence of drunkenness is frequently mentioned in the confidential inspection reports on regiments stationed at these stations. The officer inspecting the King's regiments at Poona in 1835 reported the drunkenness was a major problem in both the 4th Light Dragoons and the 2nd (Queens) Regiment. The confidential report for the 9th Regiment at Port Louis Mauritius in July 1835 commented favourably on the good conduct of the battalion, 'except for the great failing of intoxication.'

The 1836 Royal Commission on Military Punishments concluded that a great deal of the crime in the Army originated in excessive drinking and argued that a long term solution to the problem was to find more gainful occupations for the men during their leisure hours.

Lieutenant Colonel Hamilton CO 30th Foot had established a regimental garden at Secunderabad in1820, 'for healthy amusement and exercise' of the men in the hope that gardening would divert them from drinking excessively.[36] In 1826, Lieutenant Colonel FitzClarence commanding the 7th Royal Regiment of Fusiliers at Corfu instituted a library in the sergeant's mess and in 1839 the Army Estimates provided for expenditure on soldiers' libraries to combat 'crime'.[37] Libraries were gradually introduced in the larger garrisons and were followed later by the provision of reading and games rooms. The Royal Commission also recommended organised outdoor sports and games, and this was taken up from 1841, when cricket pitches were established at some barracks. There were also attempts to establish temperance societies during this period, for example in the 26th Regiment, albeit with varying degrees of success

---

36 TNA WO 27/150B: 'Confidential Inspection Reports and Returns for Regiments1820',30th Foot; TNA WO 27/199: 'Confidential Inspection Reports and Returns for Regiments1835', 4th Light Dragoons, 2nd (Queens) Regiment, 9th Foot.

37 A garrison library had been opened at Gibraltar in 1793 and by the Royal Engineers at Chatham in 1813. These were mainly for officers and the first lending library organised specifically for the men in the ranks was believed to be that of the 80th Foot at Malta in 1825. White, *The Story of Army Education*, p. 29.

during this particular regiment's stay in India. A well run regimental school could also occupy some of the men's time and divert them from drink, whilst usefully improving the educational standards of the rank and file of the regiment.[38]

The system of regimental schools in the British Army was one significant legacy of the Great Wars with France (1793-1815) that survived the demands for economy in military expenditure in the post war years. In 1840 there were sergeant schoolmasters on the establishments of the 144 regiments of cavalry and battalions of infantry on the Army List (including the colonial corps) and also with the Provisional Battalion at Chatham.[39] The charge for the salaries of these schoolmasters was little more than £5,000 per annum and this was subsumed within the overall costs for the Army and did not appear as a separate charge in the Estimates. There was no expenditure on a staff at Horse Guards dedicated to the management of the schools and although there was an annual charge in the Army Estimates for books, this small sum did not attract the attention of any Members of Parliament who were pressing for reductions in military spending.

The regimental schools were cheap and measured by the numbers on their registers were remarkably good value for money. In 1840 the Horse Guards recorded that there were some 18,500 children accompanying the Army, although not all of these would have been of an age to attend the regimental schools.[40] The War Office did not provide Parliament with a return of the numbers attending the regimental schools, but a conservative estimate suggests that excluding the colonial corps there were some 8,000 to 8,500 children on the schools' registers.[41] In addition in 1837 there were some 5,700 adults on the registers and this had increased to over 9,000 by 1841, although the demands of military service was such that not all of these enlisted men would have been able attended regularly at the scheduled lessons.[42]

---

38   E.A. Smith, 'Educating the Soldier', *Journal of the Society for Army Historical Research*, Vol. .86, (Spring 1988), pp. 35-38; P. Groves, *Historical Record of the 7th or Royal Regiment of Fusiliers* (Guernsey: B.Guering, 1903), p. 164; T .Carter, *Historical Record of the 26th or Cameronian Regiment*, p. 181.

39   The 144 regiments and battalions comprised: 3 regiments of Household cavalry, 7 battalions of Foot Guards, 24 regiments of cavalry, 103 battalions of infantry and 7 battalions of the Colonial Corps.

40   TNA WO43/752: Secretary at War, 'Appointment of Schoolmistresses throughout the Army'.

41   These estimates have been calculated taking the average numbers for 1837-41 provided by the War Office for the Treasury (Table 8).They are based on 19 regiments of cavalry in Great Britain and four in India; 20 battalions of infantry in India; 63 at other overseas stations; 20 battalions and 50 depots in Great Britain. Children have been added for the three regiments of household cavalry and the 7 battalions of Foot Guards. There were also approximately 400 children at the depots of the Royal Artillery at Woolwich and Dublin.

42   These estimates are also based on the number of units, excluding the colonial corps, and have been calculated taking the average numbers for 1837 and 1841 provided by the War Office for the Treasury (Table 8).

The effectiveness of the regimental schools during these years in providing an elementary education however was another matter. Later in the century, when a corps of trained schoolmasters had been established and measures had been put in place to regulate the curriculum, management, and inspection of the schools, it was easy to point at the limitations of the early regimental schools. Lieutenant Colonel J. H. Lefroy writing in his report on the regimental and garrison schools in 1858 thought that it was always difficult and in a battalion composed mostly of young soldiers almost impossible to find men well qualified enough for the duties of schoolmaster-sergeant. The widely expressed view later in the century, after the Normal School had been established to train the Army's schoolmasters at the RMA Chelsea, was that the schoolmaster-sergeants were inefficient and generally useless. Many doubtless were of little use and their teaching ineffective, but others regularly received praise in the half -yearly inspection reports for their conscientious efforts. The inspection reports suggest that many did their best and managed to teach the rudiments of reading, a little writing, and some simple arithmetic. It must be remembered that the situation was little better in many of the civilian schools of the era. David Stow recognised as a pioneer of teacher training did not open his 'Normal Seminary in Glasgow until 1837.[43] The first Anglican diocesan college for training teachers was not established until 1839 and what became the National Society's training college at Battersea was only established by Sir James Kay Shuttleworth in the following year.[44]

Colonel Lefroy believed that irregularity of the children's attendance at the Army's schools was no greater than in civilian schools, but there were particular circumstances that affected what could be achieved by the best of teachers in the best managed regimental school. He concluded that the incessant changes in the stations of the troops, the movement of detachments and the transfer of older soldiers between the service companies and the depots or vice-versa, resulted in few children progressing beyond the rudiments of an elementary education.[45]

The achievements of the regimental schools and their sergeant schoolmasters in the decades following the Napoleonic Wars none the less should not be dismissed. The British Army was providing schooling for soldiers' children at the tax payers expense some sixty years before publicly funded compulsory elementary education was established throughout the United Kingdom and at a time when the children of the labouring classes were put out to work at an early age. Similarly, there were very few opportunities in civilian life for working class adults to gain an elementary education, or to resume their schooling and improve on what they had already learnt.

The regimental schools had become an established part of regimental life in the British Army and although not all COs were convinced of the wisdom of educating

43   Devine, *The Scottish Nation* p. 395.
44   The British and Foreign School Society did periodically accept boys for training during these years as monitors, at its Borough Road School.
45   Lefroy, *Report on the Regimental and Garrison Schools of the Army*, pp. 35, 79.

the private soldier, most accepted that efficient children's schools bought tangible benefits. At the very least children attending school were not causing a nuisance around the barracks and soldiers' sons often enlisted and their education could thereafter continue at the regimental school preparing them for eventual promotion. Soldiers' daughters might help with the younger children in the schools and many married into their fathers' regiment. The half-yearly inspection reports show that many COs and regimental officers took a keen interest and were proud of their schools and came to see them as integral part of the regimental family. Regimental standing orders emphasised the importance of regular attendance and in some cases the children were clothed out of regimental funds. It was common for the boys and girls led by their schoolmaster to march behind the men of the regiment on the Sunday church parade. The point was well made in account in 1841 of the funeral procession of Colonel C.B. Molyneuax of the 8th Hussars who had died at Hulme Barracks in Manchester. The procession was headed by the regimental band 'bringing up the rear were the boys and girls of the regimental school in their uniforms.' [46]

The sergeant schoolmasters were untrained, and some were barely competent, but the record suggests that most within the limitations of their abilities and constraints of the military service did their best to provide some schooling for the Army's children and its young soldiers. They wore the uniforms of their regiment and shared and suffered the same conditions of service as their fellow soldiers and their women and children, but their existence during these years is largely unknown and their achievements however small have been unrecognised.

46 Rumsby, *Discipline, System and Style*, p. 250.

Part II

Years of Reform
Modernizing the Regimental Schools
1840-70

9

Some Small beginnings to a Decade of Reforms

In the decades following the Napoleonic Wars there was continual political pressure to reduce government spending. During the 1820s Joseph Hume and his fellow Radicals had regularly introduced motions in the House of Commons to reduce the size of the Army, taking as their ideal the peace-time strength of the Army in 1792, but ignoring the fact that the British Empire had doubled in size following the Napoleonic Wars. The motions were never in danger of being passed, but they did compel the War Office to steer a middle course between the Horse Guards' estimates of requirements for maintaining the garrisons at home and throughout the Empire and demands to reduce military expenditure. The Whig Governments that were in power for most of the 1830s contained a number of political economists, who were strong advocates of laissez faire policies and favoured reductions in taxation in order to encourage commerce and trade, which they considered to be essential for the maintenance of international peace.[1] Sir Henry Parnell, who was the Secretary at War from April 1831-February 1832, was a member of the Political Economy Club and during his period in office he concentrated on reducing the Army Estimates. His successors at the War Office, Sir John Cam Hobhouse (February 1832-April 1833) and Edward Ellice (April 1833-December 1834) broadly continued with this policy, but although there was no threat to the regimental schools, there was a drastic reduction in spending at the Royal Military Asylum and the Hibernian Military School.

In domestic policy the 1830s was a continually reforming decade, which is seen as the start of 'the age of improvement'.[2] There was a succession of Acts of Parliament and select committee and royal commission reports that resulted in a wide range of reform affecting, inter alia, the parliamentary franchise, local government, the poor laws,

---

1   Hew Strachan, 'The Early Victorian Army and the nineteenth-century revolution in government', *English Historical Review*, October 1980, pp. 786-7.
2   D. Cannadine, *Victorious Century: The United Kingdom, 1800-1900* (London: Allen Lane, 2017), pp. 166-7.

public health and employment in factories and mines, but there were insignificant parallel reforms in the administration of the Army. There was a broad anti-military sentiment in civil society during these years and the Army was generally despised. The poor conditions of service attracted only low quality recruits and there was resentment at the use of troops at home to cope with civil disorder. There was no apparent military threat to Great Britain from the European powers and there was no opinion in the country agitating for the reform of the Army's administration.

The frequent rotation of troops between stations at home and across the empire made the individual infantry and cavalry regiments the core of the post war British Army. It is here that one must look for the roots of reform in the early Victorian Army.[3] The problems of selecting schoolmaster-sergeants and improving the conditions of the regimental schools were not the most pressing problems facing COs during 1830s. These were insignificant concerns in comparison with the high rates of sickness that sapped the effective strength of regiments, and the effect on morale of the boredom experienced by the troops stationed for long periods in the colonial garrisons. The latter was of particular concern because the men relieved boredom by resorting to drink and the cheap liquor that was available at many overseas stations resulted in drunkenness and ill-discipline in the ranks. The concomitant and indeed the officially approved response was the 'lash', but some COs sought a variety of preventive measures to occupy soldiers' leisure time and thus maintain discipline as alternatives to corporal punishment. These included awarding medals for good conduct, introducing sports and games, establishing libraries and encouraging soldiers to attend their regiments' school.[4]

The widespread use of corporal punishment in the Army was criticised both within and outside Parliament and in 1836 the government responded by appointing a Royal Commission on Military Punishments. The Report of the Commission is replete with evidence of the schemes introduced by COs at regimental level to address the problem of boredom and indiscipline in overseas garrisons and these included the beneficial effect when soldiers attended their regimental school.[5] These schemes were introduced by regimental officers without any instructions or encouragement from the military departments. They do not appear to have been influenced by the religious and philosophical doctrines of the day and were simply instrumental responses by COs to practical problems in managing their units.

3   Strachan, 'The Early Victorian Army and the Nineteenth-century Revolution in Government', p. 798.
4   The Standing Orders of the 2nd Dragoons (Dublin: 1839). The Orders stressed that 'Prevention is the spirit of discipline.'
5   Strachan, 'The early Victorian Army and the Nineteenth-century Revolution in Government', p. 801.

The first moves to reform at the official level came in the years 1835-39 when Henry Grey, Viscount Howick, was Secretary at War.[6] He became aware of COs' concerns and the various initiatives taken by them at regimental level, in part through the influence his brother Charles Grey, who was the CO of the 71st Regiment. Howick decided to introduce measures to improve the conditions of service for private soldiers.[7] In 1817 Sir James McGrigor, the Director General of the Army Medical Department, had introduced a system of half yearly returns on the sickness of troops at home and abroad, so that an empirical basis could be established for preventive medicine in garrisons. In 1835, Dr Henry Marshall and Lieutenant A.M. Tulloch were commissioned by Howick to collate this data. The results were published in a number of Parliamentary papers between 1837-40. These lead to improvements in the soldiers' diet and the standards for the construction of barracks but did not impact on the regimental schools.[8]

In the early 1840s there was a positive change in the attitude in Parliament towards the Army. In part this was in consequence of a number of emergencies in the colonies in 1838 and 1839, particularly in North America that required the augmentation of the army, and forced MPs to accept the need for increased military spending.[9] Funding for regimental libraries had been included in the Army Estimates in 1839 and in the following year the War Office introduced the first measure to improve the regimental schools since they had been established throughout the Army in 1812.

The Cape Mounted Rifles was a colonial corps established in the Cape Colony after the territory passed into British possession during the Napoleonic Wars. It was recruited from the local 'Hoottentot' (Khoikhoi) people and was commanded by British officers. Originally it had been maintained by the Colonial Establishment, but in 1839 it was augmented to six companies under the command of Colonel Henry Somerset and transferred to the Army Estimates.[10] The War Office observed that there were two schoolmaster-sergeants on the establishment of the corps and on 23rd May 1839 Viscount Howick wrote to Sir George Napier, the commanding general at the Cape, asking whether there were any particular reasons that would justify

6   Henry Grey was the eldest son of the former Prime Minister Charles Grey, 2nd Earl Grey. Henry Grey, who held the title of Viscount Howick from 1807 until 1845, followed his father into Parliament and served as Secretary at War (1835-39) and then Secretary of State for War and the Colonies (1846-52). In 1845 he succeeded to his father's title as Earl Grey.

7   Strachan, 'The Early Victorian Army and the Nineteenth-century Revolution in Government', p. 805.

8   Strachan, 'The Early Victorian Army and the Nineteenth-century Revolution in Government', p. 785. Battalions moved from Great Britain to the Mediterranean, then to the West Indies and then to North America before returning home.

9   Fortescue, *A History of the British Army Vol. XI*, pp. 451-3, 505-514.

10 R. Cannon, *History of the Cape Mounted Riflemen* (London: Parker, Furnival & Parker, 1837), p. 26. The headquarters was at Grahams Town and the regiment saw a great deal of service in the Frontier Wars.

the appointment of a second schoolmaster-sergeant. Colonel Somerset advised Sir George that two appointments were needed because of the large number of children on the strength of the corps, but that he would much prefer the appointment of a schoolmistress with an allowance of £20 per annum to teach the girls needlework and supervise their education, in the place of the second schoolmaster. He explained that a schoolmistress had been previously employed when the corps was on the Colonial Establishment and had paid for out of private funds and that the appointment was a great success.[11]

Colonel Somerset's proposal was forwarded by Sir George Napier to the War Office and reached the desk of Thomas Babington Macaulay, who had succeeded Howick as the Secretary at War.[12] Macaulay was very taken with the proposal and wrote to Lord Hill the C-in-C at the Horse Guards suggesting that a schoolmistress should be appointed to every regiment and corps in the Army. He argued that the appointment of schoolmistresses would be well received in the ranks and believed that soldiers' families were due some compensation, because the nature of their military service denied their children access to 'a national education' in the schools in the British Isles.[13]

Lord Hill, the C-in-C, did not dissent from the proposal and Macaulay proceeded to secure the support from the Treasury to include a sum in the Army Estimates to pay the salaries of schoolmistresses. He suggested a salary of £20 per annum and was able to demonstrate that the proposal would cost only £3,000-£4,000 per annum, depending on whether the appointment of schoolmistresses was extended beyond the line regiments to the two cavalry and 83 infantry battalion depots. The War Office provided supporting evidence of the need for schoolmistresses in the form of the data collated from the inspection returns of the number of women and children who were accompanying the Army in 1839-40.

11   TNA WO 43/752, ff.167-170: 'Appointment of Schoolmistresses throughout the Army.'
12   Thomas Babington Macaulay was a noted essayist and historian alongside his political work. Perhaps best known for his book *The History of England*, he also remembered for his collection of narrative poems collectively entitled the *Lays of Ancient Rome*. It is therefore not surprising that he took an interest in educational matters.
13   TNA WO 43/752: ff. 167-170, Appointment of Schoolmistresses throughout the Army. The reference to a 'national education' refers to the network of schools of the British and the National Society in England and Wales and to the Board of National Education in Ireland that were receiving Parliamentary grants.

Table 10. Numbers of women and children with the British Army 1839-40 (TNA WO 43/752: ff.179-181)

Number of units	women	women in barracks or on rations	Boys	girls
Household Cavalry & Foot Guards (10)	1005	282	706	773
Cavalry (23 regiments & 2 depots)	1442	978	1109 & 62*	1103
Infantry (103 battalions & 83 depots)	8916	4461	6641 & 204*	7018
Colonial Corps (7)	1891	1814	600	661
Totals for 143 units and 85 depots	13254	7535	9056 & 266* (both &girls)	9555

Macaulay was ultimately successful in securing the support of the Cabinet and a vote of £3,500 for the employment of schoolmistresses was included in the Army Estimates for 1839-40. In proposing the vote in the House of Commons Macaulay explained that that there were some 10,000 female children accompanying the troops, whom he called the 'the children of the state.' He continued:

> For the public service they are hurried from place to place. From Malta to Gibraltar, from Gibraltar to the West Indies, as the commonweal might require; and it therefore would be inexcusable if we did not provide these [children] at some small expense with some means of instruction.[14]

Macaulay explained that the regimental schools had been in existence since 1811, but that they had concentrated on teaching boys and young soldiers. He argued that there should also be schools for girls under the superintendence of a schoolmistress. He thought that the schoolmistress 'might possibly be the wife of a sergeant whose duty would be to instruct them [the girls] in reading, writing, needlework and the rudiments of common knowledge; with simple precepts of morality and religion as good plain women of that rank might be supposed capable of imparting to them.' [15]

One can only speculate why the Treasury was prepared to approve the expenditure for the appointment of army school mistresses. Macaulay was aware that following

14 *Hansard*, 3rd Series, Vol. LII, 9th March 1840, p. 1091.
15 *Hansard*, 3rd Series, Vol. LII, 9th March 1840, p. 1091.

repeated economies, the Royal Military Asylum Chelsea was admitting many fewer children than in the 1820s and that only 80 girls remained at its branch in Southampton. It made financial sense to close the girls' branch of the RMA at Southampton and transfer the buildings to the Ordnance Survey. The estimated cost of maintaining the 80 girls and ten infants at Southampton was £2,847 for the financial year 1839-40 and a large part of this expenditure was for staff salaries and the upkeep of the building. Once the Southampton branch had been closed and the remaining girls had been moved to Chelsea the Treasury could anticipate further savings and these would go a considerable way in meeting the costs of appointing schoolmistresses to the regimental schools.[16] It is perhaps no coincidence that when in March 1840 Macaulay was explaining to the House of Commons why it should approve the additional expense of appointing schoolmistresses for the benefit of some 10,000 Army children, he was also instructing the Commissioners of the RMA to cease the admission of girls at Chelsea and to gradually abolish the asylum's female branch.

In October 1840, a Royal Warrant was issued authorizing the appointment of a schoolmistress in all the regiments of cavalry and infantry, including the infantry depots. The Warrant emphasized that if the girls were to be brought up as useful and respectable members of society it was essential that they were taught by females. The girls were to be taught reading writing and the 'rudiments' of arithmetic, needlework and such other parts of 'housewifery' to 'train them up in habits of diligence, honesty and piety.'[17] In order to pay the schoolmistresses the warrant provided an allowance of £20 for each regiment of cavalry and an allowance of £3 for each company in each battalion of infantry. In addition, an initial grant of £5 was made over to every regiment to cover the cost of establishing the female schools.[18]

In the following month a Circular from the War Office informed the Army about the contents and intentions of the Royal Warrant. It emphasized that the appointment of a schoolmistress was not to detract from or interfere with the duties of the schoolmaster-sergeants, although she would clearly assist him in his duties. The War Office did not expect that the appointment would require any additional accommodation and that the arrangements should be made to timetable the boys and girls schools in separate teaching sessions during the day.

Commanding officers were ordered to take 'the utmost care' in selecting a suitable person as the schoolmistress. Particular attention was to be given to the 'morals, habits and acquirement' of the appointee, but it was expected that a suitable individual could be found from amongst the wives of the NCOs and private soldiers.[19] The arrangements

16   Estimate for Army Services, April 1839-March 1840.
17   TNA WO 43/752: f.177, 'Draft Royal Warrant, dated 29th October 1840, to be given at the Court at Windsor'.
18   TNA WO 43/752: f.177, 'Draft Royal Warrant'.
19   TNA WO 43/752: ff. 182-183, 'Circular NO.874, November 1840'..

for the payment of the salaries for the schoolmistresses, which were contained in the Royal Warrant and the Circular, recognized that all the companies of an infantry regiment/battalion might be serving together in Great Britain, but more likely that the service companies would be overseas whilst the depot companies remained at home. Providing that the COs could find suitable women it would be permissible for two schoolmistresses to be appointed and paid pro rata from the regimental allowance – one with the service companies and one at the depot. The Circular however specified that the schoolmistresses would not be entitled to a pension.[20]

The case for the appointment of schoolmistresses at the regimental schools, which Macaulay presented to the House of Commons in March 1840 and the subsequent Royal Warrant were the first recognitions by government since 1812 that public had an obligation to provide an elementary education for the thousands of children who accompanied the Army as it moved from garrison to garrison across the British Empire. The appointment of a schoolmistress complemented the work of the schoolmaster-sergeant and gave him more time to concentrate on the instruction of the boys and young soldiers and in this respect strengthened the regimental schools. However, the initiative failed to address the inherent weakness of the system of regimental schools. Indeed, the CO was now charged with finding both a man and a woman from within his regiment or battalion who were suitable persons willing to teach in the regimental school. The selection of a woman from within the regiment with an adequate elementary education and the requisite personal qualities proved to be particularly difficult and was to remain a problem for many years.[21]

The improvements in the conditions of service for soldiers that had been introduced by Lord Howick and Thomas Babington Macaulay were pragmatic responses to problems faced by commanding officers at regimental level and were relatively inexpensive to introduce.[22] The military departments saw no reason to address the broader issue of the lack of any formal training for the schoolmaster-sergeants and the schoolmistresses, although teacher training schools were being established in both Great Britain and Ireland to produce qualified teachers for the civilian elementary schools.[23]

The regular attention given to the regimental schools at the half-yearly inspections and in the confidential reports that were forwarded to the Horse Guards did little more than confirm that a regiment or corps was maintaining a school and that the

---

20   Where the service and depots companies were divided the start-up costs were to be divided pro- rata.
21   Lefroy, *Report on the Regimental and Garrison Schools of the Army*, p. 47.
22   Strachan, 'The Early Victorian Army and the Nineteenth-century Revolution in Government', pp. 783, 800-801.
23   The Board of National Education in Ireland was established in 1831 with a Central Training Department in Marlborough Street Dublin in 1833. Sir James Philips Kay Shuttleworth established Battersea College, the most important of the English teacher training colleges and the model for other college in 1840.

schoolmaster-sergeant and the schoolmistress were tolerably qualified for their duties. The half-yearly returns listed the numbers on the school registers, but there was no attempt to record the take up of the children of an age old enough to attend school, or the regularity of their attendance, or also of that of young soldiers. The general officers undertaking the half-yearly inspections were not familiar with developments in pedagogy in civilian schools and there was no mechanism for systematically assessing and evaluating the educational standards of any particular school and the progress of its pupils.

These were important considerations given the frequent movement of regiments between military stations at home and abroad, which disrupted the schooling of the children and young soldiers and limited their progress. Any further reform would require pressure from regimental officers, together with an awareness of the need for improvements at senior levels in the military departments, and above all a political will in government. All of this was to come about in the 1840s and was to shape the delivery of schooling and the subsequent advances in elementary education in the Army during the second half of the Nineteenth century.

10

A Sympathetic Minister and an Ambitious Principal Chaplain

In September 1841, Sir Henry Hardinge (1785-1856) was appointed by Secretary at War in Sir Robert Peel's Tory government. He was a soldier and a competent administrator and enjoyed the confidence of both Peel and the Duke of Wellington who returned as C-in-C Horse Guards in August 1842.[1] Hardinge's contribution to the development of education in the Army is important, because he set in motion a series of events that were to result in a complete overhaul of the system of regimental schools.

Hardinge acknowledged that Army had some obligation to provide for the welfare of soldiers' children. When he served as Secretary at War from 1828-30 he had presided over a reduction in the number of children admitted to the RMA, but he was on record in stressing that '...the country was bound to provide for the orphans of those who died in its service.' He opposed Hume and his fellow 'Radicals' who were pressing for the closure of the RMA and argued that the only provision that could be made for the children of soldiers who died abroad was at a military asylum in Great Britain.[2] He had not opposed Thomas Macaulay's recent scheme for army schoolmistresses, or his assertion that the public had a wider obligation to make some provision for the education of the thousands of soldiers' children who accompanied the regiments as they moved between stations across the Empire.[3]

Soon after returning to the War Office, Hardinge began to take an interest in the regimental schools, most probably because he was aware of the difficulty COs faced in selecting and retaining competent schoolmaster-sergeants. In March 1842 he wrote to the Commissioners of the Royal Military Asylum stating that in his opinion 'the present educational system of the Army is in some respects susceptible of improvement' and

---

1   Sir Henry Hardinge, *Oxford Dictionary of National Biography* <www.oxforddnb.com/articles/12/12271> (accessed 21st July 2007).
2   *Hansard*, Third Series Vol. III, 4 March to 22 April 1831.
3   *Hansard*, Second Series, Vol.XX11, 'Debate on the Army Estimates1830-1', 8 March 1830.

asked for their advice and assistance on the training and employment of schoolmasters.[4] There was a certain irony in the War Office approaching the Commissioners for help in in addressing some of the problems in the system of regimental schools. Under pressure from the Treasury, the War Office had imposed severe reductions in the Asylum for the previous twenty years and there had been some speculation in the newspapers that the institution might be closed down.

Hardinge explained to the Commissioners that in order to establish a more uniform standard of education throughout the Army it was necessary to specify criteria by which commanding officers could judge a soldier as competent for appointment as a schoolmaster-sergeant. Also, there needed to be a system of regular inspections of the regimental schools by qualified inspectors. He acknowledged that there were not enough military chaplains to inspect all the regimental schools and that the civilian inspectors of the National Society in England would be unable to assist because most schools were in garrisons overseas. He inquired whether the Asylum might be able to provide an occasional inspector to visit the schools close to London and provide a report of any defects in their operations and suggest remedies that could then be circulated to all regiments.[5]

The commissioners, who were mainly the senior officers on the staff at the Horse Guards, replied that whilst they agreed with the Secretary at War that the competence of sergeant schoolmasters should be established before their appointment, and that it was desirable to introduce inspection of the schools by qualified persons, the number of staff at the RMA was barely sufficient for the needs of the institution and that in consequence they would be unable to offer any help with inspections. This was a predictable and understandable response given the reductions that had been imposed on the Asylum in previous years. The Commissioners suggested that the most suitable person to inspect regimental schools was a clergyman of the Church of England, but they also advised against any civilian involvement in the inspection the Army's schools. They recommended that any the inspection should be performed under the superintendence of the clergyman directing the chaplains of the Army (i.e. Principal Chaplain) as was the intention in the General Order of 1st January 1812 that had established the regimental schools.[6]

In his letter to the Commissioners, Hardinge also suggested that the instructions for conducting the regimental schools should be revised, because 'the system of Dr Bell is generally admitted to have been much improved upon in late years.' Hardinge was referring to recent developments in educational thinking and practice with regard to elementary education. Opinion in the Inspectorate of Schools, a body created by the

---

4   TNA WO 143/10; ff. 454-464, Minutes of H M Commissioners, Royal Military Asylum, 1833-1846.

5   TNA WO 143/10: ff. 454-464, Minutes of H M Commissioners, Royal Military Asylum, 1833-1846.

6   TNA WO 143/10: ff. 454-464, 'Minutes of H M Commissioners, Royal Military Asylum, 1833-1846'.

Education Committee of the Privy Council to oversee Treasury grants to the civilian elementary schools, was favouring teaching by trained teachers with the assistance of pupil teachers in place of Bell's system.[7] The Asylum however was still using Bell's system introduced more than thirty years earlier. The Commissioners replied that Bell's system had never been represented to them as 'in any material respect defective.'

Hardinge also suggested to the Commissioners that in addition to teaching reading, writing, and arithmetic, the children at the regimental schools should be trained in tailoring, shoemaking, and saddlery, because this would encourage regular attendance at the schools. The Commissioners replied that this was already the practice at the Asylum, but it would be impractical to extend this type of training to regimental schools, because regiments frequently changed their stations and it would be very difficult to replicate the specialist workshop facilities that existed at the Asylum.[8]

Hardinge concluded by asking the Commissioners for their advice on the salaries that should be paid to the teachers in the regimental schools and whether allowances currently given for books and materials were adequate. They replied that they were not competent to express an opinion, but noted that as the Secretary at War had stated that he intended to forward the Commissioners' responses to the C-in-C (Lord Hill), and they were confident that Hill would provide him with all the information that he required.[9]

The Commissioners' very guarded responses to Hardinge's request for advice and assistance were understandable. In 1839, they had reluctantly responded to a War Office request to introduce denominational instruction and religious worship for Catholic children at Chelsea. They probably resented any implied criticism or further interference by the War Office of their management of the Asylum. Nevertheless, they did express a willingness to help as far as they were able and suggested that one teacher from each regimental school could be instructed at the RMA, 'as was originally done for some years, under such regulations as may hereafter be determined upon.'[10]

Henry Hardinge did not accept this offer. The RMA was in no position to provide up to date training for prospective regimental schoolmasters. Nevertheless, the commissioners' limited offer of assistance proved to be important. The list of commissioners signing the letter to Sir Henry Hardinge was headed by the Quarter Master General Sir J. Willoughby Gordon, who had been in post since 1811. Also signing was Adjutant General Sir John Macdonald, who had been appointed in

7   G. Sutherland, *Elementary Education in the Nineteenth Century* (London: The Historical Association 1982), pp. 20-1; S.J. Curtis and M.E.A. Boultwod, *An Introductory History of English Education since 1800* (London: University Tutorial Press, 1966), pp. 59-60.

8   TNA WO 143/10: ff. 454-464, Minutes of H M Commissioners, Royal Military Asylum 1832-1846.

9   TNA WO 143/10: ff.454-464, Minutes of H M Commissioners, Royal Military Asylum, 1832-1846.

10   TNA WO 143/10,ff.454-463, Minutes of H M Commissioners, Royal Military Asylum, 1832-1846.

1830, having previously been the Deputy Adjutant General for almost twelve years.[11] Therefore, two of the most senior and long serving officers at the Horse Guards were now on the record as accepting in principle that teachers should be qualified before being appointed and that regimental schools should be periodically inspected by qualified inspectors. Moreover, the commissioners had offered some assistance in training regimental schoolmasters, albeit only through a revival of the short training courses that had operated at the Chelsea in 1812. Sidney Herbert, who succeeded Harding as the Secretary at War in 1845, was to remind the Commissioners of this when in the following year he imposed a plan to establish a training school for Army schoolmasters at the Royal Military Asylum.[12]

In the meantime, Hardinge sent copies of his correspondence with the Commissioners and their replies to Lord Hill the C-in-C at the Horse Guards.[13] In response, Lord Hill appointed Major General Brown, the Deputy Adjutant General, to lead a committee of officers and report on the state of the regimental schools. This report has not been traced, but its existence is confirmed by reference to it in a subsequent report on the regimental schools by Rev George Gleig, who was appointed the Principal Chaplain to the Army by Sir Henry Hardinge in the spring of 1844.[14]

Sir Henry Hardinge, 1st Viscount (1785-1858)
Secretary at War 1828-9, 1841-1844; Governor General
of India 1844 -1848; C-in-C of the Army 1852-56.
(Open Source)

11 'Sir James Gordon Willoughby 1772-1851', Oxford Dictionary of National Biography <www.oxforddnb.com> (accessed 21 July 2007).
12 Hardinge was appointed the Governor General of India in 1844. He was succeeded by Sir Thomas Freemantle, and in 1845 by Sidney Herbert.
13 The Commander-in-Chief was ex-officio, the President of the Board of Commissioners of the RMA.
14 TNA WO 43/796: f.150, 'Decision to upgrade following critical Report by Privy Council'; 'Correspondence and Report to the Secretary at War by the Principal Chaplain, G. R.

The Chaplain General's department had been abolished in 1830 for reasons of economy. The post of Principal Chaplain replaced that of Chaplain General. The post was independent of the Horse Guards and the Principal Chaplain was responsible to the Secretary at War and had a room in the War Office.[15] In July 1843 the Principal Chaplain, the Rev J.H. Dakins, decided to retire. Sir Henry Hardinge did not consider there was a suitable candidate among the existing military chaplains. He wrote to the Archbishop of Canterbury asking him to recommend a suitable civilian clergyman for the post and noted that the Rev George Gleig, the chaplain at the Royal Hospital Chelsea, had already written to the Archbishop expressing his wish to be considered a candidate. In February 1844, the Archbishop of Canterbury replied recommending Gleig, who was appointed to the post with effect from 1st April 1844.[16] During the next three years Gleig was involved at the centre of a series of reforms that shaped elementary education in the Army. It is therefore worth taking a little time to consider the man and his career before his appointment as Principal Chaplain.

Like Rev Andrew Bell, George Gleig was a Scottish Episcopalian. He had studied at Glasgow and Oxford Universities before securing an ensigncy in the 85th Foot in 1812. He served with Wellington in the pursuit of Marshall Soult's Army from Spain into France and, subsequently, in North America where he was present at the assaults on Washington, Baltimore and New Orleans. Placed on half pay, Gleig resumed his studies at Oxford with the intention of entering the church and graduated in 1818. He was ordained by the Archbishop of Canterbury in 1820. Being very adept at securing preferment, he acquired three livings in Kent in 1821-22, but the income from these was insufficient to support his growing family. Failing in an attempt to supplement his income from private tuition, he turned to what was to prove a prolific and successful literary career. His first success was an account of his service in the Peninsular War, *The Subaltern,* published in 1825. This provided him with an introduction to the Duke of Wellington who became, at best, his half-hearted patron. Although Gleig was a Tory who identified with the Duke on political matters and opposed parliamentary reform, they later were to differ over military matters including the direction of army education.

In 1834 Gleig was appointed to the Chaplaincy of the Royal Hospital Chelsea by Lord John Russell the Paymaster General in Earl Grey's Whig government. Gleig later claimed to be surprised by the offer of this post because of his known opposition to the policies of the Whig government. He subsequently admitted that he had written to the Duke of Wellington asking if he should accept the appointment. The Duke replied that he had been approached by Russell through Lord Fitzroy Somerset

Gleig on the Regimental Schools and the Training of Schoolmasters'.

15   The War Office was in Pall Mall, but the Chaplain General's Department had been housed in offices in Parliament Street, Westminster. The Principal Chaplain was provided with a room in the War Office and the assistance from War Office clerks to deal with his correspondence. TNA WO 43/535: ' Post of Chaplain General to be abolished'.

16   TNA WO 43/740: 'appointment of Rev George Gleig as Principal Chaplain'.

for assurances that Gleig did not write articles for the Tory press. The Duke confirmed that like most clergymen of the Church of England Gleig was sympathetic towards the conservative interest in politics, but he did not believe he had ever been 'a party writer.' However, an anonymous article in *Fraser's Magazine for Town and Country* in September 1834 confirmed his Tory leanings and praised his appointment as a staunch churchman who had an army background that would be an advantage in ministering to the old soldiers at the Royal Hospital.[17] Many years later Gleig quoted a letter from Lord John Russell that gave a similar reason for his appointment:

> I was induced to offer the Chaplaincy of Chelsea Hospital to you from reading 'the Subaltern' – not for your sake, but for the sake of the old pensioners, who I thought would like better a man who had seen battles than a high and dry churchman.[18]

George Gleig's time as Chaplain at the Royal Hospital provided him with some knowledge of the RMA, which was his close neighbour at Chelsea; but perhaps of greater significance were his contacts in London that were crucial in his subsequent appointment as Principal Chaplain to the Forces. One of his most politically influential contacts was Charles J. Bloomfield the Bishop of London who was a Commissioner of both the Royal Hospital and the RMA as well as a political friend of the Prime Minister Sir Robert Peel.[19] In many respects Gleig was well qualified for appointment as Principal Chaplain to the Army. A clergyman with parochial experience, he had served as a commissioned officer in the Napoleonic War and had established something of a literary reputation writing about the Army. His ten years as the chaplain at the Royal Hospital had kept him in touch with military matters and provided him with contacts at the Horse Guards and the War Office. Sir Henry Hardinge in a letter to the Archbishop of Canterbury in February 1844 had mentioned that Gleig had put himself forward as a candidate for the post, and the Secretary at War may have assumed that he had the support of the Duke of Wellington.[20] Sir Henry nevertheless quite properly sought advice from the three most senior Anglican churchmen and within the month they had all recommended Gleig for the post. The support of Charles J. Bloomfield, the influential Bishop of London was probably the most decisive in securing Gleig's nomination.[21]

---

17   D.R. Jones, 'The Rev. G.R. Gleig and Early Victorian Education' (M A Thesis, Belfast: Queen's University Belfast, 1983), p. 54

18   G .R. Gleig. *The life of the Duke of Wellington*, 3rd edition (London: Longman Green Longman Roberts and Green, 1864), p. 500.

19   Strachan, 'The Early Victorian Army and the Nineteenth-century Revolution in Government', p. 802.

20   It is an assumption that has been made by others. See Jones, 'The Rev G.R. Gleig', p. 55

21   Strachan, 'The Early Victorian Army and the Nineteenth-century Revolution in Government', pp. 801-2.

At this date all the indications were that Gleig's ambitions were purely ecclesiastical and he does not appear to have taken any close interest in the Anglican Church's considerable commitment through the National Society to the provision of elementary education for children in England and Wales. Indeed, it has been asserted that his ultimate ambition was to secure the diocese of Calcutta. The post of Principal Chaplain to the Army would certainly have been a recommendation for appointment as the diocesan head of the ecclesiastical establishment of the Bengal Presidency, which had the additional responsibility for providing officiating clergymen for the soldiers and families of the Queen's regiments and also the European officers and NCOs in the native regiments in the Company's army. Gleig was to be disappointed in his ambition: a failure, which in 1846 he acrimoniously blamed on Sir Henry Hardinge, who was by then the Governor-General of India at Calcutta. Sir Henry subsequently described Gleig as a 'disappointed and not at all times a very discrete man.'[22] George Gleig was astute and ambitious and above all a considerable opportunist and within a couple of years of his appointment as Principal Chaplain he had created for himself 'a unique niche at the War Office.'[23]

Hardinge's letter of appointment in March 1844 had included a list of instructions covering the various responsibilities of the Principal Chaplain and one of these was the supervision of the regimental schools. In this correspondence, Hardinge stated that he was prepared to receive and consider any suggestions regarding the various responsibilities.[24] Gleig's immediate response to this invitation was to set about preparing a report on 'the regimental schools and the training of schoolmasters.'[25] Strangely in this report he does not admit to having visited any of the regimental schools, although he certainly had corresponded with at least one officiating clergymen who had strong views about their defective state and had made some suggestions for their improvement.[26]

Gleig probably also had sight of the letters published anonymously in the Naval and Military Gazette in the spring and summer of 1843, which emphasised the defects in many of the regimental schools and argued for improvements in the pay and conditions of the Army's schoolmasters.[27] Gleig definitely had sight of the report on the regimental schools that had been compiled by Major General Brown, the Deputy

22   Douglas M. Peers, 'Gleig, Robert 1796-1888', *Oxford Dictionary of National Biography* <www. Oxforddnb.com> (accessed 11th June 2007).
23   Strachan, 'The Early Victorian Army and the Nineteenth-century Revolution in Government', p. 802.
24   TNA WO 43/740: 'Appointment of Rev G R Gleig as Principal Chaplain'.
25   TNA WO 43/796: ff. 147-161, 'Correspondence and Report to the Secretary at War by the Principal Chaplain,G. R .Gleig on the Regimental Schools and the Training of Schoolmasters'.
26   TNA WO 4/348: Secretary at War, Out letters, Chaplain General, 'Letter from Gleig to Rev Mitchell', 12th July 1844.
27   *Naval and Military Gazette*, 6th May 1843, p. 279; 15th July 1843, p. 439.

Adjutant General on the instruction of the then C-in-C Lord Hill in 1842, following Hardinge's approach to the Commissioners of the RMA. More importantly, he would have been aware of Hardinge's concern about the absence of a uniform system of regimental schools, the need for some training for schoolmaster-sergeants and also for an effective mechanism for inspecting their teaching.

Gleig's report was completed during the summer of 1844 and presented on 25 September to Sir Thomas Freemantle, who had succeeded Hardinge at the War Office. The report is a good example of his ability to write quickly and seemingly with authority on matters of which he had little knowledge or experience. He opened his report by stating that on the basis of evidence available at the War Office the education received by children and adults in the regimental schools was on the whole a good one, but that there was no uniformity of system in the management of the schools. Quoting from General Brown's report he asserted that '...even in the present imperfect state they [the regimental schools] do more for the children of soldiers than either the Royal Military Asylum at Chelsea or the Royal Hibernian School.' He noted that the only guidance ever issued to the regimental schoolmasters was in the Regulations ('the sub-joined extract' of Bell's plan) issued in 1811/ 1812, but he thought they were little used and that most units were unaware of their existence. He proceeded to commend General Brown's 'able report', which he thought had made a number of useful points, including that it was highly desirable that the Army's schools should be inspected by properly qualified persons.[28]

The main body of Gleig's report focused on the steps that would be necessary to achieve a uniform system of regimental schools. The first and most important steps were to ensure that the schoolmasters were properly educated and had mastered the knowledge they were expected to deliver and also had the skills to teach in the classroom. He thought there were two ways by which the Army could secure adequately educated and well trained schoolmasters. The first was to use the training institutions of the National Society for Promoting the Education of the Poor in the Principles of the Established Church. The second was for the Army to establish its own teacher training facility. He proceeded to consider and evaluate the provision at the three training institutions operated by the National Society in London: St Mark's Chelsea, Manchester Buildings Westminster, and Battersea (which the Society had acquired from Dr Kay-Shuttleworth in autumn 1843). All three institutions followed a broadly similar approach using lectures and essay writing to gain basic knowledge followed by teaching practice in associated local elementary schools. He thought that the Battersea institution would be the most appropriate for training regimental schoolmasters. This was because the institution had residential facilities which would ensure some measure of moral discipline and social training for the prospective army schoolmasters and thus

28   TNA WO 43/796: f. 151, 'Correspondence and Report to the Secretary at War by the Principal Chaplain, G.R. Gleig, on the Regimental Schools and the Training of Schoolmasters'.

avoid the alternative of billeting the men in taverns and inns with all the attendant temptations when residing in that type of accommodation. Furthermore, he considered Battersea to be particularly suited to 'the purposes of the Army', because it concentrated on training teachers for the poorer urban areas and manufacturing districts, which were increasingly the source of many of the Army's recruits.[29]

Gleig had visited each of the National Society's London teacher training institutions and received assurances from the Society that it would be willing to admit at least nine and perhaps more soldiers for training at its Battersea institution. He thought this option might be considered, but only as an experiment and cautioned the Secretary at War against accepting it as a permanent means of training regimental schoolmasters. This was partly on the grounds of cost as the National Society would expect to be compensated for the cost of maintenance and tuition, but also because of the specifically denominational character of the education at Battersea. A permanent arrangement with subventions to National Society would identify the British Army with the rules and ordinances of that Anglican institution. Whilst he believed that the education of young soldiers and the children of soldiers must have a basis in the 'broader doctrines of the Church of England', any regimental schoolmasters trained at Battersea would become in the strictest sense 'Church of England Teachers.' He argued that it was important to avoid an overtly 'Sectarian tendency' in the education in the Army, because there were such large numbers of Irish Catholic and 'Scotch Presbyterian or Dissenters' in the ranks.[30]

All these difficulties could be avoided by the Army establishing its own institution for the training of regimental schoolmasters with an organisation and curriculum designed by the War Office. This Gleig argued could be achieved for 'a very trifling outlay' at the Royal Military Asylum Chelsea, which had been erected for 1,400 children, but now, had only some 400 living in the building.

The staff of the Army's own training institution at Chelsea should be headed by a Principal, who would be a clergyman of the Church of England, whilst the Vice–Principal and masters of the taught disciplines would be civilians recruited on merit, as they were by the National Society in its own training institutions. The interior economy would be controlled by the Commandant of the RMA and his officers would maintain military discipline. The trainee schoolmasters would gain practical experience by teaching the boys in the Asylum in the same way that the pupil teachers at Battersea taught in the local parochial schools. The cost of subsistence for the trainees would be almost entirely covered by their ordinary pay and they would live

29   TNA WO 43/796: f. 154, 'Correspondence and Report to the Secretary at War by the Principal Chaplain, G.R. Gleig on the Regimental Schools and the Training of Schoolmasters'.
30   TNA WO 43/796: f.156, 'Correspondence and Report to the Secretary at War by the Principal Chaplain, G.R. Gleig on the Regimental Schools and the Training of Schoolmasters'.

in the training college at the Asylum in the same way as they served in barracks and depots.[31]

Gleig argued that a training school established by and answerable to the War Office and with a permanent connection with the RMA would be of incalculable benefit to that institution. He referred once again to Major General Brown's 1842 report saying that it had '…spoken very disparagingly of the sort of education which the children received at Chelsea.' Although Gleig admitted that he did not have a close personal acquaintance with the Asylum, he did not believe there was any reason to dissent from Brown's conclusions.[32] The inference here was that there would need to be some fundamental changes in the boy's schooling at the RMA to make it suitable place for the practical training of army schoolmasters. This was emphasised in a note inserted at the end of his report.

> The Military Asylum at Chelsea stands sorely in need of a complete shaking up - A better man than Mr Clark [the Chaplain appointed in 1803] never lived – but he is old and past his work and the masters under him – being chiefly Sergeants of the old school are ignorant as they are drunken - I got a servant from the School five years ago, who describes these worthies as coming generally drunk into the school - All that the boys learn beyond reading and writing they teach themselves - Mr Clark is in bad health and would probably retire were it thought advisable to adopt the plan referred to in my report.[33]

There was some substance in Gleig's reference to the behaviour to behaviour of the sergeants of instruction at the RMA. The registers of boys discharged from the RMA record that Richard Esmond was apprenticed to Rev George Gleig' at the Chelsea Royal Hospital in March 1839 and he was most probably the source of Gleig's information about the behaviour of the sergeant-instructors. The Commissioners minutes provide supporting evidence and record that in July 1843 James Rogers was suspended by the Commandant and subsequently dismissed as writing master for '… his irregular behaviour and intoxication that rendered him incapable of discharging

31   TNA WO 43/796: f. 158, 'Correspondence and Report to the Secretary at War by the Principal Chaplain, G.R. Gleig on the Regimental Schools and the Training of Schoolmasters'.
32   TNA WO 43/796: f. 159, 'Correspondence and Report to the Secretary at War by the Principal Chaplain, G.R. Gleig on the Regimental Schools and the Training of Schoolmasters'.
33   TNA WO 43/796: f. 161, 'Correspondence and Report to the Secretary at War by the Principal Chaplain, G. R. Gleig on the Regimental Schools and the Training of Schoolmasters'.

his duties.' In June 1844 Sergeant and Master Tailor Esdale was suspended and subsequently dismissed for drunkenness and ill-treating one of the boys.[34]

Gleig concluded his report by stressing that for his proposals to succeed there would have to be some mechanism of regular inspection for the regimental schools. His recommendation here followed on from Hardinge's suggestion and perhaps he saw an opportunity here to advance his own career. Referring again to General Brown's 1842 Report, he accepted uncritically that 'in most of the colonies, where there are military chaplains, this [inspection] seems by the Report of Officers, to be already cared for – but in Great Britain and Ireland it is yet to be framed.'[35] General Brown had suggested that that National Society might offer for some assistance from its own inspectors, but Gleig doubted that the National Society had sufficient inspectors for the task. He recommended that where there were garrison chaplains in the United Kingdom, they should carry out the school inspections and deliver reports; but that in order to keep the regimental schoolmasters (and their commanding officers) on their toes, it would be necessary for the Principal Chaplain to carry out an annual inspection of all the other regimental and depot schools in the Kingdom.[36]

Gleig's report is an important document, not because of what it revealed about the condition of the regimental schools [the anonymous letters published in the Naval and Military Gazette in 1843 were more informative and contained a generally damming account of the schools][37], but because of its radical proposal that the Army should establish its own school for the training of a new class of army schoolmasters at the RMA Chelsea and that these men should learn the rudiments of their trade through teaching the boys at the Asylum. His proposals for the regular inspection of the schools retained the role for the chaplaincy that had been included in the orders establishing the regimental schools in 1812 but aimed to make this more effective by augmenting the duties of Principal Chaplain by making him in effect the principal inspector of army schools within the United Kingdom. He was aware that there might be opposition to any additional spending on the Army, but argued in his report that there was no need to fear opposition to any (parliamentary) grant that might be needed

34   TNA WO 143/21: 'Discharge of boys March 1839'; TNA WO 143/10: 'Minutes of H M Commissioners of the RMA July 1843', June 1844.
35   TNA WO 43/796: f. 159, 'Correspondence and Report to the Secretary at War by the Principal Chaplain, G.R. Gleig on the Regimental Schools and the Training of Schoolmasters'. There were Chaplains at Corfu, Gibraltar, Malta, Cape Colony, Mauritius, Ceylon, Upper and Lower Canada and Trinidad. There was no mention of India where chaplains were provided by the Ecclesiastical Establishment of each of the three Presidencies. J. Smith, *In this Sign Conquer* (Oxford: A. R. Mowbray & Co, 1968), p. 48.
36   TNA WO 43/796: f. 161, 'Correspondence and Report to the Secretary at War by the Principal Chaplain G. R. Gleig on the Regimental Schools and the Training of Schoolmasters'.
37   The letters described the lack of suitable accommodation, the limited curriculum, the absence of text books and the high turnover of schoolmaster-sergeants, many of whom were unqualified to perform their duties.

'for the education of the troops', provided the objective of the moral improvement of the troops was kept firmly in mind and it was made clear that the management of this improved system of army education was 'altogether' [i.e. exclusively] in the hands of the War Office.[38] This point was included to counter any public concerns that, given the current Chartist agitation, literate soldiers might read and be influenced by seditious publications.

Gleig's report reveals his views on the purpose and priorities for the Army's schools. He emphasised that his proposals were submitted '...not so much with a view to benefit the children of soldiers, as to raise the character and enlarge the minds of the soldiers themselves' and he pointed to the large number of adults attending the regimental schools, which he asserted (without producing any evidence) in many cases exceeded the number of boys and girls. He believed that once teaching in the adult schools had been improved by a new class of trained army schoolmasters, the appetite for education amongst the troops would increase as would school attendance. This would be welcomed by the public because of its beneficial effect on '...the morale of the whole Army.' The purpose of education in the Army was to improve its moral character and thereby the conduct of the rank and file. This was something Gleig was to expand on in the articles he published anonymously in the *Quarterly Review* in 1845, 1846 and 1848, and which are considered in the following chapter.

Sir Thomas Fremantle succeeded Hardinge as Secretary at War, but only served until February 1845 and he did not take any action on Gleig's report. Fremantle's post was outside the Cabinet and his standing in the government would have made it difficult for him to proceed with Gleig's recommendations without the agreement or at least acquiescence of the Duke of Wellington, who had succeeded Lord Hill as C-in-C. The Duke may have considered General Brown's report on the regimental schools, but if so, he took no action. It does not seem that General Brown's alleged criticism of the RMA in his report caused the Commissioners any concern. On 14 July 1842 they had undertaken one of their regular inspections of the boys on parade and they witnessed an examination of their knowledge of the scriptures and noted their progress in writing and arithmetic. The Commissioners expressed their approval of the turnout and clean appearance of the boys and recorded in the Minute Book their entire satisfaction in the progress that the children were making in every part of their education.[39]

38 TNA WO 43/796: f. 160, 'Correspondence and Report to the Secretary at War by the Principal Chaplain, G.R. Gleig on the Regimental Schools and the Training of Schoolmasters'.
39 TNA WO 143/10: Minutes of H M Commissioners of the RMA, July 1842.

11

Securing Men Better Qualified to be Army Schoolmasters: The Reforms of 1846

William Gladstone's resignation from Robert Peel's government early in 1845 triggered a ministerial reshuffle and on 1st February 1845 Sidney Herbert accepted the office of Secretary at War with a seat in the Cabinet. Herbert had previously served as Secretary to the Admiralty and had been responsible for handling all naval business in the House of Commons because the First Lord of the Admiralty sat in the House of Lords. During his tenure at the Admiralty Herbert had successfully reformed the naval school for sailors' children at Greenwich. At this time he may have formed some opinion of the conditions at the RMA because in March 1843 the Commissioners at Chelsea assented to a request from the Lord Commissioners of the Admiralty for Captain Sir Thomas Hasting and two unnamed clergymen from Greenwich to visit the Asylum and examine the organisation of the establishment.[1]

Herbert's approach to public policy was pragmatic and has been described as being based on 'common sense rather than systematic reform.' This indeed was to characterise his approach to the reform of Army education.[2] Sidney Herbert's biographer has written that 'it is not too much to say that all the improvements introduced into the English system of military education between 1845-61 were due Sidney Herbert's exertion and advocacy.'[3] It was however some twelve months before Herbert addressed the issue of the training of the Army's schoolmasters. The condition of schooling in the Army was not the only or indeed the most pressing matter of concern for the War Office. During 1845 Herbert spent a great deal of time discussing with the Home Office the need to revive and re-organise the Militia, which through neglect had effectively ceased to exist. He also gave consideration to the pay and allowances of the

1   TNA WO 143/10: Minutes of H M Commissioners of the RMA, 23 March 1843.
2   H.C.G. Matthew, Oxford *Dictionary of National Biography*, <www.oxforddnb.com> (accessed 11th June 2007).
3   A. H. Gordon, *Sidney Hebert: Lord Herbert of Lea, a Memoir* (London: John Murray, 1906), Vol. II, 375.

troops, including the pay rate for the schoolmaster-sergeants and also whether adult soldiers should be charged fees for tuition when attending the regimental schools.

Sidney Herbert, 1st Baron Herbert of Lea, Minister at War 1845-46; 1852-55; Secretary of State for War 1859-61 by Sir Francis Grant. (© National Portrait Gallery, London)

The military departments were not unaware of commanding officers' difficulties in securing and retaining suitable soldiers to serve as regimental schoolmaster-sergeants. Hardinge had raised the question of their remuneration in his correspondence with the Commissioners of the RMA and this appears to have been considered by General Brown's committee of officers at the Horse Guards later that year. Gleig mentioned in his 1844 report that Brown's committee considered that the allowances for regimental schools were adequate.[4]

The matter again came to the attention of the War Office in November 1844, when a request was made by the commandant of the Provisional Battalion at Chatham to authorise Sergeant Robert Kennedy, the schoolmaster-sergeant, to be paid 2s/6d per day – the same rate as for the Sergeant Major and the Quartermaster Sergeant at the station. Sergeant Kennedy had transferred from the 58th Regiment earlier in the year on the understanding that he would receive 2s/6d per day because of the large number of pupils at the Provisional Battalion's school. On average during the previous nine months 85 boys attended the school. Sergeant Kennedy also superintended the 'writing department' of the female school where he provided tuition for 48 girls but was receiving only the usual regimental schoolmaster-sergeant's pay rate of 1s/10d per day.[5]

4   TNA WO 43/796: f. 150, 'Correspondence and Report to the Secretary at War by the Principal Chaplain, G.R. Gleig on the Regimental Schools and the Training of Schoolmasters'.
5   TNA WO 43/361: f. 276, 'Adult pupils to pay charges'.

Many regiments had allowed their schoolmaster-sergeants to supplement their income by charging fees (referred to as pecuniary allowances) to soldiers attending the schools. The fees were sometimes listed in the regimental standing orders. Queen's Regulations in 1842, however, ordered that schooling was to be given to NCOs and the rank and file 'gratis' [without charge]. The War Office turned down the Provisional Battalion's commandant's request and Sergeant Kennedy promptly asked to be released as the schoolmaster of the Provisional Battalion, because his anticipated higher salary had not materialised.[6]

The Sergeant Kennedy affair was a small event, but it started discussions in the War Office and the Horse Guards on the relative merits of granting higher rates of pay to sergeant schoolmasters and providing tuition without charge, and the alternative of requiring all adults throughout the Army attending at schools to be charged fees at a uniform monthly rate. The Adjutant General collected information from regiments and depots in the British Isles on whether pecuniary allowances had previously been received by their schoolmaster-sergeants for teaching adults. Herbert favoured the reintroduction of pecuniary allowances on the grounds of cost and argued on the basis of the Adjutant General's survey of regiments that fees had not previously discouraged ambitious soldiers from attending school. He thought that the possibility of earning additional income would be an incentive for the schoolmaster-sergeant to be proactive and zealous in his duties. Wellington concurred and a circular was issued from the Horse Guards on 16th September 1845. The circular amended Queen's Regulations and directed that Sergeants should be charged at a monthly rate of 8d, Corporals at 6d and Drummers and Privates 4d with the fees being retained by the schoolmaster.[7]

The staffing of the regimental schools was now firmly on the agenda at the War Office and in the following year Herbert addressed the problem of retaining schoolmaster-sergeants in post and introduced an allowance of 6d per day for the schoolmaster-sergeants, payable after ten years' service. This raised the pay of the long service schoolmaster to 2s/4d per day, which was the pay rate for a colour sergeant.[8] Once again it was the practical difficulties experienced by COs in operating their schools that created the awareness at ministerial level in government of the need for change.

In the meantime, Gleig was discharging his duties as Principal Chaplain, investigating and exerting his authority over the work of the military chaplaincy. On 19th May 1844, shortly after his appointment, he sent a memorandum to the military

6   TNA WO43/361: f .286, 'Adult pupils to pay charges'. Gleig had received representations on Sergeant Kennedy's behalf from the Rev. Curtois, the Chaplain at Chatham. Gleig asked Herbert to make Sergeant Kennedy a special case and pay the requested salary because of the large numbers of soldiers and children at the Provisional Battalion.
7   TNA WO 43/361: f. 286, 'Adult pupils to pay charges'. There was no change to the regulations to order the men to attend school.
8   TNA WO 43/668: Secretary at War, Regimental Pay and Allowances and Royal Warrants 1837-1846, 'Warrant, 27 January 1846'. Similar allowances were paid to schoolmaster-sergeants in the cavalry.

chaplains and officiating clergymen reminding them of their duties and exhorting them to regularly visit the regimental schools. Chaplains were to visit schools as soon as possible and thereafter twice weekly. They were to show an interest in the progress of the children and to take half an hour on each visit to examine them.[9] Gleig obtained copies of the regimental half-yearly returns and confidential inspection reports from the Horse Guards and wrote to the Adjutant General with lists of the units that had failed to submit any returns, or where the returns on the schools were irregular and incomplete. He urged the Adjutant General to exhort commanding officers to 'be a little more accurate in making returns' and generally pointed to the need for improvements at the schools:

> I cannot help offering that the general state of regimental schools as far as I have the opportunity for looking into it, is by no means satisfactory- a few brilliant exceptions there doubtless are [he mentioned the Blues, the Scottish Fusilier Guards and the 26th Foot)] – in a very large majority of the instances it appears to me that a great deal needs to be done in order to justify the expense to which the country is put in supporting them.[10]

This was written in February 1845, only a few months after Gleig had completed his report on the regimental schools, in which he stated that although there was no uniform system of management 'on the whole the education received by the children and adults in the regimental schools of the British Army is a good one.'[11] Gleig then started to canvas wider support for his ideas on the purposes of army education together with his proposals for the reform of the regimental schools in articles published in the *Quarterly Review* in 1845-46. Although these articles were anonymous, they are generally attributed to Gleig and together with subsequent articles inform much of what has since been written about the reforms in Army education in the 1840s. However, it is important to understand that Gleig's literary reputation is controversial. He has been described as a writer of 'the cut and paste school', who produced a wide variety of books and articles on military, ecclesiastical and imperial affairs often at short notice, and which were written under pseudonyms that nevertheless suggested a close familiarity with the subject matter. He also has been accused of not being averse to mixing fact and fiction with a moral message to create a good story.[12]

9   A.C.E. Jarvis, 'My Predecessor in Office, the Prebendary George Robert Gleig, MA', *Journal of the Royal Army Chaplains' Department*, Vol. IV, July 1931, pp. 324-38.

10   TNA WO4/348: Secretary at War, Out letters, Chaplain General 'Gleig to the Adjutant General, 3 February 1845'.

11   TNA WO 43/796: f. 150, 'Correspondence and Report to the Secretary at War by the Principal Chaplain G. R. Gleig on the Regimental Schools and the Training of Schoolmasters'.

12   Douglas M. Peers, 'Gleig, Robert 1796-1888', *Oxford Dictionary of National Biography* <www.Oxforddnb.com> (accessed 11th June 2007). Thomas Babington Macaulay, amongst

The first article titled, 'Moral Discipline of the Army', appeared in the September 1845 issue of the *Quarterly Review*. It is believed to have been written with Sidney Herbert's approval and in essence presents a case for an increase in the resources of the Army chaplaincy in order to address the moral and religious education of the troops.[13] This he argued was especially important in the British Army, where men enlisted for life and the young recruits were removed from parental discipline and the domestic constraints of family life, and were not able to benefit from the pastoral care provided by the local clergy. They were soon exposed to 'licentious talk, drunkenness, and all the godless behaviour' that were features of barrack room life to the detriment of the moral discipline of the service. Because of government indifference and neglect there were too few chaplains and inadequate facilities for church services in which to address the moral and religious education of the men. Gleig mentions the existence of the regimental schools but asserts that they were less than satisfactory and could be improved. He mentions the lack of provision for training schoolmasters and admits that the majority of officiating clergymen, who in effect constituted the military chaplaincy in the United Kingdom, were only paid for conducting divine service and visiting the sick and not for superintending the regimental schools. The article did contain proposals for augmenting the chaplaincy but did not include any proposal for training Army schoolmasters. However, there is a subtle appeal for reform by referring to a superior educational provision in the French Army and arguing that '... whenever the Government shall think fit to turn its attention to the subject this truth will probably appear.'[14]

There is some evidence that Gleig was becoming increasingly confident that the recommendations for the training of army schoolmasters contained in his report on the regimental schools would soon be adopted by the War Office. In October 1844, he wrote to the Anglican clergyman at Corfu in the Ionian Isles saying that the subject of the regimental school was under discussion and that he hoped that in time the education of both the men and the children would be 'carried out by a uniform and more effective system than now prevails.'[15] Gleig's room in the War Office in Pall Mall provided him with access to Laurence Sullivan, the department's long serving Deputy Secretary and from February 1845 to Sidney Herbert, so he had every opportunity to press the case for reform. It was not until early in 1846, however, that Herbert took steps to proceed with reforms in the regimental schools. Political considerations

---

others, is cited as accusing Gleig of deliberately altering or fabricating correspondence. D. Cruickshank, *The Royal Hospital Chelsea* (London: Third Millennium Publishing, 2004), pp. 139-40. The author's comments relate specifically to Gleig's *The History of the Chelsea Hospital and its traditions* (London: unknown, 1838).

13   Jarvis, 'My Predecessor in Office', p. 45.

14   G. Gleig, 'Moral Discipline of the Army', *The Quarterly Review*, LXXVI, No.15 (September 1845), p. 423.

15   TNA WO4/348: Secretary at War, Out letters, 'Chaplain General to the Chaplain at Corfu', October 1844.

probably accounted for the delay. In November 1845 Sir Robert Peel proposed to suspend the Corn Laws to deal with the famine in Ireland. The Conservative Party at Westminster was soon in a fractured and fractious state. In the following months the Cabinet was deeply divided and mainly occupied with the question of whether to repeal the Corn Laws.[16]

In March 1846 a second article attributed to George Gleig entitled, 'Education and Lodging the Soldier' was published in the *Quarterly Review*. This was a stridently polemical essay, much of which is devoted to the defects in the existing regimental schools and the several advantages that would follow from requiring all newly enlisted soldiers to attend at regimental schools staffed by a new class of army schoolmasters. This new class would be qualified by having attended a training institution that should be established at the RMA Chelsea. Perhaps to capture the attention of the reader and in deference to current concerns of the military departments, the article opened by asserting that the country's military forces were inadequate to deal with a surprise landing on the south coast of England in the event of a sudden outbreak of hostilities with France. He said it was important to augment the Army and revive the Militia. There was a pressing need to examine the moral condition of the British soldier and the attention should be given by the military authorities to the state of his accommodation in barracks. He asserted that the troops in the Royal Artillery and the Corps of Sappers and Miners were the 'most respectable body of men in the Army.' This he argued was because men enlisting in these units who could not read and write were sent to the Ordnance schools at Woolwich. In comparison, the regimental schools in the infantry and cavalry Gleig asserted accomplished 'next to nothing', because of the difficulty of finding competent schoolmasters. The schoolmaster-sergeants appointed had not been taught how to teach and in consequence the attendance of soldiers at school was 'wretchedly meagre.'[17]

> There was however, Gleig argued, a more fundamental problem with the theory and practice and the regimental schools. They were defective because, when they were established in 1811, they were mainly for the benefit of soldiers' children and he made the claim that teaching adult soldiers had never been entertained in the Army, which was of course palpably untrue.[18] Gleig was aware that many

16   B. Hilton, *A Mad, Bad and Dangerous People?* (Oxford: Oxford University Press 2008), pp. 508-9.

17   G. Gleig, 'Education and Lodging the Soldier', *The Quarterly Review*, LXXVII.No.154 (March 1846), pp. 532-42.

18   The assertion that the regimental schools were established for soldiers' children is based on the wording in Queen's Regulations, but Gleig may have been unaware of the correspondence between the Duke of York and Viscount Palmerston in 1811 in which there is mention of educating young soldiers. There were good reasons why Palmerston and York in 1812 decided to remain silent about schools for soldiers and focused on the provision for their children. (See Chapter 4)

COs encouraged their men to attend school and in his own 1844 report on the regimental schools and the training of schoolmasters he had asserted that more adults than children attended the schools. It was the case, however, that there was no separate pedagogy or curriculum prescribed for these adult students.

The article claimed that better education for soldiers would not only benefit the Army but would also bring benefits for the individual soldier. He would more easily find employment when he left the Army and thereafter would conduct himself as a responsible member of society. Again, no doubt with the current Chartist agitation in mind, he asserted that the public should not be frightened by the thought of educating the private soldier, because he would receive his education as a young recruit in a disciplined military environment.[19]

Gleig concluded the article with a direct appeal to Sidney Herbert, arguing that the only way to improve the tone of the Army and the moral and physical condition of the soldiers was to educate them. A number of suggestions followed. First, at some future date all new recruits should be required to attend their regimental school, which should have priority over schooling the children. Second, the schools should be conducted by well-educated and properly trained schoolmasters with the rank and pay equal to that of a Sergeant Major. Third, these men should be trained at the Army's own normal school that could be established without any great expense the RMA, Chelsea. The existing building had space to accommodate a normal school and a re-organised boys' school. For the boys' school to serve as a model school at which trainee army schoolmasters could practice teaching it would be necessary to replace the existing unqualified sergeant of instruction with competent schoolmasters. The boys at the RMA would continue to be educated and trained to look to the Army for a future career, but some of the more able boys might progress to the normal school and be trained as regimental schoolmasters.[20]

Gleig's focus in the March 1846 article on the need to improve the regimental schools and to address the moral tone of the Army complemented the September 1845 article in the *Quarterly Review*.[21] However, his March 1846 article makes the clear statement that the primary purpose of the regimental schools should in future be to educate the soldier and that the provision for soldiers' children should be very much a secondary consideration.

The minutes of the Commissioners of the RMA (see below) confirm that by March 1846 Herbert had decided to establish a training school for army schoolmasters at the RMA Chelsea and to undertake a re-organisation of the boys' school. Indeed,

---

19   Gleig, 'Education and Lodging the Soldier', pp. 546-7, 552.
20   Gleig, 'Education and Lodging the Soldier', pp. 548-52.
21   Gleig, 'Education and Lodging the Soldier': 'While we cultivate the intellects of our soldiers and by a well-ordered Chaplain's department nourish among them a reverence for religion', p. 553.

Rev George Gleig, Principal Chaplain of the
Forces and subsequently Chaplain-General of
the Forces 1844-75; Inspector-General of Army
Schools 1846-57. Archives of the RAEC.
(National Army Museum, London)

this probably governed the timing of the publication in the same month of Gleig's 'Education and Lodging the Soldier' in the *Quarterly Review*. The article was a call for the government to act in the national interest but did not breach any confidences. It is not known whether Herbert and any knowledge of the article prior to its publication, but it did not embarrass or compromise him politically. The timing and publication of the essay in the Quarterly Review can be seen as helpful in alerting Tory political opinion of the need for some measure of reform.[22]

Herbert would not have proceeded with any measure of reform without the support of Sir Robert Peel and the Treasury. War Office archives show that he also was careful to consult with and secure the agreement (or at least the acquiescence) of the Duke of Wellington as the C-in-C at the Horse Guards. This was essential not only to prevent any obstruction from the military commissioners of the RMA (who were on the staff at the Horse Guards), but also to ensure that Wellington did not resign from the Cabinet, because Peel was relying on the Duke to navigate the passage of the repeal of the Corn Laws through the House of Lords.[23] Herbert may have agreed with Gleig's assertions in his 1844 report on the regimental schools that the RMA was 'sorely in need of a complete shaking up', but he decided that a more authoritative

---

22   The timing of this article would have reinforced the perception that Gleig was the principal architect of Army School reform.

23   E. Longford, *Wellington: Pillar of State* (London: Weidenfeld and Nicholson, 1972), pp. 358-68.

and disinterested opinion was required before he could safely embark on a major and potentially controversial reorganisation of the Asylum.[24]

The Educational Committee of the Privy Council had been established to determine the distribution of the grants to support the capital costs of building elementary schools. The Committee decided that inspections of schools were necessary before it could award grants. In 1839 a number of 'Her Majesty's Inspectors' were appointed, and a satisfactory inspection report was made a condition for the receipt of a grant. By 1846 the Privy Council was making significant grants to educational charities to build elementary schools and these had reached almost £100,000 per annum. The steady growth in the number of schools in England and Wales required an increasing number of trained teachers. The National society and other educational charities were establishing their own teaching training institutions and from 1846, schools that had received a favourable inspection from the Privy Council's inspectors were recognised by the Education Committee of the Council as suitable for training 'pupil teachers.' Queen's Scholarships were also established to enable successful pupil teachers to attend training institutions.[25]

Herbert decided to work with the Privy Council and arranged for Professor Moseley to inspect the Royal Military Asylum and produce a report on his findings for the Councils' Education Committee. Henry Moseley, Professor of Natural and Experimental Philosophy at Kings' College London, had been appointed as an Inspector reporting to the Education Committee of the Privy Council in 1844 and was a particularly suitable civilian inspector to report on the RMA, because he had previously inspected the Royal Navy's School at Greenwich.

Professor Moseley's' inspection was not unannounced. On 31 March 1846, the Pay-Master General at the War Office, William Bingham Baring, an ex-officio Commissioner of the RMA, wrote to the Rev Dr Clarke, Chaplain of the RMA, introducing Moseley. He explained that the purpose of his inspection was to establish a case for increased spending on the 'educational part of the institution.' He wrote that it was discreditable that the Asylum had been denied the expenditure that it needed and assured the Chaplain that the inspection did not imply any criticism of his conscientious work over his many years at Chelsea.[26]

---

24   TNA WO 43/796: f.161, Report on the Regimental Schools and the Training of Schoolmasters. In the article in the March 1846 issue of the *Quarterly Review*, Gleig complained that the RMA was conducted as it had been in 1810 and that the curriculum was confined to reading, writing and arithmetic to the detriment of the intellectual development of the boys.

25   Minutes of the Committee of the Privy Council on Education (London, 1846), pp. 293-5; TNA ED17: Committee of the Privy Council on Education: 'Administrative History'; Curtis and Boultwood, *An Introductory History of English Education*, pp. 55-63.

26   TNA WO 143/39: Royal Military Asylum, Correspondence, Reports and Memoranda 1846-1852, 'Paymaster- General to the Chaplain of the RMA'; TNA WO 143/10: 'Minutes of H M Commissioners of the Royal Military Asylum 1833-1846, 31st March 1846'.

There was an entry in the Commissioners' Minute Book that indicates that they were aware of an impending inspection in early March 1846. They had received a letter from the CO of the 76th Foot Regiment requesting two or three boys from the Asylum to enlist in his regiment. The letter expressed a strong preference for boys from the RMA and thought them superior to boys that were likely to be received from the regimental or civilian schools. The Commissioners resolved on 18 March 1846 that it was desirable that the Commandant should send extracts from this letter to the Secretary at War and the Paymaster–General.[27]

The Horse Guards also knew about the inspection and Wellington received notice of it in a letter from Laurence Sullivan the Deputy Secretary at the War Office. The Duke's Military Secretary Lord Fitzroy Somerset forwarded a copy to the RMA Board of Commissioners, although it was not entered in the Commissioners' Minute Book until after the inspection had been undertaken. Similarly, there was no attempt to conceal the Government's intention to establish a 'normal school' at Chelsea. A letter from Charles Bloomfield, the Bishop of London to Quarter Master-General Sir Willoughby, discussing the Government's intention was recorded in the Commissioners Minute Book on 23rd April 1846.[28]

Moseley sent his report to the Education Committee of the Privy Council on 7th April 1846. It was immediately transmitted to the Secretary at War. The report confirmed that the RMA was totally unsuitable to serve as a model school for the army's schools. If a normal school for the training of the Army's schoolmasters was to be established at Chelsea, there would be a need radical re-organisation of the Asylum. Moseley reported that the boys' progress in reading, writing and arithmetic was in every respect grossly inferior to the naval school at Greenwich. He noted the absence of books, blackboards, globes and maps at Chelsea. More significantly, the boys' lack of progress was caused by the singular lack of qualifications of the schoolmaster sergeants and the narrowness of the curriculum. The latter was restricted by the Asylum's regulations to reading, writing and the first four rules of arithmetic. The children were taught neither history nor geography. Moreover, the boys were only in school on alternate days, the other days being devoted to the tailoring and shoemaking trades and domestic chores around the building. Moseley judged that '... in the whole of my experience - now extensive in the inspection of elementary schools - I have visited none so little deserving of commendation.'[29]

He compared the diet at the RMA adversely with that at the Greenwich school noting that the boys at Chelsea received a smaller weekly allocation of meat, bread, and milk, and a larger allocation of potatoes and beer. The incidence of sickness and

27   TNA WO 143/10: 'Minutes of HM Commissioners of the Royal Military Asylum 1833-1846, 18th March, 1846'.

28   TNA WO 143/10: Minutes of HM Commissioners of the Royal Military Asylum 1833-1846, 23rd April 1846.

29   TNA WO 43/796: ff.1-19, 'Report of Mr Moseley on the school at the Royal Military Asylum' [Moseley Report].

mortality at the RMA was higher than that at Greenwich, but he thought this might be because of the lower average age of the boys at the RMA. He was strongly critical of the disciplinary regime at the RMA, observing that flogging was more frequently resorted to than at Greenwich. He mentioned that punishments for misdemeanours included 'confinement in cage or a black hole, or by carrying a log chained to the person or by the drill.' The punishment by the log and drill was used frequently and on average was inflicted on six boys each day. His greatest concern however was that the boys spent most of the time under the direction and supervision of the schoolmaster-sergeants who always carried a cane, which they used gratuitously to deal with the most minor offences. Although he thought these retired soldiers were no better and no worse than the typical non-commissioned officer or private soldier of good character, they were neither fit nor qualified to be in charge of the moral education of children, and he did not think that the appropriate qualities and qualifications were likely to be found in men of their class.

Moseley also described the accommodation and daily routine at the RMA in some detail and his main concern was that the boys (who slept two to a bed) were locked in their dormitories without light for almost twelve hours every night in winter - a regulation which he found 'most prejudicial' as many of the boys were 14 or 15 years of age.

The main thrust of Moseley's report was that the dismal conditions of the RMA were rooted in the restrictive nature of the institution's regulations. Moseley along with his fellow Privy Council inspectors took a liberal view of what could and should be included in an elementary education for the average child. They considered that a broad curriculum involving a range of subjects delivered by trained and capable teachers would not only improve children's literacy and numeracy but would stimulate the mind and nurture intellectual growth. This applied as much to the children of soldiers as to the children of civilians and was even more necessary at the Military Asylum. This was because the boys were confined to the building at Chelsea, apart from four days holiday each year, from the time of their admission until they were discharged. During these years they were isolated from civilian life and were denied the wider experience and mental stimuli that were enjoyed by children who lived at home with their families.

Moseley had been charged to enquire into 'the extent of the instruction and the degree of religious and moral training afforded' at the RMA and not whether the boys' experience was a suitable preparation for a career as a private soldier in the British Army. He was given a paper by the authorities at the Asylum during the inspection that reported favourably on the character of soldiers serving in the Army who are alumni of the Asylum, but he observed that with the exception of their sobriety, this referred to their 'military character' and not to their 'moral character.'[30] Moseley had

---

30 This was probably an extract from the returns from regiments of the numbers, rank and character of soldiers enlisted from the RMA and RHMS that were required annually by

nevertheless identified an issue that was to re-emerge later during the 19th century in discussions about an appropriate curriculum for elementary education in the Army's schools. This centred on the balance between a broad and liberal education and one limited to the narrow instrumental needs of the Army. Sidney Herbert had chosen to seek advice from an experienced and respected Privy Council inspector and the work of the Education Committee of the Council involved the provision of education in civilian schools. It was by these standards that Moseley judged the Asylum, and on the basis what he had observed during visit, he concluded that it did not have '...the character of a model on which the public education of the country should be formed.'[31]

Armed with Professor Moseley's report, Herbert acted quickly and impressed on the Commissioners of the RMA the urgent need for reform. The monthly meeting of the management committee of the Commissioners of the Asylum was held on the 23 April 1846 when it was noted that Professor Moseley's inspection had taken place and that his report had been transmitted officially to the Secretary at War. The committee resolved that, because control and management of the RMA had been placed by Royal Warrant under a Board of Commissioners headed by the C-in-C 'for the time being', it would be improper to consider any change to the institution's regulations without the matter being considered by a Special Meeting of the Board of Commissioners summoned for that purpose. This was something which Herbert had anticipated, and the management committee's meeting was followed immediately by an Ordinary Meeting of the Board of Commissioners, which was presided over by the Secretary at War accompanied by the Paymaster General. At this meeting it was resolved to summon a Special Meeting of the Board of Commissioners for Monday 4 May 1846 in order to consider a plan to for the improvement of the boys' education and to establish a Normal School at the Asylum.[32]

Although the Secretary at War was an ex-officio Commissioner of the RMA, he rarely attended board meetings, unless politically sensitive or potentially contentious matters were on the agenda. This being one such occasion, Herbert chaired the meeting with Deputy Secretary Sullivan in attendance. Paymaster General Baring and the Bishop of London also attended along with the military commissioners including HRH the Duke of Cambridge and the Quarter Master and Adjutant-Generals.[33] The Secretary at War left the Commissioners in no doubt that the die was cast and the Government was determined to improve the regimental schools by establishing a 'normal school' at the RMA to train army schoolmasters. This would require a thorough reorganisation of the institution. Herbert asked the Paymaster General to

the War Office. 'King's Regulations and Orders 1837', p. 234.

31   TNA WO 43/796: f. 13, 'Report of Mr Moseley on the school at the Royal Military Asylum'.

32   TNA WO 143/10: Minutes of H M Commissioners of the Royal Military Asylum 1833-1846, 4th May 1846.

33   TNA WO 143/10: 'Minutes of H M Commissioners of the Royal Military Asylum 1833-1846, 4th May 1846'.

read a paper containing the resolutions on which the 'normal school' was to be based and the boys' school re-organised as a 'model school.'[34]

The paper began with the observation that in recent years important changes had been made in the objectives and character of the Asylum. It had been established as a place of refuge for the orphans of soldiers. At that time, their education was regarded '...as altogether a subordinate consideration.' Now the character of the Institution had changed: girls were no longer admitted; the infant department had been closed and boys alone were admitted when they reached five years of age. The only purpose of the institution was now the education of soldiers' sons, but so long as it remained 'organised as it was in 1804' it would never produce the results now expected from it. The sergeants were ill-educated and not qualified to teach. In consequence, and despite the zealous efforts of the Chaplain, the boys did not receive the '...full measure of the instruction sanctioned by the Board.'[35]

The Commissioners were reminded that in March 1842, Sir Henry Hardinge had asked whether it would be possible for the RMA to assist in achieving a more uniform and efficient system in the regimental schools, by providing staff to undertake periodic inspection of regimental schools and also to help ensure the competency of schoolmasters before they were appointed. The Commissioners had expressed their readiness to offer any assistance the RMA might afford in furthering these general objectives. If it was judged expedient, they would accept one teacher from each school to be trained at the RMA as had been the case when the schools were established in 1812. The Pay-Master General informed the Commissioners that the C-in-C and the Secretary at War 'wished to adopt these suggestions and were prepared to send schoolmaster-sergeants to be trained at the Asylum.' To put this into effect and to place the 'School on the footing worthy of a great national institution' it was desirable that the RMA's Chaplain should be assisted by 'well trained and adequately paid teachers.'

The paper then moved on to consider the curriculum for the boys and referred to the instruction received by the Engineers and Artillery at Woolwich. This provided examples that could be replicated at the RMA and give the boys' knowledge that would be useful for the practical duties of military life. Professor Moseley had suggested that boys would benefit from a broader curriculum and a more liberal education. The War Office, however, did not expect the majority of the boys to 'do more than just learn to read, write and keep accounts' and it was proposed that they should spend between one half and one third of their time outside the classroom learning trades and at fourteen years of age would enter the Army. Well-behaved and more able boys would (as was the present case with the boys serving in the band and the corps of drums) be excused trades and should stay at the school until they reached fifteen years of age.

---

34   TNA WO 143/10: 'Minutes of H M Commissioners of the Royal Military Asylum 1833-1846, 4th May 1846'.

35   TNA WO 143/10: 'Minutes of H M Commissioners of the Royal Military Asylum 1833-1846, 4th May 1846'.

It was hoped some few of these would qualify to remain and be trained as teachers, then go to a regimental school as assistants and after probation become schoolmaster-sergeants, returning periodically for refresher courses at Chelsea. Finally, the paper proposed that if the Commissioners were agreeable to the plan then they should appoint a committee to draw up regulations for the conduct of the reorganised Asylum and recommend a revised civil and military establishment of staff (the former to be appointed by the Secretary at War) for the institution.[36]

There is no record of any further discussion in the Commissioners' Minute book and the Board appointed a Special Committee comprising the Secretary at War, the Paymaster General and the Quarter-Master General to work out the details.[37] The committee worked quickly and Sidney Herbert presented its proposals to the Board of Commissioners on 22 June 1846.

The Asylum would be re-organised into a training school (i.e. a normal school) of '…thirty candidates for the situation of Schoolmaster Sergeant', three senior companies of boys, and one for the junior boys separate from the older boys. These four companies each of some 80-85 boys would form a model school. The staffing establishment would consist of a Head Master responsible for superintending the educational provision across the Asylum; an Assistant Master; an Upper Master for the boys' school; two Under Masters and an Infant Master. Four monitors would be employed until boys in the model school were trained to take their places. It was envisaged that the Head Master would be closely involved with the adults in the normal school aided by the Assistant Master, who would normally take his meals with the adult trainees. The trainees would have access to a library and there would be a common room for the masters and the adult trainees. Outside the classrooms the trainees would be under military discipline and would be supervised by the Asylum's Sergeant Major. The committee left open the question of whether each company of senior boys should have its own dedicated teacher or whether the Upper Master and the two Under Masters should share the teaching. Each company of the model school would be housed in a separate dormitory with a designated master sleeping in a nearby room. There would be separate dining and playrooms for both the senior and younger boys and when they were out of the classrooms a number of the adult trainees, who would have been selected by the Commandant and the Head Master, would help the Sergeant Major in superintending the boys' behaviour.

---

36   TNA WO 143 /10: Minutes of H M Commissioners of the Royal Military Asylum 1833-1846, 4th May 1846.

37   The Board of Commissioners responded immediately to Professor Mosley's observations about the boy's diet at Chelsea and requested Surgeon Laurence to consider whether any action was advisable. The meeting of the management committee of the Commissioners on 22nd June 1846 received his report and recommended to the Board that the boys' diet at Chelsea should be brought in line with that of the Naval School at Greenwich. TNA WO 143/10: 'Minutes of H M Commissioners of the Royal Military Asylum 1833-1846, June 1846'.

The Special Committee considered that it would 'not be just' to impose on the Chaplain, Dr Clarke, the additional duties of Headmaster of the re-organised institution after his long and valuable service. It proposed that he relinquish his educational responsibilities whilst retaining his ecclesiastical duties. The new Head Master would be appointed on the understanding he would eventually take over these ecclesiastical duties. The existing Sergeants of Instruction would be retired on pensions and the savings would go some way to defraying the costs of employing the schoolmasters.

Finally, the Committee proposed that the Secretary at War be requested to write to the Lord Commissioners of the Treasury to sanction the new staffing establishment and any alterations to the building at Chelsea that might be needed. Once approval had been given, selection of the schoolmasters at the salaries specified in the report would begin. The C-in-C would be requested to issue orders for regiments to send candidates for instruction as schoolmaster-sergeants as soon as arrangements had been made for their reception at Chelsea. Arrangements were to be made to provide for the remaining girls at Chelsea according to the plan (unspecified) by the Commandant, Colonel Brown.[38]

The commissioners' Minute Book for 22 June 1846 records that the Special Committee's proposals were fully accepted without discussion. The Quarter Master General then read a memorandum from the Duke of Wellington, containing his observations on the paper sent to him by the Pay-Master General, which had explained the proposals for the training college and the improvement of the boys' school at the RMA. The Duke agreed with the '…general principle of improving the scholastic discipline of the RMA that it may be rendered more beneficial and practical to the Military Service, and … also of the general outline of the arrangements for that purpose.' However, in order to prevent any misapprehension as to the meaning of the terms 'Sergeants' and 'Schoolmaster Sergeants' the Duke argued that the trainees should be designated 'Candidates for the situation of Regimental Schoolmaster.'[39]

Herbert then forwarded a copy of the Special Committee's report to Wellington together with a letter containing a number of additional proposals, which with the Duke's agreement he proposed to submit to the Treasury. These included raising the pay and military ranking of the schoolmaster-sergeants (see Royal Warrant below), the provision of schoolrooms in barracks which had none, and regular inspections of all regimental schools – including the RMA – by a qualified inspector appointed by the Secretary at War. Wellington replied on the 27th June 1846 agreeing with the first two proposals, but he was clearly unenthusiastic about the appointment of what was in effect an inspector of military schools. He wrote '…that if upon further

38 TNA WO 143/10: 'Minutes of H M Commissioners of the Royal Military Asylum 1833-1846, 4th May 1846'. In January 1846 ten girls were still in the Asylum. TNA WO 143/39, 'Correspondence, Reports and Memoranda, January 1846'.
39 TNA WO 143/10: 'Minutes of H M Commissioners of the Royal Military Asylum 1833-1846, 22nd June 1846'.

consideration, and after a reasonable time for the trial of the new plan, it shall be was judged expedient to incur the additional expense' of such an appointment on top of the supervision already provided by the military chaplains and the Principal Chaplains, the best cause of action would be to consult with the Bishop of London to nominate a suitable person for appointment.

The Duke was much more concerned about Herbert's proposal to dispose of the remainder of the lease of the land occupied by the RMA and to erect new buildings

at a cost of £45,000 on the grounds of the Royal Hospital Chelsea, instead of fitting up the present buildings at a cost of £5,000. The Special Committee of RMA Commissioners had proposed that some alterations to the RMA buildings would be needed to accommodate the proposed Normal School, but there had been no mention of a new building on the Royal Hospital site. It would appear that something similar had been proposed by the Paymaster-General in letter to Wellington dated 22nd May 1846 to which the Duke had replied that whilst he supported improving 'the scholastic discipline' of the Royal Military Asylum it was undesirable '...to amalgamate or interfere with any part of the Royal Military Hospital.' Wellington made

Arthur Wellesley, 1st Duke of Wellington (1769-1852), Commander-in-Chief of the Army 1842-52 by William Salter. (© National Portrait Gallery, London)

it plain that he would not acquiesce to any arrangements which would 'render the services of the individuals of either of these establishments in common' and it was '... not until that exception had been removed' that he would acquiesce to the plan for the reorganisation of the RMA.[40]

---

40   TNA WO 43/796: ff .48-52, 'Letter from the Commander in Chief, the Duke of Wellington to the Secretary at War 27th June 1846'.

In his 'Education and Lodging the Soldier' essay in the March 1846 issue of the Quarterly Review, Gleig had proposed that as alternative to modifying the existing RMA building to house the Normal school, consideration should be given to erecting a new building to accommodate the Normal and the Model School on Crown land attached to the Royal Hospital, releasing the existing Asylum for use as a barracks for the remaining year of its lease. The new buildings he argued could be paid for by drawing on the unclaimed Army Prize Fund money. Under Act 2 Will.IV.C.4, the Commissioners of the Royal Hospital were authorised to draw any amount they thought proper from the Prize Fund for the general purposes of the Hospital. Gleig did not see this as an obstacle and argued that '…to engraft on Chelsea Hospital both our new normal school and our military asylum would not be a task of much difficulty.'[41]   He may have had in mind some type of amalgamation or sharing of facilities and staff between two institutions on the Royal Hospital site as a means of justifying drawing down money from the Fund.

It is possible that the War Office was considering this option, but Sidney Herbert acknowledged the strength of the Duke's opposition and was not prepared to allow this to stand in the way of his plans for the Normal School at Chelsea. He therefore decided against a new building at the Royal Hospital and instead to make alterations to the existing RMA building at a cost of around £5,000.[42] Wellington's objections ensured that the Royal Military Asylum, later named the Duke of York's Royal Military School, remained in its building on the King's Road in Chelsea, where it was to remain until it moved to Dover in 1909. An Act of Parliament in 1848 authorised the use of money from the Army Prize Fund to purchase the freehold of the Asylum's building from the Earl of Cadogan and a further Act in 1855 released money from the Fund to the improve and enlarge the building with a concomitant increase in the number of boys at the Model School.

It only remained for the Secretary at War to gain the formal approval of the Treasury for his proposals. Herbert had written to the Lord Commissioners of the Treasury on 27th June 1846 outlining the rationale for a training school for prospective sergeant schoolmasters, their pay rate on qualification, and the cost implications of reorganising the RMA into a Normal and a Model School. He explained that although the introduction of trained sergeant schoolmasters would greatly improve the teaching in the regimental schools, there was also a need for their frequent examination and inspection. There were 53 regiments and 30 depots in Great Britain and Ireland, and he proposed that their schools together with the RMA and the Hibernian Military School should be regularly inspected by an Inspector of Army Schools at a salary of £450 per annum plus expenses (which was similar to the salary of the Privy Council's inspectors). Herbert proposed that the

41   Gleig, 'Education and Lodging the Soldier', pp. 549-50.
42   TNA WO 43/796: ff. 72-73, 'Letter from the Lords of the Treasury to the Secretary at War, 2nd July 1846'.

Rev George Gleig should be appointed to the post of Inspector because of his interest and commitment to the improvement of the Army's school and his acquaintance with military matters, especially the character and needs of the ordinary soldier.[43]   He considered that on occasions the post might be held conjointly with that of Principal Chaplain. The responsibilities of the Principal Chaplain, he argued were greater than that of an Archdeacon of the Church in England and he had responsibility for the work of a large number of clergymen ministering to the spiritual needs of the Army both at home and abroad. He proposed that Gleig's chaplaincy salary should be augmented to £500 per annum with the title of Chaplain–General, which would then enable him to resign the Chaplaincy at the Royal Hospital. Herbert confirmed that Gleig should conjointly hold the posts of Chaplain–General and Inspector of Schools and that this would 'lay the foundation of great moral improvements in the character of the British Army.'[44]

These arrangements were approved by the Treasury in a letter dated 2 July 1846 and the Lord Commissioners authorised estimates for the alterations to the building at Chelsea, sanctioned the salaries for the schoolmasters at the proposed Normal and Model schools and also improvements in the pay of the schoolmaster-sergeants (see below). The letter also approved the salary for the Inspector of Army Schools and an augmented salary for Gleig as the Chaplain General when he retired from the Chaplaincy of the Royal Hospital. The Lord Commissioners confirmed that they had no objection to Gleig holding both the offices of Chaplain General and that of Inspector of Schools:

> It being highly important to the successful carrying out of your (Sidney Herbert's) views that the superintendence of the education of the Army, upon the principles laid down by you, should in the first instance be confided to one at once so zealous in the cause and so intimately acquainted with the habits of the soldier.[45]

On the same day that the Treasury sanctioned the expenditure for the reforms a Royal Warrant was signed by Queen Victoria at Buckingham Palace:

> Whereas, with the view of improving the system of instruction in the Regimental Schools, we have deemed it expedient to introduce into our Army a class of men better calculated to perform the duties of Schoolmaster in the several Regiments of Cavalry and Infantry. Our will and pleasure is that such persons as, after having obtained a certificate of fitness from the training school,

---

43   Jarvis, 'My Predecessor in Office', pp. 32, 48-9.
44   Jarvis, 'My Predecessor in Office', pp. 32, 48-9
45   TNA WO 43/796: ff. 72-73, 'Letter from the Lords of the Treasury to the Secretary at War, 2nd July 1846'.

established by our authority, shall be appointed Schoolmaster Sergeants, shall be allowed the pay of two shillings and sixpence per day, with an increase of 6d per day to be granted by Our Secretary at War at his discretion for efficiency and Good Conduct. The Schoolmaster Sergeants so appointed will take rank next after the Sergeant Major and will be entitled when placed on the Pensions List to an increase of six pence per day for the services which they he would have been entitled to as Sergeant. It is our further will and pleasure that sergeant schoolmasters who shall also have gained a certificate of fitness shall be entitled to the pay of sergeant with an increase of six pence per day to be granted by the Secretary at War at his discretion for efficiency and good conduct. The Assistant Schoolmaster will have the same allowance to pension as a Sergeant. In order to secure an efficient superintendence of over the Regimental School it is Our Will and Pleasure that an Inspector of Regimental Schools shall be appointed by our Secretary at War.[46]

The reforms, including the new post an Inspector of Army Schools, held conjointly with the revived post of Chaplain-General by George Gleig, had been discussed and agreed with the Treasury as early as May 1846. Herbert had written Gleig on 4th May 1846, saying that it had been expedient to revive the title of Chaplain-General to the Forces and that Her Majesty had been pleased to confirm the title on him with a salary of £500 per annum from 1st July 1846.The duties were to be the same as that of Principal Chaplain and he was to be guided in all respects by the instructions given to him on his initial appointment in April 1844.[47] This was an important promotion because it increased Gleig's standing in the Army, which would help him in his work as Inspector of Schools.

Gleig recalled many years later that whilst he was Principal Chaplain and before he was appointed Inspector of Schools that he had been given permission by Herbert to visit a number of military stations in order to form some estimate of the educational and moral condition of the Army. However, when this came to the attention of the Duke of Wellington, the Duke ordered the commanders of the military districts not to co-operate with him in any way.[48] An addendum to Gleig's September 1845 essay *Moral Discipline of the Army*, which had been appended by the editors of the Quarterly Review, confirms that the Principal Chaplain had embarked on visits to the chaplains at the home military stations. It does not appear that any of the reports of these visits were retained in the War Office archives.[49] It would have been surprising if Sydney Herbert had not informed Wellington of Gleig's planned visits,

46   Lefroy, 'Report on the Regimental and Garrison Schools of the Army', Appendix VII. No.1.
47   TNA WO 43/740: ff.74-79, 'Appointment of Rev G. R. Gleig as Principal Chaplain ,2 July 1846'.
48   Jarvis, 'My Predecessor in Office', p. 44.
49   Jarvis, 'My Predecessor in Office', p. 44.

although it is possible that Gleig's behaviour during the visits had trespassed into areas outside the work of the chaplains and had angered the local COs. Whatever the circumstances of the visits, the revived post of Chaplain General carried the authority of a Major General in the Army, but the post was under the direction of the Secretary at War and was not under the command of, or accountable to, the C-in-C at the Horse Guards.

On the same day that Queen Victoria signed the Royal Warrant, Herbert wrote to Gleig detailing the terms and wide ranging responsibilities of his appointment as Inspector of Military Schools:

> You will inspect the training and model schools at the Asylum at Chelsea, the Hibernian School at Dublin, and all regimental schools. The regimental schools will be conducted as far as possible in conformity with the system adopted in the model school at Chelsea. After examination you will report the result of your inspections, through his deputy, to the Secretary at War for his information and that of the Commander-in-Chief, and you will submit for their consideration such suggestions for the management or improvement of the schools as from time to time you may think necessary. Your duties will be strictly confined to inspection and recommendation, as no orders can be given affecting the schools except by the Secretary at War. All communications to other Departments respecting the schools, to the Board of Governors of the Chelsea Asylum, to commanding officers of regiments, with regard to school regulations will be made by the Secretary at War, but upon matters of detail you will correspond directly with the commanding officer or the officer under whose immediate superintendence the regimental or depot school may be placed.[50]

The letter of appointment gave the Inspector specific responsibilities for advising the Secretary at War on the suitability of candidates for appointment as trainee schoolmasters at Chelsea, for advising the Commissioners of the RMA on the drafting of rules and regulations, and for establishing a new system in the Normal and Model Schools. He would attend at the Asylum for the examination of the candidates for schoolmaster (sergeant) and no certificate of fitness would be valid without his signature. In addition, the Inspector was to have responsibility for the general superintendence of the barrack and regimental libraries, recommending from time to time the books that should be purchased and attending to the libraries by ensuring that there were properly supplied. The Secretary at War would look to the Inspector for advice on the general system of education to be adopted in the regimental and depot schools and the books to be used in the classroom. The Inspector would '…in the first instance recommend to him the garrisons in which, with a view to the early

---

50   TNA WO 43/796: ff. 74-79, 'Letter of appointment from Secretary at War to Rev G.R. Gleig, 2nd July 1846'.

commencement of the new system, schools should be first established, and where it may be necessary to build or enlarge and alter or adapt existing schoolrooms for the purpose of giving the increased accommodation which will now be required.' [51] Finally, Gleig was charged with advising the Secretary at War on all matters connected with the regimental schools and he was to give his opinion of '...the efficiency and conduct of the schoolmasters and assistant schoolmasters to guide him on in his selection of those deserving of the increase in salary authorised by the Warrant of July 1846, or of promotion.' [52]

The Royal Warrant of 2nd July 1846 and Gleig's letter of appointment provide the foundations on which the reformed system of army schooling would be built. The Royal Warrant did not refer by name or title to, nor did it specifically authorise, 'a corps of army schoolmasters', but it provided the means by which one could be created through orders and regulations once significant numbers of schoolmasters had been trained. The Warrant talked only of '...a class of men better calculated to perform the duties of Schoolmaster', who after having obtained a certificate of fitness from the training school would be appointed schoolmaster-sergeants. They would receive pay of 2s/6d per day with an addition of 6d per day granted by the Secretary at War at his discretion for efficiency and good conduct and the schoolmaster-sergeants so appointed were ranked next in seniority in the regiment after the Sergeant Major. There were no specifications in the Warrant that these men had to enlist as serving soldiers before being admitted to the training school. This opened the way for the recruitment of civilians as trainee army schoolmasters through some type of competitive examination and with assurances that after graduation they would enlist as schoolmasters in the Army. In addition, the War Office Paper, which Baring had presented Commissioners of the RMA in May 1846, envisaged that some of the Asylum's more able boys could qualify for entry to the normal school to be trained as army schoolmasters.

Herbert had hoped that some suitable candidates for training at Chelsea might be identified from within the Army and that with the encouragement of their commanding officers might be persuaded to volunteer. [53] There was a financial inducement in the Warrant for existing schoolmaster-sergeants to gain a certificate of fitness, although it was not clear whether this involved attendance at the 'Training School' in the same manner as entrants who were civilians or private soldiers already serving in the ranks. Nevertheless, in the long run it was envisaged that there would be a new category of army schoolmasters, but Herbert acknowledged that it would be many years before sufficient numbers could be recruited and trained to staff

---

51   TNA WO 43/796: ff. 74-79, 'Letter of appointment from Secretary at War to Rev G.R. Gleig, 2nd July 1846'.

52   TNA WO 43/796: ff. 74-79, 'Letter of appointment from Secretary at War to Rev G.R.Gleig, 2nd July 1846'.

53   TNA WO143/10: 'Minutes of H M Commissioners of the Royal Military Asylum 1833-1846, 22nd June 1846'.

all schools in the Army. In the meantime Herbert provided some inducement for existing sergeant schoolmasters, through the additional income that could be gained from fees and also by the terms of the separate Royal Warrant of 27th June 1846, which enabled them to receive 2s/4d per day (equivalent of a Colour-Sergeant) after ten years' enlistment.[54]

Since the introduction of the regimental schools in 1811, Army Regulations had required the commanding officer of a battalion or regiment to select a soldier under his command for appointment as the schoolmaster-sergeant. Under the new system, the appointment of a schoolmaster-sergeant would be contingent on him having obtained a certificate of fitness from the training school (as per the Royal Warrant). These schoolmasters could be civilians who had passed a course at the Normal School. A commanding officer could propose a soldier for the training school at Chelsea, but his admission would depend upon the recommendation of the Inspector of Military Schools, who would also authorise his suitability for training. Moreover the Inspector would recommend to the Secretary at War the regiments and corps in which schools staffed by the newly qualified schoolmaster-sergeants would be established (as per Herbert's letter to Gleig), although in conformity with established protocols, the orders for the appointments would be made by the Horse Guards at the request of the War Office.[55]

It would be some years before sufficient graduates would emerge from the normal school at Chelsea to meet all the Army's requirements for trained schoolmasters, but the reforms pointed towards the gradual weakening of the control that the COs of regiments exercised over their schools and also possibly in the longer run their replacement by garrison schools, at least at the larger stations. In time commanding officers would cease to select and appoint a schoolmaster from their own rank and file. The trained army schoolmaster, although sometimes perhaps previously a serving a soldier, would no longer automatically have an identity with the regiment whose school he would superintend; and if he was a civilian he would quickly have to come to terms with military discipline and the particular ethos of the regiment in which he served. In all respects the trained schoolmaster would be required to conduct his school in conformity with the Army's model school at Chelsea and with such orders that might be issued to the Army following the visits to military establishments by the Inspector of Military Schools.

The complex division of responsibilities between the military departments in the first half of the Nineteenth century gave the responsibility for the civil administration of the Army (including finance) to the Secretary at War, for which he was responsible to Parliament; whilst reserving personnel matters, including command and military

54   TNA WO 43/668: 'Regimental Pay and Allowances and Royal Warrants 1837-1846, Warrant, 27th June 1846'.
55   TNA WO 43/807: 'Secretary at War, Training of Army Schoolmasters at RMA Chelsea, Letter from War Office to Commander in Chief, 2nd April 1849'.

discipline to the C-in-C at the Horse Guards under the prerogative powers of the Crown. This division of responsibilities had been acknowledged when the system of regimental schools was introduced in 1811-12. Viscount Palmerston had issued a Circular from the War Office in December 1811 announcing the establishment of the regimental schools and the selection of attested soldiers as sergeant schoolmasters to superintend them. Further details, including arrangements for the selection of the schoolmaster-sergeants and the conduct of the schools were communicated to the commanding officers of regiments and battalions in a succession of Orders from the C-in-C at the Horse Guards and these were subsequently incorporated into King's/Queen's Regulations. The half-yearly inspection returns and confidential reports on the units in the military districts and stations at home and abroad required information on the condition of the schools and the number of scholars attending and these was forwarded to the Adjutant-General at the Horse Guards.

The reforms introduced by Hebert in 1846 departed from this precedent and ignored the division of responsibilities between the War Office and the Horse Guards. The revived post of Chaplain General and the new post of Inspector of Military Schools were not part of the establishment at the Horse Guards but were housed at the War Office and the incumbents were appointed by and reported to the Secretary at War. The Secretary at War had assumed responsibility for personnel matters regarding the new class of regimental schoolmasters: this included following advice from the Inspector, the admissions of trainees to the Normal School and the determination of the suitability of the trainees for appointment as sergeant schoolmasters and also their initial postings to regiments and corps in the Army. Furthermore, the Royal Warrant gave the Secretary at War the discretion to award extra pay to the schoolmaster-sergeant for efficiency and good conduct, and in exercising this discretion he would not refer to the regiment's CO, but to guidance received from the Inspector of Military Schools. Herbert seems also to have anticipated the need for a career structure for army schoolmasters and his letter to Gleig mentioned both 'schoolmasters and assistant schoolmasters in the regimental schools.'[56]

The Inspector of Military Schools was ordered to inspect all the regimental schools and other military schools and to report his findings in the first instance to the Deputy-Secretary at the War Office for the information of the Secretary at War and the C-in-C, and not to the Adjutant-General at the Horse Guards. These reports should include suggestions for the management or improvement of the schools, but Herbert's emphasised in his letter of appointment that Gleig's duties were strictly confined to inspection and recommendation, and that no orders could be given 'affecting the schools except by the Secretary at War.' The Royal Warrant and Herbert's letter appointing Gleig Inspector of Military Schools left little doubt that the development of the reformed system of Army schools would be firmly under the civilian control of the War Office.

56   Jarvis, 'My Predecessor in Office', p. 51.

Writing some years later Gleig asserted that the Duke of Wellington's resented the reforms. The Duke was said to have been furious about '...the proposal to train masters and to open schools for the benefit of non-commissioned officers and men' and was alleged to have said that if ever there was a mutiny in the Army 'these new-fangled schoolmasters will be at the bottom of it.'[57] This has become one of Wellington's apocryphal sayings, but although he certainly had serious reservations about the innovations reforms, he had expressed agreement with the proposals to raise the status of the schoolmasters and re-reorganise the RMA and thereafter he did not obstruct the reforms.[58] Examination of the sequence of events leading up to the proclamation of the Royal Warrant in July 1846 shows that Herbert was careful to keep the Duke informed and secured his acquiescence at each stage in the proposed reforms. Furthermore, Herbert impressed upon Gleig in the letter of appointment as the Inspector of Military Schools that he must respect the existing protocols and specified that all communications to '...other Departments respecting the schools, to the Board of Governors of the Chelsea Asylum, to commanding officers of regiments, with regard to school regulations will be made by the Secretary at War, although on matters of detail you will correspond directly with the commanding officer or the officer under whose immediate superintendence the regimental or depot school may be placed.'[59] None the less the Duke of Wellington and his staff did not welcome the encroachment by the War Office and the Inspector of Military Schools into areas that had been the traditional preserve of the Horse Guards, nor the gradual diminution of the commanding officers' control over their regimental schools through the creation of what was a new class of army schoolmaster.

Rev George Gleig has been given credit as the initiator of the reforms that were to gradually transform schooling in the British Army in the second half of the nineteenth century. His literary output, prior to his appointment as Principal Chaplain in 1844, did not point towards any particular interest in elementary education, or indeed in the conditions of service of the private soldier in the British Army.[60] During years of his appointment as Chaplain at the Royal Hospital he was a near neighbour of the RMA at Chelsea and would have gained some knowledge of its interior economy and condition of the children, but he does not appear to have used his connections with the Asylum's Commissioners to press for an investigation into the condition of the establishment before he was appointed Principal Chaplain. He actively sought preferment and opportunities to increase his income to support his family and it was

57   Jarvis, 'My Predecessor in Office', p. 44; M. Gleig (ed.) *Personal Reminiscences of the First Duke of Wellington* (Edinburgh: Blackwood and Sons, 1904), pp. 304-5.
58   TNA WO 43/796: ff. 48-52, 'Letter from the Commander in Chief, the Duke of Wellington to the Secretary at War 27 June 1846'.
59   TNA WO 43/796: 'Letter of appointment from Secretary at War to Rev G.R. Gleig, 2nd July 1846'.
60   Douglas M. Peers, 'Gleig, Robert 1796-1888', *Oxford Dictionary of National Biography* <www.oxforddnb.com> (accessed 21st July 2007).

probably with the support of Bishop Charles Bloomfield that he gained the post of Principal Chaplain in 1844. His ambitions at that time were ecclesiastical and he saw the Army as his parish. He worked hard to increase the influence of his office over the military chaplains and officiating clergymen and he saw an important part of the chaplaincy's work as improving the moral welfare and conduct of the rank and file. Queen's Regulations gave the chaplaincy some responsibility for superintending the regimental schools and it was from the post as Principal Chaplain that he was able to carve out a unique niche at the War Office and establish himself as the principal adviser to Secretary at War on the improvement of the Army's schools.

Thomas Babbington Macaulay, in proposing to employ schoolmistresses in 1840, was the first Secretary at War after Palmerston in 1812, to draw the Parliament and the public's attention to the importance the regimental schools for educating the large number of children accompanying the Army. It was Hardinge, however, who first recognised the need for a uniform system for the management of the children's' and adult schools. He argued that this would require some training for the schoolmaster-sergeants and a better method of inspecting the schools. These reforms would address the difficulties faced by COs in staffing the schools, whilst justifying their expense. He started discussions about the need for reform within the military departments, but it was Herbert who with prime ministerial support took the political decision during the dog days of Peel's government to start the process of reform and enact policies that in time would transform the Army's schools.

An outline of the shape and direction of the eventual reforms introduced by Herbert can be found in Gleig's 1844 Report on the regimental schools and the training of schoolmasters. By the early 1840s most educationalists in Great Britain and Ireland were in agreement that further advances in elementary education required a supply of competent teachers and who had become qualified for their work in the classroom by attending a teacher training establishment. Gleig's particular contribution was to argue successfully that in the Army this would be best achieved by the service establishing its own teaching training school and that this could be achieved relatively cheaply by re-organising the RMA into a Normal and a Model School.

Sidney Hebert personally and with some skill drove through the re-organisation of the RMA at the series of meetings with Commissioners in May and June 1846. Gleig took no part in these meetings, although he was happy to give the impression in his writings that he played a larger and more influential part in the reorganisations at Chelsea. (See the 'Historiographical Foot' note in Appendix II below) From his room at the War Office Gleig was aware of the emerging shape of the reforms and he would have made important contributions to the detailed proposals for the Normal School. Indeed, he had difficulty containing his excitement at the progress of the reforms. On 13th May 1846, he wrote to Lieutenant Young of 2nd Foot at Winchester saying that 'in a short time I hope to tell you that a normal school for the training of regimental schoolmasters is at work' and on 17 June in a letter to Captain Moore of the 8th

Regiment, he explained in the strictest confidence that the training establishment was about to be established, adding that 'I think that a new era is dawning.' [61]

At this time Gleig knew of his impending elevation to the revived post of Chaplain General and probably also his conjoined appointment to the new post of Inspector of Military Schools. He was well placed and had astutely positioned himself to discharge the responsibilities of the new appointment. He was unrelentingly industrious in his duties and impressed others with the ease with which he conveyed a command of hitherto unfamiliar issues and material. In his position as Principal Chaplain he had gleaned information about the condition of the regimental schools from the half-yearly confidential reports and from his correspondence with the chaplains and officiating clergymen. In his published writings in 1845 he began to discuss the moral condition of the Army, but there is only his own word that he personally visited any of the regimental schools at the time that he was Principal Chaplain. However, he understood and doubtless also made Herbert understand the limitations of the chaplains in superintending the schools.

It is evident from Gleig's letter of appointment that Herbert valued his advice, although he certainly did not always accept it. For example, Gleig wished to increase the age for admission to the RMA from five to eight years and retain the boys until there were sixteen years. His primary objective in improving the regimental schools by providing training for army schoolmasters was to educate the soldier, rather than his children. He thought that classes made up of younger boys would be of no practical use in the training of army schoolmasters for this role, whereas the classes of older boys were much more useful for teaching practice. Anticipating the objection that this would place an additional burden on the widows of soldiers, who would have to maintain their boys until they were eight, he argued cynically that such women very rarely supported their children by their own exertions and such families were usually taken into a work house. Therefore, any burden would fall not on the mother but the Poor Law Union. He believed that it would be advantageous to remove the military orphans from the work house when they were a little older, because '...from five to eight boys learn comparatively little', whereas schooling at an age closer to that at which they enter the adult world would be more beneficial. This was probably too strident and insensitive an argument for Herbert and its acceptance would certainly have weakened the government's case in Parliament for justifying continuing expenditure on the RMA on grounds that it was public charity for soldiers' children. Herbert rejected Gleig's proposal and his plan for a reorganised RMA including a young boys' company with separate classes and accommodation. [62]

Nevertheless, Herbert had sufficient confidence in Gleig's abilities to make him his principal advisor on all matters relating to the management of the regimental schools

---

61   TNA WO 3/348: Secretary at War, Out letters, Chaplain General, 13th May, 17th June 1846.

62   Gleig, 'Education and Lodging the Soldier', p. 552.

and the efficiency and conduct of the schoolmasters. Herbert left the War Office on the fall of Peel's government in July 1846, but his reforms were continued by Fox Maule (later Lord Panmure), the Secretary at War in Lord John Russell's Whig government. In presenting the Army Estimates to the House of Commons in March 1847, Maule explained to the House of Commons that the plan to reorganise the RMA with a Normal and a Model School had been left to him as a legacy by Herbert. He thought that the plan did Herbert 'infinite credit' and he was sure that in the course the Army would look back on him with gratitude.[63] Gleig continued in the conjoined posts of Chaplain General and Inspector-General of Military Schools at the War Office and worked with successive governments until 1857 to build a revitalised and more efficient system of army schools.

63   *Hansard*, 3rd Series, Vol. 90, February-March 1847, p. 634.

12

RMA School Chelsea to Train Army Schoolmasters

War Office plans to reorganise the Royal Military Asylum, Chelsea were well advanced when Sidney Herbert left office in July 1846. Lord John Russell's Whig party formed the next government and Fox Maule (Lord Panmure) succeeded Herbert as Secretary at War. Maule accepted the plans and expedited their implementation. The financial arrangements had been approved by the Board of Treasury under the previous government and these were accepted without amendment by the incoming Whig administration. They were presented by Maule to the House of Commons as part of the Army Estimates in March 1847. There was a vote of £2,000 to establish a Normal and Model School at Chelsea and Maule explained that the Government proposed to establish other models schools upon which the regimental schools should be based and also infant schools for 'the orphans and children of British soldiers.'[1] Maule acknowledged that these plans had been left him as a legacy by Sidney Herbert and he believed that they would achieve a good education for soldiers' children.[2]

The Royal Warrant to reorganise the Military Asylum had been prepared by Herbert and approved by Sir Robert Peel the Tory Prime Minister. This warrant was taken up by the new government and was signed by Queen Victoria at Windsor on 21 November 1846. It established a Normal School for the training of army schoolmasters and also a Model School for boys upon which the regimental schools were to be based. The warrant authorised the appointment of a Headmaster for the Normal School at a salary of £300 per annum. He was to be assisted by a Master with an annual salary of £200 who would also act as Headmaster of the Model School. A first and a second Master were to be appointed at the Model School with annual

---

1   The reference to other model schools probably anticipated the decision to appoint the first graduates from the Normal School to the posts of garrison schoolmaster in one the larger barracks in the UK that accommodated several units.
2   *Hansard*, Third Series, Vol.190, March 1847, p. 634.

salaries of £150 and £100 respectively and there was to be a master to take charge of the Infants' School who was paid £120 per annum.[3]

An advertisement inviting applications for these new teaching posts at Chelsea had been placed in the *Athenaeum*, a literary magazine, in June 1846. Candidates were instructed to forward their application with testimonials to the Secretary at War. It was decided that the Rev George Gleig should work with Kay-Shuttleworth, the Secretary to the Education Committee of the Privy Council, and also with two of the Council's inspectors, Professor Henry Moseley and the Rev V.C. Cook, and examine the candidates and make recommendations for the appointments. The recommendations were forwarded by Gleig to Laurence Sullivan, the Deputy Secretary at the War Office on 29th August 1846.[4]

Rev William S. Du Sautoy, a Cambridge graduate was recommended and accepted the appointment as the Principal (Headmaster) of the Normal School. On the retirement of the Rev George Clarke, he would also become the Asylum's chaplain. Gleig described Du Sautoy as a gentleman of great attainments, of sound views on religion and morals, of a liberal and comprehensive mind, and entirely free from religious bigotry and sectarianism. Mr Walter McLeod, who had been trained at David Stow's teaching training school in Glasgow, was recommended as the headmaster of the Model School and 'lecturer in the art of teaching.' Stow was one of the leading influences on elementary education of the day and like Gleig viewed schooling as a means of moral and social regeneration. A firm critic of Bell and Lancaster's monitorial system, he thought it was essential that all teachers should be trained at a normal school. Walter McLeod's work at the Poor Law School at Norwood had impressed Kay-Shuttleworth and he had been appointed as the Master of the National Society's parochial school at Battersea, which was used for teaching practice by the students at the Battersea teacher training college.[5] The Battersea College and its parochial school had been visited by Gleig when he had been preparing his report on the regimental schools and the training of schoolmasters in 1844, and in his letter to Maule proposing Walter McLeod's appointment he described him as possibly the most able teacher of a parochial school in England. Gleig's confidence was not misplaced and McLeod remained in post until his death in June 1875. He was responsible for improving the educational standards of the boys at the RMA, and also for supervising the teaching practice of scores of trainee army

3   TNA WO 43/796: f. 90, 'Royal Warrant establishing the Normal and Model Schools, 21 November 1846'.
4   *Athenaeum*, 27th June 1846, No. 974, p. 641; TNA WO 43/796: ff84-85, 'Letter from George Gleig to Laurence Sullivan with recommendations for the Appointment of the Principal of the Normal School and Headmaster of the Model School, 29 August 1846'.
5   E.A. Smith, 'The Army Schoolmaster and the Development of Elementary Education in the Army, 1812-1920', PhD Thesis, London: Institute of Education, University of London 1993, pp. 72-73,76. Kay-Shuttleworth had established the Battersea College as a normal school in 1840 and it was taken over by the National Society in 1843.

schoolmasters from the Normal School. Gleig, writing some years later said: 'I held Mr McLeod in the highest esteem, both on public and private grounds; he has made his mark upon the Army and will be long remembered as one of the best teachers of elementary knowledge England has ever produced.'[6]

When in 1844 Sir Henry Hardinge had raised the question of how to provide some type of teacher training for regimental schoolmasters, he had assumed that they would continue to be recruited from the ranks of serving soldiers. This was also the Gleig's assumption in his report   on the regimental schools. When Sydney Hebert presented his plans for the Normal School to the RMA Commissioners in 1846; he announced that he would ask the C-in-C to issue a circular asking for serving soldiers to volunteer for a course of training at Chelsea.[7]

In his article 'Education and Lodging the Soldier' in March 1846 of the *Quarterly Review*, however, Gleig argued that it was rare to find men in the ranks competent to undertake the functions of a schoolmaster.[8] Moreover the Royal Warrant of 2nd July 1846 stated that with the view of improving the instruction in the regimental schools it was '...deemed expedient to introduce' into the Army 'a class of men better calculated to perform the duties of Schoolmaster.' The Warrant explained that, having obtained a certificate of fitness from the Normal School, such persons would be appointed as schoolmaster-sergeants.[9] This pointed to the recruitment of suitable civilians and in October 1846 the War Office placed an advertisement in *The Observer* newspaper seeking candidates for admission to the Normal School.[10] Applications were invited from unmarried men between 19 and 25 years of age to fill the 30 vacancies at the School. Those applying were to be 'of irreproachable character, good constitution, and not under the standard military height.' They must be able '... to read fluently, write a good hand, be conversant with the principles and practice of arithmetic, be well grounded in sacred and profane history, and have received in other respects a plain but liberal education.'[11] The applicants underwent a rigorous competitive examination conducted by Gleig lasting several days and twenty-four students were selected for the first training cohort at the Normal School, when it was opened on 10 March 1847.

The students were enrolled for a two year period and on satisfactory completion of the course would be enlisted as army schoolmasters. Although the students would not be paid whilst studying at the Normal School they would be clothed and receive board

6   Rudd, *The Duke of York's Royal Military School, 1801-1934*, pp. 101-2, 105. Rudd estimated that in the 28 years of Macleod's tenure at the Model School 2,000 boys passed into the Army and 453 young schoolmasters passed through his hands.
7   TNA WO 143/10: Minutes of H M Commissioners of the Royal Military Asylum 1833-1846, 22nd June 1846.
8   Lefroy, 'Education and Lodging the Soldier', p.541.
9   Lefroy, *Report on the Regimental and Garrison Schools of the Army*, Appendix VII, No.1.
10   *The Observer*, 10th November 1846.
11   *The Observer*, 10th November 1846.

and lodging. There was concern at the War Office that students might subsequently refuse to enlist and use the education and training received at the public expense to obtain civilian teaching appointments. After some discussion it was agreed that the students should be required to enter into a bond of £50 payable should they be dismissed for misconduct during training or fail to enlist and attest as a schoolmaster. On graduation they would be appointed by the Secretary at War at his discretion to any regiment or corps and would serve for a period of 10 years in the infantry and 12 years in the cavalry and artillery.[12]

Gleig asserted that all the successful applicants came from respectable families and he believed that '…the parents of some of the applicants had moved in superior ranks of life.'[13] When Professor Moseley made an inspection of the School in the summer of 1849, he observed that the students appeared generally superior to the students in other normal schools he had visited and that their manners and deportment suggested a respectable parentage.[14] The register of the Normal School indicates that the men in the initial cohort were largely from modest middle class backgrounds. Six had previously taught in civilian schools, nine had been clerks in a variety of businesses, and two had been surveyors. One had been a cadet at the East India Company's school at Addiscombe, but he withdrew in April 1847 after obtaining a civilian appointment with the Company. A second left in the following month when his father obtained a commission for him in the Army. John Swan who had been studying as a surgeon and was considered to be a very promising youth withdrew in September 1847 because his father refused to sign the bond guaranteeing his son's behaviour.

Gleig believed that the army schoolmasters should be well educated across a range of disciplines before they were qualified to learn how to teach. The examination and assessment of the young men who were admitted to the Normal School in 1847 revealed the limitations of their education and serious gaps in their knowledge. In 1849 Gleig issued a regulation specifying 'The System of Study and Instruction to be followed in the Normal School of the Royal Military Asylum.'[15] The regulation laid down that the students educated at the Normal School would only be considered fit to proceed to practice the art of teaching when they had been 'sufficiently' instructed in the following subjects:

12   TNA WO 43/807: ff. 87-96, 'Terms of enrolment of students at the Normal School'.
13   Jones, 'The Rev. G.R. Gleig and Early Victorian Army Education', p.92.
14   H. Moseley, 'Report on the Normal School for Training Regimental Schoolmasters, and on the Model School at the Royal Military Asylum, Chelsea ,24 August 1849', in *Minutes of the Committee of Council on Education*, 1848-50, Vol. 2, pp. 5853-5865.
15   TNA WO 43/807: ff. 87-96, Secretary at War, Training of Army Schoolmasters at RMA Chelsea.

(a) A general knowledge of the Scriptures of the Old and New Testaments;
(b) The English Language, including the ability to read correctly any word in prose; etymology, grammar, composition and accuracy in spelling and punctuation;
(c) The History of England;
(d) The Histories of Greece and Rome;
(e) The Outlines of General History-Ancient and Modern-the former partially, the latter in more detail; .
(g) The descriptive Geography of the World with a general view of the physical features and political state of its several portions;
(h) The simplest Elements of Astronomy;
(i) Arithmetic;
(j) The Four Books of Euclid or else Tate's Geometry;
(k) Algebra – as far as Equations;
(l) The Elements of Mechanics or rather the application of mechanical powers as taught by Tate.

Because British Soldiers served in all parts of the world it would be useful for the schoolmaster to be able teach lessons in Natural History (Botany, Zoology and Mineralogy inclusive) and also military drawing and field fortifications. Almost as a postscript, and perhaps in acknowledgement that army schoolmasters would spend some of their time teaching soldiers' children, the students were to be taught drawing and singing. These subjects however were regarded of lesser importance and it was thought sufficient to have lessons in singing twice and in drawing once a week.

The two year course at the Normal School was divided into four terms of six months each. The first three terms were taken up with further education in the prescribed academic subjects. In the fourth term the students moved on to 'learning how to teach' in the Model School under the supervision of the headmaster Macleod. Gleig stressed that the soldier's education on military matters was to be the preserve of the commissioned officers and NCOs and suggested that the RMA's Adjutant might be responsible for teaching Military Drawing and fortifications.[16]

The academic subjects were delivered in two departments each of two classes and the lectures in each half yearly term constituted a complete course. On satisfactorily completing the lowest course the students were to be promoted onto the higher course.

Method of instruction was mainly by oral lectures prepared to interest and 'excite the curiosity' of the students. The lessons were of one hour each with the first half -hour being devoted to an oral examination of the students' knowledge of the previous day's lecture. Prescribed reading from one of the text books in the School library

16   Gleig, 'Education and Lodging the Soldier', p. 748.

supplemented each lesson.[17] The students faced a demanding curriculum and very heavy work load and their day at the School was carefully structured and regulated in some detail.

Table 11. Timetable at the Normal School for summer months of 1847[18]

5.15	Rise
6.15	Assemble in military dress for roll call
6.30	Drill
8.00	Breakfast
8.45	Prayers
9-12 noon	Lessons
12-13.00	Recreation
13-13.45	Dinner
14-17.00	Lessons
17.00-18.00	Gymnastics or Fencing
18.00-19.00	Recreation
19.00-1930	Supper
19.30-21.30	Private study and Reading
21.30	Prayers
22.00	Bed

Despite the rigour of Gleig's selection procedure and the organised structure of the working day there was a serious problem with the behaviour of some of the young men. The Principal wrote to the War Office in September 1847 about the unacceptable behaviour of two of the students and five were dismissed by the Secretary at War for insolence or drunkenness during the first year.[19] In addition two left because they

17   The texts comprised grammatical and literary studies, mathematics and history and geography. They are itemised on purchase invoices found in Register for the Normal School. TNA WO 143/49: 'Royal Military Asylum, Register of the Normal School 1847-1851'.
18   TNA WO 43/807: ff. 32, 87-96, 'Secretary at War, Training of Army Schoolmasters at RMA Chelsea'. The Military dress for the morning assembly involved a shell jacket and a frock coat.
19   TNA WO 43/8: f.17, 'Secretary at War, Training of Army Schoolmasters at RMA Chelsea'; Jones, 'The Rev G.R. Gleig and Early Victorian Army Education', pp. 92-94.

were not happy with the course and one was advised to withdraw by the Principal. Only thirteen of the original twenty-four students made it into the second year, passed the course and enlisted in the Army.

Frederick Scrivener, who had previously worked as a surveyor in London, was the first student to graduate from the Normal School. When Gleig inspected the Normal School in 1847 and 1848, he had ranked Scrivener as the highest achieving student who excelled in every subject.[20] On 2nd April 1849 Maule informed the Duke of Wellington that he proposed to appoint Scrivener schoolmaster to the garrison school at Fulwood Barracks Preston and requested the Adjutant General to enlist him under the provisions of the Mutiny Act.[21] He reminded the Duke that it had been agreed that the new schoolmasters should rank next to the sergeant major and that he had agreed to their form of dress (which was to be the uniform of the regiment to which they were assigned) and the arrangements for their messing. He also advised the Duke that in order to uphold the schoolmasters' position in the Army and attract and retain a better class of person to the post, the trained schoolmaster should not be subject to corporal punishment should it be necessary to bring him to court martial.

Frederick Scrivener proved to be a very successful army schoolmaster and in 1853 he was sent to India. He subsequently was appointed Superintendent of Army Schools in the Bombay Presidency and established a training school at Poona for schoolmasters in the Queen's and East India Company's European Regiments(See chapter17).[22] A number of the other men in the initial cohort of trainees also had successful careers: Henry Keley who had previously worked as a clerk in a London merchant's office enlisted as schoolmaster to the 30th Foot and in 1857 was reporting to the Inspector General in London on the condition of the army schools in the Cape of Good Hope ; John Stewart, who had previously worked as a clerk for Henry Rogers, who had been an assistant at as school in Bath, progressed through the ranks of Army Schoolmasters and were appointed Inspectors of Army Schools in the 1880s.[23]

For the first three years only civilian applicants were admitted for training at the Normal School. Entrance examinations were held twice a year and a further fourteen students were admitted in 1847-48. One could not provide a bond and withdrew, two were discharged for medical reasons and four were dismissed by the Secretary at War for misconduct, leaving only seven who completed their training and enlisted in the Army.[24] In 1849 only 10 entries registered for the Normal School. There is no record

20 TNA WO 43/807: f.23, 'Secretary at War, Training of Army Schoolmasters at RMA Chelsea'.
21 TNA WO 43/807: 'Letter from Fox Maule to the Duke Wellington, 2nd April 1849'.
22 Lefroy, 'Report on the Regimental and Garrison Schools of the Army', p. 100.
23 Lefroy, 'Report on the Regimental and Garrison Schools of the Army', Appendix 9; Jones, 'The Rev. G.R. Gleig and Early Victorian Army Education', pp. 92-4.
24 TNA WO 143/49: 'Normal School Register 1847-52'. There are an additional nine names entered in the register, but without any details of the men's background. It is probable that these men had passed the entrance examination but failed to enrol at Chelsea.

of the regimental appointments of five of the men, who completed the course, but two were dismissed and one enlisted in the 12th Lancers before producing a bond.

The early years of the Normal School showed the difficulties in recruiting and retaining civilians to train and qualify as army schoolmasters. Most young men who answered the newspaper advertisements and applied for the training at Chelsea had been out of the classroom for some time and did not always find it easy to adjust to the demands of academic study. The rigorous daily regime of academic study, drill and physical training contributed to a heavy dropout rate at the School. The masters appeared to have very few disciplinary problems in the classrooms, but the military environment at Chelsea was uncongenial and many of the students resented the imposed military discipline.

In October 1849 there was a serious outbreak of insubordination amongst the students. The commandant was unable to identify the ringleaders and he confined the whole student body to the premises and withdrew privileges until the guilty parties were named or owned up to their behaviour. The students responded by writing to the commandant protesting at the punishment and requesting that the matter should be referred to the Secretary at War. Maule convened and chaired a meeting of the School Committee. This supported the commandant and ruled that the students' behaviour was insubordination and their appeal to the Secretary at War was a breach of discipline. The matter was considered sufficiently serious for Maule to address the students in person and to admonish them for their behaviour and remind them of the need for obedience both as trainees and thereafter when they became enlisted army school masters. Maule followed this with written instructions explaining that, whilst the Commandant assisted by his Adjutant had overall responsibility for discipline at the Military Asylum, the Principal and his staff were responsible for the students' behaviour whilst under their instruction in the classrooms at the Normal School. The two staffs were to cooperate to ensure the good behaviour of the students.[25]

Herbert's plan for the re-organisation of the RMA in 1846, had envisaged that some of the boys in the Model School might progress to the Normal School and train as Army schoolmasters .In December 1848 Gleig suggested that when students from the Normal School were undertaking teaching practice at the Model School it might be possible to transfer some of the school's paid monitors to study in the training establishment.[26] These boys however would be some three to four years younger than the civilian recruits entering the Normal School. It would not be feasible to reduce the age for admission to the School because the priority for the new class of army schoolmasters was to educate of the Army's rank and file rather than its children.[27]

25   TNA WO 143/51: 'RMA School Committee Proceedings 1847-1849', pp. 38,51-6; TNA WO 43/807: ff. 1054-5, 'Secretary at War to the Commandant of the RMA and the Principal of the Normal School re-their respective powers and duties'.
26   TNA WO 43/807: f.87, 'Secretary at War, Training of Army Schoolmasters at RMA Chelsea'.
27   Gleig, 'Education and Lodging the Soldier', p. 748.

One solution would be for the paid monitors at the Model School to enter into indentures and to work first as assistants (pupil teachers) to the trained schoolmasters in the regimental and garrison schools, before they themselves became of age to enter the Normal School for teacher training. In July 1849 a paper was prepared in the War Office (probably by Gleig) arguing that it was desirable that the Normal School should as much as possible be recruited from youths previously educated and disciplined at the Model School.[28] The paper pointed to the example of the Education Committee of the Privy Council whose scheme for employing 'pupil teachers' in civilian schools had shown their value working as apprentices to trained schoolmasters. It noted that many of these pupil teachers subsequently progressed into the civilian normal schools and trained successfully as teachers.

A similar scheme was suggested for the Army with a number of the monitors at the Model School being indentured with the Secretary at War as apprentices for a seven year period. After two or three years they would enter the Normal School and then be posted as 'pupil teachers' to assist the newly trained schoolmasters who were superintending the regimental and garrison Schools. They would work under the delegated authority of either the schoolmaster or an officer at the station at which they were posted, who would report back on the pupil teacher's progress to the RMA. After two or three years the pupil teachers would return to Chelsea and enter the Normal School for training as schoolmasters. The proposal would require an increase in the establishment of monitors at the Model School. The cost would be justified because each youth would serve in the Army's schools for a period of at least seventeen years. The Secretary at War forwarded the proposal to the Treasury Solicitor with a suggested form of indenture and a request to increase to sixteen the establishment of monitors at the Model School.[29]

The RMA registers record that from 1849 -58 only seven boys chose to remain at Chelsea as paid monitors and the majority of boys chose to volunteer for the Army. Similar arrangements were put in place at RHMS, Phoenix Park and during the same period ten paid monitors were appointed at the School. The establishment authorised for the 'Education Department' at the RHMS in 1858 included six monitors.[30] The Headmaster John Gibbons selected the boys and he encouraged the most promising to consider a career as an Army schoolmaster and personally coached them for the

28   TNA WO 43/807: ff. 155-158, 'Secretary at War, Training of Army Schoolmasters at RMA, Chelsea'.
29   TNA WO 43/807: ff. 155-158, 'Secretary at War, Training of Army Schoolmasters at RMA, Chelsea'.
30   TNA WO 143/18: 'Royal Military Asylum, admission of children 1826-1880'; TNA WO 143/21: 'Royal Military Asylum, discharges of male Children 1825-1867'; TNA WO 143/27: 'Royal Hibernian Military School, Boys Index Book 1803-1919'; TNA WO 143/78: 'Nominal roll of boys joining the Royal Hibernian Military School, 1847-1877'. Seven boys are recorded in the register of the RHMS as having been appointed as paid monitors from 1853 to1858. A further five were appointed in 1859 and two in 1860.

entrance examination for the Normal School. He was very successful and Hibernian boys were highly placed in the examinations for the Normal School in the 1860s and 1870s.[31]The two military schools, the RHMS and the RMA, became important sources of recruitment for the Normal School, but they could not at this time , provide the Normal School with sufficient students to meet the Army's need for trained schoolmasters. From 1846-58 the Normal School trained 178 schoolmaster and 37 of these had previously worked as paid monitors, although the majority had previously been employed in civilian schools.[32]

A War Office departmental memorandum in November 1849 discussed the vacancies at the Normal School and listed the names of 24 students in training. One was shortly discharged on medical grounds and nine were posted as regimental schoolmasters. This left 16 vacancies on an authorised establishment of 30 students, but with only five applicants seeking admission. The memorandum noted that there were two enlisted soldiers studying at the School and it suggested that other suitable young serving soldiers might recruited if the Secretary at War would give his permission. Maule scribbled a note on the memo ordering his officials to 'take some means to pick suitable young men from regiments.'[33]

In 1850 the entrance examinations were opened to sergeants and corporals with at least two years' service. Commanding Officers were requested to forward the names of suitable NCOs wishing to volunteer and who could be recommended by the regimental schoolmaster. Successful candidates would be on secondment from their regiments whilst at the Normal School. They would receive their usual payless 6d per day for their maintenance at Chelsea. Men who failed to complete the course of training for any reason would be returned to their regiments. Those who were certified fit for appointment would be discharged from their regiments and re-enlisted as schoolmasters, but without bounty and would be posted by the Secretary at War to a regimental or garrison school. As Army schoolmasters they would stand next in rank to the Sergeant Major and draw pay of 2s 6d per day and 1d per day beer money, with the addition of 6d per day after a period of service that was to be determined by the Secretary at War. They would also be entitled to receive three-quarters of the gross amount of fees paid by the soldiers they instructed. When placed on the pension list

31   Clarke, *A New History of the Royal Hibernian Military School*, p. 88.
32   Lefroy, *Report on the Regimental and Garrison Schools of the Army*, p. 67.
33   TNA WO 43/807: ff.160-164, 'War Office Memorandum December 1849'. The memorandum identifies a Sergeant Newsom and an un-named corporal, whereas the Normal School Register (TNA WO 143/49) lists only John Newsom, Schoolmaster Sergeant of the 2nd Dragoon Guards, who was admitted on 6 September1849. A Minute of the School Committee (TNA WO 143/51) dated 27th November 1849 refers to letters respecting the admission of Sergeant Newsom of the 2nd Battalion Grenadier Guards and Corporal Sykes of the 1st Royals. The RMA School Committee minute of 27 November relating to the insubordinate behaviour of the students records that Sergeant Newsom and Corporal Sykes did not sign the letter of protest and were therefore exempted from the Secretary at War's subsequent admonishment of the student's behaviour.

they would be entitled to receive 6d per day more than the pension that they would have been entitled to as sergeants. Their previous service and the time spent at the Normal School, however, would not count towards this entitlement.[34]

The War Office's request for suitable candidates was sent in the first instance to the commanding officer of the battalions of the three regiments of Foot Guards and the 2/1st, 28th, 30th, 39th, 62nd regiments of Foot and the depot of the 1st Battalion of the Rifle Brigade, all of which were stationed in the British Isles.[35] During the 1850s about one third of the candidates for the scheme were NCOs and some had already benefitted by attending classes conducted by a newly trained schoolmasters at their regimental or garrison schools. Although the pension arrangements were not ideal, the scheme was moderately successful. From 1846 to 1859, 178 army schoolmasters were trained at the Normal School and 48 of these students had previously been enlisted NCOs. Thirty-seven had been monitors or assistants in elementary schools and the balance of 93 students had entered from civilian occupations.[36]

George Gleig's appointment as the Inspector of Military Schools required him to regularly inspect the regimental schools and also the schools at RMA and the RHMS. In March 1847, he inspected at his own initiative, the schools of the 57th Foot at Dover, 31st of Foot at Walmar, the 39th Foot and the 16th Lancers at Canterbury and the Provisional Battalion at Chatham. In the following month he penned a brief report to Fox Maule highlighting the lack of suitable accommodation and the absence of books and the poor standard of teaching. He concluded that there could be no significant improvement until a trained schoolmaster had been allocated to these regiments.[37] There is no evidence in War Office archives that Gleig extended his inspections to other regimental schools. This was perhaps because little could be usefully reported until such time as trained schoolmasters emerged from the Normal School. It was only when trained schoolmasters had been posted to the garrison and regimental schools that the Inspector General could carry out meaningful inspections and assess the progress that was being made under the new system.

One of Maule's first decisions as Secretary at War had been to write to Gleig on 14 August 1846, pointing out that as the Normal School would soon be opened, he should postpone a planned inspection of regimental schools in Great Britain. Instead he should visit military schools in Belgium, Prussia, and France to learn anything

---

34   TNA WO 43/807: ff. 161-163, 'War Office Memorandum, December 1849'.
35   George Gleig had previously canvased the COs of eight regiments and the depot of the Rifle Brigade asking whether they had any intelligent and well behaved men who they would wish to recommend for training at the Normal school. Positive returns were received from 28th, 31st, 69th and 62nd Regiments and the Rifle Brigade Depot. (TNA WO 43/807)
36   Lefroy, *Report on the Regimental and Garrison Schools of the Army*, p. 69.
37   TNA WO 43/807: 'George Gleig to Fox Maule 6 April 1847', f.46.

that might be helpful to progress the reforms that were under way at the RMA.[38]This may have been a tactic by Maule to avoid Gleig offending the Duke of Wellington, who now had been persuaded of the need for trained army schoolmasters and the concomitant reforms at the RMA. Maule was questioned in the House of Commons about Gleig's overseas visit and he replied that he did not intend to publish all of his report, but that he would lay extracts before the House. There is no record that any extracts were published in the House of Commons Sessional Papers.[39] It is probable that Gleig' reports contained observations about the need for a more professional approach in the British Army in the education and commissioning of officers, which was not part of his brief, and which would have antagonized Wellington and his staff at the Horse Guards.[40]

George Gleig did pay close attention to the progress in establishing the Normal School and the reorganisation of the boys' school at the RMA into a Model School .He carried out inspections of both schools in December 1847 and again in April and December 1848.[41] His reports, which were sent to Laurence Sullivan, the Deputy Secretary at the War Office, described the students at the Normal School as keen and committed and generally making very satisfactory progress in their studies. In December 1848 he made specific reference to the students who were undertaking teaching practice at the Model School and reported that they delivered their lessons skilfully and succeeded in engaging and retaining the attention of the pupils.[42]

In April 1849, however, after a further inspection, he made a very critical report on the general condition of the Normal School. He concluded that the School was not conducted in a manner that was likely to create the habits of 'order and punctuality' amongst the students that would fit them to discharge the 'delicate duties' they would be required to perform as schoolmasters. In particular, he recorded that morning prayers were not conducted punctually. He accused the Principal, Rev. Du Sautoy, of not thoroughly preparing his lessons, and in the case of religious instruction and Ancient History, not communicating effectively with the students. Gleig also thought that Du Sautoy was a poor preacher and judged that after two years' instruction little progress had been made in the young men's moral and religious education. This he

38   TNA WO 43/807: 'Secretary at War, Training of Army Schoolmasters at RMA Chelsea', 'Letter from Fox Maule to George Gleig 14 August 1846'; *Naval and Military Gazette*,19 September 1846, p. 600.
39   *Hansard*, Third Series, Vol.190, February 1847, p.306.
40   Panmure Papers, GD 45/8/16. Quoted in Strachan, 'The Early Victorian Army and the Nineteenth Century Revolution in Government', p. 80. Gleig showed an interest in officer's education and recommendations for the education and training of commissioned officers appear in his article 'Military Education' in the September 1848 issue of *The Quarterly Review*.
41   TNA WO 43/807: ff.23-27, Secretary at War, Training of Army Schoolmasters at RMA Chelsea, Report on the   Normal and Model Schools,29 April 1848.
42   TNA WO 43/807: ff.68-71, Secretary at War, Training of Army Schoolmasters at RMA Chelsea, 'Report on the Normal and Model Schools, 8 December 1848'.

concluded was because the teaching staff did not understand the true purpose of the government in founding the Normal School.[43]

The Secretary at War was surprised and shocked by Gleig's critical comments because his previous reports on the Normal School had been effusively complimentary. A departmental memorandum noted that the Du Sautoy had been appointed on Gleig's recommendation and questioned why it had taken so long for him to inform the School Committee of his concerns. Maule wrote to the Du Sautoy on 30th April 1849 drawing his attention to Gleig's criticisms. The Principal replied with a robust defence of his teaching and conduct of the School and responded in detail to each of the Inspector General's criticisms. Regarding the criticisms of his religious instruction, he explained that he had taken the liberty of writing to the Bishop of London outlining his teaching. In response, the Bishop had promised to visit the School and observe the relevant lessons. Du Sautoy expressed his surprise that the Inspector General had conducted a number of inspections of the Normal School in the previous two years and there had not been any criticisms or expressions of concern. He was under the impression that Gleig was satisfied with his management conduct of the institution.[44]

Maule reacted quickly and ordered Gleig to produce a detailed plan for the course of instruction and a timetable of lessons for each of the classes of students in the Normal School. These were to specify the subjects that would be to be taught to each of the classes in the morning and afternoon sessions. This plan was approved by the Secretary at War and provided not only a clear statement of the students' curriculum, but also a template for future inspections.

Following Sidney Herbert's precedent in 1846, Maule also sought expert and disinterested advice from the Education Committee of the Privy Council. He asked for Dr Henry Moseley to inspect and report on the education at the Normal School, and also on the work of its students who were teaching in the Model School. Dr Moseley presented his report to the Secretary at War in August 1849. He judged that the students could write grammatically and spell correctly and that their progress in the humanities, with the exception of geography, was satisfactory. In the case of both Ancient and Modern History, Moseley reported that he had not come across pupils with such an accurate knowledge of the facts in other schools. He was satisfied with the student's proficiency in mathematics and found that the majority of those in the first class had a respectable knowledge of geometry. They were less proficient in algebra and in solving mathematical problems without the aid of text books and assistance from their teachers. He also thought that these young men might benefit from some instruction in the experimental sciences. In his examination of religious knowledge, however, he reported that the students had not acquitted themselves as well as he

---

43   TNA WO 43/807: ff.77-82, 'Secretary at War ,Training of Army Schoolmasters at RMA Chelsea, Report on the Normal School, 19th April 1849'.

44   TNA WO 43/807: ff. 122-125, 'Secretary at War, Training of Army Schoolmasters at RMA Chelsea, Letter from Rev Du Sautoy to the Secretary at War 15th May 1849'.

would have wished. He concluded that the students did not have the same knowledge of the scriptures as in other schools.[45] With this exception Moseley's report did not offer any support for Gleig's criticisms of the management at the Normal School.

It is surprising that Gleig's 1849 report made little reference to the students' progress in secular subjects, but his criticisms reflect his views of the primary purpose of army education. He saw his work as the Inspector General of the Army's schools an extension of his work as Chaplain General. In his article for the *Quarterly Review* in September 1848 he had emphasised that the main focus for education in the Army was to be on the rank and file. The function of the Normal School was not simply to produce trained army schoolmasters to take the place of the 'old fashioned' schoolmaster-sergeants. The task of the trained schoolmaster was to shape the men's intellect by making them literate and numerate, but also to develop their moral character and thus to mould their subsequent behaviour. This was to be achieved in part through religious, albeit not denominational, instruction and also through the influence and example set by his conduct as a trained of army schoolmaster. Gleig clearly had concerns that the management of the Normal School was insufficiently focused on these objectives and this was in essence the basis of the criticisms in his report to the War Office.[46]

In his 1846 scheme for the reorganisation of the RMA Hebert had intended that the Principal of the Normal School would assume the chaplaincy of the RMA when the Rev George Clarke retired. Clarke died in January 1848, but it was not until 1850 that Rev Du Sautoy combined the duties of Chaplain of the RMA with his superintendence of the Normal School. It is very probable that Gleig did not wish to see Du Sautoy appointed as the Chaplain and this was why he made such critical comments about Du Sautoy's preaching and his teaching of religious education. Gleig admitted in his correspondence with the Maule that when he had recommended Du Sautoy's appointment in 1846, initially only as Principal of the Normal School, he had relied entirely upon testimonials in possession of the Education Committee of the Privy Council.[47] In December 1856 he wrote to the War Office urging that Du Sautoy should be retired on a pension because his severe rheumatism and nervous irritability was reducing his effectiveness in managing the Normal School. Gleig urged that in future the two posts should be kept separate, thus allowing the Chaplain to concentrate on the religious instruction at the Normal and Model School.[48]

Rev Du Sautoy, however, remained in his posts at Chelsea until 1859. Lieutenant Colonel Lefroy included a section on the Normal School in his Report published in

45   Lefroy, 'Report on the Regimental and Garrison Schools of the Army', pp. 69, 70-1.
46   Gleig, 'Military Education', The Quarterly Review, LXXXIII, No. 166, (September 1848).
       Gleig argued that it was not the purpose of the Army's Schools was to give a specifically
       military education to the rank and file, because this was the business of the Officers and
       NCOs.
47   TNA WO 43/796: ff.84-85, 'Letter from George Gleig to Laurence Sullivan'.
48   TNA WO 43/796: ff.162-14, 'Letter from Geig to Lord Pamure, 30th December 1856'.

the same year and expressed his satisfaction with the educational progress and general conduct of the students at the school. Significantly he chose not to refer to Gleig's inspection reports, preferring instead to quote extensively from Henry Moseley's 1849 report. He considered that the 'present state of the institution' broadly supported Rev Moseley's earlier remarks with the students' historical knowledge once again being rated as 'highly creditable', but with their knowledge of the scriptures continuing to be 'very deficient.'[49]

In his subsequent inspection reports on the Normal School in December 1851, December 1853 and July 1854, Gleig restricted his comments to the detailed plan of secular instruction and the timetable of lessons approved by Maule as the framework for future inspections. The students were examined orally and on paper and were ranked on the basis of their performance in all the subjects. He reported in detail on the achievements of the students in each of the three classes and expressed satisfaction with the overall results of his examinations and the conduct of the students.[50]

Lieutenant Colonel Lefroy in his 1859 inspection report commented on the poor educational standards of many of the civilian applicants to the Normal School. A large part of their first term at the school was occupied with breaking them into the habits of study and in 'un-teaching' their imperfect knowledge. He however considered that it was unwise to increase the educational standards required for admission to the point where it would exclude the NCOs from the Army, who made up around one third of the applicants.[51]

In the years following the end of the Crimean War in 1856, the priorities for Army Education changed and the emphasis was on a more functional and secular education for the soldier and there was no longer a preoccupation with his 'moral education.' In 1849, acting on Henry Moseley's recommendation, physical sciences had been introduced into the curriculum of the Normal School. Lefroy noted that the students followed their lectures in Chemistry and Zoology with great interest and had gained a satisfactory knowledge of the subject matter. Military drawing and the study of field fortifications were part of the curriculum for the top two classes and a set of artillery models had been acquired to improve the students' capability in mechanics. Lefroy thought that the young men might study trigonometry, which would be useful for teaching surveying. They should also attend a programme of military lectures that would give them an understanding of the interior economy of a regiment or battalion and provide them with some familiarity with accounting and practical management of the regimental and garrison schools.[52]

49   Lefroy, *Report on the Regimental and Garrison Schools of the Army*, pp. 70-71.
50   TNA WO 43/807: 'Letters from G. Gleig to the Secretary at War, War Office relating to his inspections of the Normal School in December 1851, December 1853 and July 1854'.
51   Lefroy, *Report on the Regimental and Garrison Schools of the Army*, p. 67.
52   Lefroy, *Report on the Regimental and Garrison Schools of the Army*, p. 67.

13

The First Trained Army Schoolmasters and Organisation of Army Schools in the 1850s

During 1847-50, 22 trained schoolmasters were posted to the garrisons and regiments stationed at home. The first five men were appointed garrison schoolmasters at the large barracks in Preston, Weedon, Plymouth, Horsfield near Bristol, and the Guards depot at Croydon. In the spring of 1849 and over the next twelve months, 14 schoolmasters were posted to regiments across the British Isles. In addition, one schoolmaster was posted to the 72nd Regiment in Trinidad, and one to the 94th and 87th regiments stationed in India.[1]

In the final months at Chelsea these 22 young men had worked under the watchful eye of Walter Macleod, the Headmaster of the Model School and they relied on him for support and guidance. Once posted, they were dependent on their own resources and had no one to whom they could turn for advice in their career as Army schoolmasters. The sense of isolation of the schoolmaster in his initial posting is conveyed by Frederick Scrivener, the first schoolmaster to graduate from the Normal School. In a letter dated 6th May 1847, he appealed to Macleod for advice and assistance in his work as garrison schoolmaster at Fulwood Barracks Preston. Scrivener's immediate difficulty was that he had not been paid his salary of 2s/6d per day since he had enlisted on 2 April, nor the additional emoluments that he been led to believe that he would receive for supervising the barracks library. He asked for Macleod's help to secure the salary he expected.

Scrivener also complained that he had not received any payment from the fees charged for teaching the enlisted men who were voluntarily attending his school. As well as teaching the children, he had classes for 130 enlisted men and also six sergeants who attended school in the evenings from 1900 to 2200, three times per week. In addition, he had also agreed to give private lessons to the sergeant major of the 52nd Regiment on the two remaining weekday evenings. Furthermore, a number

---

1   Jarvis, 'My Predecessor in Office', p. 55.

of sergeants of the 39th Regiment had expressed an interest in attending school and he believed 80 enlisted men from the 52nd would also attend if they were able. Without some assistance he would not be able to teach so many scholars during a working day that extended from 0900 in the morning to 2200 in the evening. He suggested that assistance might come from one of the trained monitors at Chelsea. Scrivener had received encouragement and support from Major Davies of the 52nd Regiment and he suggested that one of the students about to graduate from the Model School might be posted to that regiment whilst it was at Preston. In all other respects Scrivener was confident that the men in his school were making good progress and that Gleig would be very satisfied when he next inspected the garrison school.[2]

Frederick Scrivener appears to have adapted well to life in the Army, but others found the transition from civilian life more difficult. James Thomson graduated in 1854 from the Normal School and was posted to Rifle Brigade and then to 55th Foot in Ireland. He wrote of his life as an army schoolmaster in the 1850s:

> An Army Schoolmaster is recognised as a soldier and not as a civilian. He wears the uniform of the regiment to which he is attached and is obliged to conform to military discipline. His position therefore is to a certain extent undefined as so much of his treatment depends a great deal on the personal feelings of his superiors, who have it in their power to be courteous or supercilious as the case may be.[3]

Thomson was an army orphan who was educated at the Royal Caledonian Asylum in London. In 1850 he became a pupil teacher at the RMA Model School and was later posted as an Assistant Schoolmaster to the garrison school at Ballincollig, near Cork, before entering the Normal School. He subsequently had difficulty in accepting the disciple of army life and was discharged, possibly for drunkenness in 1862.[4]

Wellington had been anxious to ensure that the Chelsea trained army schoolmasters had the rank and status of an NCO, taking regimental rank immediately after the regimental sergeant major. At parades, inspections, musters, and at divine service, they should always take their place at the head of the children. He ordered that the

---

2   TNA WO 43/807: ff.133-134, 'Letter from Frederick Scrivener to Walter Macleod'. It was probably as a consequence of Scrivener's that letter Schoolmaster Joseph Martin was posted to the 52nd Regiment in autumn 1849.

3   NAM, 'Records of the Royal Army Educational Corps Army, Educational Policy and Regimental Schools 1846-1920, Box 22127', 'James Thomson, Army Schoolmaster and Poet 1834-1882: A biographical note'.

4   Smith, 'The Army Schoolmaster and the Development of Elementary Education in the Army', p.124; See also First Report of the Council of Military Education on Army Schools, March 1861, App. II, pp. 61-68.

schoolmaster should eat in the mess with the other sergeants and wear the uniform of his regiment with a sash and carrying a sword to denote his rank as a senior NCO.[5]

Gleig disagreed with the Duke and argued that the trained schoolmaster should occupy a unique and distinctive rank within the Army. He was not simply '...to fill the place of one of the old fashioned schoolmaster-sergeants of regiments.' Gleig acknowledged that giving the students at the Normal School much more than an ordinary elementary education necessarily set them apart from the great majority of the NCOs, but he was adamant that they were not be placed in a position of equality with the Commissioned Officers. The young men from Chelsea would go into the Army as neither officers nor NCOs; they were trained as schoolmasters and as schoolmasters they would be enlisted.

They should not be subject to the rigid discipline and daily routine of the bugle and roll call. They must however be given a distinctive dress to identify their unique position in the Army. Their authority both in and out of the classroom must be supported by the CO. Once they had been given comfortable quarters and an adequate remuneration he believed that they would occupy their own special place in the Army without causing any trouble or harm to military discipline.[6]

All of this was accepted by Herbert and Maule and it was Gleig's vision that would eventually prevail in the mid and late Victorian Army, but in the early years the position of Chelsea schoolmaster was ill-defined and depended very much on the attitude of the CO and officers of his regiment.

Maule answering questions in the House of Commons in February 1850 referred to correspondence from the COs of regiments to which a trained schoolmaster had been posted. He explained that they welcomed these appointments and noted the beneficial impact that a higher rate of attendance at school was having on their units. Lieutenant Colonel Browne, commanding the 21st (Royal Scots) Fusiliers at Edinburgh observed:

> The Schoolmaster is behaving admirably, and the new system of education has already had a visible effect on the regiment in many ways. Many men have been able to fit themselves for promotion that were previously unable to do so; others have learned to read and write and have found occupation for time that used to be spent in public houses. It is very popular and next to the good conduct warrant is, I think, the greatest boon the Army has received since I entered it. Experience has convinced me that crime diminishes in proportion as men have rational occupation and comfort in their quarters. We have had very few defaulters during the past month and in six days none; which is very unusual

5   TNA WO 43/796: ff. 74-75, 'Letter from the Military Secretary at the Horse Guards to Laurence Sullivan, December 1848'.
6   Gleig, 'Military Education', p. 420.

in a place like Edinburgh, and is, I think, to be attributed to the school and the occupations attendant upon it.[7]

Not all COs were as enthusiastic about the new system. Charles Carnegie the Chaplain at Templemore barracks wrote to George Gleig about the difficulties encountered by one newly appointed schoolmaster. The CO made no effort to provide him with living quarters and the schoolmasters was obliged to negotiate with the staff sergeants to secure a room. Also, the CO failed to provide oil lamps for the class room and storage facilities for the teaching materials. He made it very clear in a public conversation with the chaplain that he '…did not like the new system.'[8]

Maule explained to the House of Commons that wherever a trained schoolmaster had been posted to a unit there was a large increase in the number of men attending the regimental school.[9]   Increase in attendance at the adult schools had also been helped by the order issued by the Duke of Wellington on 10th April 1849 requiring all recruits to attend lessons for two hours per day until dismissed from drill. Numbers compiled for an internal memo at the War Office in February 1853, recorded that there were 10,764 soldiers from an effective total establishment of 44,224 men attending the 65 regimental and garrison schools to which trained schoolmasters had been appointed and 2523 of these men were new recruits.[10]

Gleig's first priority as Inspector-General was the education of the private soldier, but he could not ignore the large numbers of children with the Army, many of whom attended the regimental schools. A return prepared by George Gleig and published by the order of the House of Commons in March 1852 listed the number of boys and girls instructed at the regimental and garrison schools at home and throughout the Empire (exclusive of the Royal Artillery schools) on 1st January 1851.[11]

7   Jarvis, 'My Predecessor in Office', p. 55. This correspondence was originally quoted by George Gleig in his 1852 article, 'National Education' in the *Edinburgh Review*. See Appendix II.
8   Wiltshire and Swindon History Centre, Sydney Herbert Papers, 2057/F8/111/B/6, 'Letter from Rev. Carnegie to George Gleig'.
9   Jarvis, 'My Predecessor in Office', p. 55.
10   Sydney Herbert Papers, 'War Office memoranda': 2057/F/111/B/5; 2057/F8/VII/D.
11   'Returns relating to Military and Regimental Schools', House of Commons Sessional Papers, 19th March 1852, p. 304.

Table 12 Boys and Girls Registered in Regimental and Garrison Schools

Regiments and Corps*	Boys	Girls	Total
Life Guards and Royal Horse Guards (2 schools)	73	64	107
Foot Guards (7 schools)	157	133	290
Cavalry (23 schools)	513	422	935
Infantry (109 schools)	2624	2405	5029
(141 schools)	(3367)	(3024)	(6391)
Colonial Corps (6 schools)	486	293	779
Total (288 schools)	3853	3317	7170

* Number of boys and girls on the registers of the regimental and garrison schools at home and
  throughout the Empire (Royal Artillery schools exclusive) on 1st January 1851

Under the old system schoolmaster-sergeants were appointed from the ranks of enlisted soldiers and commanding officers often expected them to exercise supervision of the children outside the classroom. Sometimes this was specified as a duty in the regimental standing orders. The first cohorts of trained army schoolmasters came from a civilian background and the expectation gained during their training at the Normal School was that their duties as army schoolmasters would be limited to their work in the classrooms. Inevitably there were instances where the newly trained schoolmaster was reluctant to exercise any general supervision of the regiment's children outside the classroom.

In November 1857, Lieutenant Colonel Shote, commanding the 6th Dragoons at Brighton, wrote complaining about the new system of regimental schools:

> I do not consider that the children are nearly so well looked after as under the old system of regimental schools. The Schoolmaster tells me that he is not in any way responsible for the conduct of the boys when out of school, whereas formerly it was considered the duty of the schoolmaster always to have them more less under his eyes and to reprimand them or punish them whenever he saw or heard of they being guilty of any impropriety. They were morally and religiously brought up better than they are at present.[12]

The newly trained schoolmasters followed the well-established practice of dividing the working day between teaching the children in the mornings and the adults in the

12   Lefroy, *Report on the Regimental and Garrison Schools of the Army*, p. 26.

afternoons and early evenings.[13] The regimental standing orders for the Scots Fusilier Guards in 1858, based on the new Army School Regulations issued by the War Office in 1854 (see below) specified that the children were to be allocated to one of three classes, each one operating for six sessions per day from 0900 to 1200, with drummers and privates in two classes from 1200 until 1300. NCOs were allocated to one of three classes that were taught in three sessions from 1430.[14] The standing orders listed the subjects that were to be studied by the children in the three classes and comprised reading, writing, grammar and poetry; arithmetic, geography and English history and some natural science, referred to as 'simple truths'. In the Saturday morning classes there was sacred history and English composition with one hour singing.[15]

The children's and adults' classes made use of text books written by Gleig and Macleod, the headmaster of the Model School. Macleod's texts covered the English language, geography and some branches of mathematics, whilst Gleig produced a large series of 45 'School Primers'. His historical titles in particular were also widely used in civilian schools.[16] There was certain simplicity in Gleig's histories which made them easy for children who were learning to read, but arguably adult learners needed a series of progressive reading books that acknowledged their wider knowledge and experience of life.[17]

Following the practice at the RMA the first session of the day in the children's schools was devoted to prayers and religious instruction. Under the existing regulations for regimental schools all the children were required to learn the catechism of the Church of England, except in the Scottish regiments were whenever possible the Catechism of the Church of Scotland was taught. Gleig acknowledged in his 1852 Return to the House of Commons that little or no care was taken to see the regulations enforced. He might also have mentioned that for some years commanding officers had allowed Catholic parents to withdraw their children from morning prayers and commence the school at the start of the second morning session.[18]

Under the new regulations, denominational catechisms were not taught. Instead the children were instructed in the main principles of Christianity and read a compendium of sacred history as a school book. Care however was to be taken to avoid controversy,

13   G.Gleig, 'National Education', *The Edinburgh Review*, April 1852.
14   NAM, 'Records of the Royal Army Educational Corps Army, Educational Policy and Regimental Schools 1846-1920, Box 22126'; 'Regulations of the Scots Fusilier Regiment of Guards (London, 1858).
15   The school subjects identified corresponded to those listed by Gleig in his article 'National Education' in the April 1852 edition of the *Edinburgh Review*.
16   These volumes were promoted in the newspapers and their military and civilian sales provided Gleig with an additional source of income. *The Times,* 21/08/1851; 19/07/1852; 31/07/1860.
17   Lefroy, *Report on the Regimental and Garrison Schools of the Army*, p. 33.
18   See Chapter 6.

and especially '...to shun debateable ground as between rival churches.'[19] Gleig dealt with this matter at some length in his article entitled: 'National Education' in the *Edinburgh Review* in 1852. He advanced the generally accepted view that elementary education could not be divorced from religious instruction and explained that the schoolmaster trained at the Normal School was taught how to place the scriptures in their grammatical and historical context and to draw moral and religious lessons from the text, but without denominational bias. He believed that religious and moral education should not be restricted to the study of the scriptures and could be delivered through all the subjects in the curriculum; but specifically denominational instruction should be undertaken by the clergy at church services and Sunday schools.[20]

Gleig has been praised for avoiding the religious controversy that beset civilian education in the UK during the Nineteenth century and his liberal attitude to religious instruction has been seen as far ahead of his time.[21] His approach to the place of religious education in schooling was to a degree reflected in the subsequent legislation governing publicly funded elementary and secondary education in Great Britain well into the twentieth century.

His approach in this matter was pragmatic. He was first and foremost an Anglican clergyman and in the later 1840s he had become a member of the National Society, but he recognised that there were large numbers of Roman Catholics and dissenting Protestants in the Army and that any successful reform of the regimental schools must avoid accusations of denominational bias. This had been one of the reasons given by Gleig in his 1844 report to Hardinge for advising the rejection of the offer by the National Society to train some army schoolmasters and for recommending that the Army should establish its own normal school.[22]

Unfortunately, strong views were developing in the Catholic hierarchy about the need for the Church to control the education of Catholic children and there was a growing opposition to 'mixed schools' in which Protestants and Catholics were taught together. Paul Cullen, the Catholic Archbishop of Dublin from 1852 (and Ireland's first Cardinal from 1866) was one the strongest opponents of 'mixed schools.' In pamphlets published in Dublin in 1857 and 1858 he criticised the Protestant character of the regimental schools and the military schools at Chelsea and Phoenix Park. He emphasised that that this was not a peculiarly Irish concern and quoted the Very Reverend Feneley, the Vicar General of Madras, who considered that the Protestant

19 'Returns relating to Military and Regimental Schools', House of Commons Sessional Papers, 19 March 1852, p. 304.
20 Gleig, 'National Education', April 1852, p. 356.
21 Smith, 'The *Army Schoolmaster and the Development of Elementary Education in the Army, 1812-1920*', pp. 109-10.
22 Gleig was a member of the National Society from early as early as February 1847, when in a letter to Laurence Sullivan, dated 20 February, he offered to obtain teaching materials for the military schools at Chelsea at a discount from the Society. TNA WO 43/807.

character of the regimental schools in India was so pronounced that soldiers who sent their children to these schools should not be admitted to the sacrament.[23]

Army School Regulations issued in 1854 and 1858(see below) addressed some of these concerns and from 1858 commissioned Roman Catholic chaplains were appointed in the Army. Even so there was continuing concern that the military schools in general, and the RHMS in particular, discriminated against Catholics and were covertly proselytising institutions. Ironically it was the widespread use of Gleig's history textbooks in these schools that contributed to these concerns. In particular, Archbishop Cullen objected to the use of Gleig's histories at RHMS, arguing that they contained many things that were contrary to the teachings of the Church and were offensive to Catholics. Suspicion and antagonism between Archbishop Cullen and the authorities at the RHMS continued throughout the 1860s and in 1871 the British Government was forced to intervene and impose a major revision to the School's Royal Charter that included additional safeguards for Catholic children.[24]

In December 1852, the Earl of Aberdeen formed a coalition government of Whigs and Peelites and Sidney Herbert returned to the War Office with a seat in the Cabinet. The Duke of Wellington died in September 1852 and he was succeeded as C-in-C at the Horse Guards by Viscount (previously Sir Henry) Hardinge, who had returned from India in 1848.The death of the Duke made army reform easier and Herbert developed a harmonious working relationship with Hardinge that ensured that two military departments avoided administrative conflict. Herbert continued with the pragmatic approach to reform that had characterised his policy when he had been at the War Office in the 1840s.[25] The Secretary at War's responsibility for the administration of the Army's schools and the training and posting of army schoolmasters was only a small part of Herbert's extensive and complex responsibilities.[26] It may have been because Herbert had initiated the reforms in army education in 1846 that he found time to introduce regulations for army schools that would ensure that the momentum of reform was maintained.

Frederick Scrivener's experience at the Preston garrison supported Gleig's conviction that whenever trained schoolmasters could be appointed to take charge of the schools there would be a large increase in attendance by enlisted men. Scrivener's

23 P. Cullen, *A Letter to Lord St. Leonards on the Management of the Patriotic Fund and the application of public money to proselytising purposes* (Dublin: James Duffy 1857); P. Cullen, *Two letters to Lord St. Leonards on the Management of the Patriotic Fund and the Second Report of the Royal Commissioners* (Dublin: James Duffey, 1858).

24 The long dispute between the Catholic hierarchy in Ireland and the RHMS is documented in Clarke, *A New History of the Royal Hibernian Military School*, Chapters10-12.

25 H. C. G. Matthew, '*Herbert, Sidney, First Baron Herbert of Lea' (1810-1861)*, Oxford Dictionary of National Biography <www.oxforddnb.com/view/article> (accessed 17th January 2015); Strachan, 'The Early Victorian Army', p. 807.

26 J. Sweetman, *War and Administration* (Edinburgh: Scottish Academic Press, 1984), pp. 97-102.

experience was soon replicated in other units, but the newly trained schoolmaster faced a number of issues in managing his school. The typical regimental school in 1851-52 contained some 40-50 boys and girls (see Table above) with enlisted men attending in the afternoons and sometimes in the early evenings. The schoolmaster might have been fortunate in finding a schoolmistress to teach the girls and the younger boys, and if posted to one of the larger barracks in the British Isles, he may also have had help from an Assistant Schoolmaster (pupil teacher) who was gaining teaching experience before proceeding to complete his training at the Normal School. Many of the early trained schoolmasters however had to shoulder the entire burden of managing both the children and adult schools.

There were also issues of remuneration. The basic pay of a trained army schoolmaster was 2s/6d per day or £45-12s-6d per annum, plus £1 for each company per annum where he instructed the female children in reading and writing. There was no possibility of promotion to a better paid post. Fredrick Scrivener had lamented in his letter to Mr Macleod at the Model School that the schoolmaster could not contemplate marriage on his basic salary.[27]

The War Office had calculated that income from the school fees paid by enlisted soldiers, three-quarters of which were retained by the schoolmaster, would encourage the schoolmaster to work hard to attract and retain adult pupils in order to supplement his income. Other than Wellington's order of 1849 requiring new recruits to attend school for two hours per day until excused drill, attendance was voluntary and depended on the encouragement exerted by COs and their willingness to arrange drill and general duties so that the men could attend. Income from fees was unequal and capricious and some of the best masters received less than their colleagues serving in other regiments where the officers took an interest in the school and were influential in securing attendance. In consequence the War Office received requests from schoolmasters asking to be transferred to regiments where they could earn more income from fees because the COs was known to encourage attendance. All of these factors could not but fail to have a deleterious effect on recruitment to the Normal School, but more worrying for the War Office there were instances of neglect of duty and insubordination on the part of a few schoolmasters.[28]

Sidney Herbert addressed these issues with a comprehensive set of Army School Regulations in June 1854, in which he replaced the ranks of regimental, garrison and assistant schoolmaster that had been introduced in 1850 with a new staffing structure

27 Scrivener wrote inquiring whether the wife of a schoolmaster might be appointed as the schoolmistress because: 'I begin to see that the schoolmaster would leave a miserable life unless he is a married man...however it would be madness to think of a man marrying on 2/6 per day.' TNA WO 43/807: ff. 133-134, 'Frederick Scrivener to Walter Macleod'.
28 NAM, 'Records of the Royal Army Educational Corps Army, Educational Policy and Regimental Schools 1846-1920, Box 22126, Memo by Sidney Herbert, January 1854'.

with opportunities for promotion within what was in effect separate corps of army schoolmasters.[29]

Table 13. Ranks and Pay of Army Schoolmasters introduced in the 1854 Army School Regulations

First Class Schoolmaster	Pay	7s.0d per day	Pension: That of a Sergeant Major plus 6d per day
Second Class Schoolmaster	Pay	5s.6d per day	Pension: Same as Sergeant Major
Third Class Schoolmaster	Pay	4s.0d per day	Pension: Same as Sergeant Major
Assistant Schoolmaster	Pay	2s.0d per day	Pension: That of a Sergeant plus 6d per day

The First Class Schoolmaster was to be a 'warrant officer' and was to rank after the commissioned officers; the Second class Schoolmasters were to rank next to the Sergeant Major; and the Assistant Schoolmaster as a Sergeant. All classes of schoolmasters were appointed under the authority of the Secretary at War and must previously have undertaken training at the 'Royal Military Asylum and have obtained a certificate of qualification.' Promotion from one class to another was made by the Secretary at War upon the recommendation of the Inspector General of Schools on merit only, and the Secretary at War could reduce the schoolmaster from a higher to a lower rank for misconduct.

The schoolmasters were not to be placed under the authority of any Non-Commissioned Officers as regards to the duties of their office. However, any cases of misconduct, which might occasion him to be placed under arrest for trial by court martial (because he was an enlisted soldier under the provisions of the Mutiny Act) the facts and circumstances of the case were to be reported to the C-in-C for such directions as he might think fit. When in the British Isles, the schoolmaster with large numbers of pupils might be allocated an assistant schoolmaster who would be under his immediate superintendence and control. The assistant was required to obey any directions he might receive from the schoolmaster, subject to such orders as might be given by the officer commanding with regard to his duties at the School. The Regulations emphasised that the assistant was attached temporarily to the regiment or garrison to assist the schoolmaster and might be removed to other stations by the

29   TNA WO 43/513: 'Army School Regulations 1854'.

Secretary at War (and only by the Secretary at War) as the circumstances required.[30] The schoolmaster was to act as mentor for the assistant schoolmaster and was to provide a monthly report to the Secretary at War on his conduct and progress.

When the assistant schoolmaster had been selected by the Secretary at War for promotion to the higher rank of schoolmaster, he was to undergo a course of instruction at the Normal School, during which period he would not be entitled to pay but would receive 'pocket money' of £4 -4s per annum. This parsimonious sum was hardly an incentive for recruitment and was a further factor contributing to discontent at the Normal School. In August 1858, 13 Army assistant schoolmasters (formerly monitors) who were training at the Normal School submitted a memorial to the War Office complaining about the withdrawal of their pay, in contrast to the enlisted army sergeants who were enrolled at the School, who retained their pay less the usual stoppages.[31]

Under the new regulations the separate status of the Army schoolmaster was emphasised by his uniform. He was no longer required to wear the uniform of the regiment to which he was posted. A uniform of the same general pattern as that provided for students at the Normal School was to be worn with distinctive badges of rank for each class of schoolmaster. Separate rooms were to be provided for each category of Army schoolmasters in which would take their meals. They could marry at the discretion of the Secretary at War, acting on the recommendations of the commanding officer with regard to the character and respectability of the intended spouse. The schoolmaster's wife was to be classed as supernumerary to the number of women allowed when proceeding overseas and the married couple were to be allocated a separate cabin on board ship. Where the wife was also the Regimental Schoolmistress she was allowed to travel at public expense when moving stations both at home and overseas.

In 1850 Regulations had been issued for the organisation of the regimental schools to which a trained army schoolmaster had been or may be appointed. These arrangements were consolidated in the 1854 Regulations. There were to be separate Children's and Adult Schools and where a trained schoolmaster was appointed there also was to be an Infants' School for both boys and girls supervised by a schoolmistress. The children were to be taught in a separate room from 0930-1200 every morning until they could read words of at least two syllables.[32] When the children had reached this standard they were to attend in the 'ordinary school room' until 1200 each morning

30   The regulations authorised the commanding officer to pay a qualified soldier 3d per day to assist the trained schoolmaster in teaching the soldiers in case of need, such as where large numbers of men were serving on detachment.

31   Royal Military Asylum, Normal School Letter Book 1853-1859, 'Memorial to the Secretary of State for War, 13th August 1857'.

32   The schoolmaster was required to visit the Infant's School every quarter and provide a written report on its condition for the CO.

to receive instruction from the schoolmaster or his assistant in what became known as the 'Grown Children's Schools'.

The hour for commencing instruction in the Children's School, whether managed by a trained Army schoolmaster or a schoolmaster-sergeant, was fixed at 0920 in the morning, but all children whose parents did not object on religious grounds were to attend at 0900 for prayers and readings from the scriptures. All children of Roman Catholic soldiers or of soldiers who were dissenters from the Church of England were allowed to be absent from this religious observance provided that their parents signified that wish in writing to the schoolmaster.

This provision did not satisfy the Catholic hierarchy. Archbishop Cullen thought that it was '...a snare for weak minded parents', because there were many '...pious Protestant Commanding Officers' who made no secret of their dislike of everything Catholic and 'the timid and weak minded private soldier' was unlikely to risk the displeasure of his CO by withdrawing his children from morning prayers.[33]

When Roman Catholic Chaplains were appointed to the Army in 1858, the War Office amended the regulations removing the requirements for parents to make a written request for their children to be absent from the Anglican morning worship. The Children's School was to commence at 0900 with half hour of payers and readings, but parents who were not Anglicans were at liberty to delay sending their children until 0930 at which time general education would commence. A period of two hours per week was set aside for religious instruction and the CO was required to provide accommodation for the different denominational classes. There was a strict injunction that secular education was not to take place in the same room during its use for religious instruction. The War Office emphasised that the intention was to remove any doubt that might exist as to the equality of treatment and freedom for members of all religions and denominations in the operation of the Army School regulations.[34]

Schools of Industrial Occupation, which had been established by the 1850 Regulations, were to continue and be managed by a schoolmistress, who would instruct the female children from 1400 to 1600 in knitting sewing and household occupations. It was expected that the school girls on the school register would attend, but boys could also attend should their parents desire it. Fees were not payable when children attended the schoolmaster's (Grown Children's) school, but parents with children at the Infant and Industrial Schools Children's were 'for the present' be charged fees at a rate of 2d per month for one child, reducing to three half pence for two children and one pence per month per child for three or more children. The fees were retained by the schoolmistress as an addition to her annual salary of £14 in each regiment of cavalry and £2 for each company of infantry. Although the schoolmaster

---

33   Cullen, *Two letters to Lord St. Leonards on the Mana Second Report of the Royal Commissioners*, p. 26.

34   War Office, Circular No. 273 (Schools), 23rd June 1858 quoted in: Lefroy, *Report on the Regimental and Garrison Schools*, p. 48.

was not allowed to retain the fees for teaching soldiers' children, he was permitted to make charges at specified rates for instructing the children of ex-soldiers employed in civilian posts in barracks. He might also instruct the children of commissioned officers at times that did not interfere with his duties for a fee to be negotiated with the parents.[35]

The 1854 Regulations had less to say about the adult schools. The CO was to decide on the time at which the school would commence for general instruction after allowing time for prayers and scripture readings for those who wished to attend. The Regulations did not specify the number of the hours that the schoolmaster should devote in the afternoons or evenings to instructing the adult soldiers. Fees continued to be charged payable at a rate of 8d per month for Sergeants, 6d for Corporals and 4d for Drummers and Privates. However, because the schoolmaster's salary had been increased, he no longer received these fee payments and the amounts collected were in future to be credited to the Treasury.

The continuation of fees for adult students and their introduction at the Infant and Industrial Schools might appear surprising given that George Gleig and others had argued that there would be benefits to the Army from soldiers attending school. This however is to ignore the pivotal position of HM Treasury in effecting any reforms in military administration. The Treasury's objective was always to limit and control cost and government grants and not to provide free elementary education, whether in civilian or regimental schools. Furthermore, the received political economy of the day argued that when a particular provision by government might bring benefit to the individual, he or she should share some of the cost with the tax payer. This argument was used to justify the retention of stoppages from soldiers' pay for bread and meat, and can also be seen in the discussions about the founding and funding of a college for training military bandsmen at what from 1857 became the School of Military Music at Kneller Hall.[36] It was the reason for requiring a bond from civilians enlisting at the Normal School and for the removal of pay for assistant schoolmasters when they entered the School for further training.[37] Similarly, although enlisted men could not be ordered to attend school, fees were justified because attendance would improve their chances of promotion, which would mean higher pay, and as Gleig had argued, would also help them to secure better paid civilian employment on leaving the Army.[38]

---

35 TNA WO 43/513: 'Army Schools Regulations 1854', para. 43-4.
36 Correspondence with regards to changes in the transactions of business relating to the Administration of the Army, House of Lords Sessional Paper, 7th April 1854. Papers Relating to Military Bands, House of Commons Sessional Papers, 15th February 1858.
37 TNA WO 143/47: 'Letter from Under Secretary of State for War to Commandant of RMA, October 1857'. It was argued that the students were receiving tuition, board and lodging and clothing and 'pocket money' of £4-4s per annum at the RMA, whereas tuition at a civilian training college would cost at least £30 per annum.
38 Gleig, 'Education and Lodging of the Soldier', pp. 546-7.

The rationale for retaining fees at the Infant and Industrial Schools is more difficult to understand. Many COs welcomed the regimental and garrison schools because they occupied children who might otherwise be a nuisance around the barracks. Also, soldiers' daughters often married within the regiment and their training at the Industrial Schools imparted useful domestic skills. The precedent of fees being charged for children at civilian schools and the objective of limiting public spending probably account for the decision to retain fees for children at the Army's schools.

Herbert's 1854 Regulations addressed many of the issues facing the reformed system of Army education in the early 1850s. They directly answered the concerns of the trained schoolmaster about his remuneration and conditions of service and provided him with career opportunities for promotion on the basis of merit. The Regulations acknowledged that he might marry, and indeed that his wife might be the schoolmistress, and he could now look forward to a pension on retirement. They stopped short however of offering the senior class of schoolmasters the possibility promotion to the rank of commissioned officer. George Gleig had expressed his strong opposition to the commissioning of the army schoolmasters and at that time any such proposal would have resulted in opposition from the C-in-C at the Horse Guards on the grounds that the War Office would be interfering with his prerogative to grant commissions.

Although the Army schoolmaster remained an enlisted soldier, the Regulations gave him a special and quasi- professional position within the Army. He was permitted to write directly to the Secretary at War and his written communications were to be forwarded immediately, with the CO's counter signature, to the War Office. He was required to forward a monthly return to the Secretary at War (on Form NO.367) countersigned by the unit's CO stating the number and progress of adults and children attending school during the previous month. Except when duty interfered, the CO was to stick strictly to the regulated hours for attendance at the Children's and Adult Schools. He was to certify in the monthly reports that the times were being adhered to, and when it was necessary to make changes. The reasons for any variations were to be specified in the next monthly report.

The schoolmaster's income was no longer dependent on the number of soldiers attending the Adult Schools and the payment of fees, but the regulations did not define the specific hours for the men's attendance. In consequence a particular schoolmaster's work load continued to depend to a large degree on whether a CO encouraged his men to attend school. A general requirement for enlisted private soldiers to attend regularly would have required primary legislation, but it is perhaps surprising that the Army School Regulations did not follow the example of the numerous regimental standing orders, which specified that promotion to the ranks of NCO would normally require satisfactory prior attendance at school. Compulsion however was contentious and was to be the subject of considerable discussion between the military departments in the following years. Herbert emphasised in his Circular accompanying the Regulations that the success of the system of instruction by trained schoolmasters continued to depend to a great degree upon the interest taken in the schools by the commanding officers of regiments and garrisons.[39]

The anonymous letter from a schoolmaster-sergeant to the *Naval and Military Gazette* in July 1843 explained that the schoolrooms were often situated in '...the darkest and worst ventilated rooms in the barracks' and that often soldiers and boys and girls pupils were taught in schoolmasters' private rooms in the presence of his wife and young children.[40] The 1854 Regulations specified that each class of schoolmaster was to have his own rooms within the barracks, but made very little reference to the type of facilities that should be available to accommodate the schools. Where the facilities were inadequate the CO was required to make representations to the Secretary at War giving their current dimensions, list any defects and suggest how these might be remedied. This was as much as could be expected given the distribution of the Army in the early 1850s. Parliamentary Return on the numbers of children at the regimental schools in 1851-52 identified 150 different stations at home and abroad and the available facilities varied widely according to local circumstances. However, where new barracks were being constructed or existing ones extended consideration could be given to the provision of dedicated facilities.

Following his appointment as Chaplain General in 1844, Gleig had expressed concern about the facilities for divine worship at barracks in the British Isles. In some cases, the men and their families were marched to the local parish church, but where this was too small the chaplain or officiating clergyman had to hold a service in whatever rooms were available in the barracks. In December 1844 he forwarded a memo to the Secretary at War proposing that a 'plain chapel' for the worship of 600 infantry, 100 cavalry and their wives and children in a new barracks that was to be constructed in the parish of Horfield near Bristol, because the local parish church was too small. He understood that barracks was also proposed at Preston and he argued that a chapel should be included in all the projects for new barracks, although at this date he did not suggest the use of the chapels as schoolrooms. Herbert conceded that where there was insufficient accommodation in the local parish church gradually barrack chapels should be erected.[41] Probably in order to counter any Treasury objections Gleig proposed that the new buildings could have a dual purpose as chapel and schools, with the chancel cut off from the nave by drop curtains or a movable screen. The west end of the chapel could be fitted with school desks and moveable chairs placed in the nave for the act of worship.[42] Herbert gave his support for this proposal and in December 1845 asked the Treasury for approval for chapel-schools

39   NAM, Records of the Royal Army Educational Corps Army, Educational Policy and Regimental Schools 1846-1920, Box 22126, 'War Office Circular 12th June 1854'.

40   *Naval and Military Gazette*, 15th July 1843, p. 439.

41   TNA WO 43/819: f. 311, Proposal to provide Chapels in Barracks.

42   St John Williams, *Tommy Atkin's Children, pp;* 46-7; Jarvis, 'My Predecessor in Office', pp. 59-6. It believed that Gleig took the idea from a temporary building seen at St John's Wood that was being used temporarily by the Guards.

in the new barracks to be erected at Glasgow and Piershill near Edinburgh, and also at Hounslow and at Parkhurst in the Isle of White.[43] In addition, Gleig and Herbert managed to appropriate rooms in the barracks that was under construction at Fulwood Preston. In the following years, chapel schools based on one of three plans devised by Gleig were incorporated in new barracks.[44] A good example is the chapel school at Lichfield Barracks that was designed for use by 521 worshippers and 175 scholars.[45]

Space had also to be found for a library and reading room. One of the first barrack chapels constructed was at Hillsborough, Sheffield. Work on the first stage of this new barracks for infantry and cavalry including a chapel was completed in 1850. However, it ceased to be used as a chapel at an early stage and the nearby St John's Church at Owlerton was used for church parades and services. The chapel was thereafter referred to as 'The Institute' and provided a reading room, a billiard room and other recreational facilities for the rank and file. It also may have been used for the adult school and perhaps for the children, because a dedicated Infant School with accommodation for the schoolmistress was not built until 1867.[46] The Wellington Lines barracks built at Aldershot Camp between September 1854-59 were provided with dedicated school and reading rooms for the adult school and a separate school room for the children.[47]

In existing barracks it was a matter of securing space to house a library and reading room and funds to convert suitable rooms into classrooms and furnish them with desks and raised platforms for the schoolmaster and schoolmistress. At Chatham two of the St Mary's Casemates, built as barracks to defend the dockyards during the Napoleonic War, were adapted to house a library and reading room for soldiers and an Infant's School for 58 children and accommodation for the schoolmistress.[48] Progress in securing suitable accommodation was however slow and uneven. The Commission for improving Barracks and Hospitals inspected 162 barracks in the British Isles between 1858-61 and only 67 had schools with adequate ventilation.[49] There were also considerable variations in the facilities available in the colonies. Frederick Scrivener when he was posted to the Bombay Presidency in 1853 found the school accommodation to be very defective and consisted of whatever rooms were available in the barracks.[50] The school accommodation in Hong Kong was totally inadequate for the numbers and was especially unsuitable in a climate with temperatures that often reached 100 degrees (F) in the shade. The visiting inspector concluded that the greatest inducement for the men to attend would be a large and well ventilated

43   TNA WO43/819: f. 349, 'Proposal to provide Chapels in Barracks'.
44   Jarvis, 'My Predecessor in Office', pp. 59-60.
45   N.T. St John Williams, *Tommy Atkin's Children*, Illustration No. 16.
46   S. Johnson, *From Bailey to Bailey-A Short History of Military Buildings in Sheffield* (Sheffield : privately published, 1998), pp. 10-13.
47   Douet, *British Barracks*, pp. 131-2,135.
48   Douet, *British Barracks*, p. 119.
49   Douet, *British Barracks*, p. 144.
50   Lefroy, *Report on the Regimental and Garrison Schools of the Army*, p. 100.

schoolroom. Similarly in the Australian colonies, the commanding officer of the 40th Foot wrote from Melbourne on 11th January 1858 complaining about the lack of accommodation offered by the colonial government with the Regiment's school housed in a tent, which in the hot climate was very trying for both the scholars and the schoolmaster.[51]

Where a number of regiments occupied one large barracks or were housed in close proximity at one station there was a strong case for establishing a garrison school with dedicated accommodation. It is interesting that Fox Maule appointed five of the first cohort of 22 trained schoolmasters as garrison schoolmasters, rather than assigning them to individual units as regimental schoolmasters. In January 1848, Lord Frederick FitzClarence, the CO of the Portsmouth district had established the Portsmouth Garrison School at his own expense. Thirty to forty NCOs and Privates attended at a time. They were taught for six hours per day and in addition to the usual elementary education the curriculum had a military bias, including instruction in trigonometry, mechanics and dynamics, field fortifications and field sketching. In 1850 a Superior School was added to give more advanced instruction school, specifically for NCOs and potential NCOs. Some of the school's success was attributed to Fitzclarence drawing off the cream of every regiment and also to the particular abilities of Frederick Scrivener, who had moved from Preston to become 'Head District School-master' at Portsmouth. Fitzclarence proposed to Fox Maule that every military district should have a similar school, so that regiments regularly changing stations could painlessly change schools. This proposal received some support in the press and Rev. George Gleig praised the Portsmouth School .However that was as far as the matter went and similar schools were not established in other districts.[52]

The proposal would have certainly encountered opposition from COs, who would have argued that it interfered with their authority over the interior economy of their regiments to the detriment of their own schools. There was also the consideration of the continuity of teaching as battalions moved regularly between garrisons at home and abroad. This favoured the retention of regimental schools and the case for garrison schools would be considered afresh and rejected by the authorities on similar grounds in the early 1860s.

51   Lefroy, *Report on the Regimental and Garrison Schools of the Army*, pp. 27, 151.
52   H. Strachan, *Wellington's Legacy: The Reform of the British Army, 1830-1854* (Manchester: Manchester University Press1986) , pp. 91-2.

14

A System for Superintending and Inspecting Army Schools

In February 1855, the Earl of Aberdeen resigned as Prime Minister following criticisms of the conduct of the Crimean War and was succeeded by Viscount Palmerston. Sidney Herbert left the War Office and Lord Panmure (previously Fox Maule) was appointed the Secretary of State for War in February 1855.[1] Palmerston decided to leave the post of Secretary at War vacant. Its various legal, financial, and administrative duties including responsibility for the posts of Chaplain General and Inspector General of Military Schools and the training and appointment of Army schoolmasters were transferred to Lord Panmure as the Secretary of State for War.[2] Panmure was determined to improve army administration by consolidating the various military departments. Herbert had already secured the removal of the Commissariat from the Treasury to the War Office and by the Order in Council of 6 June 1855 the Ordnance Department was broken up with the civilian branch placed under the Secretary of State for War and the military branch, with the appointments and promotions to the Royal Artillery, Royal Engineers and the Corps of Sappers and Miners, placed under the C-in-C at the Horse Guards.

The C-in-C at the Horse Guards retained command of the troops, but the Duke of Cambridge, when he was appointed to the post in July 1856, did not receive letters patent issued by the Crown, but a letter of service signed by Panmure as the Secretary of State for War. This emphasised that HM's Secretary of State had supreme control over the Army for which he alone was answerable to Parliament. The Horse Guards however continued to assert its independence for granting commissions and

---

1 Fox Maule had inherited the title of Baron Panmure from his father in April 1852.
2 The combined post of Secretary of State for War and Colonies was abolished in June 1854 and was replaced by a Secretary of State for War and a Secretary of State for the Colonies. The office of Secretary at War, which had always been subordinate to the Secretary of State of State for War and the Colonies, was not formally abolished until 1863. For some years the terms 'War Office' and 'War Department' were used synonymously.

determining appointments and sought to protect the authority of commanding officers in determining promotion within their battalions and regiments.[3]

The War Office had been given the control of the selection, training and appointment of Army schoolmasters in 1846, but the jealousy of the C-in-C protected the prerogatives of the COs to select suitable private soldiers for promotion as NCOs. On 18th August 1856, the C-in-C, the Duke of Cambridge, was informed by the Under-Secretary for War that Lord Panmure was minded to order that from August 1857, the promotion of soldiers to the ranks of corporal and sergeant should be dependent upon their possession of certain unspecified educational qualifications. He had presented a similar proposal to the Duke of Wellington in July 1851 and the Duke had replied that he was opposed to anyone other than the commanding officer having the power or influence in the appointment of NCOs. The Duke of Cambridge was not prepared to dissent from Wellington's opinion on the matter, but he was prepared to suggest an alternative way forward.

He observed that young soldiers were keen to attend the new regimental schools and that many COs had introduced standing orders and regimental regulations specifying that soldiers who wished to be promoted should be able to demonstrate their proficiency in reading and writing. Viscount Hardinge, when he was C-in-C had been opposed to issuing any further orders on the matter. He had observed that as a general rule, soldiers were not promoted unless they could demonstrate these competencies. Cambridge emphasised that there were occasions when men showed leadership by their meritorious conduct in the field and it was important that COs should be not be prevented by any requirements for educational qualifications from promoting these men. Cambridge declared that he wished to work in his capacity as the C-in-C hand in hand with the Secretary of State in promoting a sound and beneficial system of education for the soldier, but he was not prepared to interfere with the prerogative of the CO to select the best men under his command for promotion as NCOs. Rather than issue a general regulation, Cambridge argued that it was far better to continue to give encouragement to the 'new improved educational system' and allow it to work its own way forward to the benefits of the soldiers at large, rather than imposing an arbitrary educational standard on men recommended for promotion.[4]

Panmure does not appear to have pursued the matter, but in 1857 he abolished Schools fees for men without any elementary education who were prepared to attend school to learn reading, writing and elements of arithmetic. Although Wellington

3   Sweetman, *War and Administration*, pp. 96, 106, 124-27. The tensions between the two
      military departments and the ambiguities about their respective responsibilities were to
      continue for many years and were not finally resolved until the abolition of the office of
      Commander- in-Chief in1904.
4   TNA WO 43/513: ff.305-308, 'Letter from the Horse Guards to the Under Secretary
      of State at the War Department'. Panmure left the War office in February 1858 on the
      resignation of Palmerston's government and he did take his proposals any further during
      his final months in office.

in 1849 had ordered that all recruits should attend school for two hours per day, the Secretary of State's legal advisers remained of the opinion that the Mutiny Act did not impose the military discipline of attendance. An order was issued to commanding officers requiring them to arrange duties so that men who did not have any elementary education would be able to attend school gratis for four hours per week. However, if they wished to continue to a higher standard they would still have to pay fees.[5]

In the early years following his appointment at the War Office in 1846 George Gleig had managed to combine the work load of the two separate posts of Chaplain-General to the Forces and Inspector General of Military Schools. However, the number of paid Anglican Army Chaplains was growing and the steady appointment of trained schoolmasters to the regimental and garrison schools greatly increased the burden of inspection.[6]

It is difficult to establish the extent of Gleig's inspections of the regimental and garrison schools throughout the United Kingdom in the early 1850s. He made inspections of schools in the Cork Military District in 1851 and the Dublin District in 1856, but there is evidence that he was struggling with the demands of his dual responsibilities. There were suggestions in the newspapers that he was neglecting the efficient supervision of the military schools and that there would be advantages in separating the two posts.[7]

In 1856, Panmure appointed three Assistant Inspectors of Military Schools in the British Isles. Captain Alexander Cameron Gleig[8] (An officer in the Royal Artillery and Rev George Gleig's nephew) became responsible for schools in Southern Britain, whilst two civil servants from the War Department, Mr J. P. Sargeaunt and Mr E. A. Vicars were given responsibility for the North of Great Britain and Ireland respectively.

In March 1856 Gleig drew up a set of Instructions to regulate the reports by the Assistant Inspectors: they were to ensure that the school's timetable was strictly adhered to; that only approved books were used; that the schoolmaster and mistress were fit for their work and that they taught in suitable accommodation. The Assistant Inspectors' reports were forwarded to the Inspector-General who consolidated them into an annual report for the Secretary at War.[9]

---

5   First Report of the Council of Military Education, 1862, p. xiii.

6   In October 1856, the Army List contained the Chaplain-General and twenty Chaplains and thirty-five Assistant Chaplains to the Forces (all Anglican); quoted in Jarvis, 'My Predecessor in Office', p. 321.

7   *Morning Advertiser*, 14th August 1851, p. 6; *The Times*, 11th June 1856; *Lloyds Weekly Newspaper*, 30th December 1855, p. 4.

8   Alexander Cameron Gleig with henceforth me referred to by his military rank, to distinguish him from George Gleig. Alexander Gleig was appointed Major in June 1862 and then Lieutenant Colonel in July 1864.

9   Lefroy, *Report on the Regimental and Garrison Schools of the Army*, Appendix 1, pp. 85 6.

Panmure's decision to appoint Assistant Inspectors was not without its critics. One newspaper argued that Gleig's salary as Chaplain General should be increased to reflect his increased workload in managing the chaplaincy and that he should relinquish the post of Inspector General of Military Schools. The superintendence of the regimental schools should be given to an efficient trained inspector or to the Committee of Education of the Privy Council. The newspaper caustically commented that this would not suit Gleig, who wished '...to retain the honour-and of course the emoluments-of an appointment, the duties of which he cannot perform, and at the same time to provide a snug birth for one of his family.'[10]

Sidney Herbert, speaking from the back benches in the House of Commons in June 1856 acknowledged that the Inspector-General was not able to inspect all the numerous schools throughout the Army. He welcomed the appointment of additional inspectors, but the appointment of the two civil servants was in his opinion a grave mistake as they had no particular qualifications for inspecting regimental schools. In his view inspectors should be selected from military officers who had distinguished themselves in '...the higher and more scientific branches of the profession of arms', and who therefore would carry more weight with Army than anyone appointed from the Civil Service.[11] The same might have been said of the qualifications for the post of Inspector-General of Military Schools and if so, it would follow that the post should not in future be occupied by a clergyman who was also the Chaplain-General. Ironically, Gleig advanced a similar argument in correspondence with Panmure later in the year on the matter of a successor for Dr Du Sautoy, as the Chaplain of the RMA and Principal of the Normal School. Gleig argued that Du Sautoy should retire on grounds of ill-health and that the rubrics of the RMA should be amended to separate the two posts. There should be a Chaplain who would have nothing to do with discipline or secular instruction and would be responsible only for the religious instruction of the students and boys in the two schools at the RMA. The Headmaster (Principal) of the Normal School should be an Army Officer of '...known ability and judgement', not below the rank of Captain, who would infuse '...what is now wanting; a right a military spirit into the (Normal) School.' Gleig argued that such a person would probably be 'far better qualified than any clergyman to instruct in those subjects which are especially required in military teachers.'[12]

Lord Panmure had shown himself to be a firm supporter of the reforms introduced into the Army's schools and when questioned in the House of Commons had explained that many commanding officers welcomed the introduction of trained schoolmasters because of the beneficial effects of the increased attendance by soldiers at the adult schools. Shortly after he returned to office in 1855, he decided that the time was right for further reform and that the superintendence of all aspects of education in

10   *Lloyds Weekly Newspaper*, 30 December 1855, p. 4.
11   *Hansard*, Third Series, 5th June 1856, Vol. CXLII, pp. 980-1023.
12   TNA WO 43/796: ff.162-164, 'George Gleig to Lord Panmure'.

Fox Maule, 2nd Baron Panmure (1801-74) Minister at War 1846-52; Secretary of State for War 1855-58 by Maull & Polybank. (© National Portrait Gallery, London)

the Army should be brought together in one post at the War Office. He began to develop the view that the responsibility for inspection and superintending all aspect of education in the Army should be in the hands of a serving officer drawn from 'the higher and more scientific branches' of the service.

Panmure was fortunate in finding a suitable person on the War Office Staff. Major John Lefroy RA had been appointed as senior clerk in the War Office in December 1854 as confidential adviser in artillery matters.[13] He was promoted Lieutenant Colonel in September 1855 and quickly gained Panmure's confidence. In October of that year he was sent to Constantinople to confer and report on the condition of hospital staff in the East and the accommodation of the sick in Scutari.[14]

Sometime in the summer of 1856 Panmure had 'private and confidential' talks with Lefroy about his plans to bring education throughout the Army more directly under the control of the Secretary of State. Panmure explained that he wished to abolish the Board of Commissioners for the Royal Military College at Sandhurst and to take control of the regimental schools from the Chaplain General (i.e. from Gleig).

13   Lefroy was gazetted as 'scientific adviser on subjects of artillery and inventions', and for reasons of pay and military precedence, he was made a senior clerk. Lefroy had served overseas for a number of years working on magnetic observations and surveys, but he had shown a continuing interest in the professional development of the artillery's officers and was co-founder of the Royal Artillery Institution. In 1854 he compiled 'The Handbook of Field Artillery for the use of Officers' that remained as a text book for artillery officers until 1884.
14   R. H. Vetch, 'Lefroy, John Henry', *Dictionary of National Biography*, Vol. .32 (Oxford: Clarendon Press, 1885-1900).

He asked Lefroy to draw up a scheme for his consideration.[15] Lefroy submitted a substantial memorandum in which he proposed that the administration of military education at the Royal Military College (Sandhurst), the Royal Military Academy (Woolwich), the RMA and the RHMS and the Garrison and Regimental Schools should be conducted by one authority under the Secretary of State for War. This would be achieved by establishing an 'Educational Department' in the War Office with a Director- General of Military Education and a staff of Assistant Inspectors, with overall responsibility for the education of officers, soldiers and their children.[16] Lefroy wrote to his wife on 10 September 1856 saying that Panmure was minded to offer him the post of 'Inspector-General' and that Gleig was prepared to give up his superintendence the Army's schools in order to concentrate on his increasing work load as Chaplain-General.[17]

It is not known exactly when Gleig became aware of Panmure's intentions to unify the administration of military education, but he certainly had sight of Lefroy's memorandum and its proposal for a Director-General of Military Education, which would take over his responsibilities as Inspector -General for Military Schools. George Gleig was opinionated, forthrightly assertive, and arrogantly self-confident, but Sidney Herbert had found ways of working with him and harnessing his ambition and capacity for hard work to implement the reforms in the Army's schools. Herbert was known for his tact and common sense and his cool and subtle approach when handling difficult colleagues.[18] He respected Gleig's opinions even if he did not always accept them and speaking in the House of Commons in 1857 publicly acknowledged the benefit that he had derived from his advice and assistance.[19] In many ways the two men complemented each other, although it was always Herbert who was in command and had control over policy and the details of any reform. Once sure of his ground, Herbert worked quietly but effectively in gaining the support of the Treasury, his colleagues in Cabinet and the other military departments to effect change.

Lord Panmure was a different character; he was famous for his hot temper and was known in political circles as the 'the Bison'. It not surprising that the working relations between Panmure and Gleig were tetchy. Panmure had been annoyed by Gleig's vociferous and unexpected attack on Dr Du Sautoy's management of the Normal School in his 1849 report and he had sought an independent opinion from Professor Moseley, the Privy Council inspector. Moseley's report had cast doubt on

15   Lady Lefroy (ed.), *The Autobiography of General Sir John Henry Lefroy* (London; privately published, 1895), pp. 191-1

16   TNA WO 33/3B: War Office 'Reports and Memoranda, pp. 5-6. The memorandum deals with the arrangements for the selection, education and training of Commissioned Officers.

17   Lady Lefroy, *The Autobiography of General Sir John Henry Lefroy*, pp. 191-192.

18   H.C.G. Matthew, Herbert Sidney, First Baron Herbert of Lea (1810-1861) <www.oxforddnb.com/view/article> (accessed 17th January 2015).

19   Debate on staff training in the Army 28th July 1857, Hansard Third Series, Vol. 157, pp. 569-608.

Gleig's judgement and subsequently Panmure issued guidance about the format that he was to follow in future inspections.

Panmure had little patience with Gleig's penchant for expressing unsolicited opinions, especially on matters that were outside his competence.[20] Both men were assertively self-confident, with strong and ambitious personalities. The relationship between the two had probably been deteriorating for some years and there was a growing animosity between them.

Gleig may have had some inkling that Panmure was considering changes in the administration of army education when in March 1856 he wrote to the Secretary of State with an observation about the Army Estimates. He noted that the Chaplain-General and Director of Schools was 'particularised as Head of a combined department' in the Estimates and wished to know the date when the combined department would come into operation and when he could begin to run it without reference to other 'authorities.' He believed that there was inconvenience and delay in having to submit every detail for his decisions for approval by the Secretary of State. Panmure replied by referring Gleig to his letter of appointment of July 1846 and reminded him that he was '…the mere adviser to the Secretary at War' and that with some specified exceptions all his 'official correspondence must be to and from the Secretary of State.'[21] Any other arrangement would be impossible, because only the Secretary of State was accountable to Parliament. Gleig replied by asserting that he was now to be designated 'Director of Schools' and not merely the inspector of army schools and that the restrictions original letter of appointment therefore could no longer apply. He asserted that he had no objection to referring or deferring to a higher authority on matters of policy, but unless the need to refer continually on trifling matters was removed, he could see no public advantage from the reorganised post. Panmure replied that he agreed that the Secretary of State should not be bothered with trifling matters, but what was a trifling matter remained to be defined. He then challenged Gleig to make a statement of what he considered should be the duties of a Director of Schools, indicating the matters the Director should deal with and those that should be referred to the Secretary of State.

Gleig responded with his usual energy and at the end of 1856 submitted a paper entitled: 'Army Education' in which he outlined detailed proposals for the Director's Responsibilities. He argued that military education should be under the control of the Secretary of State for War and must not be transferred to the Privy Council.[22] He

20   J. Sweetman, *Maule, Fox, second Baron Panmure and eleventh earl of Dalhousie (1801–1874)* <www.oxforddnb.com/view/article> (accessed 17th January 2015).

21   Correspondence between Gleig and Panmure, quoted in Jarvis, 'My Predecessor in Office', pp. 322-33; G.D Bart and G.D. Ramsey (ed), *The Panmure Papers* Vol. 2 (London: Hodder and Stoughton, 1908), 'Letter from Lord Panmure to Queen Victoria', 20 January 1857, pp. 341-2.

22   There was some speculation in 1856 that the Government might be considering placing the regimental schools under the inspection of the Education Committee of the Privy Council. Sidney Herbert in the debate in House of Commons on army education in June

insisted that the direction of army education should only be conducted by a responsible officer under the authority and responsible to the Secretary of State. The Secretary of State would issue regulations that the Director would have to obey and which he would enforce, but as the responsible officer the Director would receive all reports and carry out all correspondence on military education. He would also undertake all appointments and transfers and other personnel matters in the name of the Secretary of State. He would report directly to the Secretary of State or through the Under Secretary.[23]

Gleig was certainly playing for very high stakes by contending that he should no longer be a mere adviser to the Secretary of State but should have executive authority with regard to military Schools. He was prepared to go even further and argued in his paper that it was the duty of the Secretary at State to inaugurate an efficient system of education for the officers as well as the private soldiers in the Army.

In his *Quarterly Review* articles published in the 1840s Gleig had strongly criticised the education given to the officer cadets at the Royal Military College and the work of its senior department in preparing officers for staff appointments.[24] It is likely that when Herbert was at the War Office in the 1850s, Gleig had pressed for reforms in the education and training of officers, although this did not fall within his remits either as the Chaplain General or the Inspector- General of Military Schools.[25] Always ambitious and with an eye for new career opportunities, this now appeared to be Gleig's main interest in the field of military education. Moreover, during the winter of 1856-57, he submitted further memoranda criticising proposals made by Lieutenant Colonel Lefroy and the C-in-C, the Duke of Cambridge, for the administration of military education and the education and training of army officers.[26]

It is difficult to believe that Gleig seriously expected Panmure to concede such extensive powers over the regimental schools or to sanction his involvement in any the discussions about reforms in the education of commissioned officers. He surely would have been aware that his relations with the Secretary of State were fragile, and by asserting that the holder of the new post should be granted executive responsibility for Army schools, he was implying this was a necessary condition for his continuation in office. He must have known that this would have been unacceptable and had probably

1856 explained that he had seen a minute of the Privy Council to this effect. He described the proposal as both objectionable and fanciful because commanding officers would be totally opposed to the involvement of civilians in regimental matters. Frederick Peel, the Under Secretary of State for War replied assuring Herbert that the idea had never seriously been entertained. Nevertheless, Gleig felt it necessary to oppose the idea at some length in his paper: 'Army Education'.

23   TNA WO 33/3A: ,'G. Gleig, Memorandum on Army Education', pp. 72-96.
24   Gleig, 'Moral Discipline of the Army', pp. 387-424; 'Education and Lodging of the Soldier', pp. 526-63; 'Military Education', pp. 419-50.
25   'House of Commons Debate on Staff Training in the Army, 28th July 1857', Hansard Third Series, Vol. 147, pp. 569-608.
26   TNA WO 33/3B: Section 73/98.

concluded that Panmure intended to replace him as Inspector General of Military Schools and nothing would be lost by placing his views on the administration of army education on record. This fencing between Gleig and Panmure about the extent of the proposed Director of Education's powers was soon overshadowed by a larger and more fundamental disagreement about the control of military education.

The education and training of officers had surfaced as a politically sensitive issue following the criticism in the press and parliament about Army's performance during the Crimean War. William Russell, the war correspondent of *The Times* was scathing in his criticism of the military administration and the efficiency of the commanding generals and their staff in the Crimea. A leading article in the newspaper in December 1854 declared that '...the noblest army England ever sent from these shores has been sacrificed to the grossest mismanagement.' Although the Royal Military College at Sandhurst which trained officer cadets (other than for the artillery and engineers) was under the jurisdiction of the C-in-C, the Prime Minister Lord Palmerston could not ignore the public criticisms of the Army's leadership and he appointed a Select Committee to inquire into the work of the College. Its report of July 1855 contained some highly critical testimony on the current state of military education and the low value that was placed on professional training for officers. The Government responded by establishing a commission under the chairmanship of Lieutenant Colonel W. Yolland, Royal Engineers, to consider the best mode of reorganising the system of training officers and for the scientific corps. Its report in 1857 recommended, inter-alia, a single authority to oversee all aspects of military education, by which time Panmure had already reached a similar conclusion.[27]

The Duke of Cambridge was opposed to greater political control of the Army by the War Office and was certainly unwilling to allow the education of officers to be taken out of his hands. He quickly had produced a memorandum setting out proposals for a 'Special Educational Department' presided over by a Director-General for the selection, education, training, and the promotion of officers under the control of the C-in-C at the Horse Guards.[28] He then appealed directly to his cousin Queen Victoria outlining his opposition to Panmure's proposals. There was a copious exchange of correspondence on the matter between the Queen and Panmure during the early part of 1857, with the Queen suspicious of any attempt to curtail her prerogative powers and the C-in-C's authority. For his part, Panmure insisted that only the Secretary of State could be answerable to Parliament for the administration of the Army. The impasse did not arise from the Queen's objection to Panmure's wish to place Colonel Lefroy in charge of the regimental and garrison schools, but to his proposal to create a post of Director-General of Education at the War Office, which included

27 Report of Commissioners Appointed to Consider the Best Mode of Reorganising the System for Training Officers and for the Scientific Corps, House of Commons Sessional Papers 1857, pp. xix –xxi.
28 TNA WO 33/3A: Section 73/98.

responsibility for the education of army officers. The Queen protested that the transfer of this responsibility from the Horse Guards to the Secretary of State would weaken the C-in-C's authority over the Army and endanger the exercise of her prerogative powers.[29]

In the end a compromise was agreed. Panmure explained to the Queen that Gleig held '...the double appointment of Chaplain-General and Inspector-General of Schools', but that this had become too great a workload for one person. He therefore proposed that the two posts should be separated. Gleig would relinquish the post of Inspector-General of Schools to concentrate on his responsibilities as the Chaplain -General for the growing number of chaplains in the Army. He dropped the proposal for a Director General of Army Education and proposed that Colonel Lefroy should be appointed to the lesser post of Inspector-General of Army Schools, with responsibility limited to the regimental and garrison schools, military libraries and reading rooms. A Council of Military Education would be established, but with responsibility initially only for the education of officers. The C-in-C would be its President subject to the overall control of the Secretary of State.[30]

In February 1857, the Queen approved Colonel Lefroy's appointment and he was gazetted as Inspector-General of the Regimental and Garrison schools, Military Libraries and Reading Rooms on 6th March 1857.[31] Gleig ceased to be Inspector General of Military Schools, but he retained the post of Chaplain-General for the next eighteen years. The War Office quickly issued an order to the Army Chaplains stating that they no longer had any responsibility for regimental schools. This order may have been issued to prevent Gleig from using his position as Chaplain-General to meddle in the schools, but it was also a statement of the underlying reality that there was now an embryonic system of inspection for the work of the trained army schoolmasters in some 150 regimental and garrison schools.[32] There has been a failure to acknowledge that from July 1846 Gleig held two appointments at the War Office. His important contributions to the reform of army education had been made in his capacity as the Inspector General of Military Schools, and not in the revived post of Chaplain General. This has been the source of much subsequent misunderstanding.

There had been good reasons in July 1846 for George Gleig to be appointed to the new post of Inspector of Military Schools, whilst also holding the post of Chaplain-General, but Herbert had never intended that they would always be conjoined appointments. In 1857 the pioneering days in the reform of army education were over and good progress had already been made in embedding the new system of army schools. The students who were educated and trained at the Normal School were

29   G.D. Bart and G.D. Ramsey (eds.), *The Panmure Papers*, Vol. 2, pp. 341-42, 351-2.
30   G.D. Bart and G.D. Ramsey (eds.), *The Panmure Papers*, Vol. 2, p. 352.
31   G.D. Bart and G.D. Ramsey (eds.), *The Panmure Papers*, Vol. 2, p. 355. Lady Lefroy (ed.) *The Autobiography of General Sir John Henry Lefroy*, p. 194.
32   Lefroy, *Report on the regimental and Garrison Schools of the Army*, p. 67.

appointed to the post of army schoolmaster and were enlisted as soldiers under the Mutiny Act. Almost one third of the trained schoolmasters had been serving NCOs and a growing number had been paid monitors at the RMA and RHMS and had served for two years as assistant Army schoolmasters before entering the Normal School. All schoolmasters could earn promotion on merit and become First Class schoolmasters with the warrant officer rank. A small number of trained schoolmasters were in effect already acting as assistant inspectors in the colonies and in time more would assume this responsibility in Great Britain and Ireland the British Isles and across the Empire.

The increasing army chaplain supervision workload for the Chaplain-General, the growing animosity between Panmure and Gleig, and the emergence of what was in effect of an embryonic corps of army schoolmasters, was sufficient reason for Gleig to be replaced as Inspector General. He was to be replaced by a professional soldier, with the rank and a record that would ensure his standing throughout the Army, and who could in the aftermath of the Crimean War, bring about a more secular and military focus to education in its schools.

15

Lieutenant Colonel Lefroy's 1859 Report

Lieutenant Colonel Lefroy served as Inspector-General of Army Schools until the post was abolished in 1860 and during this short time at the War Office he produced the seminal *Report on the Regimental and Garrison Schools of the Army and on Military Libraries and Reading Rooms, 1859,* which drew together the main achievements of the reforms implemented from 1846 and identified the obstacles to further progress. He personally visited 26 stations in England and 12 in Ireland and incorporated reports from the three Assistant Inspectors in the British Isles, and others from India, Gibraltar, Malta, and a number of other colonial garrisons to produce a detailed picture of the education provided for the British soldier and his children.[1]

Despite the difficulties of attracting sufficient suitable candidates for training at the Normal School, 178 schoolmasters had been trained by 1858, and 157 were still in post. There were trained schoolmasters with the three regiments of Household Cavalry, all the battalions of the Foot Guards, seven of the stations of the Royal Artillery; with six regiments of cavalry, 91 service battalions of the infantry of the line, 19 depot battalions, and with five colonial corps.[2] Although the work was incomplete, the creation of such a large body of trained army schoolmasters stands as a fine tribute to the work of Dr Du Sautoy at the Normal School, who gave these men a much needed further education, and arguably more so to Walter McLeod at the Model School under whose supervision and guidance they gained the skills and confidence to teach large classes of children and adults in the Army's schools across the Empire.

In April 1858, the War Office removed the post of sergeant schoolmaster from the establishments of the regular cavalry and infantry of the line. In 1857, however, in

---

1 Major T.A. Bowyer-Bower, 'Some Sources for the History of Education in the British Army during the 19th Century', *British Journal of Educational Studies,* Vol. 4, No 1 (November 1955), p.72. Lefroy's Report was quoted extensively in 'The Report of the Commissioners appointed to enquire into the State of Popular Education in England (The Newcastle Commission), Vol.1, Part IV, and State Schools'.
2 Lefroy, Report on the Regimental and Garrison Schools, pp. 15-24.

Lt Colonel J. H. Lefroy (1817-1890), Inspector General of Military Schools (1817-90), by J.W. Beattie c. 1880. (J.W. Beattie, *The Governors of Tasmania: from 1804 to 1896*)

order to augment British troops in India following the Mutiny and the subsequent uprising the 2nd to the 25th regiment's of foot were given a second battalion. Lefroy reported that 55 infantry battalions, 47 of which were overseas remained without schoolmasters. Unless there was a trained garrison schoolmaster, these regiments had to rely on their own resources and continue to appoint one of their NCOs to conduct the schools. It was always difficult and in young battalions almost impossible, to find men qualified for the duties of schoolmaster.[3] The problem did not stop with the Regular Army. There were also regiments of the embodied militia requiring masters for their schools. In the Militia regiments an allowance of £60 per annum had been made available for engaging a civilian teacher, but such was the demand for good masters in civilian schools that many COs reported that they were unable to do so and only six trained masters had been attached to them.

This was at the expense of providing trained schoolmasters for the same number of battalions of the line.[4] Lefroy calculated that at least 60 more trained masters were required to meet the demands of the regular regiments and embodied militia and that this number could not be supplied from the Normal School at Chelsea in less than three years.[5] In the meantime the Inspector-General could only recommend that the allowance payable to the soldier assistants sanctioned in the 1854 Army School Regulations should be increased to encourage their recruitment and retention.[6]

---

3   Lefroy, *Report on the Regimental and Garrison Schools*, pp. 15-24; TNA WO 380/3: pp. 3,4.
4   The County Militia had been revived in Great Britain in 1854 and in Ireland in 1855.
5   Lefroy, *Report on the Regimental and Garrison Schools*, p. 82.
6   Lefroy, *Report on the Regimental and Garrison Schools*, pp. 82-3.

Colonel Lefroy provided information in his report to show the extent of challenge facing the military authorities in improving army education. Statistics compiled by the Adjutant General based on returns from regiments showed that 20.5 percent of the enlisted men could neither read nor write and a further 18.8percent could read but barely sign their name. During the Crimean War the British Government resurrected the practice adopted during the Revolutionary and Napoleonic Wars of establishing corps of foreign volunteers to deal with the Army's shortage of manpower. The literacy rates in the British regular regiments and corps compared very unfavourably with those of the recruits for the 'British Foreign Legion.' In 1855, 4,312 German recruits passed through the Heligoland recruiting depot, but only 3percent could neither read nor write.[7] In total slightly more than 39 percent of the men in the British Army were classed as 'uneducated' [could neither read nor write] and were in urgent need of an elementary education, although the situation showed wide variations across the various regiments and corps.

The Corps of Engineers rarely accepted recruits who could neither read nor write and the Brigade of Guards had a much higher proportion of men who could both read and write (79 percent) than the line infantry(55.4percent), even though most of the Guards' recruits came from agricultural areas. Lefroy believed this was because of the encouragement given to the men in the Brigade's battalion schools and also the efficiency and high rate of average daily attendance at the Guards' depot school at Croydon. In 1858, 2,250 out of the 4,200 men in the Brigade attended school and the average daily attendance was 41 percent.

The largest number of men in the Army served in the infantry and 44. 6 percent of these men were classed as 'uneducated.' The proportion of men in the cavalry who could neither read nor write was some four percentage points below the figure for the Guards, which stood at (24.8 percent) and was well below that for the infantry. Lefroy however did not choose to comment on the relative figures for the cavalry.

There were also a surprisingly large proportion of uneducated men (40.4 percent) in the artillery. Lefroy speculated that this was because 11,985 men had been recruited into the regiment from 1854-57 to meet the needs of the Army in the Crimea and India. These men had little opportunity to attend school because they were often dispersed in small detachments. He recommended that the elementary education of the gunners should be made a priority.[8]

Soldiers who were illiterate and wished to attend the adult school were enrolled in the fourth or lowest class to learn how to read and write and master the first four rules of arithmetic. According to the regimental returns submitted in 1857 all the men attending school in 49 battalions of the infantry were in the lowest class. When a soldier could read '...tolerably well and write a little from dictation' and had mastered the basics of arithmetic, he joined the third class where he started the

7   Lefroy, *Report on the Regimental and Garrison Schools*, p. 8.
8   Lefroy, *Report on the Regimental and Garrison Schools*, pp. 6-7.

study of history and geography. Further progress in literacy and numeracy earned promotion to the second class and then to the first, where in addition to history and geography, he learnt elements of grammar, simple equations and some geometry and mechanics.[9]

Colonel Lefroy asked a number of the most experienced Army schoolmasters for their views on the length of time that was needed to teach an uneducated young man to read and write intelligibly and to master the four simple rules of arithmetic. His report contains a reply from Army Schoolmaster First Class John Little, who was in charge of the garrison school at the New Barracks at Limerick. Little was rated one of the best army schoolmasters and was in charge of the largest adult school in Ireland. He reported that he had 31 men in the school who had an average attendance of less than three hours per week and were able to read fluently, write pretty correctly from dictation and had mastered multiplication, all in six months. These men however were prepared to do homework in their barrack rooms when off duty. Little also reported that there were 140 men who attended his school on average for less than two hours per week over the same six-month period and were barely able to read and write and do any additions. He admitted that it required greater ingenuity to manage a class of soldiers than of children; but he believed that more could be achieved with smaller classes, especially where there were not more than ten men in each class of beginners. Although he was able to rely upon trained assistant masters to manage the advanced classes in his schools, Little considered that they were of little use and generally could not be trusted. He concluded that a young man of even a very moderate intelligence who attended regularly for two hours per week over nine months ought to be able to master the basics of literacy and numeracy under a well-trained master. He regretted however that many soldiers did not do so well because regimental duties prevented regular attendance.[10]

Following the advice from John Little and other army schoolmasters, Lefroy concluded that it was reasonable to expect that a trained schoolmaster could teach soldiers of average intelligence to read and write and do simple arithmetic in around twelve months, provided they attended regularly for four hours per week.[11] The available returns for the regular army in 1857 recorded that there were 26,918 soldiers on the books of the regimental and garrison schools, but the average daily attendance was only 9,623 men. In short regularity of attendance was the main obstacle to progress.

The long voyages under sail between stations across the Empire had seriously affected attendance the men's attendance at school and their progress, but the introduction of large steam troopships for the passage to India in the 1850s enabled schoolmasters to organise schools for the men during the voyages. From December

9   Lefroy, *Report on the Regimental and Garrison Schools*, p. 12.
10   Lefroy, *Report on the Regimental and Garrison Schools*, pp. 173-5.
11   Lefroy, *Report on the Regimental and Garrison Schools*, p. 8.

1857 to January 1858 the trained schoolmaster attached to the 44th Foot organised a school attended by 189 men on the regiment's voyage to Madras. The schoolmaster of the 95th managed a school attended by three hundred and twenty men on route to Bombay from July to October 1857.[12]

More generally however the frequent movement of regiments and the stationing of men in small detachments to assist the civil authorities at home and abroad continued to disrupt schooling. Attendance was not always treated as a priority and men were often pulled out of schools by NCOs for the most trivial reasons that would not have been accepted during parades, drills and rifle practice. Men became discouraged by their lack of progress and the schoolmasters found it difficult to manage their schools. On some days they had few pupils, whilst on others they had too many. The result of all of this was that the instruction of the men in the adult school rarely extended beyond the lowest class. This was illustrated by the experience of the School of Musketry at Hythe in 1856-57, which was able to find only 44 suitable recruits from 121 applicants for its corps of instructors, because of deficiencies in the candidate's reading and writing.[13]

Lefroy identified two obstacles in the way of introducing a well-regulated system of attendance for soldiers at the adult schools. The first was legal, and he sought professional advice on the question of whether enlisted men could be ordered to attend school. He was advised that the situation had not changed since the judgement in the Warden v. Bailey case in 1811, and that neither NCOs, privates, drummers nor enlisted boy soldiers, could be lawfully disciplined for refusing to attend. Lefroy observed that for many years however the practice had been at variance with the 1811 Ruling. Some COs exerted considerable pressure on recruits to attend and many regiments had adopted standing orders requiring attendance as a condition for promotion to the rank of NCO for those men who could not demonstrate a satisfactory standard of elementary education.

In June 1857 the Duke of Cambridge ordered that no man who had not satisfactorily passed out of the lowest class at the regimental school and was not 'tolerably advanced' in reading and writing could be promoted corporal, although he was not prepared to make this a requirement for promotion to sergeant.[14] Lefroy concluded that further progress could only be made by amending the Articles of War and the Mutiny Act to introduce the legal power to order men to attend school.

The second obstacle was the contentious issue of charging fees for instruction in the regimental and garrison schools. In 1857, fees had been abolished for men in the fourth or lowest class at the schools but remained payable by those studying in the more advanced classes. Lefroy concluded that the abolition of fees for the lowest class

12   Lefroy, *Report on the Regimental and Garrison Schools*, p. 19.
13   Lefroy, *Report on the Regimental and Garrison Schools*, pp. 9, 27-9.
14   Lefroy, *Report on the Regimental and Garrison Schools*, p.13; 'War Office Circular from Lefroy, 20/7/1857' and 'General Order 686, 19/6/1857', p. 11.

had encouraged men to attend, but the retention of fees for the higher classes was a tax on progress and a disincentive to attendance. He thought that the revenue yielded from fees, which was an average of £2,300 per annum in the years 1854-56 when fees were paid by all adults, was trivial. He recommended their total abolition.[15]

Most of Colonel Lefroy's report was devoted to the adult schools and the training of Army schoolmasters at the Normal School, but he also dealt with the new arrangements that had been introduced for the children's schools. Although Gleig asserted that the Army's schools were intended primarily for the education of NCOs and private soldiers, the 1850 and 1854 Army School Regulations had established separate 'Infant' and 'Grown Children' schools. The infant schools were managed and taught by a schoolmistress leaving the trained army schoolmaster free to run the 'Grown Children' and Adult schools. Children were normally admitted to the Infant School around five years of age and progressed into the Grown Children School when they could read words of two syllables. The majority of children in the schools were between five and twelve years of age, but a small proportion remained at school until they were fifteen years.

The Army School Regulations specified that the children's classes should take place in the mornings after prayers. In India the hours were varied because of the climate with sessions taking place in the early mornings and late afternoons. Boys and girls were taught together in most schools, although the girls were taught separately in the large schools at Woolwich Depot of the Royal Artillery. Lefroy recommended that where there were large numbers of girls and staffing was available boys and girls should always be taught in separate classes.[16]

Gleig had provided the House of Commons with a return of the number of boys and girls at the regimental and garrison schools for 1851-52. Lefroy attempted to arrive at comparable figures for the Infant and Grown children schools for 1858 but was unable to obtain returns from 68 units. A large proportion of these were regiments sent as reinforcements to India. They had left their women and children at home and some of these children were counted as attending the depot and garrison schools. In other cases the regiments were composed largely of young soldiers without wives and children. From the available returns Lefroy was able to record a combined total 11,062 children on the registers of both categories of school. He thought it reasonable to conclude that the actual figure was probably around 12,000, which was a considerable increase (approximately 5,000 children) above the numbers recorded in Gleig's earlier return.

15   Lefroy, *Report on the Regimental and Garrison Schools*, p. 13.
16   Lefroy, *Report on the Regimental and Garrison Schools*, pp. 34-37. The trained schoolmaster was expected to make regular visits to the infant schools.

Table 14. Number of children at the regimental and garrison schools 1858

	Boys	Girls	Total
Infant schools	2661	2689	5350
Grown children	3122	2590	5712
Total	5783	5279	11062

It is not possible to make a direct and meaningful comparison between Lefroy's estimate of the numbers of children on the registers of the army's school for 1858 and number recorded in Gleig's Parliamentary Return for 1851. The establishment of the regular army had been increased from 130,000 in 1851 to 223,000 in 1858. This increase included the Royal Artillery and Engineers and the recently embodied militia.[17]

There was no legal obligation for solders to send their children to school, although many COs continued to place considerable pressure on the families to do so. Some parents objected to their children attending on religious grounds and this was invariably respected. In 1858 the Army School Regulations were amended to make it easier for parents to withdraw them from prayers and religious education. Lefroy thought that most parents were keen for their children to attend and that absence and truanting by children on the school registers was probably no more frequent than in civilian schools. However, as with the Adult schools, irregular attendance caused by incessant changes of station of the troops was a significant issue that limited the children's' progress, with very few advancing beyond the elementary stage.[18]

The 1850-54 Regulations had authorised industrial schools to provide instruction by the schoolmistress in needlework and knitting and this was scheduled to take place in the afternoons after the infant and grown children's schools. Lefroy commended Gleig's work in establishing the industrial schools and considered that they were especially important in providing useful occupational training for girls. He acknowledged that Gleig had hoped to introduce additional trades specifically for boys at a later date, when resources became available. Meantime boys were allowed to attend at the industrial schools along with the girls and Lefroy reported that in total around 5,000 children were receiving instruction at these schools.[19]

Teaching trade skills to soldiers' children was not a new idea and was a well-established practice at the RMA and the RHMS. In his correspondence with the commissioners of the RMA in 1842, Sir Henry Hardinge had envisaged that the practice might be extended to the regimental schools. Extending instruction beyond

17   Fortescue, *A History of the British Army*, Vol. XIII , pp. 21,526.
18   Lefroy, *Report on the Regimental and Garrison Schools*, pp. 34-7.
19   Lefroy, *Report on the Regimental and Garrison Schools*, p. 36.

needlework and knitting was hardly a practical proposition when soldiers and their families units moved regularly, sometimes in detachments, between stations. Even in the larger barracks there would have been considerable expense in establishing garrison workshops to instruct the boys in trades and occupations.

Colonel Lefroy was impressed with a scheme that had been introduced by the Second Class Schoolmaster at the Colchester barracks, where 18 children were assigned to domestic duties in the Women's Wash Room on one day each week.[20] In a similar vein, Mr Sargeaunt, the Assistant Inspector for North Britain, proposed that on one afternoon per week a number of boys and girls might be employed in scrubbing the schoolroom floors, cleaning grates and learning every aspect of household work that presents itself. He argued that this would be useful training for boys, because the sons of soldiers were likely to earn a living doing unskilled or manual labour. Domestic work around the barracks would make them strong and give them an aptitude for hard work. This not untypical view that the children of the labouring classes needed only the rudiments of an elementary education and that for a good part of each day their might be more usefully employed in domestic work was something that was to feature in discussions about the content of army education well into the 1880s.

More immediately, the success of the new system of schooling for the children in the regimental and garrison schools depended on recruiting suitably qualified schoolmistresses to take charge of the infants and industrial schools. The scheme for the employment of paid schoolmistresses, introduced by the War Office in 1840, had specified that the persons appointed should be qualified to teach the girls reading and writing, a little arithmetic and needlecraft and other useful household skills. A Circular in November 1840 had ordered that COs in making appointments should pay careful attention to the morals and habits of the applicants and they were advised that they were likely to find qualified persons amongst the wives of their NCOs.[21] It would be necessary to interrogate the pay rolls of all the regiments and corps on the Army's to identify how many paid schoolmistresses were engaged during the 1840's, but probably most of those appointed were the wives or daughters of soldiers in the regiment.

Lefroy explained that candidates for appointment as army schoolmistresses, who were not otherwise specifically qualified, were sent at the public expense to one of the following teacher training institutions for a six or twelve months course: Home and Colonial Training Institution, Grey's Inn Road, Middlesex; Wesleyan Training Institution, Westminster; National Society's Training Institution in Dublin ; Free Church National Training in Glasgow and Free Church National Training Institution in Edinburgh.

20   Lefroy, *Report on the Regimental and Garrison Schools*, pp. 22-3. Six girls were occupied for two hours on laundry work and six worked for two hours cleaning plates and cutlery. Six boys were assigned to clean brasses and candlesticks.
21   TNA WO 43/752; ff. 182-183, 'Circular No. 874, November 1840'.

The candidates were not to be under eighteen, or over thirty-five years of age. They were to have a good standard of literacy and numeracy, knowledge of sacred history and geography, be competent in needlework and ideally also have a taste and ear for music, especially singing. A certificate from a clergyman of their denomination was required declaring that they were of good moral character and 'in disposition and temper' were fit for the duties of an infant schoolmistress.[22]

In 1858 there were 44 trained schoolmistresses (excluding the artillery) attached to regiments and depots. A further 31, many of whom were the wives of trained army schoolmasters, were rated as trained because of their merit and efficiency. There were always difficulties in securing the requisite numbers of trained schoolmistresses. There was no shortage of candidates for training, but very often they were the wives and daughters of NCOs and although these women often possessed the personal qualities that were required, they generally had a poor standard of education.

Qualified married women wished to remain with their husbands' regiments where their services as a schoolmistress might not be required, but they could not be posted to other units where there were vacancies. Simultaneously, the authorities were reluctant 'for reasons of prudence' to undertake the widespread employment of young single women. The Inspector reporting on the regimental and garrison schools in Ireland commented: '...the peculiarities of their position in the barracks, the temptations to which they are exposed, render it expedient that schoolmistresses should be either married women or women of advanced years.' The majority of units therefore remained without a trained schoolmistress and their infant's schools was superintended by the schoolmaster and where there was an industrial school this was conducted with the assistance of one or more women from the regiment.[23]

Colonel Lefroy's Report is important because it draws together a great deal of information about the results of the reforms in Army education that had been introduced since 1846 and had been consolidated and extended by the first Inspector-General working under the firm leadership and with the political support of Herbert and Panmure. The description of the elementary education provided by the garrison and regimental schools was extensive and was quoted at length in the 1861 Report of the Commissioners appointed to enquire into the State of Popular Education in England (the Newcastle report).[24]

Lieutenant Colonel Lefroy's account of the Army schools however was incomplete because of the embryonic arrangements for inspection and the difficulty in securing detailed returns from all the military stations throughout the Empire. None the less he identified what already had been achieved and identified the obstacles to further progress. He pointed to the limitations in the arrangements for the inspection of the

22 Lefroy, *Report on the Regimental and Garrison Schools*, pp. 174-5.
23 Lefroy, Report on the Regimental and Garrison Schools, pp. 47, 94.
24 1861 Report of the Commissioners appointed to enquire into the State of Popular Education in England. (The Newcastle Commission), Vol. 1, Part IV, 'State Schools'.

schools and recommended the creation of a class of commissioned army schoolmasters to superintend and report on the larger garrisons such as Aldershot and Dublin with their thousands of adult scholars and large numbers of children.[25]

25   Lefroy, *Report on the Regimental and Garrison Schools*, p. 83.

16

Consolidation: The Regimental Schools in the 1860s

The considerable advances in the provision of army education since 1846 owed a great deal to the work of the two successive Inspector-Generals of Army Schools, both of whom had enjoyed the political support and leadership provided by Sidney Herbert and Lord Panmure at the War Office. Herbert had continued to take an interest in the Army after leaving office in 1855. When Palmerston formed his second government in 1859, Herbert was appointed Secretary of State for War. His immediate priorities were to consolidate the new office, transfer the Indian army from the East India Company to the Crown, and introduce new rifled ordnance. There was also a highly controversial war with China from 1859-60, but more important was a growing fear of war with France and Herbert began work on a programme of military expansion, with increases in the army estimates and a programme of coastal fortifications.[1]

It was decided to free Lieutenant Colonel John Lefroy from his responsibilities for the Army's schools to work on improving coastal fortifications.[2] In 1860 the Council of Military Education took over the supervision of the Army's schools and libraries. The post of Inspector-General was abolished and for the next ten years the Council was responsible for the selection, training, discipline, and promotion of the schoolmasters and the superintendence of the regimental, depot and garrison schools.[3] The Council was responsible to the Secretary of State through its President who was the C-in-C, but in practice its work was handled by a small number of members, who with one exception were all senior army officers.[4] The Council had only limited

---

1   Sidney Herbert, *Oxford Dictionary of National Biography* <www.oxforddnb.com/articles/13/13047> (accessed 17th January 2015).
2   Lefroy left the Army in 1870 with the honorary rank of Major General and entered the Colonial Service, subsequently serving as Governor of Bermuda (1871-77) and Administrator of Tasmania (1880-81).
3   War Office Circular 566, 10/03/1860.
4   The original membership in 1857 included a major general commanding a brigade, a colonel of engineers who had experience of inspecting the RMA at Woolwich and a Lt Colonel on the Staff. In 1858 this was augmented with a colonel of artillery with

executive authority and no financial powers. It operated on an ad hoc basis, without a formal agenda, resolving issues through discussion as they arose. The Council did not include any senior civil servants from the War Office. The only civilian member was Rev Henry Moseley, who had extensive experience of inspecting civilian schools and also was well acquainted with the RMA. He helped with the examination of candidates for entry to the Normal School and continued to inspect the Model School but had no experience of inspecting the regimental and garrison schools.[5]

For the regimental and garrison schools the Council relied on reports from three permanent Assistant Inspectors in the United Kingdom. Captain (subsequently Lieutenant Colonel) A.C. Gleig was responsible for inspecting Division 1. This covered London, Aldershot, the South-eastern Military District, Woolwich, Chatham and Colchester and was the largest division normally containing 61 adult, 63 grown children's and 58 infant and industrial schools. Mr J.P. Sargeaunt was responsible for Division 11, which covered Scotland, the Northern, Western and South Western Military Districts. This division usually contained 39 Adult, 44 Grown Children's and 30 Infant and industrial schools. Mr E. A. Vicars was responsible for Division 111, which covered all the military stations in Ireland and contained usually 40 Adult, 40 Grown Children's and 34 Infant and Industrial Schools.

In the larger garrisons abroad such as Gibraltar, Malta, and Corfu (until the Ionian Islands were transferred to Greece in 1864) reports were provided by inspectors selected from the staff and regimental officers of the local garrisons. Superintending schoolmasters were subsequently appointed for Upper and Lower Canada and occasionally visited other military schools in North America.[6]

A separate system of inspection and superintendence was developing in the three Indian Presidencies. An Inspector of Army Schools was appointed by the Government of India for the Madras Presidency and superintendents of schools were selected from Army schoolmasters and granted the local rank of captain in the Bombay and Bengal Presidencies. They could inspect schools but could not issue instructions and only make recommendations to the higher authority in each presidency.[7] Reports on the schools in India were received by the Council from time to time, but they were not in the form that enabled the Council to amalgamate them with the report from the Divisional inspectors in the UK. In 1863 the Council proposed a scheme for amalgamating the inspectors on the Imperial and Indian establishment, but this required the approval of the Secretary of State for India, which remained in abeyance

experience of inspecting the RMA Woolwich and the Rev Moseley who was involved inter alia in the competitive examinations for entry to Woolwich.

5   *First General Report by the Council of Military Education 1860*, p. i.
6   *Fourth Report by the Council of Military Education on Army Schools, Libraries and Recreations Rooms 1866*, pp. vi-vii.
7   *First Report by the Council of Military Education on Army Schools, Libraries and Recreations Rooms 1862*, p. ii.

throughout the 1860s.[8] The largely separate development of the system for the Army schools in India is considered in the following chapter.

In 1861 Sidney Herbert, now created Lord Herbert of Lea, decided it was time to evaluate the changes in the management of the regimental schools that had been introduced since 1846, their effectiveness in providing education for soldiers and their children, and the cost and value for money of the new system. In February 1861, the Secretary of State requested the C-in-C to direct the Council to ask for reports from each of the assistant inspectors of schools. They were asked to reflect on information gained from inspecting the regimental schools and make suggestions for improvements in the system. Reports on the working of the system were also requested from a few of the most experienced schoolmasters and the COs of some of the larger depots. The Council was requested to consider the reports and send its observations and recommendations for change to the Secretary of State.[9]

The assistant inspectors interpreted their briefs widely and produced lengthy reports characterised by some plain speaking. It appeared that the reformed regimental schools had not met with universal approval in the Army and that there were a number of major obstacles to further progress. The assistant inspectors and schoolmasters' reports were published as an appendix to the First Report of the Council on Army Schools in 1862, but it was decided in a Council Minute dated 31st July 1861 that any recommendations for consideration by the Secretary of State should not be included in the initial report. During 1862 and early 1863 there were discussions between the Council, the C-in-C, and the Secretary of State for War regarding projected changes in organisation of the Army's schools. These changes were finally agreed by the Government and promulgated in a new set of Army School Regulations in May 1863.[10] The Council Minute however was not published until 1865, when it was included in its Second Report on Army Schools. One factor for this delay was the heavy workload at the War Office following the re-organisation of the military department exacerbated by a succession of Secretaries of State.

Unfortunately, ill-health forced Lord Herbert to resign in July 1861. He was succeeded, reluctantly, by Sir George Cornewall Lewis until his death in April 1863, when he in turn was succeeded by Earl de Grey. The Assistant Inspectors' and Army schoolmasters' reports raised a number of sensitive issues for the military departments and some of the Council's responses and recommendations were critical of COs and others would prove to be unpopular with many of the serving Army schoolmasters.

8   *Fourth Report by the Council of Military Education on Army Schools etc.*, pp. vii-viii. Any reports received on schools in India were included as appendices in the Council's Reports on Army Schools.

9   *First Report by the Council of Military Education on Army Schools etc.*, Appendix II, p. 32.

10   *Second Report by the Council of Military Education on Army Schools, Libraries, and Recreation Rooms1865*, p. i. The Council's Minute of July 1861 was included as Appendix No I of this report.

The Council's 1861 Minute paid attention to the issues around the appointment, status, pay, and pension of the schoolmaster and was careful to ensure that its recommendations were in harmony with the Army's regimental system. Over the years two routes had developed by which a candidate could become qualified as an army schoolmaster. The first was by competitive examination for appointment as a monitor at the Model School at the RMA or at the RHMS.[11] The candidates for the posts were 16 to18 years of age and after serving for two years at Chelsea or Phoenix Park they were enlisted in the army as an assistant schoolmaster (Fourth -Class). They served in that capacity for two years at pay of 2s per day under the supervision of a First Class Army Schoolmaster at a garrison or depot school. On satisfactory completion of this apprenticeship they became a student at the Normal School at the RMA, where they remained for one or one and a half years, followed by six months teaching practice at the Model School. On passing the course they were appointed Third Class Schoolmasters. They were not paid as assistant schoolmasters during their time as students at Chelsea and received only a uniform, board and lodging, and 'pocket money' of £6.6s 0d per annum.[12]

The second route was by direct entry to the Normal School through a competitive examination without an apprenticeship as an assistant army schoolmaster. The competitions were advertised and candidates had to be between 19 and 25 years and unmarried. The examination was open to civilians and also NCOs, not below the rank of corporal. Successful candidates remained as students at the Normal School for one and a half years and after being examined by independent civilian examiners moved to the six-month's teaching practice at the Model School. Those successful were appointed Third-Class Schoolmasters. The NCOs were on furlough from their regiments whilst at the Normal School and wore the uniforms of their regiments and drew army pay less stoppages whilst at the School. If unsuccessful during training or dismissed for any reason they were returned to their regiment. Those who were successful resigned from their regiments and re-enlisted as army schoolmasters. The civilian students were not paid, but like the ex-monitors they wore the uniform of the School and received board and lodging and 'pocket money' of £6.6s.0d per annum.[13] They were not enlisted in the Army as schoolmasters until they had passed out from the Normal School.

On 31st March 1861, there were 39 students at the Normal School of who nine were on teaching practice in the Model School. Fourteen were from the RMA or RHMS and had previously served monitors before enlistment as assistant schoolmasters. Seven were NCOs in the Army and two were NCOs in the Royal Marines. The other

11   Many of the successful candidates for the post of monitor were boys already at the Model School and the RHMS.
12   *Second Report by the Council of Military Education on Army Schools etc.*, p.i.
13   *Second Report by the Council of Military Education on Army Schools etc.*, p.i.

16 were civilians and with three exceptions, all had previously been pupil teachers or certificated schoolmasters in civilian schools.[14]

There was still difficulty in attracting civilian candidates to train as army schoolmasters. Most applicants had only a limited education and the Council began to show a marked preference for applicants who were serving NCOs. This was probably because as enlisted soldiers with experience of serving under military discipline, they adapted more easily to regimental life. It however was thought that some promising NCOs did not apply for entry to the Normal School because they feared that they would not be as well prepared for the examination as the civilian candidates. In consequence, an experiment was tried in August 1860 and again in the February 1861, whereby three places in the examinations were reserved for applications from NCOs and seven for civilians. It was found that under this system some NCOs who would have gained a place in an open competition had to be rejected. In a minute of July 1861, the Council decided to return to an open competition and argued that with proper encouragement there were sufficient men in the Army with the potential to be successfully trained as schoolmasters. It was noted that four of the most eminent schoolmasters, who were superintending the schools at Aldershot, Dublin, the Curragh and Limerick, were formerly NCOs.[15]

A significant number of the Fourth Class (Assistant) Schoolmasters expressed dissatisfaction when they entered the Normal School. In a large part this was because their pay was withdrawn and they received only board and lodging and 'pocket money'. This contrasted unfavourably with the treatment of the NCOs, who drew their regular pay whilst at the Normal School on furlough from their regiments. Some Assistant Schoolmasters also resented the restrictions that were imposed on them when they became resident at Chelsea. The commandant of the RMA wrote to the Council in April 1861 recommending that Fourth Class (Assistant) Schoolmasters should not be admitted as students, because they were '...generally dissatisfied with the restraint that was imposed on them, and that this had a detrimental effect on other students.' The Council agreed and in its July 1861 Minute recommended that this mode of entry should be discontinued and the post of Fourth Class Schoolmaster should be abolished.

Soldiers who volunteered to assist the schoolmaster in the regimental schools received a supplement to their pay of 3d per day. These men had some elementary education and many were soon promoted as NCOs. The Council argued that there would be an advantage in insisting that all soldiers wishing to become Army schoolmasters should first complete a certain period as an assistant in a regimental school before being eligible for entry to the Normal School.

14   *First Report by the Council of Military Education on Army Schools etc.*, pp. xi-xx.
15   Second Report by the Council of Military Education on Army Schools etc., Appendix No.1, pp. 5-10.

In essence, the Council was recommending that other than students from the RMA and RHMS, entry to the Normal School should be restricted to: NCOs or Soldier Assistants who had at some time during their service had performed the duties of soldier assistant in a regimental school for a period of not less than twelve months; pupil teachers who had completed an apprenticeship in a civilian school and certificated civilian schoolmasters. All candidates should be unmarried and be from 19 to 25 years of age.[16] These recommendations were accepted by the Secretary of State and incorporated in the revised Army Schools Regulations that were issued by royal warrant on 19th May 1863. (See below).

The reports received at the Council from the assistant and local inspectors of schools expressed general satisfaction with the efficiency and effectiveness of the trained army schoolmasters. There was however criticism from COs that on occasions some schoolmasters had an unacceptably narrow view of their duties, seeing the post as 'a mere trade' and repudiating any responsibility for the conduct of the children outside the classroom.[17] Major General Eyre, the CO of the large Chatham depot considered that the young men from Chelsea '...did not take the same interest in the classwork or the progress of the pupils as the old Sergeant Schoolmasters.'[18] Captain Gleig, the Assistant Inspector for South Britain, did not accept that these criticisms applied to the majority of the Army's schoolmasters. He pointed out that they were much more occupied than the old schoolmaster-sergeant used to be in instructing the adult classes and they did not have the same time to monitor and control the general behaviour of the children. Nevertheless, whatever the cause, he agreed that the schools were not succeeding in training the children 'sufficiently in habits of politeness and deference to their superiors in age and position.'[19] These observations about the behaviour of the children outside the classroom were included in the council's 1861 Minute to the War Office. It is significant that the Council did not attribute the children's behaviour to any faults on the part of the Army Schoolmistresses, who were responsible for early years' education in the regimental schools. The Council did however regret that so few schoolrooms had playgrounds attached to them and thought that the moral education of the children would benefit if they played under the supervision of the schoolmaster or mistress, instead of loitering in the barrack's square.[20]

Although there were no concerns reported by the inspectors about the education and training that the schoolmasters received at the RMA, there were serious concerns in some quarters about the 'regimental position of the (Chelsea) trained schoolmaster.' The Council in its 1861 Minute explained that the schoolmaster was often represented as occupying an '...isolated and ill-understood position'; that he was neither a

---

16   *Second Report by the Council of Military Education on Army Schools etc.*, Appendix No.1, p. 8.
17   *Second Report by the Council of Military Education on Army Schools etc.*, p. 6.
18   *First Report by the Council of Military Education on Army Schools etc.*, p. 66.
19   *First Report by the Council of Military Education on Army Schools etc.*, p 44.
20   *Second Report by the Council of Military Education on Army Schools etc.*, p. xxiv.

commissioned officer nor an NCO; that he did not identify with the regiment and lacked the *espirit de corps* that came from personal friendships gained through years of service in the same regiment. Unlike the NCOs he did not look to the regiment's CO and his fellow officers for promotion and because he had not served in the ranks he was not well placed to deal with either the officers or the men.[21]

The Council believed that there was some truth in these observations and would appear to have been strongly influenced by the submissions from Major General Eyre commanding at Chatham and from Major Pitcairn, the CO of the Depot of 23rd Regiment at Aberdeen. Eyre complained that the trained Chelsea schoolmasters did not identify with their regiment, had no military training and were unused to military discipline, whilst their 'extreme youth' made their privileged rank objectionable. Major Pitcairn argued that the schoolmasters occupied an anomalous position and that in most instances they displayed a sense of self- importance that made them unpopular with both officers and men.[22] Schoolmaster (First Class) W. Kemshead serving at the Depot of the 23rd Regiment went further and blamed the attempt by the military departments to give the schoolmaster a separate and distinctly 'middle class position' that made him 'neither fish nor fowl.' In his experience, many officers refused to recognise the warrant rank and the NCOs and men resented the schoolmaster's pay and privileges. He asserted that the Army schoolmasters were the most unpopular body of men in the Army: two-thirds of them were regarded by the COs as a nuisance and by the officers generally as upstarts; and they had failed to command the respect of the rank and file who considered that they thought too much of themselves.[23]

Captain Gleig agreed that in the years immediately following the 1846 reforms some COs had resented the independent position of the schoolmaster and in particular their exceptional privilege of being able to communicate directly with the War Office. The Duke of Cambridge (C-in-C) believed that the newly trained schoolmasters had been encouraged to write to the War Office with complaints about their COs and that this resulted in some trouble in certain regiments.[24] Captain Gleig accepted that this privileged arrangement may have been necessary in the early years in order to establish the new school system, but it had certainly ceased to be so. Indeed, this had been acknowledged by the War in its Circular of 31st May 1858, which ordered that all correspondence relating to the schools should be conducted by the COs of regiments and garrisons and not as previously by the schoolmasters. The C-in-C acknowledged that this had improved matters and Gleig thought that this and other changes in administrative procedures had reduced the resentment of COs and had induced them to take a much greater interest in their regimental schools. Occasionally he still met a CO who complained about the impositions placed upon

21   *Second Report by the Council of Military Education on Army Schools etc.*, Appendix No.1, p. 6.
22   *First Report by the Council of Military Education on Army Schools etc.*, pp. 60, 66.
23   *First Report by the Council of Military Education on Army Schools etc.*, pp. 60, 63, 66.
24   *Second Report of the Royal Commission on Military Education 1870*, p. 91.

him by the Army School Regulations and the independence of the schoolmaster, but this was a rare exception. Although Gleig considered that the working relationship between the CO and the schoolmaster had now been placed on a sounder basis, he thought that it was time to re-visit the Army School Regulations. In particular he believed that the promotion and pay of the schoolmaster should be determined by merit and his record of managing the school and not the length of his service as was the case with the 1854 Regulations.[25]

The Council acknowledged in its 1861 minute that the schoolmaster's 'isolated' and semi-detached position within the regimental system was a cause for concern. It believed that some of the issues identified in the reports would resolve themselves over time. For example, the gap between his education and that of his colleagues in the regiment would diminish as the education of the typical NCO progressed. The schoolmaster's isolated position in the regiment was to some degree exacerbated by his distinctive uniform, which the Council thought resembled 'too closely' that of an officer, and also by the 'high pay' received in his first posting, which was more than a sergeant major of infantry.[26]

The 1854 regulations prescribed a uniform consisting of a blue frock coat, heavily braided in black, and worn with gold shoulder-knots; a sword and crimson silk sash; and a cap with scarlet band, bearing a crown in gold thread. Although stars that indicated rank (three, two and one for First, Second and Third Class Schoolmasters respectively) were worn on the collar and not on the shoulder, this uniform was otherwise indistinguishable from that of many officers. It seems that a number of the young schoolmasters wore their warrant rank and new uniform with panache and adopted an air of superiority that was objectionable to officers and long serving NCOs. The superiority of his education set the schoolmaster apart from the rank and file and in a few cases they displayed 'the arrogance of education, thinking because they were better educated they were better men than others around them.'[27] This was certainly the view of the Duke of Cambridge, who had commanded the Dublin garrison in 1854 and in his evidence to the Royal Commission on Military Education in 1870 described the young Army Schoolmasters as '...considering themselves more like gentlemen than anything else.'[28]

The criticisms about the anomalous and semi-detached status of the Army Schoolmaster within the regimental system implicitly questioned the wisdom of the changes that had been introduced by Sidney Herbert in the 1854 Army School

25   *First Report by the Council of Military Education on Army Schools etc.*, pp. 41-44; *Second Report of the Royal Commission on Military Education 1870*, p. 91.
26   *Second Report by the Council of Military Education on Army Schools etc.*, p. 6.
27   Sir Beauchamp Walker was a Commanding Officer in 1854 and a future Director-General of Military Education. Quoted in White, *The Story of Army Education*, pp. 264-5.
28   *Second Report of the Royal Commission on Military Education 1870*, p. 91.

Regulations and the Council was cautious in its response.[29] It did however suggest that it might be sensible to revise the regulations for the dress of the schoolmaster in order to remove from it any unnecessary similarity with that of the regimental officer.

The issues surrounding the rank, relative pay, and privileges of the Army schoolmaster were much more difficult to resolve. The Council proposed that the small numbers of experienced schoolmasters superintending schools in the larger stations should, with its recommendation, be promoted to a commissioned rank with the eligibility for a pension similar to that of quartermasters. This had originally been proposed by Lieutenant Colonel Lefroy in his 1858 report and had been advocated by Captain Gleig and schoolmaster Kemshead in their written submissions to the Council. The commissioned schoolmaster would be appointed on merit and the number would be limited to the camps, such as Aldershot and the Curragh, and the larger garrisons such as Dublin.[30]

Army Schoolmaster First Class with Warrant Rank, 1854. There was an entitlement to wear a red sash not depicted in this image. (Watercolour by Alan. M Gladwell reproduced by kind permission of the Adjutant General's Corps Museum, Winchester)

It was the warrant rank and its associated pay and privileges that, however, were cause for the greatest resentment. Major Pitcairn the CO of the Depot of the 23rd Regiment recommended abolishing the rank and argued that the Army schoolmaster should only rank as a staff sergeant. The Council did not explicitly call for the removal of the warrant rank but recommended the abolition of the four classes of schoolmaster. The current army schools' regulations

---

29   The Council's Minute was dated 31st July 1861.By this date Lord Herbert was terminally ill and had resigned from the War Office. He died in August 1861. This may have influenced the Government's decision to delay the publication of the Council's Minute until the Second Report of the Council on Army Schools that was submitted to Parliament in 1865.

30   *Second Report by the Council of Military Education on Army Schools etc.*, pp. 6-9, 20.

limited the number of schoolmasters who could be promoted to the First and Second Classes to a fixed proportion of the schoolmaster establishment – one-tenth for the First Class and two-tenths to the Second Class. For a number of years promotions had been accelerated by the augmentation of the overall establishment, but once the establishment of trained schoolmasters had been completed promotion would be much slower. Moreover, in most cases promotion meant only additional pay without any additional responsibilities. The Council therefore recommended that the three classes should be replaced by a single class of Army schoolmaster with a starting salary of three shillings per day with pay increases of 6d per day every two years up to the current salary of Second Class Schoolmaster, which stood at 5 shillings and six pence per day. The increases would be subject to positive reports from both the CO and the assistant or local inspectors supported by a recommendation from the Council to the C-in-C at the Horse Guards. In a note of dissent to the Council's minute, Major General J.E. Portlock pointed out that this involved a reduction in the starting salary of a schoolmaster from 4 shillings to 3 shillings per day, and this would lower the number of applications from civilians and NCOs for places the Normal School.[31]

There is evidence that some of the serving schoolmasters were dissatisfied with their existing levels of pay, lack of opportunities for promotion, and eligibility for a pension. First Class Schoolmaster W. Kemshead in a letter to the Council gave these as reasons why he was not prepared to re-enlist for second term as a schoolmaster in August 1861.[32] This discontent was exacerbated by a suggestion in the United Services Gazette in July 1861, that the War Office was contemplating cancelling the warrant of 1854 and downgrading Army schoolmasters to the position of staff sergeants (i.e.to below the rank of Sergeant Major), with the consequent loss of status and privileges. This prompted an anonymous letter to *The Times* newspaper, purporting to be from 200 serving Army schoolmasters, protesting that this proposal was a breach of faith and an attack on the dignity of educated servants of the Crown.[33]

The Council accepted that its proposals with regard to the new ranking would be unpopular with the existing trained Army schoolmasters and recommended that they should only be applied to future graduates from the Normal School, whereas existing schoolmasters should have the choice of remaining with their present conditions or transferring to the new conditions of service.[34] With this proviso, the War Office accepted the recommendations of the Council of Military Education for the pay and conditions for schoolmasters and schoolmistresses and incorporated them in revised Army Schools Regulations that were issued by royal warrant on 19th May 1863. The number of classes of Army schoolmasters was reduced from four to two: Superintending schoolmasters, who were commissioned officers with the relative rank

---

31 *Second Report by the Council of Military Education on Army Schools etc.*, pp. 6-9, 20.
32 *First Report by the Council of Military Education on Army Schools etc.*, pp. 61-65.
33 *The Times*, July 31st 1861, p.6.
34 *Second Report by the Council of Military Education on Army Schools etc.*, pp. 6-9, 20.

of Ensign; and Army schoolmaster, who had graduated from the Normal School at the RMA, with the rank of NCO next below that of sergeant-major.

The starting pay for Army schoolmasters was 3s 0d per day increasing by biennial increments of 6d to 6s 6d per day after fourteen years' service. These increments were granted by the Council of Military Education on satisfactory reports on the general conduct of the schoolmaster and the management and progress of his schools. Where no special quarters for the schoolmaster were provided at the barracks he was entitled to a furnished staff sergeant's room with provision for fuel and lighting. An orderly was to be allocated to keep the schoolroom and his quarters clean and tidy. Army schoolmasters were placed on the pensions list after twenty-one years' service and were entitled to apply to the Chelsea Hospital Commissioners for early pensionable discharge in cases of ill-health or disability.[35]

Superintending schoolmasters would be selected on merit from the body of serving schoolmasters and paid 7s per day on appointment rising to 8s per day after fourteen years' service, five of which was as a superintending schoolmaster. They were entitled to an allowance of 1/0s per day in lieu of a servant. Provision was made for superintending schoolmasters with at least ten years' service as a trained schoolmaster, five of which was as a superintending schoolmaster, to move onto half pay in cases of ill-health or disability. After thirty years' service they were eligible to retire on a pension.[36]

It is significant that the War Office did not use the Royal Warrant enacting the revised Army Schools Regulations to formally establish a Corps of Army Schoolmasters, following the precedent in the Royal warrant of 1857 that had established the 'Army Hospital Corps' for the care of sick and wounded soldiers in the military hospitals[37] Most of the Army's schoolmasters were assigned to specific regimental schools and COs were concerned about their anomalous and semi-detached status within their regiments. The 1863 Army Regulations and subsequent circulars attempted to address these concerns, whereas the formation of a separate Corps of Army Schoolmasters would have exacerbated them.

A War Office circular on 25th May 1863 accompanying the new regulations explained that no serving schoolmaster was compelled to accept the new terms regulating pay, pension and promotion. A period of six month was allowed for serving schoolmasters to decide whether they wished to transfer to the new regulations or remain on their existing pay and conditions under the 1854 Regulations. Schoolmasters who did not transfer would be ineligible for promotion as superintending schoolmasters and would be bound by the new regulations with regard to their conduct, discipline, and general duties.[38]

35 *Regulations for the Management of Army Schools 19th May 1863*, pp. 2-5.
36 *Regulations for the Management of Army Schools 19th May 1863*, pp. 2-5.
37 *Regulations for the Army Hospital Corps* (London: War Office, 1857).
38 War Office Circular No.485, 25th May 1863.

The circular offered reassurance to the serving schoolmasters and sufficient encouragement for the majority to transfer onto the new regulations. There were 191 trained schoolmasters on the establishment in 1861. The 1854 Regulations gave 70 percent of these men (about 133) the rank of Third Class Schoolmasters at a salary of 4s per day. Serving schoolmasters with four years' service received this remuneration under the new regulations and had every chance of earning 6s 6d per day of the after fourteen years' service. On 31st March 1864, only 36 Third Class Schoolmasters had elected to remain under the old regulations. Most of the Second Class Schoolmasters (approximately 42 men) who were earning 5s/6d per day however elected to remain with the old regulations. This was because these schoolmasters would have to serve a full ten years under the new regulations before receiving this salary. In 1863 seven First Class Schoolmasters who had been appointed under the 1854 Regulations were promoted to the commissioned rank of Superintending Schoolmaster. The remaining First Class Schoolmasters elected to retain their pay and conditions under the old regulations and forgo the chance of promotion to the new commissioned rank.[39]

There were now Army schoolmasters who were serving with units in the same garrison under different regulations and this contributed to a continuing and widespread dissatisfaction about pay and conditions. This was a matter that would be discussed in the Second Report of the Royal Commission on Military Education published in 1870. (See Chapter 18)

The new regulations laid down that schoolmasters serving under both sets of regulations were not to be placed under the authority of any NCO with regard to the duties of their office, but all were subject to any directions specified in the new regulations relating to conduct, discipline and general duties. They were to wear uniform at all times and were to salute officers. They were subject to Queen's Regulations regarding attendance at divine service. They were to march to church with the children of their religious persuasion and were expected to assist the chaplain of their persuasion in conducting his Sunday school.[40]

In 1863 the military departments approved a form of dress 'more in accordance with the rank of the schoolmaster', which was a blue frock coat as before, with chevrons (on both arms) of the colour and pattern of chevrons worn by rifle regiments. The sash was suppressed, except for the commissioned Superintending schoolmasters, who wore the uniform of an ensign of the infantry of the line.[41] By March 1866 Superintending schoolmasters had been appointed at Woolwich, Aldershot and Dover; at Edinburgh, Plymouth and Portsmouth and the Curragh and Dublin in the three Inspectional Divisions in Great Britain and at Toronto and Montreal in Canada.[42]

39 *Second Report by the Council of Military Education on Army Schools etc.1865*, pp. iv-v.
40 Regulations for the Management of Army Schools (London: War Office, 19th May 1863).
41 *Second Report by the Council of Military Education on Army School, etc 1865*, p. v; Circular No.352, Horse Guards 18th August 1865.
42 *Fourth Report by the Council of Military Education on Army Schools, etc 1866*, pp. vi-vii.

Table 15. Establishment of Army Schoolmasters 1861-68[43]

	March 1861	March 1864	March 1865	March 1866	March 1868	March 1870
Establishment of Schoolmasters	191	226	238	235	259	270
Under 1863 Regulations: Superintending Schoolmasters		7		10	10	12
Army		128		152	203	217
Under 1854 Regulations 1st Class Schoolmasters	20	13		9	14	11
2ndClass Schoolmasters	}	42		39	30	29
3rd Class Schoolmasters	} 171	36		25	2	1
Total	191	226	238	235	259	270

The establishment of schoolmasters in the table, which excludes those trained in India, increased to 1865 and although there was a small reduction in 1866, it continued to increase thereafter to the end of the decade. Reductions in the number of schoolmasters through death and discharge averaged around ten per annum until 1865, increased to 20 in 1866, before falling to nine each year in 1867 and 1868.

The Normal School produced 56 trained schoolmasters in the three years to 1865, a further 19 in 1866 and a total of 42 in 1867 and 1868.This was more than sufficient to replace the 'casualties' through death and discharge during 1862-1868, whilst also ensuring that most of the Army's schools could receive a trained schoolmaster. The margin however was tight and if there was a large drop in the supply of trained schoolmasters graduating from the Normal School it would be difficult to fill all the annual vacancies that could be expected to occur in the service.

---

43   *Second Report by the Council of Military Education on Army School etc.1865*, p. iv; *Third Report 1866*, p. iii; *Fourth Report 1866*, p. iii; *Fifth Report 1868*, p. iii; *Sixth Report 1870*, p. iii.

Under these new regulations future competitions for admission to the Normal School were restricted to certified schoolmasters and civilian pupil teachers who had completed their apprenticeship; pupil teachers from the RMA and RHMS; and to sergeants, corporals and privates who possessed a good conduct badge. The restriction on civilian applicants to those with some prior teaching experience reflected the pattern of civilian applications to the Normal School in recent years. There had been a growing number of entrants who had been monitors at the RHMS and RMA and had subsequently worked for three years as assistant schoolmasters. Following the abolition of the class of assistant schoolmasters (Fourth Class), these boys were required to remain at the RHMS or the Model School at the RMA as salaried pupil teachers until they were old enough to complete for entry to the Normal School.

The extension of eligibility for entry to the competition to private soldiers reflected the confidence of the Council of Military Education that military candidates would have a fair chance of success and prove effective schoolmasters. It also reflected the view in the military departments that schoolmasters who had experience as enlisted soldiers would adapt and work more harmoniously within the regimental system.

The new regulations acknowledged the value of soldiers who were prepared to volunteer and help as assistants in the regimental schools. The qualified schoolmaster had the duty of selecting one or more men from the regiment for training so that they will be competent to assume the position of acting schoolmaster.[44] The War Office however did not adopt the Council's recommendation that experience as an assistant or acting schoolmaster should be made a qualification for private soldiers competing for entry to the Normal School.

The 1863 regulations covering the appointment, pay and promotion of schoolmasters marked a departure from Rev George Gleig and Sidney Herbert's ambition '...to introduce into the Army a class of men' better qualified to manage the regimental schools.[45] The open competitions in the early years for admission to the Normal School had aimed to attract civilian recruits who would enlist in the Army only after they had qualified as teachers at the Normal and Model Schools. The difficulty of attracting sufficient applicants had resulted in the recruitment of NCOs, and under the new regulations, private soldiers.

The War Office had no intention of abolishing the system of regimental schools and had developed a marked preference for entrants to the Normal School, who were already enlisted soldiers and had imbued the military discipline and the ethos of the regimental system. The question remained whether serving soldiers could be attracted to the Normal School to train in sufficient numbers to staff all the regimental and depot schools. The establishment of the Normal School remained at 40 students

---

44 *Regulations for the Management of Army Schools 1863*, pp. 8-9. There was an authorised schedule of payment whenever these men assumed the duties of acting schoolmaster in a detachment or regimental school.
45 Royal Warrant, 2nd July 1846.

throughout the 1860s, but there was increasing difficulty in attracting candidates. In March 1864, 15 of the students at Chelsea were civilian entrants, and 12 were NCOs, whilst 14 had been monitors at the Model School and had subsequently served three years as assistant Army schoolmasters. In addition, a number of boys had been sent from the West Indies to the Normal School in 1864 and after completing their training were enlisted as army schoolmasters and posted to battalions of the West India Regiment.[46]

In March 1866 only three of the students admitted were civilians, nine were NCOs and 25 had previously been monitors in the two residential military schools before serving three years as assistant schoolmasters. The decision to abolish the rank of assistant Army schoolmaster would in time end this source of recruits for the Normal School. The young men would have to elect to remain at the two Military Schools as pupil teachers, subject to provision of funding by the War Office, until they were old enough to compete for entry to the Normal School.

Between April 1866 and March 1868 the Normal School admitted 40 students. Fifteen of these were described as pupil teachers and civilians, 23 were NCOS and private soldiers, and only two had previously been assistant schoolmasters. Two thirds of those admitted in 1868 and 1869 were soldiers. However, by March 1868 the number of students at the Normal School had fallen to 29 and in 1870 there were only 16 students, 13 of whom were serving soldiers. The Council in its final report on Army schools published in 1870 concluded that the supply of candidates for the post of schoolmaster appeared to be sufficient to meet the needs of the service, but clearly the recruitment from the Army had not met expectations. Inevitably questions would be raised about the wisdom of maintaining an expensive teacher training establishment for the Army at the RMA.[47]

The Council noted in its 1862 Report that returns to the Adjutant General on the condition of the soldiers' education in 1860 showed little change from that recorded by Lieutenant Colonel Lefroy in his 1858 report, with around 38.0 percent of the men in the ranks continuing to be classified as 'uneducated' and in need of an elementary education.[48] The assistant inspectors and superintending officers were unanimous that this was caused by irregularity of attendance at school. The Council's 1861 Minute described this as 'unquestionably the greatest difficulty in the educational system.' Attendance fluctuated widely from day to day with the average instruction in some cases amounting on average to less than two hours per week. The soldiers often made little progress and schoolmasters became disheartened. In some regiments, however, difficulties around attendance had been overcome by the positive 'influence' of their

46   TNA WO 143/48, 'Normal School Letter Book 1859', pp. 305-306.
47   *Second Report by the Council of Military Education on Army School etc,1865*, p. xxv; *Fourth Report1866*, p. xxxii; *Fifth Report 1868*, p. xxiii; *Sixth Report 1870*, p. iii; *Second Report of the Royal Commission on Military Education*, p. xxviii.
48   *First Report by the Council of Military Education on Army Schools etc.1862*, pp. ii-iii.

CO's, Some regiments organised the duty rotas so that men could regularly attend at the adult schools and the Council suggested that consideration should be given to extending this good practice throughout the Army.[49]

The Council recognised that a soldier's general duties around the camp or barracks were often the cause of his irregular attendance at school. This difficulty could be overcome by adopting the practice that had been introduced in some regiments of establishing special classes in addition to the ordinary adult classes. These Special Adult Classes would contain a small number of men (about three per company) selected for their good conduct and who were promising candidates for promotion to the higher non-commissioned ranks. Men would attend these classes for two or three hours every day for as many days as their duties would permit. They would reach a good standard after six to nine months, when they could be dismissed and another class formed. The Council issued a circular in May 1862 urging COs to introduce these Special Classes and argued they would produce a large field from which to select adequately educated NCOs.

Mr Vicars observed that success of Special Classes in Ireland depended very much on the co-operation and commitment of COs in ensuring that men could attend school for at least 16 hours per week. He pointed to the example of the 32nd (Cornwall) Light infantry, stationed in Dublin. From a class of 30 men (three from each company) organised in May 1863, 18 men had been promoted and two appointed school assistants. Assistant Inspector Gleig, in a supplementary report on Special Classes in England in 1863, pointed to the progress made by men attending these classes, which was much greater than for men attending ordinary schools. He particularly, commended those established in the Royal Artillery at Woolwich. He regretted that they had not been more widely adopted by units in his division, and he believed that this was more frequently caused by the opposition of the captains of companies, than from that of COs of regiments.[50]

According to the information received by the Council there were 93 Special Classes in the Army on 1st January 1866, but most of these were maintained only during the winter. This was notably the case for regiments stationed in Canada where the long winters enabled classes to continue for up to seven months. Elsewhere the classes varied considerably in strength and attendance and some existed in name only.[51]

Local circumstances could disrupt attendance at the Special Classes. This was a particular problem In Ireland where the Fenian disturbances during the mid-1860 seriously interfered with the operation of the regimental schools. It was necessary to deploy troops in detachments over a wide area to garrison outlying towns and villages and the strengths of regiments at their headquarters were materially reduced. COs

---

49 *Second Report by the Council of Military Education on Army Schools,1865, Appendix No.1*, p. 10.
50 *Second Report by the Council of Military Education on Army Schools etc.*, p. xviii.
51 *Fourth Report by the Council of Military Education on Army Schools etc.*, pp. ix-xxii.

struggled to keep open detachment schools and these were often staffed by untrained masters. In April 1868 Mr Vicars reported that in consequence the special classes had been almost suspended across the island.[52]

The introduction of Special Classes contributed to the increase in the number of candidates sitting the examinations for the Army Certificates of Education. Initially, these had been granted at the discretion of the COs, on the recommendation of the schoolmaster. There were three classes of certificates. The lowest or Third Class was awarded to a soldier who could 'read tolerably, write a little from dictation' and had thoroughly mastered the four simple rules of arithmetic. The Second Class was awarded when the soldier was a 'good reader' and could '...write well, fluently and with correct spelling from dictation'; had thoroughly mastered the 'four elementary rules of arithmetic, simple and compound' and had a fair acquaintance with geography. The highest or First Class Certificate required the soldier to 'write a letter in a good hand with correct spelling grammar and composition', to 'thoroughly master of vulgar and decimal fractions' and be generally well informed in history geography and other subjects.[53]

The Certificates had not been widely used and in 1864 the Council proposed and the military departments accepted that they should granted by COs on the recommendation of the divisional and local inspectors after each inspection or an examination.[54] In 1866 and 1867, 3,910 certificates were awarded. There was however no uniform style or set standard for the examinations and in consequence the proportion of grades awarded varied. Nearly 17 percent of those granted by Mr Vicars in Ireland were 1st Class certificates compared with little over 9 percent in Mr Sergeaunt's Division. Lieutenant Colonel Gleig's examinations were regarded as more stringent and in his Inspection Division there were 2,895 candidates, but only 80 (4.25percent) obtained a 1st Class certificate and 1,008 failed to obtain any certificate at all.[55]

Some regiments adopted standing orders that required men to attend a Special Class and achieve a certificate before they could be promoted as NCOs. The 26th Regiment (Cameronians) stationed at Belgaum in the Bombay Presidency issued orders in 1864 for an 'Educational Scheme of Promotion' establishing a special class for men who were recommended as promising material for promotion by their company officers. All Lance-Corporals were selected from men who had passed out of the Special Class. Promotion to a higher rank of NCO depended upon the possession of a certificate of education, in addition to a satisfactory knowledge of the regiment's interior economy and the ability to command drill, guard duty and bayonet and musketry exercises. Promotion to Corporal required a third class certificate; to Sergeant a second class

52 *Fifth Report by the Council of Military Education on Army Schools etc.*, p. 36.
53 *First Report by the Council of Military Education on Army Schools etc.*, pp. 32, vi-vii.
54 *Second Report by the Council of Military Education on Army Schools etc.*, p. xiv.
55 *Fifth Report by the Council of Military Education on Army Schools etc.*, p. xv-xvi.

certificate and to Colour sergeant a First Class Certificate. A similar educational scheme for promotion was adopted by 1st Battalion of the 16th Regiment.[56]

Awarding of certificates of education and introduction of Special Classes for men who sought promotion could only make a small contribution to the wider problem of low participation and irregular attendance at the adult schools. The Council considered that the succession of General Orders regarding attendance had not been helpful. Wellington's 1849 Order had required recruits to attend school for two hours until their basic training had been completed (until dismissed drill). This was cancelled by a General Order in June 1857 because of the legal ruling that men could not be compelled to attend school and attendance at school and the new order was limited to exhorting COs to encourage their men to attend. It had also introduced the requirement in peacetime for the possession of at least a 4th class certificate of education for promotion to corporal.

Subsequently, Clause 37 of the Articles of War authorised COs to order school parades and to enforce attendance at school and a General Order in February 1860 reminded them of this power. In the following January, a General Order was issued to clarify the matter. This explained that it was not incumbent on COs to '…order all men indiscriminately, and against their will to attend.' Rather, Clause 37 was intended to ensure that soldiers who had volunteered for school should remain under the command of the CO with regard his discipline whilst in the classroom.

Some COs interpreted this to mean that they did not have the power to compel men to attend school. Others interpreted it to mean they did have the power to require newly enlisted men to attend and also to exempt older soldiers who volunteered to attend from parades and other duties, whilst ensuring that these men attended diligently to their studies.[57]

There was broad opposition from COs to newly enlisted men being compelled to attend school because this interfered with basic training. Some COs chose to ignore the 1857 Order requiring them to encourage soldiers to volunteer for school after being completing drill and failed to arrange duties so that they could easily attend.[58] The Council argued that this state of affairs was unsatisfactory. The public was paying for the Army's schools, but whether soldiers attended school and improved their education depended on the attitude of the COs. The question therefore was whether COs should be directed to exercise their powers under Clause 37 of the Articles of War to compel attendance at school. The Council was firmly of the opinion that this should be the case and argued that it was essential for the soldier to be able to read and write. An elementary education was required for the soldier to be effectively instructed in the use of the newly introduced rifled fire-arms. The Army would ultimately benefit

56   *Fifth Report by the Council of Military Education on Army Schools etc.* pp. 53-55, 81.
57   *Second Report by the Council of Military Education on Army Schools etc.*, p. 11; General OrderNo.775, 16th January 1861.
58   *First Report by the Council of Military Education on Army Schools etc.*, pp. 34, 47.

because there would be a larger pool of educated men for promotion as NCOs. There would also be less drunkenness and crime because the educated soldier would make greater use of libraries and reading rooms in his leisure time.

The Council recommended that all illiterate recruits should be compelled to attend school for at least six hours per week until they were able to read and write. In the case of men who volunteered to continue with their education, COs should give them the opportunity to attend school for at least four hours per week in accordance with the General Order of June 1857. In addition, the half-yearly inspection reports of regiments, which were transmitted to the Adjutant General, should record the extent to which this order was being carried out and whether the system of school certificates conferring eligibility for promotion was being implemented in conformity with the order.[59]

The question of soldiers' attendance at the adult schools remained controversial. The 1863 Army Schools Regulations did not place any obligations on the enlisted soldier to attend school and advance his education, nor give any directions to COs ordering them to encourage soldiers to attend. There also was no mention of the certificates of education, which although sanctioned by the Council, continued to be awarded at the discretion of the COs. The War Office accepted that any stricter regulations regarding attendance at the ordinary adult school would be unpopular with the Army and was reluctant to place any additional duties on COs, most probably in deference to the views of the C-in-C, the Duke of Cambridge. The Duke was strongly of the opinion that school attendance should not be compulsory. New recruits should first master drill and thereafter should be ordered to attend school, but only if they were illiterate. COs should decide whether men should attend and for how long in order to qualify them for promotion as NCOs.[60] Nevertheless, the regulations issued by the War Office for military prisons in April 1863, which established the post of 'Schoolmaster Warder', ordered that prisoners were compelled to attend school at such hours as were prescribed by the prison governor.[61]

The Council agreed with Colonel Lefroy that charging soldiers fees for attending school was 'a tax on progress' and endorsed his recommendation that they should be abolished. It judged that the abolition of fees in 1857 for soldiers attending the Fourth Class and the subsequent abolition for those attending the Third Class had been beneficial. The evidence from the assistant inspectors and superintending officers indicated that most men stopped attending school once fees became payable. Little revenue therefore would be lost through their abolition. This would also improve the effectiveness of the teaching by placing men in different classes for instruction in different subjects according to their progress. Finally, the Council argued that the

59   Second Report by the Council of Military Education on Army Schools etc., pp. 11-12.
60   Second Report of the Royal Commission on Military Education 1870, p. 89.
61   Regulations for Military Prisons (London: War Office, 1st April 1863).

abolition of fees would send out the message that government valued the educated soldier.[62]

The War Office accepted this recommendation and in September 1862 remitted the payment of fees for adults studying in the First and Second Classes.[63] A royal warrant in May 1863 stated that all NCOs, drummers and privates were to be admitted without payment of fees.[64]

Table 16. State of Education in the Army, 1860-68[65]

	% 1860	% 1864	% 1865	% 1866	% 1868
Class 1: Who can neither read nor write	18.95	13.44	12.97	12.25	9.46
Class 2: Who can read but Not write	19.72	17.30	16.55	16.12	10.59
Class 3: Who can read and write	53.89	64.05	63.67	65.47	73.80
Class 4: Who have a superior degree of education	7.44	5.18	6.80	6.16	6.14

The Council in its reports on Army Schools in the 1860s included a representation of the educational standards of the enlisted men based on returns received from the Adjutant-General. These returns, although frequently incomplete, show a general improvement in the educational standards of the rank and file. Nevertheless in 1868 33,934 men, or slightly more than one fifth, of the rank and file in the units that had submitted returns were unable to read and write satisfactorily. These men and were placed in Classes 1 and 2 and thus needed further education. There were also significant differences in educational attainment between the different branches of the service throughout the decade.

62   *Second Report by the Council of Military Education on Army Schools etc.*, pp. 12-14.
63   War Office Circular 783, 17th September 1862.
64   *Regulations for the Management of Army School 1863*, p.16; *First Report by the Council of Military Education on Army Schools etc.*, pp. vi-vii.
65   First, Second, Fourth and Fifth Reports by the Council of Military Education on Army Schools, passim.

Table 17. Classes 1 and 2, (Uneducated Men) in the Army 1860 and 1868

	% 1860	% 1868
Cavalry	22.03	10.90
Royal Artillery	25.65	18.30
Royal Engineers	5.36	1.34
Foot Guards	10.96	8.12
Infantry of the Line	42.37	23.54

In percentage terms the largest improvements were in the engineers and the cavalry. Captain F. Scrivener writing in October 1861 and reflecting on his experiences in inspecting Army schools over some fifteen years at home and in the Bombay Presidency in India, observed that in cavalry regiments there were 'always a considerable number of exceedingly well-educated men serving in the ranks as privates or as NCOs.'[66] In consequence he observed that the adult schools in the cavalry were seldom well attended. Nevertheless, there were many men who would benefit from further tuition and he thought that with certain inducements, such as exception from some parades, many more might be persuaded to attend.

There was substantial progress in reducing in the number of uneducated men in the cavalry during the 1860s, but the largest number of uneducated men was to be found in the much more numerous battalions of infantry. There were 37,840 men on the registers of the Army's adult schools in September 1867 and 22,386 of these were infantrymen. The recruits to the infantry were typically less well educated, but irregularity of attendance continued to be the main obstacle to their progress at school.

The high proportion of uneducated men in the regiments of artillery in 1868 was perhaps more surprising. The corps was recognised as having some very good schools, but it had expanded during the Crimean War and because of the need to replace the native batteries in the Indian Army following the Mutinies (See Chapter 17). Outside the major depots the batteries were often dispersed in small detachment, which presented difficulties in providing schoolmasters and maintaining teaching.[67] The situation was sufficiently serious in the Bombay Presidency in 1866 for the C-in-C of the Bombay Army to submit a memorandum on the matter to the Secretary of the Council of Military Education.[68] In September 1867, there were 37,840 men on the books of the Army's adult schools and 5,442 (14percent of the total) were serving

---

66   *First Report by the Council of Military Education on Army Schools etc.*, p.136.
67   *Fourth Report by the Council of Military Education on Army Schools etc.*, p. lii.
68   *Fourth Report by the Council of Military Education on Army Schools etc.*, p. 37.

in the Royal Artillery. Captain Dunn in his report on the regiments in the Bengal Presidency thought that the schools of the Royal Artillery had the best attendance.[69]

The difficulties schoolmasters encountered in securing regular attendance of the men on their school register in the ordinary classes at the adult schools in all branches of the service meant that very little was taught beyond reading, writing and arithmetic. From 1 January 1866 separate classes were introduced in reading and arithmetic and soldiers moved from a lower to a higher class in each subject depending on their progress.[70] There was also some attempt to make the men's schooling relevant to their military service. Schoolmasters were ordered to make themselves familiar with the system of issuing and accounting for the men's pay, maintaining savings bank books and other regimental accounts, and to teach these subjects to the men whenever their writing and arithmetic were sufficiently advanced.[71] Sometimes history and geography was added, but in general only by basing reading lessons on a page in a text book of one of these subjects. In 1867 Hindustani was taught at 38 schools in the Bengal Presidency, but the inspecting officer reported that progress was slow because many of the regimental "moonshees" (native teachers) had a poor command of English.[72]

There were frequent references by the inspectors in the Council's reports to the progress that was made when COs took an active interest in their schools and provided incentives and encouragement for men to attend. For example, the Council's 1866 Report noted that special classes were generally established in the regiments of the Gibraltar garrison because the commanding officers were '...very favourably disposed towards the education of the soldier.'[73] These were presented as examples of good practice that should be emulated across the Army, but it could be inferred from the reports that the indifference of some COs and company officers was a significant obstacle to further reductions in the number of uneducated soldiers.

The Council, in its 1868 Report, regretted that there was no visible improvement in attendance at the adult schools, but in a marked change of emphasis asserted that this was because of 'the indifference with which the British soldier regards the advantages of education.' The report quoted instances of regiments in Canada with men on the school registers who attended no more than once or twice per month and one case of seven men who managed only 23 attendances in six months. The local inspector at Malta mentioned that a CO had been 'indefatigable in his exertions to induce men to attend.' He had established night classes and restricted promotion as much as possible to men who had gained certificates of education, but the results were not encouraging. When he offered monetary rewards regular attendance improved, but when these

69   *Fifth Report by the Council of Military Education on Army Schools etc.* pp. xiv-xv.
70   *Second Report by the Council of Military Education on Army Schools etc.*, p. xv.
71   War Office Circular 360,10th August 1863.
72   *Fifth Report by the Council of Military Education on Army Schools etc.*, p. xi.
73   *Fourth Report by the Council of Military Education on Army Schools etc.*, pp. 17-18.

were removed attendance dwindled. The Council argued that: 'For education itself the men cared little. A limited number had no objection to it provided it was worth their while, but partial exemption from general duties formed no inducement in itself, schooling being only another kind of work.' The Council expressed its firm conviction that a full return for the money expended on the adult schools would never be attained until '…compulsory attendance becomes the rule of the service.'[74]

The Council had strongly favoured compulsory attendance in its recommendation to the military departments in July 1861, but it is not clear why the Council waited until 1868 to repeat this recommendation and why it then shifted the focus of its argument away from the indifference of some COs to the indifference of many of the rank and file. The common factor was Council's concern about public expense and a fear that unless there was there was a significant improvement in attendance questions might be raised at the War Office and in Parliament about the value for money of maintaining the adult classes in the regimental schools. This fear was not unfounded. The Tory government of 1866-68 had been parsimonious in military matters and Gladstone's Liberal ministry that would take office in December 1868, with Edward Cardwell as the new Secretary for War, was determined to be more parsimonious still.[75]

Rev George Gleig had shown little interest in soldiers' children and saw improving the 'moral education' of the soldier as the main reason for reforming the regimental schools. Sidney Herbert however had recognised the importance of the children's schools and his 1850 and 1854 Army School Regulations had established separate 'Grown Children's, Infant and Industrial Schools' as integral components in the reformed system. The children's schools flourished during the 1860s. The numbers increased in all three categories of schools, but the largest increase was in the infant schools. In 1860 the returns from regiments, depots and garrisons recorded that there were 3,110 boys and 3,000 girls in the infant schools. The Council was determined to encourage the expansion of the infants' schools and instructions were given '…to admit children as soon as they are able to dispense with assistance.'[76] Many parents responded by sending their children as soon as they were able to walk often in company with older brothers and sisters.

74 *Fifth Report by the Council of Military Education on Army Schools etc.*, pp. xiii-xiv.
75 K.T. Hopen: *The Mid-Victorian Generation 1846-1886* (Oxford: Oxford University Press, 2008), p. 602.
76 *Fourth Report by the Council of Military Education on Army Schools etc.*, p. xxix.

Table 18. Children at the Army Schools 1860, 1863, 1865, 1867

	1860 (i)	1863 (ii)	1865 (iii)	1867 (iv)
Infant boys	3110	4027	4402	5051
Infant girls	3005	4240	4847	5400
Infant Total	6115	8267	9249	10451
Grown Schools Boys	3440	4212	4535	4960
Grown School Girls	2691	3402	3379	3614
Grown School Total	6131	7614	7914	8574
Total at Children's Schools	12246	15881	17163	19025
Industrial Schools	7052	9402	NA	10681

(i) First Report by the Council of Military Education on Army Schools 1865
(ii) Second Report by the Council of Military Education on Army Schools 1865
(iii) Fourth Report by the Council of Military Education on Army Schools 1866 (Average attendance for May and October 1865)
(iv) Fifth Report by the Council of Military Education on Army Schools 1868 (At 1st September 1867

The infant schools were staffed by an Army Schoolmistress and for many years it had been difficult to secure enough qualified women for the post. There continued to be large number of applications (many from the daughters or widows of former NCOs) for places at the four designated colleges that trained schoolmistresses. The period of training at the colleges varied between sixth months and one year and the earliest age for admission had been raised to 20 years. The newly qualified schoolmistresses therefore would be not less than 21 years of age, but the Council thought that this was too young, given the '...peculiar position of the young schoolmistress in a regiment or garrison.' Wherever possible the Council endeavoured to restrict appointments to older women and favoured the appointment of the wives of NCOs but was unable to secure sufficient qualified applicants.[77]

Many applicants to training colleges had little education and twelve months training was insufficient to prepare the young women to take charge of an infant's school. Captain Gleig proposed the infant's schools at some of the larger garrisons might act as 'model schools' at which the newly appointed schoolmistress could work as the assistant to an experience schoolmistress before being posted to a regiment. The

77   *Second Report by the Council of Military Education on Army Schools etc.*, Appendix No.1, pp. 16-17.

Council thought that there was merit in this proposal but recommended that it should not extend beyond the training of the wives of NCOs, because it would be difficult to give 'adequate protection' to large numbers of young unmarried women in the large camps and garrisons.[78]

The shortage of staff was a particular problem in the larger infant schools, where there could be a class of 40 or more children, many who were at different levels of education. The War Office permitted the appointment of 'pupil teachers' to assist the schoolmistress in this case, but it was very difficult to find sufficient recruits at the paltry salary of £4 per annum.[79] The Council suggested the appointment of two additional categories of auxiliary teachers to assist in the larger infant schools where there were at least 25 children. Girls from the age of 13 who had been educated at Army schools could be appointed as 'monitoresses'. They could serve until they were 17 years of age and would be paid a salary of at £4 per annum. These girls would attend the grown school and receive instruction from the regimental schoolmaster in the mornings and for the rest of the day they would work assisting the schoolmistress in the infant and industrial schools. In the case of the garrison and depot schools it might be possible to recruit the daughters of soldiers and NCOs from the age of 17 as pupil teachers. They would live with their parents and assist the schoolmistress in her various schools. They would receive a salary of £6 per annum rising to £18 and to £21 at the age when they would be eligible for entry to the training colleges and graduate for employment as a trained schoolmistress.

Where there were 50 or more children in the infant and industrial schools the Council suggested that it also should be permissible to appoint the wife of an NCO as an 'assistant schoolmistress.' She would be certified as fit for the duties of the post by the Assistant Inspector and receive the same pay as the pupil teacher. The assistant schoolmistresses would be eligible for promotion to regimental schoolmistress by attending either one of the training colleges or by means of special certificate of competence issued on the authority of the Assistant or Local Inspector of schools. The Council hoped that these two proposals would address the shortage of schoolmistresses, whilst limiting direct entry to the training colleges to older and more experienced applicants.[80]

The 1863 Army Schools Regulations acknowledged the crucial role of the schoolmistresses in managing the infant and industrial schools. They did not make any changes to the rank and status of the trained schoolmistress but drew extensively on the recommendations of the Council of Military Education to establish a larger and more effective teaching establishment.

78 *Second Report by the Council of Military Education on Army Schools etc.*, Appendix No.1, pp. 17-18.
79 *Second Report by the Council of Military Education on Army Schools etc.*, Appendix No.1, pp. 17-18.
80 *Second Report by the Council of Military Education on Army Schools etc.*, Appendix No.1, pp. 17-18

Women aged between 21 and 30 thirty years and holding a certificate of teaching proficiency from the Committee of Council of Education could be appointed as Third Class Schoolmistresses at a salary of £24 per annum. They would be eligible for promotion by the Council for Military Education 'according to their merit and service' to the posts of Second Class and First Class Schoolmistress at a salary of £30 and £36, respectively. The regulations were silent on the how the recommendations for promotion were to be determined but provided the schoolmistress with a pension after twenty one years' service or earlier in cases if ill-health and disability.[81]

The regulations continued to look to the Army's families to provide large number of women who could be trained as schoolmistresses. Girls who were 13 years of age and educated at the Army's schools could be appointed to the post of Monitoress to assist in the children's schools at an annual salary of £4 until they reached seventeen years of age. They would be taught by the regimental schoolmaster for one and a half hours per day in the mornings in the grown children's schools and would learn needlework from the schoolmistress in the evenings.[82] Young women between the age of 17 and 21 years of age could be appointed as pupil teachers to assist in the infant and industrial schools at a salary rising from £6 to £18 per annum. It was expected that many these pupil teachers would be soldiers' daughters and would have previously worked in the schools as Monitoresses.[83]

Since 1815 the military departments had looked to soldiers' wives to play a part in providing some formal instruction for the regiment's daughters. The 1863 regulations permitted the employment of the wives of NCOs in the children's schools as Assistant schoolmistresses with the same pay and conditions as pupil teachers. Where a trained schoolmistress could not be found an Acting Schoolmistress could be appointed as temporary schoolmistress by the Council of Military Education at a salary of £18 per annum. Both the Assistant schoolmistresses and the pupil teachers could be admitted to the training colleges, but on the recommendation of an assistant inspector to the Council of Military Education they could be appointed Third Class Schoolmistresses without further training.[84] In the short run the new regulations were more important for inaugurating new classes of teaching assistants and acting schoolmistresses for the Infants' and Industrial schools than in increasing the number of trained schoolmistresses.

81   *Regulations for the Management of Army Schools 1863*, pp.10-15.
82   *Regulations for the Management of Army Schools 1863*, pp.10-15.
83   *Regulations for the Management of Army Schools 1863*, p.14.
84   *Regulations for the Management of Army Schools 1863*, p. 13.

Table 19. Staff in the Infant and Industrial Schools 1864-68[85]

	March 1864	March 1866	March 1868
Trained Schoolmistresses	205	208	225
Pupil Teachers and Assistant school mistresses	27	26	33
Monitoresses	98	162	182
Acting Schoolmistresses	-----	83	76
Total establishment	330	479	516

By 1867 the numbers in the infants' schools had risen to 5,051 boys and 5,400 girls. There was a particular difficulty in securing sufficient pupil teachers and assistant school mistresses in India because most soldiers daughters there were married by the age of sixteen. Elsewhere the employment of auxiliary teachers was essential to the successful management of the growing number of children in the infant schools.[86] Children normally remained in the infant schools until they could read words of two syllables when they moved to the grown children's schools where they would be taught by the regimental schoolmaster. The Council however ordered that boys should not be kept in the infant schools after attaining the age of eight.[87]

The 1863 regulations did not change the organisation of the schools or the hours when they were open. In the UK the infant and grown children's schools were operated from 9.00 to 12.00 in the mornings and the industrial schools between1400 and 1600 in the afternoons. When regiments were abroad the COs were allowed to vary the hours according to local conditions. The regulations specified that morning schools were to commence with prayers and bible readings, but in deference to Catholic and non-conformist opinion, parents who were not of the same religious persuasion as the schoolmaster or mistress were free to delay sending their, children to school until 0930hrs, when the secular lessons commenced. The regulations permitted the unit's officiating chaplain, Catholic priest or non-conformist minister to give religious instruction for one hour on two days each week (excepting Saturdays). The schoolmasters, mistresses and pupil teachers were expected to attend and assist the clergymen of their respective religious persuasions. COs were given the power to specify and vary the timings and locations for these assemblies, which also could be

---

85 *Second Report by the Council of Military Education on Army Schools etc,*1865, p. vi; *Fourth Report1866,* pp. v-vi; *Fifth Report 1868,* pp. v-vi.
86 *Third Report by the Council of Military Education on Army Schools etc.,* p. xviii; *Fourth Report on Army Schools etc,* p. 37.
87 *Fifth Report by the Council of Military Education on Army Schools etc.,* p. xviii.

attended by adults. All the schools were closed for three weeks in December and again in July to allow the schoolmaster and mistress to take leave.[88]

Most of the School Inspectors were in favour of the abolition of school fees for the children on the grounds of the poverty of their parents. They noted that some parents sent the children to nearby civilian school because the fees were lower and argued that abolition would be a boon to soldiers' families and would be at little cost to the government. The Council did not dismiss these arguments, but also recognised the counter argument that was advanced by the National Society for charging fees in its schools, that knowledge paid for was more prized than when it was free. The Council was concerned that abolition of fees would lower the status of the regimental schools in the eyes of the soldiers and their families and place them below that of the 'humblest of the paid- for schools outside the barracks.' It therefore decided on balance to retain fees and did not recommend any changes in the school regulations.[89] The War Office agreed, and the 1863 regulation specified the fees that were to be charged for children attending the schools. These were 2d per month for one child; 1.5d for each child if two children were attending from the same family and 1d per month for each child if three or more children from the same family were attending.[90]

When reinforcements had been dispatched to India in 1857, the War Office had made provision for all legitimate children who were precluded from travelling with their fathers to be educated gratuitously in the Army's schools. This provision had been extended in 1862 to the legitimate children of all soldiers who were serving abroad and who were precluded from accompanying their fathers to any the overseas station. This provision was included in the 1863 regulations.[91]

The number of children in the grown children's schools increased during the decade but at a slower rate than in the infant schools. This differential can be explained by the smaller number of girls progressing into the grown children's schools each year, whereas the number of boys in the infant and grown children's schools was broadly similar in each of the Council's reports (Table 18). It is possible that girls were allowed to stay in the infant schools, perhaps in order to remain with their younger brothers and sisters beyond the age when they could read words of two syllables, whereas boys were ordered to move to the grown children's school when they were eight years of age.[92] Gleig, now a Lieutenant Colonel, commented in his 1866 report that younger children were often kept too long in infant schools and in some of these schools he had seen children learning arithmetic, a subject that was usually reserved for the curriculum of the grown children's schools. His concern was that the children

88   *Regulations for the Management of Army Schools 1863*, pp. 10-15.
89   *Second Report by the Council of Military Education on Army Schools etc.*, p. 15.
90   *Regulations for the Management of Army Schools 1863*, p. 16-17.
91   War Office Circular 753, May 1862; Regulations for the Management of Army Schools 1863, p.16.
92   St John Williams, *Tommy Atkins' Children*, p. 80.

might be badly instructed in the infant schools, thus making it more difficult for the schoolmaster to teach the basics in the grown children's schools.[93]

The continuation of fees may have been a factor for some families deciding not to send their daughters to the grown children's schools. There were instances of parents complaining that in comparison with the civilian schools the children were spending too much time studying subjects such as geography and history that were not 'useful to their station in life.' These subjects were however limited to the more advanced classes with the lower classes concentrating on the basics in reading, writing and arithmetic.[94] The Council favoured the retention of these subjects because they stimulated and broadened the intellect but cautioned that the inspectors must also ensure that the schoolmasters and mistresses were giving proper attention to the children's proficiency in reading, writing and arithmetic.[95]

The grown children's school were co-educational and the children were divided into classes according to attainment, advancing from the lower to the higher classes as was the practice of the day, on the basis of progress and not age. There were exceptions in the schools of the Royal Artillery at Woolwich and the Royal Engineers at Chatham where there were separate classes for boys and girls. This may have been with a view to teaching boys subjects (such as more advanced arithmetic) that would be useful if they subsequently enlisted in their fathers' corps. The Council noted that these were large and stationary schools that could justify the expense of additional staff. Mixed classes in the grown children's schools at the ordinary regimental schools were unavoidable, because otherwise in would be necessary to employ second schoolmistress with a high level of education to teach the girls.[96]

Some parents certainly had reservations about mixed classes for older girls and the Council admitted that there was considerable prejudice against them in India and at many of the cantonments there the girls were always taught by the schoolmistress. The Council considered that this was very detrimental to the education of girls and quoted Captain Dunn who spoke strongly of the disadvantages that this was causing to the girls of the schools in the Bengal Presidency.[97] The regimental returns for 1860 record that 7,052 children were being instructed mainly in sewing in the industrial schools.[98] These schools had originally been intended only for girls, but the 1854 school regulations had permitted boys from the grown children's schools to attend. It would appear that boys' attendance was being strongly encouraged by the COs in some regiments, possibly because this made them less of a nuisance around the barracks. The War Office made a capitation grant to the regiment of 5s per child

93 Fourth Report by the Council of Military Education on Army Schools etc., p. xxix.
94 St John Williams, Tommy Atkins Children, pp. 95-7 (See ttimetable for six classes for grown children of the 1st Battalion the Grenadier Guards, November 1869.
95 Second Report by the Council of Military Education on Army Schools etc., pp. 13-14.
96 Second Report by the Council of Military Education on Army Schools etc., pp. xx.
97 Fourth Report by the Council of Military Education on Army Schools etc., pp. xxi-xxii.
98 First Report by the Council of Military Education on Army Schools etc., pp. xv-xvi.

attending to cover the cost of materials. In December 1862 the War Office issued a Circular noting that the expenditure on these grants had increased and that grown boys' education would better served by remaining under the instruction of the schoolmaster in the afternoon school.[99] The Council disagreed and thought that the schoolmaster's time might be better used in giving extra tuition to his adult students.[100] Afternoon schools for grown boys were nevertheless established in a number of units depending on the availability of accommodation and whether there was sufficient staff time available after having provided for tuition in the adult schools. The timetable for afternoon lessons for the 1st Battalion of the Grenadier Guards at Beggar's Bush Barracks Dublin, dated 26 November 1869, shows that the boys were largely occupied with writing from dictation, copying and transcribing, reading and spelling and practicing writing and arithmetic on slates. It is very probable that these classes were taken by the assistant schoolmasters whilst the regimental schoolmaster was teaching the adult classes.[101]

Industrial schools were popular with parents. The children were encouraged to bring in their own work and were frequently given permission by COs to retain the articles made by them from the material provided. Many parents sent their children at a very early age and some were too young to take part in any practical work. These children sat in the same room as the older girls and in effect were merely childminded by the female staff. The Council found instances where capitation grants were being claimed for these very young children and instructed the schoolmistresses to maintain to maintain separate registers for the infant and industrial schools.[102] The returns for September 1867 show that there were 10,681 children attending the industrial schools. (Table4) The Council's reports commented that it was widely agreed that these schools were beneficial to the Army and wished that they could be extended to instructing boys in tailoring and shoemaking.[103]

The inspectors' reports on the children's schools were consistently favourable and there was a general agreement that they were on the whole superior to 'ordinary National Schools.'[104] The Council believed that this was because most of the children attended regularly at lessons. Attendance at the children's schools was always more regular than at the adult schools, although from time to time the schools were closed because of outbreaks of measles and scarlet fever. In 1867, Colonel Gleig expressed

99   War Office Circular No.795, 2nd December 1862.
100 *Second Report by the Council of Military Education on Army Schools etc.*, p. 16.
101 St John Williams, *Tommy Atkins' Children*, p. 95.
102 Fourth Report by the Council of Military Education on Army Schools etc., pp. xxix-xxx.
     The 1863 Regulations included detailed instructions for the schoolmasters and mistresses
     on keeping records and forwarding returns of the numbers of pupils on the school
     registers and their attendance, and also for the collection and accounting for fees at the
     children's schools.
103 *Second Report by the Council of Military Education on Army Schools etc.*, p. 16.
104 *Second Report by the Council of Military Education on Army Schools etc.*, p. 14.

concern about the irregularity of attendance of the grown children who appeared in some cases to attend or not 'according to their own or their parent's inclination.' The Council thought that the solution was in hands of the commanding officers and appealed for their assistance.[105]

There was no legal obligation for soldiers to ensure that their children attended regularly at the regimental school and the state expected them to pay for the privilege, unless their children were forced to remain at home when they were posted abroad. A number of regiments had adopted standing orders requiring soldiers to ensure that their children regularly attended school. The Standing Orders of the Scots Fusilier Guards issued in 1858 laid down that that all children were required to attend the school and held the parents responsible for any irregularity of attendance. Schoolmasters was to report cases of non-attendance to the Adjutant who would report any irregularities to the CO. Behind this was the veiled threat that where the soldier did not comply with the standing orders his family could be denied the privilege of living in barracks.[106]

There was discussion from time to time in the Council and with the assistant inspectors on relative merits of garrison and regimental schools for the children and infants. The dispersal and movement of the Army across a large number of stations at home and abroad favoured the regimental school, but garrison schools had been retained at the Aldershot Camp and in some of the larger barracks, for example in Dublin. The Council was aware that these were superintended by some of the most effective schoolmasters and were '...models of instruction and discipline.'[107]

The Council thought that there were advantages in garrison schools for infants, but on balance favoured the regimental school. It was argued that the teachers in these schools had a better knowledge of their pupils and could more easily supervise their classes. Many officers and their wives took an interest in their regiment's school and would be more reluctant to attend a large garrison school containing children from different regiments. The Council believed that the regimental system created sense of community between officers and the men and their families. There was a danger that the interest taken by officers and their wives in the welfare of the soldiers and the children of their regiment would be endangered by a more general system of garrison schools. Furthermore, the Council argued that the absence of the active involvement of officer's wives would not help to overcome the 'defect of training of the children, before noticed, to habits of politeness and deference to their superiors.'[108]

There was nevertheless recognition that when a regiment was quartered in one of the larger stations there could be advantages for the teachers and the children in merging the various regiments' schools into a larger garrison school. Major General

105 *Fifth Report by the Council of Military Education on Army Schools etc.*, p, xiii.
106 NAM, Army Educational Policy and Army Schools 1846-1920, Box 22126, 'Regulations and Standing orders of the Scots Fusilier Guards' (London, 1858).
107 *Second Report by the Council of Military Education on Army Schools etc.*, pp. 10, 14-16.
108 *Second Report by the Council of Military Education on Army Schools etc.*, pp. 10, 14-16.

J. E .Portlock stressed the advantages of the garrison and depot schools: he argued that mixing children from different regiments under the supervision of a senior and experienced schoolmaster provided a richer learning environment, which benefited both the pupils and their regimental schoolmasters. This, the Council cautioned, should not extend to withdrawing the children altogether from the supervision of their regimental schoolmaster or the exclusion of the active interest and support of the officers of the regiment. The Council did not propose to disband the existing garrison schools but argued that they should not be extended beyond the largest camps and stations, because a system of garrison schools would not be 'in harmony with the regimental system of the army.'[109]

The Woolwich Garrison's schools for the children of soldiers in the Royal Artillery and Royal Engineers constituted one of the largest of the garrison schools and provided for around 1,000 children from six to 14 years of age, in addition to children in its infant schools. There was a strong sense of community between officers and the men and their families at the garrison and an annual feast for the children was held in the garrison's riding school, followed by prize giving in the garrison's assembly rooms attended by a large number of the officers and their families and friends. These schools were however a special case and arguably the exception that proved the rule, because the majority of the children were from Royal Artillery families who did not move between station with the same frequency as the infantry and cavalry.[110]

It is believed that Lieutenant Colonel Lefroy's appointment as Inspector-General in succession to Rev George Gleig was widely welcomed. Colonel A.T.C. White in *The Story of Army Education* writes that he was very popular with the Army's schoolmasters who regretted his loss. Inspector-General Lefroy's influential presence in the War Office gave the Army schoolmaster's confidence that their interests would be well represented, and that priority would be given to the continuing development of the regimental and garrison schools. Captain Gleig in his March 1861 report to the Council, written in response to Lord Herbert's request for an evaluation of the reformed management of the regimental schools, had strongly opposed the abolition of the post of Inspector-General. He believed that the duties of the inspection and superintendence of the schools could only be effectively performed by one person, assisted by a deputy, who would be able to devote his undivided attention to the task. The council disagreed and thought it better to receive reports from the assistant inspectors, which could be considered and discussed by a small group of disinterested persons, who would then report any recommendations for action to the higher authorities in the military departments. It argued that it would be sensible for individual members of the Council to visit the military districts in the British Isles

---

109 *Second Report on Army Schools by the Council of Military Education etc.*, pp. 10, 14-16; *Second Report by the Council of Military Education on Army Schools etc.*, p. 20.
110 *Illustrated London News*, 21st January 1865, p. 51.

each year in order to gain insights that would assist in their moderation of the assistant inspectors' reports.[111]

The council acknowledged that there were great variations in their reports, because the duties of the Assistant Inspectors had never been adequately defined. A standardised system was needed, and the council recommended that there should be twice yearly inspections of schools in each military district and that the inspector should devote at least one day to the examination of the adults and children in each of their respective schools. The Council thought it essential that commanding officers should be encouraged to take a close interest in their unit's schools. It recommended that when a school was scheduled to be inspected its CO should receive notification two weeks prior to the visit. He would be provided with forms for completion by the schoolmaster entering the number of students in the classes of each of his schools. At the start of the inspection the inspector should meet with the CO to discuss the attendance at his schools and the conduct of the schoolmaster. The inspectors' report including statistical information about student attendance and progress should be prepared for the CO before being forwarded to the Council. Where a commissioned schoolmaster had been appointed, he should visit the regimental schools in the camp or garrison every month and give a written report to the regiment's CO and to the general officer commanding the military district, who would forward this to the Council.[112]

In the case of the three Inspection divisions in Great Britain and Ireland each school was inspected by the Assistant Inspector or by one of the superintending schoolmasters at least once a year, with the assistant inspectors visiting the schools that had previously been inspected by the superintending schoolmaster. The regimental schoolmaster examined and assessed the pupil's progress in reading writing and arithmetic twice a year and the visiting inspectors examined and assessed around 40 percent of the pupils in each subject during their visits. This process provided for some degree of moderation of the assessments of progress made by the schoolmaster.[113]

There was however concern about the differing standards applied by the three Assistant Inspectors in the United Kingdom when awarding the certificates of education and also the disparity in the number of candidates examined in each division.[114]

In 1869 Mr J.P. Sargeunt retired from his post of Assistant Inspector of Division II and this gave the War Office the opportunity to make some changes in the arrangements for inspection of schools in the British Isles. Lieutenant Colonel Gleig, whose testimony figured increasingly in the Council's reports and clearly was a major influence on its conclusions and recommendations, was appointed Inspector of Army Schools throughout Great Britain. Superintending Schoolmasters were

---

111 *Second Report by the Council of Military Education on Army Schools etc.*, p. 2.
112 *Second Report by the Council of Military Education on Army Schools etc*, p. 3-5.
113 *Fourth Report by the Council of Military Education on Army Schools etc.*, pp. vii, xxxii.
114 *Fourth Report by the Council of Military Education on Army Schools etc.*, pp. xvi-xvii; *Fifth Report*, pp. xv-xvi.

appointed from the establishment of Army schoolmasters to every military district and they were given the responsibility for inspecting all the Army's schools in their districts. The Inspector visited every station in Great Britain at which superintending schoolmasters were appointed and the schools at all outstations at least once per year and reported annually to the Council. Mr E. A. Vicars retained all his responsibilities for inspections of schools in Ireland with the exception of those relating to the certificates of education. In order to ensure that all the certificates were of the same standard, Colonel Gleig would classify the candidates and recommend the awarding of certificates to all the NCOs and men throughout the United Kingdom.[115] In the following year Mr E. A. Vicars died and this furnished the opportunity to extend the system of inspecting Army schools that was operating in Great Britain to Ireland. This was only a small step away from creating a post that would be similar to that of 'Inspector-General' for army schools.[116]

Distribution of prizes to the children of the Royal Artillery and Royal Engineers at the Woolwich Garrison Assembly Rooms, January 1865. (*Illustrated London News*, 21st January 1865)

115 War Office General Order (G 100,) 1st October1869.
116 War Office General Order (G 73), 1st October1870.

The Council of Military Education in its final report on 31st March 1870 detailed the considerable progress that that had been made in the Army school system since it had been placed under its superintendence in March 1860. It noted the increase in the number of trained schoolmasters; the large increase in the number of children under instruction; the reduction in proportion of uneducated men in the Army; the introduction of Special Classes and the certificates of education and the contribution that these were making by creating a body of educated NCOs and men qualified for promotion. Although there were issues that remained unresolved, the Council concluded that on the whole the system had progressed satisfactorily, and the Army had benefited to no small degree from the reforms.[117]

117 *Seventh Report by the Council of Military Education on Army Schools etc.*, p. iii.

17

Army Schools in India

In 1850 the control of the British territories in India rested with the Honourable East India Company, which maintained separate armies in its three Presidencies of Bengal, Madras and Bombay. These were composed of locally recruited native regiments, with a small number of European regiments recruited in the Great Britain and India. Since the 18th century these had been supplemented by an increasing number of King's/Queens regiments from the British Army's regular establishment. The territories controlled by the East India Company had increased significantly during the early 19th Century and in the post Napoleonic Wars years a large proportion of the British Army was stationed in India. As a private venture the East India Company paid for the soldiers in its native and European regiments and also the King's/Queen's regiments supplied by the British Army. The British Army Estimates during the late 1840s usually provided for garrisons of 30,000 men paid for by the Company, from a total Army establishment of around 130,000.[1] It was usual for the Queen's regiments to serve in India for long periods. For example, in 1844, 16 battalions of infantry had been stationed in the country for 15years or more years. There had been very little mention in the discussions at the War Office or elsewhere in government in about the provision for the superintendence and inspection of the Army's schools and the newly trained schoolmasters at the various stations in India, or indeed for those posted to stations elsewhere in the British Empire.

A small number of the first cohort of trained schoolmasters graduating from the Normal School at Chelsea were sent to join the Queen's regiments stationed in India, and others slowly followed when their regiments sailed to join one of the three Presidencies' armies. Many regiments already in India however remained without a trained schoolmaster and their schools continued to be staffed by schoolmaster sergeants selected from the ranks.

---

1   A.J. Guy & P. B. Boyden, *Soldiers of the Raj* (London: National Army Museum, 1997) p. 79; Fortescue, *A History of the British Army*, Vol. XIII, pp. 5-15.

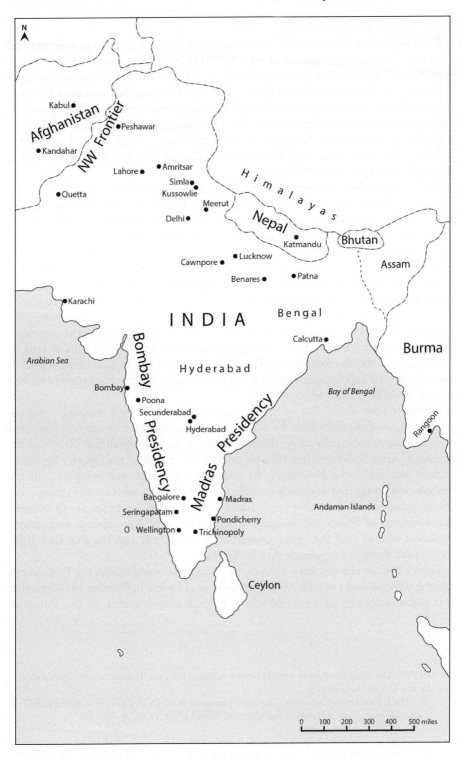

India in the 1860s.

Each Presidency had its own C-in-C, but from 1831 the C-in-C in Calcutta had exercised command and control of all the British and Indian troops in the country regardless of the Presidency in which they were stationed There does not however appear to have been any attempt by the military authorities in London or Calcutta to introduce a uniform system for superintending and inspecting the numerous regimental and garrison schools across the vast distances in the presidencies. Instead a system for the Army's schools was allowed to develop, which was not only semi-detached from that being established in Great Britain, but also differed to varying degrees between the three Presidencies.

In 1852 Lord Frederick FitzClarence, who had established the successful garrison school at Portsmouth in 1848 was appointed C-in-C of the Bombay Army[2]. FitzClarence immediately approached the C-in-C in Calcutta suggesting the appointment of a trained schoolmaster as superintendent of the regimental schools of the European Corps in the Bombay Presidency and he recommended Frederick Scrivener, who he had known during his time at Portsmouth for the post. Approval was granted and in March 1853 Scrivener was appointed garrison schoolmaster at Poona and superintendent of the schools of the European regiments in the Presidency at a salary of 200 rupees per month, with extra payments when inspecting the regimental schools. Following the precedent set by the appointment of the Instructor of Naval Gunnery for the Indian navy, Scrivener was granted the official rank of Lieutenant in the Bombay Army. The military authorities in Calcutta decided to sanction similar appointments in the other presidencies 'whenever a properly trained person' could be provided.[3]

Scrivener later wrote that on his arrival in Bombay he had received a request from the CO of the 64th Foot for advice on a replacement for its recently promoted schoolmaster-sergeant, because there was not a suitably qualified NCO in his regiment. After Scrivener's initial inspections of the schools of the Queen's regiments at nine stations in the Presidency, he concluded that with one exception, all the schoolmaster-sergeants were useless teachers and were incapable in maintaining order in the schoolrooms. Scrivener immediately embarked on a programme of training schoolmasters at Poona and recorded that in 1853-4 he had selected and trained sufficient men to staff the entire Queen's Regiments, and also the five East India Company's European regiments then in Bombay.[4]

Lord FitzClarence was keen to improve educational standards in the Presidency's army and established a number of military schools at Poona. In October 1854 Scrivener was placed in charge of a normal school to train schoolmasters for the European

2   In 1895 the three Presidency armies were combined into the 'Indian Army' commanded by the C-in-C in Calcutta.
3   BL: IOR, East India Company General Correspondence 1602-1859, E/4/ 820, pp. 547-9.
4   Lefroy, *Report on the regimental and Garrison Schools of the Army*, pp. 100-10.

and native regiments of the Bombay Army.[5] Scrivener was also given responsibilities at the 'Central School for Military Instruction' where he taught officers and NCOs mathematics, surveying and civil engineering.[6] In 1855 a school of civil engineering for the instruction of the civilian staff of the Department Public works was added and Scrivener was appointed Professor of Drawing and Surveying. Mr Brett was appointed to assist Scrivener in teaching surveying and also in the administration involved in superintending and inspecting the Army's schools.[7] In recognition of these responsibilities Scrivener was promoted to Captain in the Bombay Presidency Army in 1857 with the designation of Local Inspector and Superintendent of Army Schools.

In addition to supervising the training schools at Poona during the summer months, Scrivener inspected as many of the regimental schools as possible during the dry season, which usually lasted from December to March. The Bombay Presidency was organised in geographical divisions with European troops in garrisons at a large number of stations in each division. The Head Quarters was at Bombay; the Poona Division in the Western Ghats had six stations; there were four stations in the Northern Division; two stations in the Southern Division; five stations in the Sindh Division, three stations in the Central Division and there was a brigade of detached units at Aden. During the winter of 1855-56, Scrivener covered vast distances by sea and road to inspect schools at Karachi in Sindh, Deesa in the Northern Division, Belgaum in the Southern and Ahmednugger (Ahmednagar) in the Central Division.[8]

Copies of the Army Schools Regulations were dispatched by the War Office in London to Calcutta and were then circulated to the C-in-C of each of the three presidency armies with orders that they should be implemented. The schoolmasters trained at the Poona were appointed and served under the 1854 Army School Regulations and these were also applied in the Presidency's European regiments.[9] In other respects progress was slow. There was a shortage of school text books and delays in obtaining copies from Great Britain. Lack of suitable accommodation however was the most pressing problem. Schools were often conducted in barrack rooms that were not adequately furnished. In 1856 a proposal was considered by the government in Calcutta for building chapel schools in India. This was rejected and it was ordered that no new school buildings were to be erected until a standard plan has been agreed. In

---

5   Strachan, 'Wellington's Legacy: The Reform of the British Army', pp. 78-80.

6   *First Report by the Council of Military Education on Army Schools*, pp. 131-2. When Scrivener successfully applied for admission to the Normal School in 1846 his occupation was described as a 'surveyor' This presumably qualified Scrivener for his appointment as Professor of Drawing and Surveying.

7   House of Commons Sessional Papers 1859, Accounts and Papers Part III, East Indies (Education), Bombay.

8   *The Bombay Calendar and Almanac 1856*, p.321; *First Report by the Council of Military Education on Army Schools*, pp. 131-32.

9   BL: IOR, East India Company General Correspondence 1602-1859, E/4/804, 517-8; E/4/826/1419-20.

the meantime temporary accommodation was constructed where required.[10] Scrivener reported in 1858 that purpose built schoolrooms had been constructed at Poona and Karachi and that alterations had been made to accommodation in Bombay and four other stations in the presidency and that all the schoolrooms were furnished as in England with a raised platform and low desks.[11]

Scrivener makes little mention in his reports to the War Office of the impact on the schools of the European regiments of the mutinies in the native regiments of the East India Company's armies. The mutinies are usually described as starting at Meerut in the Bengal Presidency in May 1857 and then spreading rapidly resulting in a general rebellion and extensive fighting in the Presidency.[12] The native regiments of the Bombay and the Madras Armies largely remained loyal and many of their European regiments were dispatched north under Sir Hugh Rose to deal with the mutineers in the Bengal. The men's families remained at depots in Bombay and Madras, and where several regiments were located at one station, it was usually possible to maintain schools for the children and sometimes for recruits and other soldiers who were not on active service. In most cases the adult schools were suspended whilst men were serving in the field. There is no evidence that Lt Frederick Scrivener served in the field in India during the mutinies and subsequent rebellion. He most probably remained in Poona, where in addition to conducting the correspondence and supervising matters relating to the regimental schools, he managed the normal school and the schools of military and civil engineering.[13]

At the outbreak of the mutinies in the Bengal Presidency, the local arrangements for training schoolmasters and the supervision of schools were not as well advanced as in Bombay. In 1854 the government in Calcutta decided to establish a normal school for training schoolmasters and mistresses at the Lawrence Military Asylum at Sanawar in the hills on the road to Simla. The Asylum had been founded as a public charity in 1847 by Lieutenant Colonel Sir Henry Lawrence to '…provide for the orphan and other children of soldiers serving or having served in India' with the objectives of freeing them from 'debilitating effects of a tropical climate, and the demoralizing influence of barrack life.' It offered the '…benefits of a bracing climate, a healthy moral atmosphere, and a plain, useful and above all a religious education, adapted

---

10   BL: IOR, East India Company General Correspondence 1602-1859, E/4/835, 1219-1221.
11   Lefroy, *Report on the regimental and Garrison Schools of the Army*, pp. 100-110.
12   W. Dalrymple, the Last Mughal (London: Bloomsbury Publishing 2006), pp. 3-23. The use of the term 'Indian Mutiny' has been criticised for ignoring the wider uprising amongst the civilian population in the Bengal Presidency. Many contemporary historians prefer to use the term 'The Rebellion' and in India often the 'War of Independence'.
13   Scrivener's service papers record that he had accompanied General Outram's expeditionary force on the Persian campaign in 1856 and 1857. He was present at the action at Moohumrah (Mohumrah), a town at the junction of the Euphrates and Karen Rivers. This however was prior to the rebellion in India.

to fit them for employment, suited to their position in life...' and 'to make them consistent Christians, and intelligent and useful members of society.'[14] The institution was co-educational, but organised on quasi-military lines with the boys dressed in the blue uniform of the Bengal Artillery (Lawrence's old regiment). The government in Calcutta decided that the Asylum should be developed as a model school at which the students of the associated normal school would obtain their teaching practice. Schoolmaster E.H. Rogers, who had trained at the Chelsea Normal School, was seconded from the 87th Fusiliers to serve as Headmaster of the Asylum boy's school for the remaining seven years of his enlistment. He quickly trained a number of schoolmasters to work as his assistants.

In 1854 most of the children who had been accommodated at public expense at the Bengal Military Orphan Society's Lower Orphan's School at Alipore near Calcutta were transferred to the Lawrence Asylum and the government provided funds to build additional accommodation. In 1857 there were 143 girls and 198 boys in residence at Sanawar, most of who were complete or partial orphans.[15] The plan was that some of the senior boys would be apprenticed as pupil teachers to assist in the Normal School for four years and it was hoped that they would then enter Normal School to train as Army schoolmasters. Other trainees would be secured from volunteers serving with the European regiments. The COs of European regiments were requested to encourage men to volunteer for the Normal School. The initial response however was disappointing, and the authorities noted a marked reluctance for men in the Company's regiments to volunteer.[16]

In the case of the girls it was expected that once a headmistress was appointed some of the more able pupils would progress into the Female Normal School and qualify as schoolmistresses or assistant mistresses of regimental schools. Other students would be obtained from the women and daughters of soldiers in the European regiments. Regulations were issued requiring women trained at the Normal School to serve for a minimum of five years. They would be permitted to marry a man of respectable character during this period.[17]

Schoolmaster F.W. Dunn of HM 32nd Regiment, who was assisting teaching and examining the pupils at the Asylum was appointed to head the Normal School. On 20th May 1857 the government's military department confirmed his appointment

14   BL: IOR, East India Company General Correspondence 1602-1859, E/4/835,260-1; H. M. Lawrence, *The Lawrence Military Asylum being a brief account of the past ten years of the existence and progress of the institution established in the Himalayas by the late Sir H. M. Lawrence for the Orphan and other children of European Soldiers* (Sanawar: privately published, 1858), Appendix I.

15   Lawrence, *The Lawrence Military Asylum etc.*, pp. 12, 26, 33-7, 41-2, 66.

16   Lawrence, *The Lawrence Military Asylum etc.*, pp. 43, 55, 66; BL: IOR, East India Company General Correspondence 1602-1859, E/4/844,242.

17   Lawrence, *The Lawrence Military Asylumetc.*, p. 58; BL: IOR, East India Company General Correspondence 1602-1859, E/4/851,122.

as Superintendent of regimental schools in the Bengal Presidency with the rank of Lieutenant and an office and rooms at the military station at Kussowlie (Kasauli), which was close to the Lawrence Asylum.[18]

Lawrence Asylum at Sanawar near Kussowlie (Kasauli). (*Illustrated London News*, 12th January 1867)

The news of the mutinies at Meerut and the rebellion in Delhi caused great anxiety at the Lawrence Asylum and there was fear that the hill stations would be attacked. The pupils and staff were ordered to leave and move to the nearby military station at Kussowlie where there was a garrison of one hundred men of the Queen's 75th regiment. The Company's native regiment at Shimla did not mutiny and the local population did not join the rebellion. After a fortnight at Kussowlie the pupils and staff of the Asylum were able to return to the undamaged school buildings at Sanawar.[19]

The hostilities in other parts of the Bengal Presidency had a much greater impact on the regimental schools. The safety of the regiments' women and children was paramount. Most of the regimental schoolmasters had enlisted as private soldiers and in the desperate circumstances in the early months following the mutinies the schools were closed and the masters fought with their regiments. For example, schoolmaster Sergeant Vaughan was wounded whilst serving with the 32nd Foot in the Residency at Lucknow.[20]

18   Lawrence, *The Lawrence Military Asylum*, p. 27; BL, IOR, East India Company General Correspondence 1602-1859, E/4/844 ,626.
19   Lawrence, *The Lawrence Military Asylum*, pp. 68-69.
20   White, *The Story of Army Education*, p. 263.

When regiments had been dispatched to the Crimea in 1854 there had been concern expressed in the newspapers that soldiers' children left behind would no longer be able to attend their regimental school .This concern grew when reinforcements were sent to India following the mutinies and subsequent rebellion. Lord Panmure responded in October 1857 by assuring the troops that any children left at home would be entitled to attend the schools at their nearest garrison without the payment of fees.[21]

Frederick Scrivener's reports to Lieutenant Colonel Lefroy, and subsequently to the Council of Military Education, are the main sources of information about the condition of the Army's Schools in India in the years following the rebellion. After the rebellion had been suppressed it was very difficult to open the adult schools. In 1856 there had been around 36,000 British and European soldiers across the three Indian Presidencies, distributed in two Queen's and three Company regiments of cavalry and 20 Queens' and nine company battalions of infantry. Reinforcements from all arms were sent from Great Britain and other stations in the East Indies and by the end of 1858, in addition to batteries of the Royal Artillery, there were eight British cavalry regiments and 68 battalions of infantry.[22] Many regiments, although not actually in the field, were marching back to their peacetime stations. Some were accommodated in temporary barracks or housed in tents and in the case of the Bombay Presidency, it was not until early in 1860 that all the regiments were settled into permanent quarters and were able to re-open their schools.

In the Bombay Presidency, in addition to the local European forces recruited by the East India Company, the army included ten battalions of infantry, three regiments of cavalry and several batteries of the Royal Artillery and companies of the Royal Engineers sent from the home commands of the British Army. There was a serious shortage of qualified staff to manage these units' regimental schools. The situation was so desperate that in June 1860, the C-in-C of the Bombay Army wrote to the Secretary of the Council for Military Education conveying the urgent need for more trained schoolmasters. Until these men arrived Captain Scrivener had to extemporise and make do with the manpower available in the Presidency.

The troops that had been sent as reinforcements to India following the rebellion typically sailed without their families or a trained schoolmaster.[23] For example, the 6th (Inniskilling) Dragoons was without a schoolmaster when it arrived in India. During the time that the regiment was stationed at Kirkee (Khadki) in the Bombay Presidency its adult school was very badly managed by a corporal. The regiment's children joined from England in June 1860 and Scrivener was fortunate in obtaining the services of schoolmaster Walker of the 95th Foot. Walker had been on leave at Poona and because

21 *Naval and Military Gazette,*21 October 1857.p.1
22 Fortescue, *A History of the British Army*, Vol. V, pp. 243, 391-2.
23 *First Report by the Council of Military Education on Army Schools etc.*, p. 139.

of the monsoon he was unable to re-join his regiment. He successfully managed both the adult and children's schools until schoolmaster Robinson arrived from England.[24]

Poona was a large station and its garrison included three of the Queen's infantry regiments. Scrivener had managed to secure competent teachers for schools of the 56th Regiment when it had arrived in India early in 1858 and whilst it was at Poona they were managed by schoolmaster Duffield and his wife, both of whom were trained teachers. By contrast, the 31st Regiment was also without a schoolmaster when it reached India, but Scrivener had great difficulties in securing a competent teacher to open a school. He eventually secured the services of provisional Third Class Schoolmaster Parkhill, a sergeant of the 83rd Regiment. Parkhill managed the school very effectively for some time before he was court marshalled and reduced to the ranks for drunkenness. When the families of the 31st Regiment had arrived from England they were accompanied by a schoolmistress who managed the infants' school. In 1860 the regiment were ordered to embark for China. The families remained at Poona and the older children joined the school of the 57th Regiment under provisional 3rd Class Schoolmaster Smith, who had formerly been a sergeant in the 64th regiment.

In other units Scrivener had no alternative but to appoint an NCO to manage the schools until a trained master became available. An acting schoolmaster managed the schools of 33rd Regiment at Deesa in the Northern Division from 1859-61. He was very conscientious, but the pupils made very little progress until he was replaced by 2nd Class Schoolmaster Carroll. The 4th King's Own regiment stationed at Ahmedabad in the Northern Division during 1860 was without a schoolmaster. The CO recommended one of his sergeants who ran the schools quite effectively until schoolmaster Morgan and his wife, both qualified and experienced teachers, arrived at the station in the following year.[25]

When trained schoolmasters eventually arrived it took time to re-establish the schools and for the pupils to make significant progress. The 83rd Regiment had been in the field for three years and had marched several hundred miles before it arrived at Belgaum in May 1860. The children had been in school with a trained schoolmaster at Deesa, but when the regiment settled into permanent quarters at the Belgaum the barracks were overcrowded and there a lack of suitable accommodation for its schools. It was not until January 1861that 3rd Class Schoolmaster Annett was able to report that all the schools were in suitable accommodation and that the adults and children were making satisfactory progress. Matters were much better in the schools of the 72nd Highlanders, the 28th, and 95th regiments. Each had competent and hardworking schoolmasters and also suitable accommodation and the pupils in all these regiments' school made very satisfactory progress.[26]

24   *First Report by the Council of Military Education on Army Schools etc.*, pp. 136-7.
25   *First Report by the Council of Military Education on Army Schools, etc.*, pp. 133-9.
26   *First Report by the Council of Military Education on Army Schools, etc.*, pp. 140-1.

In 1858 the East India Company's territory was transferred to the Crown. The Government of India Act replaced the old Board of Control with the India Office, and the East India Company with the Government of India in Calcutta. In the Cabinet, the Secretary of State for India replaced the President of the Board of Control. The India Office and the Government of India inherited the existing military contracts, so that the Government of India and not the Imperial Government paid for the entire Army in India, both the native and the British regiments serving in the country.[27]

The permanent British Army garrison in India almost doubled after the mutinies and rebellion and in 1861 accounted for 69,000 men from an Army establishment of around 215,000.[28] During the early part of the nineteenth century the annual movements of British units on relief between the United Kingdom and India had involved long voyages in sailing ships with the men and their families travelling in a number of transports and the regimental schools were closed during the voyage. In the 1850s a number of large iron steam vessels were purchased specifically to transport troops across the Empire.[29] In 1857 a school was attended by 320 men of the 95th Regiment during its voyage to Bombay and in the following year the 44th Regiment managed to operate a school that was attended by 189 soldiers during its voyage to Madras.[30] Whenever troops were on board ship for long voyages, the War Office encouraged the COs to open schools. The 1863 Army School Regulations ordered that when a trained schoolmaster or mistress embarked with troops for long voyages the CO was to open a school for adults and children and to provide a supply of school materials. When trained teachers were not on board the CO was authorised to select an NCO to act as schoolmaster with the payment of 6d per day. Where there were young children on board the CO could select a suitably qualified woman person as acting schoolmistress on the same pay.[31]

In 1866, the first of a fleet of five screw-driven steam troop ships entered service and it became easier to keep the schools open. Each of these vessels was designed to carry a full battalion of infantry and the men's families (about 1200 persons) with some degree of comfort on the passage to and from India.[32] When the Suez Canal was opened in 1869 these five fast troop ships could complete the round trip from Portsmouth to Bombay in seventy days. The movement of troops and their families

27 Guy and Boyden, *Soldiers of the Raj*, p. 79.
28 Fortescue, *A History of the British Army*, Vol. XIII, p. 532. The 69,000 regimental men allocated to the Indian garrisons included those remaining of regimental depots in Great Britain.
29 H.C.B. Rogers, *Troopships and their History* (London: Seeley Service 1963), pp. 105-110. These ships comprised the screw propelled iron ex-frigates, the *Megara* and *Simoom*, and the ex-P&O ship the *Himalaya*.
30 Lefroy, *Report on the regimental and Garrison Schools of the Army*, pp. 15-24.
31 Army School Regulations 1863, p.9.
32 J. J. Colledge, *Ships of the Royal Navy* (London: Greenhill Books, 1987). The fast troop ships ordered in 1863 and entering service from 1866 were: *Crocodile, Euphrates, Jumna, Malabar*, and *Serapis*.

within India continued to be a slow and arduous process entailing the prolonged closure of the schools. There were no railways before 1850, and at the time of the mutinies and rebellion only 570 miles of track, rising to 6,541 by 1875 and 25,000 miles of trunk and branch lines by 1900.[33] Following the 1858 Government of India Act, the East India Company's nine European infantry regiments were incorporated in the British Army as the 101st to 109th Foot and the cavalry as the 19th, 20th and 21st Hussars. The Indian Artillery disappeared and was replaced by a brigade of field and a brigade of garrison artillery of the Royal Regiment.[34] In the Bombay Presidency, three European infantry battalions together with companies of the Bombay artillery and engineers were incorporated into the British Army. The schools of these units were staffed by trained and experienced teachers. For example, the schools of the 2nd European Regiment (later the 106th Regiment) at Bombay were ably managed by Schoolmaster Wolfe and his wife. The children of the headquarters of the Bombay Horse Artillery and the 1st and 3rd Battalions of the Foot Artillery were under the able supervision of 2nd Class Schoolmaster Clifford at the garrison school at Kirkee in the Poona Division.[35]

The incorporation of the Company's units into the British Army did not always go smoothly causing additional problems for the schoolmasters. When the 3rd European Regiment (later the 109th Foot) moved to Karachi in Sindh following active service in Central India, many of its men declined to transfer to the British Army and elected to take their discharge. They were replaced by German soldiers from the Jaeger Corps recruited during the Crimean War.[36] First Class Schoolmaster Brett had been appointed to the regiment in July 1860, but soon after he became sick and remained in hospital until the following April. During his illness the schools were managed by Colour Sergeant Roller who taught schools of 52 adults (many of whom were Germans learning English) and also 26 six children.[37]

Long years of service in India continued to affect the health of the schoolmasters. Schoolmaster Eaglesome had been trained in India and was in charge of the Headquarters' school of the 2nd Foot Artillery at Bombay. In 1861 his health deteriorated and Captain Scrivener transferred him to the healthier climate of the artillery school at Belgaum in the Southern Division.[38] Schoolmaster Stuart, formerly a soldier in the artillery had been trained at the Presidency's normal school and proved an able teacher of the adult and children's schools of the 1st Bombay Fusiliers (later

33   D. Gilmour, *The British in India* (London: Alan Lane 2018), p. 152.
34   Fortescue, *A History of the British Army*, pp. 528-30.
35   *First Report by the Council of Military Education on Army Schools etc.*, pp. 132, 134,135.
36   T. Royle, *Crimea* (London: Little, Brown and Company, 1999), pp. 303, 365. The 1853 Foreign Act Enlistment was designed to address the shortage of manpower during the Crimean War. By the summer of 1855, 5,659 men had been enrolled in the British German and British Swiss legions.
37   *First Report by the Council of Military Education on Army Schools etc.*, pp. 142-43.
38   *First Report by the Council of Military Education on Army Schools etc.*, p. 141.

the 103rd Regiment); but when the battalion moved to Bombay in 1861 Stuart was admitted to hospital suffering from the effects of his heavy drinking and Scrivener was forced to recommend his dismissal.[39]

Table 20. Number of pupils attending Schools of the European Forces in the Bombay Presidency, September 1861

	NCOs	Privates	Total Adults	Boys	Girls	Total Children
British Home Troops	354	1374	1728	272	287	559
Local European Forces						
(ex- East India Company)	99	610	709	201	148	349
Total	453	1984	2437	473	435	908

Schooling in the regiments of the Bombay Army had been seriously hindered by the need to dispatch troops to deal with the mutinies in the native regiments, but by April 1861 Captain Scrivener was able to report that a great deal of progress was being made once units returned to their peacetime stations. The request for additional schoolmasters from England had been answered and there was a trained schoolmaster and a number of schoolmistresses on the establishment of every European unit. Instruction in needlework was provided for the girls and the government was in the process of establishing workshops for several trades in each regiment for the instruction of some of the older boys.

Approximately 23 percent of the 7,403 NCOs and private soldiers in Queens's regiments sent from Great Britain to the Bombay Army were on the school registers compared with only some 18 percent of the 3,900 strong local European forces. Captain Scrivener concluded that much work still remained to be done and pointed out that around 3,200 men in the home based regiments and almost 1,200 in the European local forces were unable to read and write. Once again, the main problem was irregularity of school attendance and Scrivener recommended to the Council of Military Education that men should be ordered to attend school for six hours per week until they were able to read or write. Thereafter he considered that attendance should be voluntary, but if inducements for promotion from one grade of NCO to another by

39   *First Report by the Council of Military Education on Army Schools etc.*, p. 141.

means of examinations were made standard throughout the Army, he believed that there would be no lack of volunteers who would be prepared to attend.[40]

Scrivener's reports speak with the authority of an experienced and effective practitioner. He had been the first schoolmaster to graduate from the Normal School at Chelsea in April 1849 and had served with distinction as the garrison schoolmaster at Preston, Portsmouth, and Dublin. During the following nine years as the local inspector and superintendent in Bombay he was responsible for increasing the number of trained schoolmasters in India and improving the effectiveness of the Army's schools in the Presidency. Dedicated and conscientious, there is no doubt that Scrivener willingly took on a punishing work load. During the summer months he was busy with the Central School of Instruction and the Normal School at Poona and from November to the middle of April of each year he inspected the schools at as many stations as possible and worked to ensure that they were conducted in conformity with the Army School Regulations.

During these winter months in 1860-61, he travelled upwards of 3,400 miles visiting at least some of the schools in all parts of the Presidency, with exception of those at Aden.[41] He was now a married man with two young daughters, and it was perhaps for this reason that in August 1862 he resigned his post and transferred without purchase to the less demanding position of Paymaster of 103rd Foot with the rank of Captain. He subsequently served as paymaster with the 97th, 95th and 83rd regiments, but he took no further part in the management or inspection of the Army's schools. In April 1878, he was appointed Staff Paymaster in the Army Pay Department in England. He retired on half pay with the honorary rank of Lieutenant Colonel in November 1879.[42]

In 1862 Lieutenant J.A. Jacob replaced Captain Scrivener as the superintendent and local inspector for the Bombay Presidency. He provided the Council of Military Education with regular reports on the state of his schools until 1868, when he was granted leave of absence and his duties were assumed by staff from the Presidency's civilian education administration. By June 1865, most units had trained schoolmasters. There were ten Chelsea trained masters: the 33rd, 72nd and 95th regiments had Second Class masters and the 44th, 56th, 1/4th, 26th regiments and 6th Dragoons had Third Class masters. In addition, 3rd Dragoon Guards and 45th Foot had schoolmasters who serving under the revised 1863 Regulations. There were also Bombay trained masters with the 106th and 109th Regiments and a further twelve locally trained masters and acting masters, mainly serving with detachments of the Royal Artillery and the Sappers and Miners.[43]

40   *First Report by the Council of Military Education on Army Schools etc.*, pp. 131-50.
41   *First Report by the Council of Military Education on Army Schools etc.*, pp. 131-150.
42   TNA WO 76/106: 'Records of Officers' Services, 95th Nottingham and Derby Regiment (45th and 95th Foot) 1825-1878'.
43   *Third Report by the Council for Military Education on Army Schools etc.*, pp. 46-47.

Jacob's report in 1865 included a letter from Lt General Robert Napier, the C-in-C of the Bombay Presidency, regretting that were not enough trained schoolmasters to staff all the schools of the detached batteries of the RA in the Presidency. Many of these units had to turn to an untrained NCO simply to keep their schools open and in consequence the educational attainment of both the soldiers and their children in these units left a good deal to be desired.[44]

In contrast the schools of the 26th Cameronians at Belgaum were very well managed and the adult schools were judged to surpass all others in the Presidency. The regiment had adopted regulations specifying the educational attainments required for promotion though the ranks of NCOs and the CO took a personal interest in the school and did everything in his power to assist the schoolmaster and encourage attendance. Schoolmaster Walters was very conscientious teacher, who gave so many hours to this unusually large school of 386 adult pupils, that Jacobs feared that his health would suffer.[45] The COs of other regiments however were not so committed. Circulars had been issued by the C-in-C India and also by the C-in-C Bombay encouraging the introduction of 'Special classes'. This had not been popular with a number of COs. In 1865 five of the 25 regiments in Bombay did not have any special classes, and in the 20 that did, only 14 supported attendance by exempting the men from duties.[46]

In the same year there were seven trained schoolmistresses in the Presidency's schools. Three were Second class mistresses and, four were Third class. There were also three assistant mistresses.[47] Jacob did not comment in his reports on the condition of the infant schools, but he reported that the school of the 26th (Cameronians) was particularly well managed and the children were ably taught by the wife of the schoolmaster, who was a trained schoolmistress.

In the same report Lt General Napier regretted that he was not able to appoint more assistant mistresses. He noted that it was unusual for girls in the line regiments to remain unmarried after the age of sixteen and it was therefore difficult to retain their services as monitoresses or assistant teachers. Consequently, if a schoolmistress should become sick there was seldom anyone properly qualified to take her place.[48]

F.W. Dunn continued as the Superintendent and Assistant Inspector of Army Schools in Bengal during the 1860s and was promoted with the local rank of Captain. His responsibilities extended from Assam in the east to Khyber Pass on the North West Frontier. Although he was assiduous in his duties it was impossible to inspect all the schools each year. In most years he managed to inspect and report on upwards of thirty schools and the Council of Military Education included a selection of these in its Reports.[49]

44 *Third Report by the Council for Military Education on Army Schools etc.*, pp. 37-8.
45 *Third Report by the Council for Military Education on Army Schools etc.*, pp. 45-47.
46 *Third Report by the Council for Military Education on Army Schools etc.*, pp. xxi –xxii.
47 *Third Report by the Council for Military Education on Army Schools etc.*, p. 46.
48 *Fourth Report by the Council for Military Education on Army Schools etc.*, pp. 37, 47.
49 *Fourth Report by the Council of Military Education on Army Schools etc.* p. viii.

The Council's Third Report published in 1866 included a letter from General Sir H. Rose, the C-in-C in India, enclosing reports on schools in the Bengal Presidency inspected by Captain Dunn. The Schools of the Royal Artillery, 19th Hussars, 2/ Rifle Brigade, 1/20 Foot and the 94th Foot at Meerut, Rookee and Kussowlie were inspected in November and December 1864. These units had adopted regulations requiring young soldiers to attend school until they could read and write and had a fair knowledge of the simple rules of arithmetic. Other regiments required soldiers seeking promotion as NCOs to pass examinations showing that they were literate and numerate.[50]

Between January and July 1866 Dunn inspected the schools in Central India and the Punjab and produced synoptic reports on the progress of the pupils. He examined work produced by 2,664 adults. In reading, about 42 percent achieved the two highest standards indicating the ability to read an ordinary book very fairly, while 38percent were below the lowest standard and were unable to read the easiest book with any facility. There were lower proportions reaching the highest standard in dictation, whilst attainments in arithmetic were generally below those in reading and writing. Special classes existed in 14 schools comprising 300 scholars, but these men were handicapped by not being exempted from routine military duties.[51]

Dunn also examined 436 children in the grown children's schools. Some 22 percent had not achieved the lowest standard, and this increased to 49 percent in writing from dictation and to 56 percent in arithmetic. He believed that the attainments of these children suffered wherever they were taught by schoolmistresses. He confessed that he did not have a high opinion of the regimental schoolmistresses as a body but acknowledged that they did valuable work in charge of the infants.[52]

In the following year (1867), he inspected some thirty schools in the Lower (eastern) Provinces, where regiments were much more scattered and broken up into detachments than in the Upper Provinces and the Punjab. He apologized to the Council for the delay in submitting his reports. He explained that the work of inspection without assistants was heavy and he earnestly hoped that the '…arrangements under consideration for the more effective superintendence of schools in the presidency may not be much longer delayed.' The majority of the 1,550 men he examined were attending school because they were ordered to do so by their COs. In general a smaller proportion of the men had failed to achieve the lowest standard in reading, dictation and arithmetic than in the previous year. Dunn made few comments regarding the children. Attendance was generally good, but their progress was hindered by the climate with comparatively little instruction given during the summer months. In addition, the schooling was interrupted by long marches when regiments moved between stations and there was

---

50   *Third Report by the Council of Military Education on Army Schools etc.*, pp. 20-33.
51   *Fifth Report by the Council of Military Education on Army Schools etc.*, pp. 73-75.
52   *Fifth Report by the Council of Military Education on Army Schools etc.*, p. 75.

often also a need to close down classes because of outbreaks of cholera.[53] Cholera was a major cause of school closures until well into the 1870s. In 1862-63 the 1/19 Foot lost 87 men and five wives and 11 children to the disease and ten years later the 2/19 Foot in one year lost 25 men and five women and seven children.[54]

In 1868-69 Dunn visited 37 schools, including those at Peshawar on the North West frontier. In response to his representations, the military authorities acknowledged the heavy demands placed on Dunn in attempting an annual visit to all schools in the Presidency and he was given permission to limit the number of stations visited each year. He reported that trained schoolmasters had been provided for all units including the detached batteries of artillery. Attendance at the adult school was compulsory in some 70 percent of the units, but there was little improvement in the overall attainment in the basic subjects. Although Special Classes had been established in most units the average annual attendance of the men was barely eight months.

Once again Dunn had very little to say about the grown children's schools, but he was concerned that the boys and girls were not adequately prepared in the basic subjects before transferring from the infant schools. He was still not thoroughly satisfied with the results of the teaching in the infants' school. He considered that there was no clear statement of the standard of literacy that should be achieved in these schools.

Dunn's reports do not give any information on the number of schoolmasters and mistresses who were trained at the Normal Schools of the Lawrence Military Asylum or the regiments and corps to which they were posted. The standard period of training for the schoolmasters was two years and Captain Dunn would have taken a major part in the half -yearly examination of the students. Like the students at Chelsea their teaching practice was probably restricted to children at the Asylum, although there were adult schools close by at Kussowlie.

Sergeant William Bartram of the 52nd (Oxford) Light Infantry volunteered to train as an army schoolmaster at the Sanawar School in September 1859 and was a student there until 28th September 1861. Born in 1835, he was orphaned when an infant and grew up in the Rochford Union Workhouse Essex. He enlisted as a boy soldier in the 52nd in December 1851. In July 1849, the regiment had been allocated one of the first of the Army schoolmasters trained at Chelsea. William as a boy soldier would have attended the regimental school and it probably provided him with the standard of elementary required for entry to the Normal School at Sanawar. He accompanied the regiment when it moved to the Bengal Presidency and joined the garrison at Umballa in the Punjab. The regiment was heavily involved in the fighting

53 *Fifth Report by the Council of Military Education on Army Schools etc.*, p. 76-80.
54 T.A. Heathcote, *The Indian Army: The Garrison of British Imperial India 1822-1922* (London: David & Charles, 1974), p. 158.

during the rebellion and took part in the siege and capture of Delhi.[55] On passing out from the Sanawar School, he was posted as a Third Class Schoolmaster to the first battalion of the 23rd Foot. Before joining this regiment, he was given permission to marry Emma Caroline Malone, who was a 17 year old ward of the Guardians of the Lawrence Military Asylum. The marriage was conducted by the chaplain of the Asylum. Subsequently, Emma was appointed as an Army Schoolmistress and the couple managed the battalion's schools. Three sons were born in India and the couple continued to be in charge of the regiment's schools when the battalion was stationed in Newport Monmouthshire after its return to Great Britain. Interestingly, William elected to remain as a 3rd Class Schoolmaster until he retired in 1876.[56]

William Bartram, Army schoolmaster Third Class, c.1874. (Reproduced by kind permission of the Adjutant General's Corps Museum, Winchester)

Dunn conducted the half-yearly examinations of the trainee schoolmistresses at the Normal School at the Lawrence Asylum and in 1869, 35 of the 48 regiments and artillery brigades in the Presidency had been provided with trained schoolmistresses. Fifteen had been trained in Great Britain and 20 at the Normal School of the Lawrence Asylum. There were no details of how many of the Lawrence Asylum alumni were married to Army schoolmasters. The remaining 13 units without trained schoolmistresses had an unqualified acting schoolmistress who had been appointed by the C-in-C India. There was a serious shortage of teaching assistants in the regimental infant schools throughout the Presidency. The Indian government would not agree to the appoint pupil teachers until 1869 and because their pay was the same as for a monitoresses no applications were forthcoming.

55   W.S Moosom, *Historical Record of the Fifty-Second Regiment* (London: Richard Bentley, 1860), p. 339.
56   BL: IOR, 'Marriages at the Lawrence Military Asylum Kussowlie,1861'; Census of England and Wales 1871; TNA WO12/6290: 'General Muster Book and Pay Lists, 52nd Foot, 1st Batalion 1861-1862'.

In general, Dunn was satisfied with the conduct of the schoolmistresses and schoolmasters, although three of the masters, two of who were locally trained, were reduced to the ranks in 1868 by a general court martial for unspecified misconduct.[57] The Council did not include any reports on the schools in the Madras Presidency until its Fifth Report published in 1868. This Presidency covered a large area across Southern India stretching from the Bay of Bengal to the Malabar Coast on the Arabian Sea. It included the barracks at St Thomas and Fort George Madras and the large stations at Bangalore, Secunderabad (near Hyderabad) and at Wellington in the Western Ghats. It also extended across the Bay of Bengal to Rangoon and lower Burma. Unlike the other two presidency's armies the Madras army included a European Veteran battalion with its own depots and schools. Initially, the schools of the European Regiments had been placed under the presidency's civil inspectors, but in 1859 a military superintendent was appointed. This person was removed from office in October 1861 and the superintendence reverted to the government's civil inspectors. It was not until March 1867 that Lieutenant Colonel Lawrie was appointed Superintendent of Army Schools in the Madras Presidency.[58]

In his first report to the Council in May 1868 Lawrie emphasised the limitations of using civilian inspectors to superintend the Army's schools. Not only were they unaware of the amount of education that was generally useful for private soldiers and NCOs, but because their priority was with their civil duties, they had little time to gain an understanding of the particular characteristics of the Army's schools. During his appointment Lawrie arranged for monthly written reports to be sent from the regimental and depot schools to his HQ at Bangalore. He also completed a comprehensive tour of inspection, reporting that he had travelled nearly 6,000 miles, which included visits to the schools in Burma. Colonel Lawrie relinquished the post in August 1868 and was succeeded by Major H. L. Grove, who continued the work of establishing a system of military supervision of the presidency's Army schools. In winter months of 1868 -1869 Grove visited the schools of every depot, regiment and battery with the exception of those in Burma and two battalions of infantry that were marching between stations. He claimed that the distance travelled by sea amounted to 1,100 miles and 4,200 miles by rail and road. Grove acknowledged that that it would be impossible to visit all the stations each year. He announced that in the future he would only visit the stations in Burma every second year but would undertake an annual visit to Secunderabad which was home to the second largest European garrison in India and had several large schools.[59]

Colonel Lawrie had stated that his priority was to prepare the way 'for amalgamating the Indian with the Imperial Establishment', which had been recommended by the Council of Military Education in 1864. He was acquainted with the reports of the

57 *Sixth Report by the Council of Military Education on Army Schools etc.*, pp. 55-59, 68-72.
58 *Sixth Report by the Council of Military Education on Army Schools etc.*, pp. 66-71.
59 *Sixth Report by the Council of Military Education on Army Schools etc.*, p. 108.

Council of Military Education and in his short time in post worked to introduce the standard documentation for reporting that was in use in Great Britain. Although the current Army School's Regulations had been sent to the C-in-C India and copies dispatched from Calcutta to Bombay and Madras, a number of the standard War Office forms covering the returns of school attendance, examinations of pupils and the reporting of inspections had not been circulated. Colonel Lawrie had WO Form 1060(with the return of the numbers of pupils on the registers and in attendance) printed at his own expense and Major Grove ensured that the standard documentation for the monthly (Form 367) and the half yearly reports (Form D) and for the examination of pupils were printed locally on government presses. In May 1869 Grove reported that the War Office forms were in use in every school; however he expected that it would be some twelve months before those schoolmasters, who had not previously served in Great Britain would have thoroughly mastered the detail of the documentation. In the meantime he advised the Council to approach the forms returned to London with caution.[60]

Irregular attendance was a serious issue at most of the adult schools in the presidency. Colonel Lawrie's' first visit was to the Convalescent Depot School at Wellington in the Ghats, which enjoyed a relatively benign and pleasant climate. The children's school was in good condition, but although there were nominally more than 50 soldiers on the books of the adult school, he did not find any men attending classes. He was not surprised and accepted that the climate in India made regular attendance at the adult schools even more unpredictable than it was in England. He acknowledged that some COs were prejudiced against army education and observed that attendance was better whenever the CO took an interest in his regiment's school. Major Grove quoted the example of a cavalry regiment, very probably the 18th Hussars, where nominally school attendance was compulsory. However, during a five month period 32 of the 65 NCOs never attended the schoolroom and the attendance of the remainder was derisory. When a new officer assumed command however there was a significant improvement in attendance. The situation was much better where there were Special classes, which Lawrie described as indispensable and the 'life and soul of the military educational system.' Both Lawrie and Grove shared the growing consensus amongst the Army's inspectors that that real progress could be only be made when the possession of a school certificate was made essential for promotion in peacetime.[61]

There was general satisfaction with the children's schools. Grove concluded that the standard of education in the grown children's schools was often superior to that at the adult schools and the boys trained in them readily found employment in the telegraph, survey, engineer, medical, and postal departments in the Presidency. A number of the infant schools did not have trained schoolmistress and were often

60   *Fifth Report by the Council for Military Education on Army Schools etc.*, pp. 66-72; *Sixth Report by the Council of Military Education on Army Schools etc.*, pp. 84-114.
61   *Sixth Report by the Council of Military Education on Army Schools etc.*, pp. 84-114.

taught by assistant mistress and soldier's wives. Many of these women were poorly educated and the schools often fell well short of the required standard. There was also shortage of classroom assistants. Grove noted that the appointment of pupil teachers, which had been authorised by the 1863 Army School Regulations, had not taken place and the schoolmistresses were assisted only by monitoresses on a salary of £4 per annum. These girls were young and were generally left the moment they received an offer of marriage. Grove considered that absence of trained female staff was serious but admitted that given the particulate circumstances in India he did not see how the staffing requirements could be met.[62]

Colonel Lawrie and Major Grove both agreed that well ventilated school rooms were essential in the climate of India, but they found that most of the accommodation was unsatisfactory. There was no standard specification for the schoolrooms and in May 1868 Lawrie recommended the adoption of a plan drawn up by the Quarter Master General's department at Bangalore for a school for the 16th Lancers with space schools to accommodate 100 pupils in four classrooms.[63] In the following year Major Grove was reporting continuing difficulties. There were 90 boys in the European Veteran Company's school at Palaveram, which was temporarily housed in a barracks which was available for only six months of the year. The barracks was soon to be required for accommodating troops and an order was issued to rent the most commodious dwelling available. Apparently the presidency's government was unwilling to go to expense of building a school house, because the veteran parents would in due course die or be absorbed in other units.[64]

The Council of Military Education in its Second Report on the Army's schools published in 1865 had admitted that it was uncertain about the particular arrangements for supervision and inspection of the schools in India. It also observed:

> In India there is, it is believed, one assistant inspector, whose district comprises the whole of the Bengal, Agra, and Punjab Presidencies. An officer of the army officiates as acting Superintendent of the Bombay Presidency; while the army schools of the Madras Presidencies are understood to be under the Civil Commissioners.[65]

The difficulty was that the Council did not have the executive powers to impose a common system of inspecting and reporting on the schools in India. The Council did receive reports from all three Presidencies, but not in the form that could be easily amalgamated with the other reports it had received for the superintending inspectors in the British Isles and the garrisons in the colonies in the Mediterranean and Canada.

---

62   *Sixth Report by the Council of Military Education on Army Schools etc.*, pp. 84-114.
63   *Fifth Report by the Council of Military Education on Army Schools etc.*, p. 69.
64   *Sixth Report by the Council of Military Education on Army Schools etc.*, p. 95.
65   *Second Report by the Council of Military Education on Army Schools etc.*, p. viii.

The reports from India in the early 1860s often contained a large amount of statistical information on the numbers on registers and the average attendances and detailed reports on individual schools, but there was little attempt to synthesise and evaluate the material. In consequence it is difficult to piece together a comprehensive account of the progress of the regimental schools across the three presidencies.

The Council of Military Education was concerned about the development of the separate systems of inspection and reporting within the three presidencies in India and that these differed from the arrangements in Great Britain and garrisons in other parts of the Empire. In 1864 the Council had submitted a scheme to the C-in-C at the Horse Guards for amalgamating the Indian and the Imperial systems.[66] This was approved by the War Office and was forwarded to the India Office, which presumably passed it on to the Government in Calcutta. The Council in successive reports during the 1860s noted with regret that the proposed scheme for amalgamating the Indian and the Imperial establishments had not yet been sanctioned by the Secretary of State for India.

The Superintendent and Inspectors of Army Schools in the three Presidencies were appointed by the Government of India and the Superintendents in Bombay and Bengal held local army ranks. In 1865 the Superintendents in the presidencies, together with 41 schoolmasters who had been appointed by the Government of India, formed what was referred to as the 'Indian establishment.' These men were serving under the 1854 Regulations: three held the rank of First Class Schoolmaster, four were Second Class, 18 were Third Class and 15 held the Fourth Class Rank.[67] They had been trained at the Normal Schools at Poona and the Lawrence Military Asylum. The Third Report of the Council of Military Education published in 1866 listed 44 schoolmasters on the 'Indian establishment' – the majority serving as Third and Fourth Class masters.[68]

On 31st March 1866 there were 228 schoolmasters on what was referred to as the 'Imperial establishment' who had been trained at the RMA Chelsea and the majority was serving under the 1863 Regulations. Only 76 of the schoolmasters on the 'Imperial establishment' had chosen to remain with their ranks and serve under the 1854 Regulations. The 1863 Army School Regulations had been forwarded to India, but the military authorities in Calcutta appear not to have implemented them until 1867. Most locally trained masters chose to transfer to the new regulations. It however took some time for those who had agreed to transfer to the 1863 Regulations to receive the increases in pay and there was understandably some discontent until the increases were implemented. Colonel Lawrie had reported that 19 of the schoolmasters under his superintendence in Madras had decided to move on to the 1863 regulations,

---

66   *Fourth Report by the Council for Military Education on Army Schools etc.*, p. vii.
67   Editorial note: Readers will note that when added together the total number is 40 and not 41 as the author asserts. In normal circumstances this query would be referred to the author, but with his tragic and untimely death this has not been possible.
68   *Third Report by the Council for Military Education on Army Schools etc.*, p. iv;19.

whilst 11 had elected to remain under the old regulations, but some of these had been trained at Chelsea, and therefore would not have been counted part of the Indian establishment.[69] Major Grove reported in May 1869 that all the masters attached to the Royal Artillery's schools in Madras and those managing the schools of six battalions of British infantry and one regiment of cavalry had been trained in India. Significantly he noted that the training of men at the normal schools in India had been discontinued and the number of schoolmasters on Indian establishment would steadily diminish. In future all vacancies for regimental and depot schoolmasters would have to be filled by men sent from England who had trained at the RMA Normal School.[70]

There had been a rationale for the retention of a separate 'Indian establishment' when there were European regiments recruited and maintained by the East India Company and the normal schools in India providing trained schoolmasters for their depot and regimental schools. The 1858 Government of India Act and the incorporation of the Company's European regiments into the British Army, followed some ten years later, by the closure of the local arrangements for training schoolmasters in India ended this rationale. All the Army schoolmasters were now serving under the same set of Army School Regulations and it was sensible that there should be a common system of superintendence and inspections for the Army's the schools at all stations at home and abroad. Moreover, the existing arrangements with only a single superintendent for each of the Indian Presidencies were clearly unsatisfactory given the huge distances between the Army's schools.

This was the view of the Royal Commission on Military Education ,which in its Second Report in 1870 (see Chapter18), observed that the system of Army schools in India was not under the direct control of the War Office. The Commissioners had been told by the military authorities in London that this caused 'great inconvenience' and they also received testimony   from at least one schoolmaster, who had served both at home and in India, that the system of superintendence there was 'inferior', and that the schools were 'conducted in a less satisfactory manner than at home.' The Commission accepted that there may be '...local difficulties in effecting an amalgamation of the system in India with that at home' but concluded that this would be extremely desirable and recommended that the government should give it immediate consideration. Nevertheless, for unspecified reasons the proposal was not acceptable to the India Office and it was not until February 1874 that the two establishments were unified and Superintending officers and the schools in India were placed laced under Director General of Military Education at the War Office.[71]

69 Fifth Report by the Council of Military Education on Army Schools etc., p. 69.
70 Sixth Report by the Council of Military Education on Army Schools etc., p. 114.
71 TNA WO32/6079: 'Second Report of the Royal Commission appointed to inquire into the present state of Military Education 1870', pp. vii, 27; Army List, February 1874.

Part III

Regimental and Garrison Schools in the Late Victorian Army

18

The Royal Commission on Military Education 1870

When the Liberal Party under William E. Gladstone's leadership decisively won the general election of 1868, they suffered a significant electoral causality in the loss of the Marquis of Hartington, their military spokesman in the House of Commons. In the circumstances Gladstone readily accepted the offer from Edward T. Cardwell to assume the post of Secretary of State for War. Cardwell was an old Peelite ally of Gladstone and had served as Colonial Secretary (1864-66) and was competent in financial and administrative matters. He had never previously promoted any contentious army reform, but like Gladstone he sought reductions in military expenditure in order to enhance the Army's efficiency.

Cardwell quickly came to the view that the reorganisation of the army administration in the wake of the Crimean War had produced a costly and cumbersome bureaucracy. Although the Duke of Cambridge, the de facto C-in-C, had conceded that the supreme control of the Army rested with the Secretary of State, there continued to be two distinct military departments with overlapping responsibilities. The Horse Guards and the War Office each had its own expensive establishments, each monitoring the other and duplicating the transaction of business.[1] One of Cardwell's first decisions was to appoint a committee chaired by Lord Northbrook to review the constitutional control and administration of the Army. This recommended that the Secretary of State should be formally confirmed as the responsible Minister with all departments subordinate to him within a unified administration at the War Office in Pall Mall. It proposed that the new department under the authority of the Secretary of State of State should contain three divisions: Military, Supply and Finance. The C-in-C would head the military division with responsibilities inter alia for discipline, appointments and promotions recruiting, training and education.[2] These recommendations were included in the War Office Act 1870.

---

1   Edward. M. Spiers, *The Late Victorian Army* 1868-1902 (Manchester: Manchester University Press,1992), pp. 2-4.
2   Spiers, *The Late Victorian Army*, p. 6.

In 1868 the Government had appointed a Royal Commission to enquire into the present state of Military Education and the training of candidates for Army commissions. The Commissioners recommended that the Council of Military Education should be replaced by a single head and a Director General of Military Education (Major General William Craig Emilius Napier) was appointed in 1870.[3] This officer was housed in the Military Department of the War Office which was headed by the C-in-C. He was assisted by a military secretary and was given the general superintendence of everything connected with Army Schools. This included the appointment of teachers at home and in the colonies and issuing general regulations that ensured that the schools was uniformly conducted throughout the Army.

The Royal Commission on Military Education was subsequently instructed to extend its enquiries to the Army's schools for soldiers and their children. The Commissioners in their Second Report published in 1870 were surprised that the arrangements for the immediate supervision and inspection of the schools varied within Great Britain and across the British Empire.

In October 1869, a step had been taken to standardise the arrangements when Lieutenant Colonel A.C. Gleig RA was appointed Inspector of Army Schools in Great Britain. Also, superintending schoolmasters with the rank of ensign had been appointed for each military district in England, Wales, and Scotland and they were required to regularly examine the schools in their districts. The Inspector was responsible for visiting every station in Great Britain that had a superintending schoolmaster at least once per year, and to report to the Director-General upon this and on such other visits as he had deemed necessary. Separate arrangements had been retained for inspection in Ireland where there was an Assistant Inspector of Army Schools, but Gleig was given responsibility for awarding Certificates of Education to soldiers in all the military districts throughout the UK. The Royal Commission on Military Education in its 1870 Report recommended the abolition of the post of Assistant Inspector in Ireland and following the death of Mr Vickers in the same year, Lieutenant Colonel Gleig was made responsible for inspecting all the schools in the UK. In conformity with the arrangements in Great Britain additional superintending schoolmasters were appointed to the military districts in Ireland.

The Royal Commission in its Second Report strongly supported the separation of the duties of general inspection from the examination of the pupils in the schools. The superintending schoolmasters were responsible for visiting every school in their districts and examining the pupils and the commission recommended that they should be designated Sub-Inspectors reporting to the Inspector of Army Schools. The Commissioners recommended that the Sub-Inspectors should visit and thoroughly

---

3   Napier was already serving as Vice President of the Council of Military Education and had been since April 1866. Before the Director General was established the President of the Council had been the Commander-in-Chief. In reality much of the work and responsibility therefore fell upon the Vice President of the Council.

inspect the schools and examine the pupil's half-yearly. This should take place a short time previous to the half-yearly visit by the inspecting general officer, who would then have be able to judge the state of the regiment's schools and the progress of the pupils based on the evidence in the Sub-Inspector's report.[4] These arrangements for the inspection of the Army's schools and the examination of pupils were incorporated in amendments to Queen's Regulations in October 1871.Sub-Inspectors were appointed to the following districts: Aldershot (two Sub-Inspectors);Cork ; Curragh; Devonport; Dover; Dublin; Edinburgh; London; Manchester; Portsmouth and Woolwich. Subsequently a thirteenth Sub-Inspector was appointed for the Eastern District.[5]

The Royal Commission explained, and Queen's Regulations emphasised, that the regimental schools had been are established to give NCOs, soldiers and their children the opportunity to gain a sound and useful education.[6] The commission in its Second Report devoted considerable attention to the children's schools. It estimated that around 20,000 children attended these schools, and this included some 3,000 children whose fathers were not serving soldiers but were employed in various capacities in barracks and army camps. Although Queen's Regulation did not place a duty on enlisted men to ensure that their children attended the regimental schools, in effect attendance was compulsory. This was because the Regulations specified that '…all married soldiers shall send their children to the school of the regiment or garrison, on pain of being liable to be deprived of privileges attendant on the residence of their wives in barracks.'[7]

The commissioners explained that COs were directly responsible for the proper management and conduct of their regimental schools and concluded that in general they showed an interest and gave them their support and encouragement. Regular attendance was enforced by the COs and this contributed greatly to the pupils' progress and gave the schoolmasters a considerable advantage over their contemporaries in the National Schools. The subjects taught were suited to the 'social condition and future wants of the children and were well devised and practically successful in their results.'[8]

There were a few issues relating to the infant schools. The Regulations did not specify the age for admission and parents frequently sent very young children to school with their elder sisters. These children were often too young to benefit from the teaching and caused problems for the schoolmistress. The commissioners recognised that it

---

4   TNA WO: General Orders: GO100, October 1869; WO, General Orders GO73, 1870; WO 32/6079, 'Second Report of the Royal Commission of Military Education 1870', pp. vi-vii.

5   First Report of the Director-General of Military Education on Army School, Libraries and Recreation Rooms1872, p. iv.

6   Queen's Regulations 1871; TNA WO General Orders, GO70, 71, October 1870.

7   TNA WO 32/6079: Second Report of the Royal Commission of Military Education 1870, p. viii; Queen's Regulations 1871, Para. 454.

8   TNA WO 32/6079: 'Second Report of the Royal Commission of Military Education 1870', p. ix.

would be inconvenient for the parents should these young children be excluded and recommended that they should be placed in the charge of a pupil teacher or monitor in a separate classroom. At some of the larger garrison the infant schools of a number of regiments had been amalgamated, but the commissioners were unimpressed with the results. They argued that it was preferable for the infants to remain with their own regiment's schoolmistress as was unavoidably the case when the regiment moved to a smaller and isolated station. They strongly supported the system of regimental schools and argued that it stimulated the commitment and zeal of the teachers and created an interest on the part of the officers and others connected with the regiment in the success of its schools.[9]

The classes of the co-educational infant schools were held from 9 to 12 in the mornings under the charge of a schoolmistress. The elder children of both sexes attended school together under the schoolmaster in the mornings, but were separated in the afternoon, when the boys remained with the master and the girls were joined by infants to form the industrial school. The Commissioners believed that the scope of the industrial schools could be increased. Girls might be taught some domestic duties in addition to needle work and some kind of industrial training might be given to boys in the regiments' workshops. The latter was encouraged by Queens' Regulations, but they could find no evidence of any systematic attempt had been given to put the suggestion into effect.[10]

Regulations continued to specify when the children should transfer from the infant to the grown children's schools, but in practice the transfer was arranged on an ad hoc basis by the regiment's schoolmaster and the schoolmistress. The Commissioners saw no reason to interfere with this arrangement.[11]

The ccommissioners emphasised that the children's subsequent progress in the grown children's schools depended upon the earlier work of the schoolmistresses in the infant schools.[12] In December 1869 there were 208 schoolmistresses on the imperial establishment. This comprised two Superintending Mistresses, 20 First Class, 49 Second Class and 145 Third School Class Schoolmistresses. There were also 277 teaching assistants. These were made up of: 39 pupil teachers and assistant schoolmistresses; 162 monitoresses and 76 acting schoolmistresses. In total there were

9   TNA WO 32/6079: 'Second Report of the Royal Commission of Military Education 1870', p. x.
10   TNA WO 32/6079: Second Report of the Royal Commission of Military Education, p. xi. The Commissioners argued that the costs of extending industrial instruction could be met by reducing the capitation grant, which more than covered the cost of materials used in teaching needlework. The capitation grant was subsequently reduced in Queen's Regulation, but there is little evidence the savings were used to increase the industrial instruction.
11   TNA WO 32/6079: 'Second Report of the Royal Commission of Military Education', pp. vii, x.
12   TNA WO 32/6079: 'Second Report of the Royal Commission of Military Education', pp. x–xi.

485 women and girls teaching in the infants' and industrial schools.[13] These women and girls were appointed and served under the Army Schools Regulations, but there was no military Normal School in Great Britain for their training. Schoolmistresses were appointed between the ages of 21 and 30 either from persons holding a civilian Certificate of Proficiency under the Committee of the Council on Education or from those employed as assistant teachers who had passed an examination proving that their education and teaching skills were satisfactory.[14]

There had been particular difficulties in securing sufficient numbers of trained schoolmistresses in India and this had resulted in the formation of a training school at the Lawrence College. The commissioners were apparently unaware of this and did not express any concern about a shortage of trained women teachers in the Army's schools in India. They however noted the inequities in the remuneration received by married and unmarried women. Both categories of teachers received the same modest salary, but there was a generous lodging allowance for the single teachers. In some cases the unmarried Third Class mistress was in a better pecuniary position than a married schoolmistress of higher class to whom the lodging allowance was not granted. The commissioners recommended that the situation could be improved by increasing the salaries and making a small reduction to the lodging allowance. There were also other differences between the treatment of unmarried and married women that the Commissioners wished to see removed. When travelling, married teachers were treated merely as one of the women of the regiment, but unmarried teachers were entitled to superior accommodation. They recommended that married schoolmistresses should be placed in the same position as regards quarters, allowances and all privileges such as drawing rations as the unmarried irrespective of whether the husband was entitled to any allowances. In addition, they considered it was undesirable that the unmarried schoolmistress or married schoolmistress whose husbands were absent should be required to live in barracks and instead recommended that they should be permitted to draw lodging allowances. In making these recommendations the Commissioners were aware that some schoolmistresses were married to the regiment's schoolmaster, whilst others were widows who wished to remain with their late husband's regiment and work in the regimental school.[15]

The commissioners did not discount the important part played by the teaching assistants in the infant and industrial schools and observed that pupil teachers were invariably recruited from the monitoresses, who themselves were selected from the girls attending a regiment's school. There however was a shortage of monitoresses

13 *Sixth Report by the Council of Military Education 1870*, pp. v, vi.
14 TNA WO 32/6079: 'Second Report of the Royal Commission of Military Education', pp. xxii. The Committee of the Council on Education was the Committee of the Privy Council that had been set up by Order in Council in 1839 'to superintend the application of sums voted by Parliament for the purpose of promoting Public Education.'
15 TNA WO 32/6079: 'Second Report of the Royal Commission of Military Education', p. xxiii.

and the Commissioners recommended that the minimum age for recruitment should be reduced from 13 to 12 and that their pay should be increased after the first year of appointment.[16]

The Commissioners considered that in general the children's schools met their objectives and provided a 'sound and useful education' which was highly appreciated by the parents. In these circumstances there was little justification for charging fees. The sums collected were trifling, around £1,400 per annum, but there was a cost in collecting, accounting and remitting the fees. The Commissioners argued that as the privilege of free education had very properly been granted to the soldier the same privilege should be granted to his children.[17]

Rev George Gleig, when he was Inspector-General had had shown very little interest in the children's schools, but in his evidence to the Royal Commission he compared them very favourably to the generality of civilian schools. He also praised the moral influence of the regimental and Sunday schools on the children. The Commissioners noted that there were still those who regretted the passing of the old class of schoolmaster sergeants, who with the encouragement of their COs could be relied on to supervise the children's behaviour outside the classroom. They did not believe that the new class of trained schoolmasters should be required to extend their duties beyond the classroom and concluded that the direct responsibility for the moral welfare of the children could only rest with the parents.[18]

The Commissioners were much less confident about the adult schools. The abolition of fees had been followed by little improvement in the regularity of attendance. In 1867 there had been nearly 39,000 men on the adult schoolbooks, but Colonel Pocklington, the member of the Council of Military Education who had special responsibilities for Army Schools, doubted if more than 30 men out of 200 or 300 on the school-books of a regiment attended on average each day. Queens Regulations gave COs some powers to enforce attendance, but they were reluctant to use them. Practice varied between regiments: some required recruits and NCOs to attend school until they were considered to be 'duly qualified'; others restricted compulsion to newly enlisted men and in some cases attendance was voluntary. Special Classes, which encouraged attendance by exempting men from regimental duties, improved attendance and their number was increasing, but they had not been established in all regiments. Some regiments insisted on the possession of one of the Certificates of Education for

16   TNA WO 32/6079: 'Second Report of the Royal Commission of Military Education', p. xxiii.
17   TNA WO 32/6079: 'Second Report of the Royal Commission of Military Education', p. x.
18   TNA WO32/6079: 'Second Report of the Royal Commission of Military Education', pp. x-xii.

promotion, whilst others set their own exams or simply promoted men on personal recommendation.[19]

The regimental schools had been staffed with trained masters and the Army was providing plenty of opportunities for men to improve their education, but the results were disappointing. The commissioners argued that a modern army required intelligent and self-reliant soldiers with at least the rudiments of an elementary education. Following the Cardwell's reforms (see below) more men would be enlisting for 'short service' and the Army could play its part in 'promoting popular education' with all its benefits for society. The system of education for rank and file would not be placed on a satisfactory footing until there was a uniform set of arrangements based on common principles applied across every regiment and corps in the Army.[20]

The commissioners discussed whether attendance at school should be made compulsory. Based on the testimony presented to them they concluded that this would be inadvisable for men who were already in the service. Many of these men were not ambitious and saw little point in education and would resent compulsion. The same could not be said for new recruits. All newly enlisted men should be required to attend school until they gained a Fourth Class Certificate of Education. This new certificate would be awarded by the CO on the recommendation of the Sub-Inspector and would demonstrate that the recruit could read and copy an easy narrative and work the four simple rules of arithmetic. Attendance would become an integral part of the basic training for the soldier and would be undertaken alongside learning drill. COs should ensure that instruction was systematic and uninterrupted, and attendance should not as a rule be less than five hours per week. Enlisted boys between fourteen and seventeen years would be required to attend until they had obtained a Second Class Certificate. Recruits who could pass the examination for the Fourth Class Certificate should be encouraged to attend on a voluntary basis and work towards a higher class certificate. The Commissioners believed that every encouragement should then be given for the soldier to further improve his education and this could be achieved through greater use of the certificates of education for promotion. In peace time and except when on active service, possession of a Third Cass Certificate should be necessary for promotion to full Corporal and a Second Class Certificate for promotion to Sergeant. They considered that this would be within the spirit of Queen's Regulations, because possession of the certificates would not be the only condition for promotion and would continue to give CO's discretion in selecting men as NCOs. The commissioners believed that these measures would result in a considerable improvement in the standard of education

19   TNA WO32/6079: 'Second Report of the Royal Commission of Military Education', pp. xii–xxii.
20   TNA WO32/6079: 'Second Report of the Royal Commission of Military Education', pp. xii–xxii.

in the Army, but they warned that this could not be achieved without an adequate number of well qualified teachers.[21]

In December 1869, the imperial establishment of Army schoolmasters (not including those appointed locally by the government of India) stood at 270. This comprised 12 Superintending schoolmasters and 217 Army schoolmasters appointed under the 1863 Regulations and 41 schoolmasters who had elected to remain under the 1854 Regulations. The latter was formed of 11 First Class, 29 Second Class and one Third Class Master. The Commissioners had collected a great deal of evidence that there was widespread dissatisfaction amongst the schoolmasters about their position in the Army. Some of the alleged grievances they thought were more imaginary than real and some arose from the inevitable circumstances of army life, but they believed that the position of the schoolmaster was such that it failed to attract the same class of men who formerly entered the service. They received testimony that the various changes in the conditions of service for schoolmasters introduced during the 1860s had reduced their status in the Army. The Council of Military Education had been confident that although there were only 11 students in training in the Normal School at Chelsea and the majority of those admitted were serving soldiers, the supply of trained masters from Chelsea was continuing the meet the needs of the Service.[22] The commissioners disagreed and pointed to the reduction in the number of civilian applicants to the Normal School from 34 in 1861 to three in 1869. Although the qualifications required from serving soldiers had been lowered, the number of military competitors for admission had fallen from 32 in 1867 to 14 in 1869. There were upwards of 500 soldiers serving as assistant in the schools, but in 1870 there were only 13 soldier candidates for admission to the Normal School. The Commissioners concluded that unless measures were taken to attract a larger number of applicants, in a few years the supply of trained schoolmasters would be inadequate to meet the annual vacancies arising from the discharges and deaths in service.[23]

The commissioners had received representations that the principal cause of the existing dissatisfaction amongst the schoolmasters was the abolition the warrant rank, granted previously to those promoted to First Class Schoolmaster, with the loss of attendant privileges and the prospect of advancement within the service. The commissioners were well aware of the opposition at the highest levels in the Army, including the C-in-C the Duke of Cambridge, to the imposition of an intermediate rank between the commissioned officer and the sergeant major. They pointed out that the schoolmaster held a position superior to all NCOs other than the regimental sergeant major and this was unlikely to cause any issues of command or discipline,

21   TNA WO32/6079: Second Report of the Royal Commission of Military Education, pp. xiv-xvii.
22   *Sixth Report by the Council of Military Education on Army Schools, 1869.*
23   TNA WO 32/6079: 'Second Report of the Royal Commission of Military Education', p. xix.

provided he confined himself to his proper sphere of duties in the classroom. Moreover the 1863 Regulations, whilst abolishing the warrant rank, offered the prospect of greater advancement by creating the grade of superintending schoolmaster with the higher rank of a commissioned officer.

The commissioners argued that it was preferable to address the dissatisfactions by making more substantial and tangible improvements in pay and conditions of service.[24] They recommended that as enlisted soldiers the Army schoolmasters should continue to be subject to the Mutiny Act and the Articles of War as regards military discipline, but otherwise their conditions of service should recognise their non-combatant status and the distinctive position in the Army. They suggested a number of changes to increase their status including the ending of the requirement for unmarried schoolmasters to mess with the sergeants. The commissioners also considered that it was desirable to make some improvement in pay and pensions. The increased responsibilities of the superintending schoolmasters for inspecting the schools was recognised by their designation as Sub-Inspectors of Army Schools and the commissioners recommended an increase in their pay and improvements in their pensions. They also considered that the pay on entering the service was insufficient to enable the young Army schoolmaster to maintain his position. He no longer received the fees paid by soldiers for their children's schooling and introduction the Special Classes entailed a lengthening of his working day.[25]

There were good reasons for increasing the schoolmaster's salary and in making recommendations the Commissioners were guided to some extent by the salaries offered to civilian schoolmasters in analogous positions. The pay of the newly qualified Army schoolmaster was considerably below that of the trained civilian schoolmaster in the National Schools, but the Army schoolmaster received, clothing, fuel and light, and rations. He could look forward to periodical increases in pay and a pension after 21 years' service. The Commissioners proposed increases and changes to the pay scales that were designed both to attract and retain the schoolmaster. They recommended a 33.3 percent increase in the Army schoolmaster's starting salary, with triennial increases after three years' service, rising to £99 per annum after 21 years, which with contingent allowances amounted to about £114 and a pension on retirement. This final sum exclusive of the pension was in excess of the salary of the typical trained civilian teacher and the Commissioners also proposed shortening Army schoolmaster's working week by ending the requirement that he should assist in the Sunday Schools.[26] Moreover the Army schoolmaster was spared from serving under the 1862 Revised Code that made his civilian counterpart's salary and tenure

24   TNA WO 32/6079: 'Second Report of the Royal Commission of Military Education', p. xix.
25   TNA WO 32/6079: 'Second Report of the Royal Commission of Military Education', pp. xx-xxii.
26   TNA WO 32/6079: 'Second Report of the Royal Commission of Military Education', pp. xx-xxii.

of employment dependent on the results of his pupils. The Revised Code replaced the payments made directly to certificated teachers in elementary schools with grants to managers of the schools, which depended on the number of pupils attending regularly and their annual performance in examinations in reading, writing, and arithmetic conducted by government inspectors (HMIs). The majority of managers related the teachers' salaries to the amount of grant they earned for the school and failure to maintain results or a critical inspector's report could result in dismissal.[27]

The Commissioners gave a great deal of consideration to the future of the Normal School at Chelsea and concluded that in recent years it had not '...fulfilled the expectations of its founders.' They were very concerned that although the authorised establishment was placed at 40 students, the number of candidates had greatly decreased and at present consisted of only 16 students. Of this number, 13 were soldiers and only three were civilians who previously had been employed as pupil teachers. It was hoped that the measures proposed for improving the pay and conditions of service of the Army schoolmaster would make the position a more attractive career prospect and thereby increase the number applicants for admission to the Normal School. In its current state however the Commissioners questioned whether the institution justified the cost of its maintenance. It was apparent that the Commissioners were not confident that their proposed improvements in pay and condition would significantly increase the number of applicants for School. They went further and questioned whether the system of training provided by the Normal School was the best preparation for the duties of an Army schoolmaster. The institution was small and although the students spent twelve months on teaching practice in the Model School, the experience there extended only to teaching children. It was invariably the case that the young schoolmaster was first employed teaching adults under the guidance of an experienced master, but there no actual regulations to ensure that this was carried out. The Commissioners considered that the civilian training colleges could supply some qualified candidates for appointment but believed that it would be inadvisable to exclude serving soldiers from becoming trained schoolmasters. These men accepted military discipline, understood the private soldier, and were familiar with army life and were more likely to be successful in teaching the adult classes. Indeed, one of the strongest arguments in favour of maintaining the Normal School was the facilities that it provided for soldiers to qualify as schoolmasters. This argument however lost its force if, as the commissioners believed, a scheme could be devised that offered every encouragement to civilian candidates, whilst offering reasonable opportunities for soldiers to qualify for appointment.[28]

27   G. Sutherland, *Policy-Making in Elementary Education 1870-1895* (Oxford: Oxford University Press, 1973), pp. 66-67.

28   TNA WO 32/6079: 'Second Report of the Royal Commission of Military Education', pp. xxviii-xxxi.

The Commissioners proposed abolishing the Normal School and recommended a tripartite scheme in its place. Appointments would be thrown open to public competition by civilians who had spent at least twelve months in a teacher training establishment, and soldiers who had either been employed as school assistants for the same period or had passed sixth months in this capacity and six months in a teacher training establishment. Pupil teachers the RMA Model School and Monitors at the RHMS would continue to be admitted to the competition on reaching 20 years of age. Candidates who passed the competition would be appointed on probation for sixth months under an Army schoolmaster with not less than five years' service. During this time they would gain practical experience of teaching both adults and children. On the successful completion of the probation the Inspector of the district would make a report on the probationer to the Inspector of Army Schools and if approved would be sent by him to the Director-General of Military Education with a recommendation for appointment as an Army schoolmaster. The cost of sending soldiers to a civilian teaching establishment would be offset from the savings gained from abolishing the Normal School and the Army would benefit from the work of the candidate schoolmasters during their probationary period.[29]

The Second Report of the Royal Commission was presented to Edward Cardwell, the Secretary of State for War, on 14th July 1870 and he asked for comments from the senior officials and officers at the War Office together with any notes of disagreement and alternative recommendations. There was broad agreement on most of the Commissioners' recommendations and these were incorporated in the revised Army School Regulations issued in October 1871 and subsequently in amendments to Queen's Regulations.

The C-in-C, still The Duke of Cambridge, and the Director General of Military Education expressed their disagreement on different points of detail but were in one voice in their total opposition to the proposal to close the Normal School. The Director General considered that the improvements in Army education were mainly due to this School and he could see no reason for its abolition. The alternative arrangements proposed by the Commissioners were inferior to the status quo. Civilians admitted to the Normal School gradually gained experience of military discipline and an initiation into military life before their initial posting to a regiment or depot school. A young man moving straight from a civilian training institution to a barracks would be 'completely lost and bewildered.' This he argued was in itself a sufficient reason for maintaining the Normal School. In the case of serving soldiers, the proposals for a twelve month period as an assistant schoolmaster was a very poor substitute for the twelve months currently spent at the Normal School and the twelve months at the Model school. The soldier candidate would be much less educated than the civilian and be unlikely to pass the prosed qualifying examination. He feared that as

29   TNA WO 32/6079: 'Second Report of the Royal Commission of Military Education', pp. xxviii–xxxi.

a consequence soldiers who would have succeeded at the Normal School and qualified as Army schoolmasters would be lost to the service. He doubted whether the civilian training establishments would be willing to accept soldiers as students, or whether with regard to matters of discipline these establishments would be desirable places for soldiers to study. He hoped that the Secretary of State would seek the views of the members of the late Council of Military Education, including Rev Moseley and Major General Pocklington, before deciding on the abolition of the Normal School.[30]

---

30   TNA WO 32/6079: Memorandum Number 2, 'Dissent by the Director-General of Military Education from the recommendations of the Royal Commission on Military Education in its Second Report'.

19

Army Schools at Home and Abroad 1870-82

The Director General of Military Education in his First Report on Army Schools published in 1872 confirmed that Royal Commission's recommendations regarding the Inspectorate and inspections, the pay and pensions of schoolmasters and mistresses and the children's schools had been implemented. The Secretary of State for War however had decided not to proceed with Royal Commission's recommendation to abolish the Normal School.[1]

During 1870-76, 134 students were admitted to the Normal School and 87 of these were NCOs and private soldiers. The successful civilian applicants already had some teaching experience mainly as pupil teachers. The RHMS become an established source for these entrants during the 1860s and the Headmaster, John Gibbons, encouraged his more promising boys to remain at the School as monitors, as pupil teachers were called at the Phoenix Park School. He then coached these boys for the entry for the Normal School with a high degree of success and some of the Hibernian boys regularly gained the highest marks in the entry examinations.[2] In 1874 the Government made took one additional measure to make training at the Normal School and enlistment as an army schoolmaster a more attractive career. Army schoolmasters became eligible to sit the annual examinations of the Committee of Council on Education and to receive the certificate of merit if found qualified. This offered the young schoolmaster the possibility of finding a post in the public elementary schools in England and Wales after the expiration of his initial twelve-year term of enlistment or after subsequent enlistments and on leaving the Army with a pension.

On 31st December 1876 there were 248 schoolmasters in post and 23 students under instruction at the RMA. There were also 947 soldier assistants to help in the adult and Elder Children's schools, but these men were frequently moved by their COs to other

---

1   In September 1876 schoolmasters'pay was increased by 2d per day and a further 2d per day after two years' service.
2   *First, Second and Third Reports of the Director-General of Military Education on Army Schools etc.*, 1872, 1874 and 1877, passim.

duties and often contributed little to the effectiveness of the schools. In addition, there were 148 'Acting and Detachment Schoolmasters' in charge of the smaller depots and of detachment schools to which trained schoolmasters were not usually posted. They sometimes temporarily took charge of the regimental and artillery brigade schools when a trained master was not available. These men, although untrained, had higher qualifications than soldier assistants but they were in short supply, especially in the artillery where their service was most frequently required.

All new recruits were now required to attend school until they had obtained a Fourth Class Certificate and generally soldiers were required to have gained a Third Class certificate before promotion to Corporal and Second Class Certificate before promotion to Sergeant. All regimental certificates of education were abolished, and the general Army certificates were a requirement for promotion in all regiments and corps. The Director-General reported that these changes were already having an '… invigorating effect on adult attendance at schools' and that a total of 12,766 Certificates of Education had been awarded in the UK, India and the colonies in 1870 and 1871. He was also able to report that the proportion of uneducated men who could neither read nor write fallen from 9 percent in 1869 to 6.89 percent in 1871 and he speculated that with the introduction of compulsory schooling for new recruits there would soon be very few entirely uneducated men in the Army.[3] The introduction of compulsory schooling for recruits however was not without difficulties.

Colonel Gleig in his February 1874 reports on the adult schools in Great Britain and Ireland expressed his growing concern about the consequences of requiring recruits to achieve a Fourth Class Educational Certificate before being excused school. There were large number of recruits in some regiments and their schools were very overcrowded. He observed that many of the recruits had little elementary education, or any interest in further schooling. COs were anxious to reduce the numbers and free the recruits to spend more time in the hands of the drill sergeants. All these factors he believed contributed to an unduly large number of candidates being entered for the Fourth Class examination. Men were often entered who not ready for the examinations and in consequence they failed to obtain the certificate. Gleig urged that entry for the examination should be postponed until men were better prepared and had a chance of passing and he acknowledged that this might sometimes require an increase in the number of adult classes.[4]

On 31st December 1876, the Infant and Industrial Schools were staffed by 249 trained schoolmistresses and they were also 80 untrained Acting and Detachment mistresses. These teachers were assisted in the classroom by 112 pupil teachers and assistant school mistresses and 420 young girls who acted as monitoresses. The reports of the Director General had very little to say about the adequacy and sufficiency of teaching staff in these schools, but many of the untrained class room assistants

3   *First Report by the Director-General of Military Education on Army Schools etc.*, 1872, p. xii.
4   *Second Report by the Director-General of Military Education on Army Schools etc.* p. 25.

probably contributed more to the care than the instruction of the children. More trained staff was required and one of the Infant Schools at Aldershot was designated as a Model School under the supervision of First Class Schoolmistress Davies to train infant school mistresses.[5]

The Royal Commission on Military Education had recommended the abolition of school fees for children on the grounds that the privilege of free education had been granted to the soldier and the same privilege should be granted to his children, and also that the sum of money involved was trifling. Few people outside philosophical circles however paid even lip service to free education and the Liberal Government under the terms of the 1870 Education Act was committed to a policy of 'fees as a rule, but remission and help in case of need.'[6] The War Office therefore decided to continue to charge fees for children and the 1871 Army School regulations required the schoolmasters and mistresses to collect and account for the fees and the regiment or depot schoolmaster was responsible for remitting them to the Paymaster.

Queen's Regulations continued to require married soldiers to send their children to the regimental school on pain of loss of privileges. This principle of ' indirect compulsion' had been included in the 1870 Education Act, which gave the elected School Boards powers to decide whether attendance at their schools should be compulsory for children of specified ages and the grounds for exception. A number of School Boards allowed exemption for children who had reached a certain age so that they could obtain paid employment.[7] Colonel Gleig observed that there were children with the artillery brigades and at other depots whose families were likely to be in the same barracks for some time. He argued that the older children at these stations should be excused school upon the CO receiving 'trust worthy evidence' that they were engaged in paid employment and that the law of the land in relation to school attendance was being complied with.[8]

There were few other developments of note in the children's schools during the 1870s. The schoolmasters were urged to follow the practice of some civilian schools and include a session of drill for both the boys and girls each day. This was not only useful for instilling discipline but ensured that children had some regular exercise. It was adopted by some schools, but in 1876 Colonel Gleig regretted that it had not become part of the regular curriculum of all schools. He supported increasing the number of trades taught in the Industrial Schools and also suggested that some of the older girls could usefully be instructed in domestic duties such as cooking, scrubbing, cleaning grates, washing, ironing and getting up linen. However, there was little

5   *Third Report by the Director-General of Military Education on Army Schools etc.*, p. viii.
6   Sutherland, *Policy-making in Elementary Education*, pp. 163-9.
7   Sutherland, *Policy-making in Elementary Education*, pp. 115-21.
8   *Second Report by the Director-General of Military Education on Army Schools etc.*, pp. 26-7.

progress in diversifying the curriculum and most of the instruction in the Industrial Schools continued to be limited to needlework.[9]

The machinery of imperial government was slow to implement the recommendations of the Royal Commission that the Army School system in the United Kingdom and colonies should be extended to India. This would facilitate the appointment of sub-inspectors in the three Presidencies and improve the supervision of the Army's schools in that country. In the meantime, the three superintendents had to manage a heavy work load and to travel large distances to inspect as many schools as possible each year. Captain Jacobs usually managed to visit the schools in all but one of the Districts in the Bombay Presidency during the dry season, but his inspections were sometimes restricted by the movement of regiments between stations.[10] Captain Dunn based at Kussowlie decided to inspect the schools to the west of Delhi, in the Punjab and the North-Western Provinces and those in the 'lower provinces', which were to the east of Delhi, in alternate years. During the dry season in 1869-70, he inspected 44 schools in the Punjab and North West Provinces and in the following year 1870- 71 he managed to visit 37 schools in the lower provinces, although these were scattered over much greater area than in the Punjab.[11]

The absence of common regulations caused problems for the schoolmasters when their regiments arrived in India. They found that British regulations for awarding certificates had not been adopted and they were often uncertain about how they should proceed in preparing soldiers for the examinations.[12] The majority of men on the school registers were under orders from their COs, but the actual attendance showed wide variations. An order from the C-in-C India in Calcutta specifying that as a general rule the possession of a school certificate was required for promotion was a mixed blessing. The order encouraged men to attend school and make progress with their studies, but as Captain Dunn reported at the same time it increased the number of candidates to be examined by the Superintendent. Captain Dunn looked forward to the appointment sub-inspectors so that he did not have to examine so many soldiers and had more time to observe the general workings of the schools.[13]

The Government of India introduced revised Army School Regulation in 1873 with higher pay for schoolmistresses and increases in the allocations of assistant teachers and monitoresses and thus broadly placing the schools in India on the same footing as in Great Britain. It was however some time before a full complement of sub-inspectors could be appointed and were ready to commence their duties.[14] The Director-General in his Third Report detailed the names of four sub-inspectors under Major F.W.

9   *Second Report by the Director-General of Military Education on Army Schools etc.*, pp. 26-7.
10   *First Report by the Director-General of Military Education on Army Schools etc.*, pp. 74, 76.
11   *First Report by the Director-General of Military Education on Army Schools etc.*, pp. 54, 59.
12   *Second Report by the Director-General of Military Education on Army Schools etc.*, p. 69.
13   *First Report by the Director-General of Military Education on Army Schools etc.*, pp. 58, 65.
14   The revised Army School regulations issued by the Secretary of State for War in London in 1871 were made applicable in India by an order of the Government in Calcutta.

Dunn, in what was now designated the Bengal Command; two sub-inspectors under Major G.A. Jacob in the Bombay Command, and two under Lieutenant Colonel H.L. Grove in the Madras Command. Altogether the three Superintendents were responsible for 130 adult school, 114 Elder Children, and 108 Infant and Industrial Schools across India. This compared with the 227 adult schools, 184 elder children schools and 166 Infant and Industrial schools that were the responsibility of Colonel A.G. Gleig, the Inspector of Army Schools in Great Britain and Ireland.[15]

The adult schools in India were now rarely without a trained schoolmaster, but following death or sickness of a master, teaching devolved temporarily on a soldier assistant. In some regiments these men had received little training and there was a general complaint that the assistants were often removed from the classroom by their COs to undertake other duties. It was often necessary, especially in the artillery, to detach men from their units to serve with native regiments and the schools in these detachments were often managed by soldier assistants. In Bombay, detachment schools were taught by NCOs or men who had passed through the Central Military School at Poona.[16] The superintendents in all three commands expressed satisfaction about the work of the schoolmasters, but there were occasional instances of misconduct-often through drunkenness- that resulted in disciplinary action.[17]

Not every regiment sent out from Great Britain was accompanied by trained schoolmistress and it was unusual for a schoolmistress to be posted unaccompanied to India. In Bengal in 1870, there were 46 infant schools, but only 34 had trained mistresses and the remainder were conducted by acting mistress. In case of the trained mistresses, half their number had been trained at home and half were locally appointed. The Female Normal School at Kussowlie continued to operate in a small way during the early 1870s, with an average of eight students in training each year. The introduction of the revised Army School regulations in 1873 was followed by the closure of the Female Normal School. Thereafter any vacancies would be filled by direct examination according to the standards laid down in in the Army School Regulations or by acting (unqualified) schoolmistresses. The direct examinations were demanding, and Captain Dunn expressed concern that there were very few opportunities for British women to study in India. He decided that the best way forward was to encourage the wives of trained schoolmasters to volunteer and study for the examinations. In 1876 there 20 home trained mistresses and 26 who had been locally appointed and Dunn was confident that sufficient well qualified candidates could be found for future appointments.[18] Major Grove in Madras however was not

---

15   *Third Report by the Director-General of Army Schools etc.*, pp. x-xi.

16   *First Report by the Director-General of Military Education on Army Schools etc.*, pp. 71, 86.

17   *First Report by the Director-General of Military Education on Army Schools etc.*, pp. 73,75; *Second Report of the Director-General of Military Education on Army Schools etc.*, pp. v, 51; *Third Report of the Director-General of Military Education on Army Schools etc.*, p. 79.

18   *First Report of the Director-General of Military Education on Army Schools etc.*, p. 5; *Second Report of the Director-General of Military Education on Army Schools etc.*, p. 51; *Third Report*

impressed with locally appointed untrained schoolmistresses and judged them to be ineffective teachers. He argued that this soon became apparent when the children moved from the Infant into the Grown Children's Schools.[19]

The Director-General of Military Education judged that bringing the schools in India under the 1871 Army School Regulations and the appointment of Sub-Inspectors had produced good results. Nevertheless, attendance continued to be irregular at some of the Adult Schools. The school attendance of the older children was generally good, but less so at the Infant Schools. Some parents had difficulty in delivering their children to the early morning classes during the hot season and sickness, especially in the summer months kept the children from school. There was often a lack of specialist accommodation for the infants and frequent instances of the infants sharing classrooms with the older children. Wherever new barracks were constructed, especially in the Punjab and the North West Provinces they were well equipped with classrooms, but accommodation was less than ideal in the older barracks.[20]

Edward Cardwell's policy at the War Office had been to make reductions in the Army Estimates by reducing the colonial garrisons outside India and concentrating more soldiers at home. The home army was deployed in a larger number of smaller formations: 105 batteries, 19 cavalry regiments and 68 infantry battalions in 1870-71 compared with 97 batteries, 16 cavalry regiments and 46 infantry battalions in 1868-69.[21] As of 31st December 1876, these units were served by 227 adult, 184 elder children and 166 infant and industrial schools. The inspection of these schools was the responsibility of thirteen Sub-Inspectors (one for each military district) who were answerable to Colonel Gleig, the Inspector of Army Schools within Great Britain. The second largest number of troops was stationed in India, with 130 adult, 114 elder children and 108 eight Infant and Industrial Schools across the Bengal, Bombay and Madras armies. Each presidency in India continued to have is its own Superintendent of Army Schools stationed at its HQ. Approaching two-thirds of the schools were in the Bengal Command and the Superintendent was assisted by four Sub-Inspectors and there were two Sub-Inspectors for each of the smaller Bombay and Madras Commands.

There continued to be substantial garrisons at Gibraltar and Malta. The Gibraltar garrison was served by 10 Adult, nine Elder Children and eight Infant and Industrial Schools and there were 11 Adult, seven Elder Children and seven Infant and Industrial Schools at Malta. The schools at these stations were superintended and inspected by a garrison staff officer. There were also 40 Adult, 21 Elder Children and 21 Infant and

of the Director-General of Military Education on Army Schools etc., p. 79.

19   Second Report of the Director-General of Military Education on Army Schools etc., p. 62.
20   First Report of the Director-General of Military Education on Army Schools etc., pp. 56-7;
     Second Report of the Director-General of Military Education on Army Schools etc., pp. 45,50;
     Fourth Report of the Director-General of Military Education on Army Schools etc., pp. vi, 82.
21   Spiers, The Late Victorian Army, p. 4.

Industrial Schools at other colonial stations, but the Director General's reports were silent about the arrangements for the inspection of these schools.[22]

The inspection of the Adult schools and the awarding of educational certificates continued to be made twice a year. This constituted a heavy work load for the Sub-Inspectors in the larger military districts and in consequence it was decided that the pupils in the children's school should only be examined once a year. A total of 57,213 Educational Certificates were awarded to soldiers in 1874, 1875 and 1876.This however could not be taken as a measure of the improvement state of education in the Army since the introduction of compulsory attendance for new recruits in October 1871, because there were large numbers of men still in service who had enlisted before that date .

The Director-General continued to rely on the returns from the Adjutant –General. On 1st January 1876 returns from regiments and corps amounting to 172,392 men was used to deduce the level of education of men in the Army.[23]

Table 21. Educational Standard of the Troops 1872-76

	Number returned 1st January 1876	% In 1876	% In 1875	% In 1874	% In 1873	% In 1872
Class 1: Who can neither read or write	8540	4.95	5.25	5.37	6.01	18.95
Class 2: Who can read, but not write	7614	4.41	4.47	4.59	5.35	19.72
Class 3: Who can read and write	78748	45.68	48.41	40.1	36.02	53.89
Class 4: Who are better educated	77490	44.95	41.86	40.01	32.61	7.44

There was a slow but steady reduction during the 1870s in the number of soldiers who could not read and write (Classes 1 and 2) and a considerable advance in the overall level of literacy since 1860. What is surprising is the large increase in the proportion that was judged to be 'better educated'. These figures need to be approached with some caution. There is no information on the criteria that was used by COs to place soldiers

22 *Third Report by the Director-General of Military Education on Army Schools etc.*, pp. ix-xi.
23 *Third Report by the Director-General of Military Education on Army Schools etc.*, p. xii. The returns for 1876 had not been made for 1858 men in Great Britain and for all the men in the Colonial Corps. The data for 1860 is from the Second Report by the Council of Military Education on Army Schools, p. x.

in Class 4 or whether their regimental schoolmasters contributed to the classification. Colonel Gleig's reports on the results of the examinations for Army Certificates of Education shows a very different picture.

Table 22. Awards of Army Certificates of Education

	Entered	1st, 2nd & 3rd Class	4th Class	Not awarded
1872	23000	8586	7432	6982
1876	22348	6339	9214	6795

A significant minority of the candidates entered for the Certificate examinations in the United Kingdom in 1872 and 1876 failed to obtain even the Fourth Class Certificate, which involved only simple reading, a little writing and some basic arithmetic. The Director General reported that only 10,191 of the 57,213 Certificates awarded in the years 1874, 1875 and 1876 were First and Second Class.[24] Colonel Gleig nevertheless was confident that educational standards in the Army would continue to improve. Writing in 1874, he envisaged a time, perhaps only some ten years away, when as a consequence of the 1870 Education Act, all recruits would have passed through one of the civilian elementary schools and some would have progressed to a higher grade. It would then be reasonable to assume that the Second Class Certificate of Education would easily be within the reach of the average soldier without any further instruction by the regimental schoolmaster. When that day arrived, many men could be successfully taught to gain a First Class Certificate and then this should be made a requirement for those aspiring to become sergeants. In these circumstances the curriculum for the First Class Certificate should be broadened to include useful military subjects that have would a direct bearing on the men's professional duties, such as surveying and measurement, map reading and mechanics and even the study of a modern language. This would require the Army schoolmasters to be trained to teach these subjects, but in the meantime they could not be better employed than teaching the masses of illiterate recruits.[25]

Colonel Gleig's views were not untypical of the confident optimism of liberal reformers in middle years of Victorian Britain and he would have been surprised at the continuing poor levels of soldiers' literacy during the 1880s and 1890s, and even more so at the low standard of education after decades of compulsory elementary education of many regular soldiers and conscripts serving in the Army in the 1940s and 1950s.[26]

---

24 *Third Report by the Director-General of Military Education on Army Schools etc.*, p. xiii, 25.
25 *Second Report by the Director-General of Military Education on Army Schools etc.1874*, p. 26.
26 Spiers, *The Late Victorian Army*, p. 145; R. Vinen, *National Service: A Generation in Uniform 1945-63* (London: Penguin Books, 2014), pp. 156,240.

Important questions about the future provision of elementary education in the Army arose not only from the 1870 Education Act, but also from the reforms in military organisation introduced by Edward Cardwell between 1868-74. The Army Enlistment Act of 1870 had introduced a flexible system of short service enlistment. The initial term of enlistment in the infantry was 12 years, with the first six years to be spent with the colours and the remainder with the reserve. The War Office gradually extended shorter terms of enlistment to the cavalry and artillery. Although soldiers of every corps could still extend their service to 21 years, it was expected that most infantrymen would pass out of the regular Army into the Reserve at the end of the first six year period of their enlistment. It could be argued that adult classes in the regimental schools would still be needed to improve these men's education and assist them in finding employment when they returned to civilian life. Otherwise they would join the ranks of the unemployed and bring no credit to the Army.[27] There is no evidence that the War Office considered providing classes to help support short service men in finding employment when they returned to civilian life. The profession of soldiering may not have been highly regarded, but there were some employers who were happy to recruit ex-soldiers of good character for a variety of manual occupations, especially if they were prepared to also enlist in the local Volunteer Rifle Corps.[28]

During the 1870s, and confounding expectations, a quarter of infantry enlistments extended their service to 12 years with the colours and the Army could look to these men to provide its senior NCOs.[29] This pointed to the continuing need for Special Classes and the possession of Certificates of Education as a prerequisite for promotion and perhaps, as Gleig argued, for a curriculum that was more focused on the professional needs of the Army. The important question however was whether this education should continue to be provided at the regimental schools.

Edward Cardwell's primary objective for short term service was to create an Army Reserve and his Localisation Act of July 1872 divided Great Britain into 66 territorial districts, each of which would contain a brigade depot for the infantry. Two line battalions, two militia infantry battalions and various volunteer units would be based in each district. One of the regular battalions was to be based at home whilst the other served abroad, but each was to retain two companies at the depot, which would serve as a training base for new recruits for the line battalions and also as the reception centre for the reservists when they were recalled to the colours. It was felt there might

27   E.A. Smith, 'Educating the Soldier in the Nineteenth Century', *Journal of the Society for Army Historical Research*, Volume LXV(Spring 1988), p. 206.

28   The author's great-grandfather left the Army in 1879 after 25 years' service in the 22nd Foot and obtained employment as a labourer with a large Sheffield iron and steel manufacturer and subsequently enlisting in the Yorkshire Rifle Volunteers. Successive Secretaries of State encouraged government departments to employ ex-servicemen, but only the Post Office responded on a significant scale. Spiers, *The Late Victorian* Army, p. 146.

29   Spiers, *The Late Victorian Army*, p. 10.

be an advantage in providing a combined adult depot school, and thus in effect form a small garrison school, for the recruits enlisting in the two battalions. A brigade depot schoolmaster might also be able to provide special classes for its aspiring NCOs in both companies of the two battalions allocated to the depot. Where the depot was located in one of the larger barracks men from other battalions could join these classes within a larger garrison school. This would reduce the need for soldier assistants and also possibly achieve additional economies by reducing the establishment of schoolmasters needed to staff the Adult Schools.

The Army continued to accept that some of the men enlisting for longer periods of service would wish to marry and have their families live with them in barracks. The presence of women and children however was generally considered to adversely affect the 'mobility, discipline and efficiency' of the service. The importance of providing separate married quarters was increasingly, if reluctantly, recognised and these were included in newly constructed barracks, but the renovation of existing accommodation was costly and proceeded slowly. Only soldiers who had married with the permission of their COs were allowed to bring their wives into barracks and feed free on half rations and enrol their children in the regimental schools. There would be no benefit to the service in encouraging infantrymen during their initial six year term of enlistment to marry 'on the strength' of their battalion.[30] The impact of Cardwell's reforms on the children's schools therefore would depend very much on the numbers of men re-enlisting for a further period of service with the colours. Any reduction in the number of children on the strength of regiments and the introduction of system of localisation might however re-open the question of whether their schooling might be more cheaply provided in larger garrison schools, at least in the barracks in the British Isles.

Edward Cardwell hoped that short service enlistment introduced by the 1870 Army Enlistment Act would popularise service in the Regular Army. The Army would attract a better class of recruit and by doing away with the prospect that soldier would spend most of his adult life overseas there would be a reduction in the losses from desertion. Most soldiers would be in their mid or late twenties at the end of their service with the colours and would still be young enough to take up another occupation. In consequence savings would be made in the Army Estimates by cutting the size of the pension bill.[31]

Several aspects of the Cardwell Reforms attracted growing criticism during the 1870s. Initially the move to short service caused a crisis in recruitment. Between 1861-65 the Regular Army needed to enlist 12,500 men per annum. Short service meant that between 1876-79 it needed 28,800 per annum. Recruitment did increase, but not enough to make good the losses through death, discharge and desertion, which in the case of the latter rose from 3,332 in 1870 to 7,493 in 1878.There, was also a

30   Spiers, *The Late Victorian Army*, p. 139.
31   D. French, *Military Identities* (Oxford: Oxford University Press, 2005), pp. 13-14.

worrying increase in the disciplinary offences by young soldiers. This was attributed to the harsh living conditions in barracks and a disciplinary code that severely punished men for minor misdemeanours: for example, men who arrived back in barracks a few minutes late were liable to be placed in cells overnight.[32]

One reason frequently mentioned for exacerbating this disciplinary problem in the post Cardwell army was that it lacked sufficient NCOs who through dint of experience born of long service knew how to manage men. Under short service enlistment this had been lost. Before 1871 promising soldiers were normally promoted lance corporal after three to four years' service and sergeants were mature and experienced men. Following the Cardwell reforms many men saw little advantage in accepting the extra responsibilities during the final years of a short service enlistment and preferred to remain with their friends in the ranks. Consequently, in order to fill the gaps in the cadre of NCOs there was no alternative but to promote any young man willing to accept promotion into the junior ranks often after less than one years' service.[33]

Hugh Childers, who became Secretary of State for War in 1881, chose to address the Army's problems of recruitment and retention by increasing the initial period of enlistment with the colours from six to seven years and by improving the condition of service of NCOs so that experienced men would be retained to fill these vital ranks. In 1881 Childers improved the pay and prospects of junior NCOs by allowing them to extend their service to twelve years after one years' probation. The status of the NCO was raised by transforming the most senior NCOs into the new rank of Warrant Officer. Pensions for these ranks were improved and half of the sergeants and all the Warrant Officers were permitted to marry on strength and receive separate married quarters in the barracks. There would in consequence be a continuing need for classes for infants and older children of these marriages at the regimental schools.[34]

As part of Childers' improvement in the conditions of service for NCOs, Army schoolmasters were initially enlisted for twelve years with the rank of sergeant and with an order of precedence amongst NCOs second only to that of Master Gunner (3rd Class) .On a second term of enlistment they were appointed as a Warrant Officer and their rank was placed next in order of precedence to a regimental sergeant major. After 21years service they could retire on the maximum pension of 3s6d per day.[35] The Army List for 1881 contains the names of 104 Army schoolmasters who were promoted to this new warrant rank.

In 1882 Childers appointed a departmental committee chaired by Lord Morley (the Under Secretary of State at the War Office) to inquire into the RMA and the

---

32   French, *Military Identities*, pp. 16-17.
33   French, *Military Iden*tities, pp. 16-17
34   French, *Regimental Identities*, pp. 20-21.
35   TNA WO 30/39: 'Report ordered by the Secretary of State to consider the Precedence and Command of Warrant Officers and NCOs'; TNA WO 33/39, 'Report of the Committee on the Royal Hospitals at Chelsea and Kilmainham, Royal Military Asylum, Chelsea, and the Royal Hibernian Military School, Dublin etc.1882', p. 26.

RHMS. The committee was also asked to report on the effects of the extension of elementary education in the civil population and the introduction of short service in the Army on the provision for the education of soldiers at the Regimental Schools and whether Army's schoolmasters should continue to be trained at the Normal School.[36]

In 1882, the 1870 Education Act had not been in operation for long enough to affect the men who were then enlisting. In 1881 the CO of the 2/18th (Royal Irish) estimated that over one third his recruits were illiterate. Since 1871, the Army had compelled all men to attend school until they obtained the 4th Class Certificate of Education. The large number of recruits required by the short-service system resulted in a marked increase in the number of adults attending the regimental schools and in 1880 there were 40,715 adults on the school registers. In the same year 44 percent of the Army did not possess this basic certificate, which was broadly equivalent only to the 2nd Standard of the Civil Code in civilian elementary schools. Furthermore, only 29 percent of the men in the Army possessed the 3rd Class and 2nd Class certificates that were requirements for promotion to the ranks of Corporal and Sergeant respectively.[37]

The Morley Committee accepted that as long as so many of the recruits had little elementary education the regimental schools would have to be retained, not least in order to ensure that sufficient men would qualify for promotion.[38] The committee believed nevertheless that when the generation of boys that had been subject to compulsory education reached the age for enlistment very few recruits would not have reached the moderate educational standard required of sergeant. This was about equivalent to the 4th standard of the civil educational code in the Board Schools. Provided that there were sufficient qualified soldiers in the ranks to keep up the supply of NCOs, the committee concluded that at some date in the not too distant in future, there would little reason to retain the adult classes in the regimental schools. It did however consider that in garrison towns and at the important Army Camps such as Aldershot and the Curragh, it would be desirable to provide opportunities for men to attend voluntary classes to further their education and qualify for promotion.[39]

More controversially the committee believed that it would be possible to dispense with the regimental schools for soldiers' children. Short service enlistment would result in a large reduction in the number of married private soldiers and it would be more economical to pay fees to enable the few children that remained with their father's regiment to attend civilian schools in the garrison towns. The committee accepted that this would not be easy when regiments were stationed overseas and in these circumstances some teaching would have to be provided. Surprisingly, the committee did not make any specific recommendations for the many units stationed

---

36   TNA WO 33/39, Committee on the Royal Hospitals, etc., 1882.
37   French, *Regimental Identities*, pp. 33-5.
38   This should not be confused with the 1887 *Report of the Committee appointed to inquire into the Organisation and Administration of the Manufacturing Departments of the Army* that is often referred to as the Morley Committee.
39   TNA WO 33/39: 'Committee on the Royal Hospitals etc. 1882', p. 26.

in India, but its conclusions pointed to making provision wherever possible in garrison schools.[40]

In 1880 there were 175 Army schoolmasters on the Home Establishment and 81 in India and there were some 18-20 vacancies each year. The abolition of the regimental schools and their replacement by a shared provision at the garrisons and military camps would reduce the number of schoolmasters required and bring into question the continuing need for the Army's Normal School. The Royal Commission on Military Education some twelve years previously had recommended the closure of the Normal School, but no action was taken because of the strong objection by Major General William Napier, the then Director General of Military Education. The Morley Committee agreed with the conclusions of the Royal Commission that the Normal School was on too small scale to fulfil the various objectives that the training school had been designed for. It considered that the civilian training colleges could provide an ample supply of schoolmasters at least as well trained as those currently emerging from the Normal School. Anticipating previous opposition to this move, it argued that discipline at the civilian colleges was quite as strict in their discipline as the Normal School and that they would provide the prospective Army schoolmasters with a much better education. Men could be admitted into the Army from the training colleges though a competitive examination and appointed as schoolmasters on probation for six months, during which time they would rank as ordinary sergeants and be employed as assistant masters in Army's Schools. On satisfactorily completing probation they would confirmed as Army schoolmasters.[41]

There had been a significant reduction in the number of serving soldiers volunteering for training at the Normal School and in 1881 only three enlisted men were in training. The Committee received evidence that the fall in the number of enlisted men applying was because COs were reluctant to encourage applications, preferring to retain promising young soldiers as NCOs in their regiments. The Morley Committee nevertheless hoped that young soldiers of good character might be attracted by the improved conditions of service and that they would be encouraged by their CO to volunteer for training at the civilian colleges. Similarly, pupil teachers at the RHMS and the RMA who had reached the age of 20 and wished to train as Army schoolmasters should be encouraged to compete for entry. A portion of the money saved from the closure of the Normal School could be used to use to defray the expenses of enlisted soldiers and pupil teachers from the two military schools attending the training colleges.

40   TNA WO 33/39: 'Committee on the Royal Hospitals etc. 1882', p. 26.
41   TNA WO 33/39: 'Committee on the Royal Hospitals etc.1882', p. 27

20

The Dilemma: Regimental Schools or Garrison Schools?

Between December 1882 and January 1887 there were three changes of government and five Secretaries of State for War and there was no attempt to implement the recommendations of the Morley Committee.[1] It was not until the final months of 1886 that War Office, under pressure from the Treasury to reduce the Army Estimates, further considered the Army schools and the training of its schoolmasters. A small committee under Lord Harris, the Under Secretary at War in Lord Salisbury's Government, was appointed to 'enquire into certain questions affecting Army Schools and Schoolmasters.'[2] This was a broad remit and the Committee decided to focus on the system of providing education for soldiers and their children, the training of the Army's schoolmasters and the supply of school accommodation. Evidence was taken from officers with specialist knowledge and experience of Army education, including a number of inspectors, and from regimental officers and the Committee's report containing a number of radical recommendations was delivered to the Secretary of State in July 1887.[3]

The Harris Committee considered that it would be helpful to set its recommendations in the context of the origins and subsequent development of the regimental schools. It concluded from reading the Horse Guards' Order of 1st January 1812 that the regimental schools had been established to educate soldiers' children and 'not the soldier himself.'[4] The Royal Commission on Military Education in its 1870 report had focused on the importance of making education compulsory for recruits who did not

---

1   The Secretaries of State for War were: Marquess of Hartington (December 1882 to June 1885), W.H. Smith (June 1885 to February 1886), Henry Campbell-Bannerman (February 1886 to August 1886), W.H. Smith (August 1886 to January 1887) and Edward Stanhope (January 1887 to August 1892).
2   Harris is perhaps better remembered for his services to cricket both as a player and an administrator. He captained both Kent and England.
3   TNA WO 32/6952: War Office, 'Report of the Committee appointed to enquire into certain questions affecting Army Schools and Schoolmasters'; Harris Report, pp. i-iii
4   TNA WO 32/6952: Harris Report, p. iv.

possess the rudiments of an elementary education, because the modern army placed greater demands on the intelligence and self-reliance of the private soldier. This had been accepted by the military departments and from 1871 schooling had been made compulsory for recruits until they had gained a 4th Class certificate of Education. This had been modified by Regulations in 1884 and thereafter attendance was made compulsory for six months, or a lesser period if the newly enlisted soldier obtained the 4th Class Certificate. The Harris Committee concluded that the original objective of establishing army schools for soldiers' children had been extended to include a period of compulsory education for the private soldier and, therefore its recommendations would have to address both these objectives.[5]

The War Office had expected that the provision of public elementary education following the 1870 Act would ensure that the typical recruit would have an elementary education that was not only sufficient for the needs of the private soldier but was also of the standard required for promotion to NCO rank. The Harris Committee believed that the typical recruit in 1887 could read and write better than those enlisting 1878, but the improvement in educational attainment was less than had been expected. In the first half 1886, 14.71 percent of the recruits were totally illiterate, and 27.1 percent could read but not write, or could read but were only able to sign their name. Many boys in the social classes from which the Army obtained its recruits had left elementary school at the age of ten. Others who had remained until the age of 12 had forgotten much of what they had learnt in reading and writing by the time they enlisted at the age of 18 or 19. A short time in the Army's classrooms enabled these boys to reach the standard of a 4th Class Certificate in reading and writing, but this was rarely the case in arithmetic. Schoolmasters and their assistants spent much of their time endeavouring to teach the four rules of arithmetic with little positive result.

In 1886, 36 percent of the rank and file were unable or unwilling to obtain a 4th Class Certificate. Many recruits viewed schooling as no more than one disagreeable part of their daily duties and therefore attended lessons, but made no effort to learn, knowing that after six months they would be excused school. Harris reported that many of the 'better men' chose to voluntarily attend school and study for the 3rd and 2nd Class Certificates that were required for promotion as NCOs. In 1886 there were 18,526 men in voluntary attendance at the regimental schools compared with 17,195 in 1885 and there was a small but steady increase in the number of men gaining the 3rd and 2nd Class certificates.

The Harris Committee believed that much time and expense was wasted on teaching for the 4th Class Certificate and the Army schoolmasters could be more effectively used teaching the volunteers who wished to work towards the higher certificates. It recommended that compulsory schooling for recruits should cease and that the 4th Class Certificate of Education should be abolished. COs should continue to offer every encouragement for enlisted men to voluntarily attend school. On the basis of existing

5   TNA WO 32/6952: Harris Report, p. iv.

attendance, there should be no greater difficulty than currently existed in attracting sufficient men who would voluntarily study to gain the educational qualifications required for promotion.[6]

The interior economy of the infantry battalions certainly allowed sufficient time for men to attend school. John Lucy who joined the 2/Royal Irish Rifles in 1882 observed that that working hours of the fully trained soldier were not excessive, and he had sufficient time to educate himself in the 'Regimental School' and prepare for promotion.[7] Financial savings in the Army Estimates would follow from ending compulsory schooling. In 1886, 17,080 recently enlisted men were compelled to attend school and not all of these would volunteer to attend when compulsion was abolished. This would allow the adult classes in the regimental schools to be abolished with the tuition for the remaining educational certificates taking place in garrison schools were soldiers from a number of different units could be combined in single classes. Once the garrison schools had been established it should be possible to dispense with the soldier assistant bringing savings of around £4000 per annum. Also, less accommodation would be required.

The Royal Commission on Military Education had recommended the abolition of the Chapel Schools because it believed it was undesirable to use the same building for secular and religious purposes. The Harris Committee agreed and argued that once compulsory schooling for soldiers had been abolished it should be possible to find sufficient school accommodation in most garrisons allowing the use of the military chapels to be confined to the purpose for which they were originally intended.[8]

The Morley Committee had concluded that short service enlistment would result in a large reduction in the number of married private soldiers and in consequence the number of children on the strength of each regiment and corps. In time it should be possible in most instances to dispense with the children's classes at the regimental schools. The Harris Committee noted that the attendance of the older children at many of the regimental schools was quite small and considered that these children would receive a better education if they were combined with children from other regiments in a garrison school. Harris accepted that many COs had a keen attachment to their regimental schools and were strongly opposed to their abolition. They argued that the children's education would suffer by being taught by a succession of teachers rather than by their own regimental schoolmaster. Harris countered this concern by pointing out that this was no different to what happened each year to children in the large civilian schools in urban areas.

Harris however did not agree with the Morley Committee's recommendation that the older children should attend the local civilian schools. Instead he proposed that children's schools should be established alongside the schools for soldiers at each

6   TNA WO 32/6952: Harris Report, pp. v-vii.
7   J. Lucy, *There's a Devil in the Drum* (Sussex: Naval and Military Press, 1993), p. 5.
8   TNA WO 32/6952: Harris Report, pp. vii-viii.

garrison. The Army was the children's home and it was important that they absorb its ethos. They therefore should go to school in the barracks and be taught by Army schoolmasters. It accepted that in some depots and for detached units this might not always be possible and in these cases the state should pay the fees required for the children to attend a civilian school.[9] The War Office would have to devise a scheme for placing the garrison schools at the various military stations at home and abroad. It was considered essential that the children and soldiers should not have to travel more than one mile to attend classes, which was about half the distance that many children had to travel to attend civilian schools in country areas in Great Britain.[10]

For practical reasons, the Committee favoured the retention of the regimental schools for the infant classes. The Committee however looked to ways of reducing the cost of these classes. There were currently 258 schoolmistresses in pensionable posts on an average salary of £66 per annum including allowances. They only instructed the infants up the 1st Standard of the code in the civilian schools and at around the age of seven the children transferred the schoolmaster's school. In some cases, there were acting schoolmistresses, generally the wives of NCOs appointed on the recommendation of the COs, who taught the children to what the Committee implied was an acceptable standard. The Committee, without any further explanation, decided that it was unnecessary to employ college trained schoolmistresses to do such elementary work. It recommended that in future acting schoolmistresses should be employed at an annual salary of £25 per annum, subject to whatever tests of competency that the Director of Military Education considered to be necessary.[11]

The move from regimental to garrison schools would have significant implications for Army schoolmasters. Instead of being posted to a battalion or regiment and staying with that unit as it moved between military stations, the schoolmaster would now be posted to a particular garrison school. The Education Department in the War Office would allocate schoolmasters according to a rota that would from time to time include a posting to garrisons in India or one of major colonial stations such as Malta or Gibraltar. Harris argued that this would not be an unattractive prospect for both serving and prospective army schoolmasters, but the abolition of compulsory classes for enlisted men and the concentration of teaching in garrison schools would allow for a reduction in the number of masters. This would be achieved overtime by natural wastage with annual variations in recruitment depending on the number of soldiers volunteering to attend at the garrison schools.[12] Harris then turned to recruitment of the schoolmasters and the future of the Normal School.

The Royal Commission on Military Education and the Morley Committee had been critical of the Normal School and both had recommended its closure. Harris

9   TNA WO 32/6952: Harris Report, pp. iv-v.
10   TNA WO 32/6952: Harris Report, p. viii.
11   TNA WO 32/6952: Harris Report, p. viii.
12   TNA WO 32/6952: Harris Report, pp. ix-x.

noted that the competitions for entry to the School were restricted to civilians who held '...the parchment certificate of the Education Department of the Privy Council' and were trained teachers, together with pupil teachers from the RHMS and RMA and serving soldiers. Successful candidates spent two terms at the Normal School under the instruction of Mr Reynolds, the Headmaster, and a further term as instructors at the Model School under Mr Lamb, its Headmaster. Mr Reynolds taught an essentially academic curriculum and he was not responsible for teaching the students how to teach, although in his evidence to the Committee he explained that he organised the subject material in ways that would be helpful when the students became teachers. Staffing reductions had been made at the Normal School and Mr Reynolds had a punishing workload, teaching all 23 students currently at the School without any assistance. The only teaching practice undertaken by the students was at the Model School where they only taught boys and they had no experience of teaching adults before appointment as Army schoolmasters.

The Harris Committee believed that the requirement that certificated schoolmasters had to compete for entry to train as Army schoolmasters, and if successful to spend two terms under instruction at the Normal School, deterred applications from the best civilian teachers. Also, in recent years there had been very few applicants from enlisted soldiers. Harris therefore recommended that the Normal School should be closed. Certificated civilian teachers should be appointed on probation as 'assistant masters' and work under the supervision of an army schoolmaster. They would teach both adults and children in a garrison school for six months before being accepted and enlisted as an army schoolmaster. Soldiers up to the age of 23 who had obtained a 1st Class Certificate of Education, which should be expanded to include English Literature, History and Geography, would similarly be accepted as assistant masters. After successfully serving 18 months at a garrison school they would be re-enlisted as schoolmasters and be able to count up to five years previous service towards their pension entitlement.

There was no doubt that the Committee looked to the pupil teachers from the RMA and the RHMS as the most promising source of future army schoolmasters. It noted that some of the best masters had commenced their career as pupil teachers at these schools. It suggested offering incentives for pupil teachers to enter the Model School at Chelsea and the RHMS and at the age of 19 plus, and that after around one year they should be sent to work as assistant teacher at a garrison school. They should not be required to compete against certificated civilian candidates and once having passed this probation should be enlisted as Army schoolmasters.[13]

The War Office accepted the Harris Committee's recommendations and through General Order 198 confirmed that the system under which the Army Schools were now conducted would cease from 31 December 1887. Army Schools would be established in all garrison towns and at other stations where necessary for the education of adults

13   TNA WO 32/6952: Harris Report, pp. ix-x.

and older children. They would take the place of the regimental schools. For the present, regimental schools would be retained for children under the age of eight. The compulsory education of recruits would cease and the 4th Class Certificate of Education abolished. COs were ordered to use every means at their disposal to induce men to attend school voluntarily in order to improve their education and to obtain the certificates necessary for promotion. The 1st Class Certificate would in future include examinations in English, Geography, and History. This certificate had hitherto been required only for NCOs seeking a commission, but in future it would also be needed by soldiers who sought an appointment as schoolmaster in a garrison school. Soldiers acting as School Assistants would be to be returned to their regimental duties on 1 January 1888 and no more would be appointed without the special authority of the Director General of Military Education. Finally, all school returns that presently were forwarded to the War Office by COs would in future be forwarded by an officer of the Adjutant-General's Department on the staff of the District in which the school was situated.[14]

It was subsequently decided that the Order to establish garrison schools for soldiers and older children should not apply in India. There were stations in India where there was only one British regiment and very often the exigencies of climate and disease resulted in the frequent temporary closure of the schools. The War Office on the recommendation of C-in-C in India sanctioned the continuation of the regimental schools in the sub-continent.[15]

Although regiments at home stations retained their infant schools, many COs were strongly opposed to the abolition of the regimental schools for the elder children and soldiers and there was widespread criticism of their replacement by garrison schools over which they had no authority.[16] The Harris Committee had used the example of the civilian schools to counter the concern that children's and soldiers' education would suffer by having a new schoolmaster every year. Regiments however frequently moved between stations during the Army Schools' year, which ran from the date of one annual inspection to the next. In consequence the garrison schools sometimes experienced one regiment quitting a station and another arriving in the middle of the year. This made it difficult for any one schoolmaster to assess the children's progress. In case of soldiers preparing for the examinations for the Certificates of Education, they would be liable to be taught by a different master half way through their course, which could hinder their progress and eventual success. An attempt was made to address these problems by requiring that the annual examination of pupils should in normal circumstances take place at the same time in schools throughout the service, as late as possible in the second half of the year.[17]

14   TNA WO, General Orders 1887, pp. 227-8.
15   *Fourth Report by the Director-General of Military Education on Army Schools*, pp. 6-7.
16   *Fifth Report by the Director-General of Military Education on Army Schools*, p. 3.
17   *Fifth Report by the Director-General of Military Education on Army Schools*, p. 4.

The Director General of Military Education, reporting March 1889, agreed that the COs' objections to the closure of regimental schools had some weight, but considered that on balance the Harris Committee's reasons for replacing the regimental schools with garrison schools were sound. Successive reports concluded that the system of garrison schools permitted a better classification of pupils' progress and consequently they received more appropriately focused instruction. Nevertheless, the War Office accepted that COs were less likely to take an interest in garrison schools and it was therefore necessary to introduce stricter regime of inspections and examinations in order to prevent laxity, maintain standards, and ensure the efficiency and effectiveness of the teaching.[18]

The general duties of the Sub-Inspector of Army School were extensive and included: the inspection of every army school in his military district every half-year and reporting on their general condition and on the competence of the teaching staff; the examination of candidates for the posts of acting schoolmistress, pupil teacher and monitors (see below); the periodical examination of soldiers for the Certificates of Education and the marking and setting of all the examination papers. The examination of candidates for the 4th Class Certificates of Education had involved a great deal of work by sub-inspectors and their abolition made it possible to reduce the number of sub-inspectors serving at home from 14 to 10, by making some sub-inspectors carry out their duties in two military Districts. There was a separate inspectorate in India and the duties of sub-inspectors in the colonies were performed by regimental officers appointed by the general officer commanding. These men although often conscientious did not have the technical knowledge to carry out the inspection work effectively. Their reports on the efficiency and workings of the schools and on the masters and mistresses were not always reliable. Soldiers were awarded certificates when not educationally qualified for them and children moved up to higher standard classes when they should have been kept back. It was therefore decided to combine the colonial stations into groups and appoint a sub-inspector to each group in order to achieve more uniformity in the inspections and the awarding of certificates. In 1888-89 four sub-inspectors were appointed: for the West Indies, Bermuda and Nova Scotia; for South Africa, St Helena and Mauritius; for China, Singapore and Ceylon and for Malta, Gibraltar, Cyprus and Egypt.[19]

Colonel Gleig retired as 'Inspector of Army Schools' in 1881. He had conducted school inspections for some 25 years and more recently had superintended the work of the sub-inspectors. His long tenure of appointment had given him a detailed knowledge of all aspects of the Army's Schools and the relative merits of individual masters and mistresses, who he ensured were promoted on merit and not by seniority. During 1881, the post of 'Inspector of Army Schools' was abolished and replaced by an

---

18   *Fourth Report by the Director-General of Military Education on Army Schools*, p. 7.
19   *Fourth Report by the Director General of Military Education Army on Army Schools*, pp. 8-9. An additional inspector was appointed to the Madras Presidency in 1892.

Assistant-Director of Military Education, which was a fixed term staff appointment, usually for four years. For the next eleven years the schools were supervised by a succession of staff officers and the Director-General, reporting in 1893, concluded that this had resulted in deterioration in the efficiency of the Army's Schools. Some of these staff officers were not interested in army education and viewed the post as just another staff appointment. Their short tenure in the post prevented them from gaining the specialist knowledge that was required for administering the schools. This was exacerbated when the regimental schools were replaced by garrison schools and the Director-General of Military Education had more need than ever of the assistance of an officer who was acquainted with the personnel of the education division.[20]

In 1892 it was decided that a more permanent appointment was required. The post of Assistant Director of Military Education was abolished and replaced by a Director of Army Schools, appointed initially for a term of five years, and renewable for a second and third term subject to satisfactory performance. The officer appointed was selected because of his interest in education in the Army and the aptitude to quickly gain an understanding of the work of the schools. Over time he would be able to assess the relative merits of individual masters and mistresses and through experience gain a very comprehensive knowledge of the administration and inspection of the Schools. At the same time the standing of the inspectorate in the Army was enhanced by the abolition of the title of 'Sub-inspector' and its replacement by that of 'Inspector of Army Schools.'[21]

In the following year surprise inspection visits without notice and at irregular intervals were introduced. These were judged to be particularly successful. The practice was continued throughout the 1890s and ensured that the schoolmasters and mistresses were consistent in their working practices across the school year and that their pupils were attending punctually and regularly at all times.[22]

The procedures to be followed by the inspectors had been codified in the 1888 Army School Regulations and remained largely intact until the first decade of the twentieth century. At the annual inspection the inspector observed the regular workings of the school and if there was any doubt about the teachers' abilities, he would observe a complete lesson. At the children's schools he would ensure that the timetable reflected the prescribed course of instruction and also check the attendance over the previous year. The central feature of the inspection was the individual examination of each child at his or her appropriate standard. A child of seven to eight years was expected to pass in Standard 1 and to attain a higher standard each year until, at the age of fourteen, Standard VII was passed. Children were expected to have passed standard 1 in the Infant School before going up to the Elder Children's School. In order to obtain a

20   St John Williams, *Tommy Atkin's Children*, p. 102.
21   *Fifth Report by the Director-General of Military Education on Army Schools*, pp. 16-17.
22   *Fifth Report by the Director-General of Military Education on Army Schools*, pp. 17-18; *Sixth Report by the Director General on Army Schools*, p. 9.

pass at any one standard a child had to achieve the requisite level of proficiency in two of the three elementary subjects. If a child failed in more than one elementary subject he/she was usually presented again in the same standard.

Table 23. Average daily attendance at the Army Schools[23]

	1888	1892	1895
Adults and enlisted boys	6,750	13,315	14,345
Elder children	4,614	5,718	5,988
Infants	5,154	6,403	6,801
Total average attendances	16,518	25,436	27,314

There was some uncertainty about the number of soldiers who would voluntary attend school following the ending of compulsory attendance for recruits. Compulsory schooling was retained for soldiers who were selected for promotion and had not obtained a 2nd and 3rd Class Certificate. Previously some men had been able to work towards a 3rd Class Certificate during their period of compulsory schooling, but under the new system many soldiers chose not to attend school until appointed acting NCOs. Regular attendance thereafter was often difficult because of their regimental duties and some men had to attend school for long periods before achieving the relevant certificate. In April 1892, the War Office issued a circular authorising COs to excuse selected NCOs and soldiers who were working for a 2nd Class Certificate from all guards and other duties that would prevent their attendance at school, especially during the winter months. Those excused were obliged to attend twice daily in the hope this would help men to obtain the certificate and be quickly appointed to the active rank. Similar exemptions were available to encourage selected NCOs to gain a 1st Class Certificate, which the War Office decided was a requirement for promotion to Warrant officer and the higher ranks of NCOs, such as Paymaster and Quarter -master sergeant. It was hoped that these measures would encourage COs to take an interest in their soldier's education and thus identify the most promising men for promotion.[24]

The War Office recognised that many regimental officers had little interest in the education of the private soldier and considered that all that was required was a high standard of physical training. The Director of Military Education disagreed and in his

23 *Fourth Report by the Director General of Military Education on Army Schools*, p. 17; *Fifth Report by the Director General of Military Education on Army Schools*, p. 12; *Sixth Report by the Director General of Military Education on Army Schools*, p. 6.
24 *Fourth Report by the Director General of Military Education on Army Schools*, p. 15; *Fifth Report by the Director General of Military Education on Army Schools*, p. 5.

1893 report argued that the development of a soldier's intellectual education alongside his physical education achieved the best results. This he argued was understood in the German Army and he quoted the contemporary proverb that it was the 'Prussians schoolmaster' that had won the battle of Koeniggratz (Sadowa). He argued that the British Army also now needed to rely more on the soldier's 'intelligence and enlightenment.' Attention was drawn to the Infantry Drill Book of 1892, which explained that '…the conditions of modern warfare render it imperative that all ranks should be taught to think and, subject to their general instruction and to accept principles act for themselves.' [25]

Although there was a suggestion that the abolition of regimental schools might have deterred some soldiers from attending school, because they could have to change out of barracks clothes into a walking out uniform to attend their nearest garrison school, overall attendance increased between 1888 and 1895 (Table 23).[26] The most important obstacle to progress however was the typical recruit's low standard of elementary education. The successive reports had recorded that the educational standard of recruits had been gradually increasing since the 1870 Education Act, but not by as much as had been expected. The 1896 Report concluded that nearly all boys were receiving some type of education in the public elementary schools and the number of absolute illiterates was very small, but a large number could only read printed matter and had difficulty in reading manuscript. They could barely do more than write their name, whilst they had forgotten all the arithmetic they had learnt. This was perhaps not surprising given that attendance at elementary school was irregular and the boys often left at the age of eleven, twelve, or thirteen in order to obtain paid employment.[27] Typically there was a period of five to eight years or more between leaving school and enlistment.

The standard of the Army's 2nd and 3rd Class Certificates that were required for promotion was low. The examination for the 3rd Class Certificate, which was needed for promotion to corporal, consisted of writing to dictation from a book of easy words arranged for children of nine years of age and the paper in arithmetic included calculations suitable to children in the civilian Board Schools in England and Wales who were 10 years of age. The higher 2nd Class Certificate needed for promotion to Sergeant was in all essential points similar to Standard V of the civilian Education Code, which children in civilian schools were expected to pass before reaching the age of 12. The great of majority of soldiers selected for promotion had to attend school for a considerable time before they were able to obtain a 2nd Class Certificate and the Director-General feared that the day when the Army's schools could be dispensed with was as far away as ever.[28]

25   *Fifth Report by the Director General of Military Education on Army Schools*, pp. 7, 28.
26   *Fourth Report by the Director General of Military Education on Army Schools*, pp. 6-7;
27   *Sixth Report by the Director General of Military Education on Army Schools*, p. 5.
28   *Fifth Report by the Director General of Military Education on Army Schools*, pp. 7-9.

Nonetheless, the Army was offering opportunities to the rank and file for further education in 'continuation schools' at a time when very little similar provision was available for civilians. There were large employers who were seeking men with a good standard of elementary education and COs were exhorted to encourage their men to attend school not only because this would increase their prospects of promotion within the Army, but also because on leaving the service they would increase their chances of employment with the Post Office, the larger railway companies, and other employers.[29]

29   *Fifth Report by the Director General of Military Education on Army Schools*, p. 5.

21

Final Years

The War Office soon realised that the formation of garrison schools and the abolition of compulsory attendance at school for recruits, would not materially reduce the number of schoolmasters required. In the past illiterate recruits had often been taught for some of their lessons by Soldier Assistants and the requirement of an Educational Certificate for promotion ensured that there was no shortage of work for the schoolmasters. Furthermore, in 1888 the possession of a 1st Class Certificate had been introduced for Warrant Officers and some of the senior NCOs appointments. In 1887 only 480 candidates had sat the examinations for the 1st Class Certificate and 203 were awarded, whereas in 1895 there were 1,418 candidates and 1,143 certificates were awarded.[1] In consequence there was very little change in the size of the establishment of schoolmasters during the 1890s, with some 15-20 vacancies arising each year.

Table 24. The Establishment of Army Schoolmasters 1889-96[2]

	Home Stations	Colonies	India
1889	149	32*	82
1893	148	34	84
1896	153+	33	79

* Three locally enlisted schoolmasters in the West India Regiment inclusive.
+ 123 schoolmasters in Great Britain and 30 in Ireland inclusive.

1   *Sixth Report by the Director General of Military Education on Army Schools*, p. 8.
2   For particulars see, Fourth, Fifth and Sixth Reports by the Director-General of Military Education on Army Schools.

The Normal School was closed in December 1887 and thereafter all candidates selected for the 'Corps of Army Schoolmasters' (this designation first appeared in the Fourth Report by the Director General of Military Education in March 1889) were appointed assistant schoolmasters on probation in the garrison schools at Aldershot.[3] Candidates were selected by competitive examination and were either: serving NCOs recommended by their CO, not under the rank of corporal and possessing a 1st Class Certificate of Education; or pupil teachers at the Duke of York's Royal Military School (previously titled the Royal Military Asylum) and the Royal Hibernian Military School. Both categories of candidate had to pass examinations in each of the following subjects: reading, dictation, composition and grammar; geography and English History; arithmetic, algebra Euclid, mensuration; scripture and music. No candidate was accepted who did not demonstrate a proficiency in singing. Civilian certificated teachers recruited by newspaper adverts filed the remaining vacancies, and they only had to satisfactorily complete the probationary period. All candidates had to be unmarried and between 20 and 24 years of age; be physically fit and of 'unmixed European blood' and of English, Scottish or Irish parentage.[4]

An important criticism of the training at the Normal School had been that it had only provided teaching practice with the boys of the Model School at the Military Asylum, whereas much of the schoolmaster's work involved teaching adults.[5] The probationary year at Aldershot included experience of teaching both children and adults and also learning something of the practicalities of managing an Army school. At the end of their probationary year all the assistant schoolmasters sat an examination in teaching and school management and if successful were enlisted as Army schoolmasters for a period of twelve years. Serving NCOs were discharged from their regiments and re-enlisted for general service as schoolmasters.[6]

The Normal School was mainly closed for reasons of economy, but there was always a concern about how to recruit sufficient men of the right calibre as schoolmasters and who would be comfortable with the demands of military service. The pay and conditions of service were periodically reviewed in order to attract suitable candidates and encourage enlistment. From1895 schoolmasters who were judged to be especially effective could be promoted to warrant rank after eight rather than 12 years' service.[7] From 1895-1900, 100 schoolmasters were appointed, split almost equally between a civilian teachers and pupil teachers from the two residential military schools, with only one-solitary NCO. It was thought that many of the civilian entrants were attracted because of the possibility of a pension and there was concern when it was suggested

3   *Fourth Report by the Director –General of Military Education on Army Schools*, pp. 10-11.
4   *War Office, Instructions for the Guidance of Candidates for Admission to the Army as Schoolmasters, and for Admission into the Duke of York's Royal Military School and the Royal Hibernian Military School as Pupil Teachers 1894*, para, 4-6.
5   TNA WO 32/6952: Harris Report, p. 43.
6   *Fourth Report by the Director-General of Military Education on Army Schools*, pp. 10-11.
7   *Sixth Report by the Director-General of Military Education on Army Schools*, p. 18.

that pensions might become available for long service teaching in the civilian schools.[8] Appointments however were increasingly made from pupil teachers at the Duke of York's Royal Military School and the Royal Hibernian Military School.

The pupil teachers at both these schools were recruited by open competition from boys who were serving monitors at the two schools or had been educated at civilian schools. In 1902 the establishment of pupil teachers at each school was increased: in the case of the RHMS from 16 to 32. The designation 'Pupil Teacher' was abolished and replaced by 'Student in training for Army Schoolmaster.' After 1902, recruitment for the 'Corps of Army Schoolmasters' hardly extended beyond the students from the two residential Army schools.[9]

For many years the Army schoolmasters had relied upon help in the classroom from 'Soldier Assistants' and the War Office anticipated that the ending of compulsory schooling and the formation of garrison schools would make it possible to dispense with the greater part of the 508 soldier assistants employed in December 1887. Although the numbers were soon reduced, in December 1888, 217 soldier assistants were still being employed. This was partly because of the increase in the soldiers voluntarily attending at the garrison schools and also because the regimental schools had not been abolished in India. New recruits passed quickly out of the regimental depots, but there were NCOs and other soldiers at these depots who wished to attend school. There were also stations with small detachments of troops - especially batteries of the Royal Artillery-where schools might be needed. In both cases it would have been expensive to deploy an army schoolmaster because of the small numbers involved. In these cases, when sufficient number of NCOs and soldiers wished to attend school, NCOs with 2nd Class Certificates were appointed as acting schoolmasters. In December 1888, 65 of these NCOs were employed on the teaching establishment.[10]

There was a continuing need to employ soldier assistants and acting schoolmasters throughout the 1890s.Under the old system of regimental schools the schoolmaster had been able to advise the COs on the selection of soldiers as assistants and these men usually remained in post for some time, enabling the schoolmaster to exercise supervision over their work in the classrooms. Where now there were garrison schools, the assistants were often detailed to the school under orders from the HQ of the Military District. Sometimes soldiers who subsequently did not prove to be capable teachers were selected, whilst more competent assistants were often removed and allocated to other duties. This had a very detrimental effect on the efficiency of the schools and on the progress made by the men.

8   *Sixth Report by the Director-General of Military Education on Army Schools*, p. 19; White, *The Story of Army Education*, p. 272.
9   Clarke, *A New History of the Royal Hibernian Military School*, pp. 424, 444, 446; War Office, *Report of the Inter-Departmental Committee on Army Schools*, 1901 (Dassent Report); White, *The Story of Army Education*, p. 272.
10   *Fourth Report by the Director-General of Military Education on Army Schools*, p. 12.

In 1888 the Royal Artillery at Woolwich had initiated an annual course for training assistant schoolmasters. The course lasted for six months, mostly covering the winter months. The subjects studied were those required for the 1st Class Certificate with the addition of grammar and school management. Those who qualified received, in addition to the 1st Class Certificate, a 'battery schoolmaster's certificate' and their names were recorded for employment in Army schools as required whether as acting schoolmasters or as soldier assistants.

In 1893 it was decided to establish a similar course for 60 NCOs of the cavalry and infantry at Aldershot during the winter months, and in 1895 this was supplemented by summer courses which could train an additional thirty NCOs. These courses built up a small cadre of trained men who were able to assist the schoolmasters in the garrison schools and were qualified as acting schoolmasters to teach classes up to 2nd Certificate standard in detachment schools. These men however were not considered qualified to teach the elder children and could only be appointed as acting teachers, when they were detailed as part of a detachment and were not required for other duties elsewhere.

Although Regulations prescribed that Soldier Assistants were not to be appointed for a period of less than one year, this could not always be guaranteed because of the frequent moves of units between stations. The pressures on the Army schools increased during the 1890s and there was a growing demand for acting masters and soldier assistants. In 1896, the Director-General reported that there were 97 acting schoolmasters and 262 soldier assistants employed in the Army's Schools. Many of these men had not been trained at Woolwich or Aldershot and the inspectors reported that their teaching was generally indifferent and that in consequence it was difficult for men to obtain the education certificates for which they were studying. This could only be remedied by employing many more Army schoolmasters, but this cost was unacceptable to government.[11]

Average attendance at the children's classes in the regimental schools was increasing at the time of the introduction of short-service enlistment. In 1867 10,451 infants and 8,574 elder children were attending and by 1876 the numbers had increased to 12,028 infants and 10,117 elder children. Over time the number of private soldiers marrying whilst serving with the colours was expected to fall. The majority of the married men would be NCOs and the number of children attending the regimental schools would decrease. When the regimental schools were abolished at the home stations in 1888, the Director-General reported that the average daily attendance was 5,154 infants and 4,614 elder children.[12] The new system required the elder children

11   *Fifth Report by the Director-General of Military Education on Army Schools*, pp. 19-21; *Sixth Report by the Director-General of Military Education on Army Schools*, pp. 6-8, 18-21.
12   *Fifth Report from the Council of Military Education 1868*; *Third Report by the Director-General of Military Education on Army Schools 1877*; *Fourth Report by the Director-General on Army Schools, 1889.*

to attend the garrison schools, whilst infants under the age of eight remained with the regiment in classes taught by an Army schoolmistress. There were difficulties at the smaller stations where soldiers were being taught by acting schoolmasters, who were generally judged to be unsuitable to take charge of teaching the older children. In these circumstances, the elder children had to attend a local civilian school, and this also was the case for infants when a schoolmistress was not available.[13]

The War Office however had no intention of adopting the Morley Committee's recommendation to send all the Army's children to civilian schools. The Director-General in his 1889 report explained that this proposal had been examined by the Harris Committee, but had been rejected. It was evident that it would only be practical in Great Britain when civilian schools existed in a parish and it was considered inadvisable to send the children to the National Schools in Ireland, which had developed differently from those in Great Britain. A supply of army schoolmasters had to be maintained in Great Britain to staff schools in India and the colonies. These masters also taught NCOs and men in the garrison schools and it was more economical to use them to teach the elder children, because otherwise the state would have to defray the cost of the fees charged for attendance at the civilian schools.

There were other difficulties in sending children to civilian schools. In the larger garrison towns, the existing school accommodation would have to be enlarged to take in soldiers' children and this would materially increase the local rates. Civilian school managers would object to the removal and addition of children during school year as this would upset the regular work of the school. Also, government grants to the schools and often the teachers' salaries were dependent on 'payment by results' (the pupils' success in examinations) and they could hardly be expected to take pains with children whom they might lose any day and thus prove to be unprofitable scholars.[14]

Nevertheless, questions continued to be asked why, given that there was a national system of elementary education, soldier's children could not be sent to public elementary schools instead of educating them in Army schools. This question persisted because the War Office considered that it was too expensive to establish a school for small numbers of children under a fully qualified schoolmaster at each of the regimental depots. The depots mostly housed recruits, who after basic training were quickly passed onto their regiments, and as there was only a small number of NCOs at each depot, they only merited a detachment school under an acting schoolmaster. These men were not considered to be qualified or suitable to teach the NCOs' children and hence the only alternative therefore was to send the children to the nearby civil school.[15]

The Director-General in his May 1896 report thought it necessary to reiterate and expand on the reasons why it would be impractical and undesirable to send the

13 *Sixth Report by the Director-General of Military Education on Army Schools*, p. 27.
14 *Fourth Report by the Director–General of Army Education on Army Schools*, p. 7.
15 *Sixth Report by the Director-General on Army Schools*, pp. 27-29.

majority of soldiers' children to local civil schools when their fathers were stationed in the United Kingdom. In addition to the reasons enumerated in his predecessor's March 1889 report, he explained that parts of the curriculum in the civil schools differed widely in different parts of the country. Hence, when the children moved with their father's regiment, they would study different subjects at different schools and would experience discontinuities in their education that would be disadvantageous in later life. The scheme of education in the Army's schools, whilst based on the Civil Educational Code, had been modified to meet the particular circumstances of soldiers' children. The curriculum was identical throughout the Army and the schools used the same text books (see below) whether at home, in the colonies, or in India.[16]

More significantly the Director-Generals' reports stressed that the Army's children schools were highly valued by warrant officers and soldiers of all ranks and quoted from the Lord Harris Committee Report:

> We are convinced that the existence of Army Schools is appreciated by the married men as a reward for their long and good service, by the children as tending to encourage in their minds the feeling that the Army is their home, and by the service in general, as in many ways raising its tone.[17]

These were essentially the reasons given by the Duke of York and accepted by Viscount Palmerston in 1812 for establishing of a system of regimental schools and they remained the ultimate rationale for retaining the Army's schools well into the 20th century.

The Harris Committee's primary concern had been to achieve savings by making the system of Army Schools more cost effective. It considered that the 250 Army Schoolmistresses imposed 'an unnecessarily heavy cost' because they only instructed the infants until they were passed over to the schoolmasters at the age of seven. The Committee without further consideration recommended the employment of assistant schoolmistresses, usually the untrained wives of NCOs, to undertake this work at a considerably lower salary.[18] The Committee appears to have been unaware that some thirty years previously the Inspectors of Army Schools had reported the schoolmasters' complaints that untrained mistresses in the infants' school, who were invariably soldiers' wives, often failed to give the children a satisfactory grounding in reading and writing. Trained schoolmistresses had been subsequently appointed and the Model School at Aldershot gradually produced very competent teachers. The efficiency of the infant schools improved and compared very favourable with similar civil schools. The Director-General in his 1889 report had noted that it was widely recognised that the educational progress and success of elder children depended on good foundations of

16 *Sixth Report by the Director-General on Army Schools*, pp. 27-29.
17 *Sixth Report by the Director-General on Army Schools*, pp. 27-29.
18 TNA WO 32/6952: Harris Report, p. viii.

learning in the infant schools. In the civilian schools, infant teachers were trained and well remunerated and every effort was made by the school managers to increase their efficiency. Unfortunately, the rates of pay offered to trained army schoolmistresses were well below what was paid a competent teacher in the Board Schools that had been established under the 1870 Act. It was thought that suitable candidates were only attracted to the Army's schools because of the retirement pension.

In 1888 the War Office issued a circular asking COs to submit names of candidates who could be recommended for the post of acting schoolmistress. From the 222 officers addressed only 53 made a recommendation; 44 candidates submitted themselves for examination, but only 13 were successful and appointed. This numbers did not meet the requirements of the service and the War Office decided to maintain the model school at Aldershot and to revert to the former system of appointing trained schoolmistresses.[19]

One difficulty that had not been foreseen was that many of serving schoolmistresses were the wives of Army schoolmasters. This practice had been encouraged by the military authorities and generally worked well and had been particularly cost effective with regard to the allocation of quarters under the system of regimental schools. Under the new system a schoolmaster might be serving in a garrison school and his schoolmistress wife might be serving at the infant's school of one of the regiments in the garrison. When her regiment moved to another station the schoolmistress would be expected to move with it, but the schoolmaster would be required to remain at the garrison school.[20] This difficulty could only be overcome by careful rostering that ensured that the husband and wife were always moved together between stations.

Table 25. Establishment of Army Schoolmistresses[21]

	December Home	1888 Colonies	India	December Home	1896 Colonies	India
I Class	18	1	6	20	2	6
2 Class	50	5	20	52	10	23
3 Class	66	26	55	98	24	50
Total	134	32	81(247)	170	36	79(285)

---

19 *Fourth Report by the Director-General of Military Education on Army Schools*, pp. 12-14.
20 *Fourth Report by the Director-General of Military Education on Army Schools*, p. 10.
21 See Fourth and Sixth Reports by the Director-General of Military Education on Army Schools.

In the early 1890s the War Office experienced great difficulty in finding sufficient schoolmistress candidates to meet the needs of all the army's schools at home and abroad. The principals of the larger female civil training colleges were approached to inquire whether some of their students might consider employment as Army Schoolmistresses. Their replies were all to the same effect: Army pay was too low and the frequent moves between stations and the long periods of 'foreign service' were a disincentive. There was also the predictable anxiety of parents that when their daughters became Army Schoolmistresses they would in inevitably associate with private soldiers in the barracks. Better and more respectable employment was always to be had in the civilian schools close to the parental home.[22]

The War Office responded to the shortage by increasing the pay and pensions of the schoolmistresses and in 1896 the Director-General was able to report that the compliment of schoolmistresses was up to the full establishment. However, there was some concern about the ability to fill future vacancies. Most of the successful candidates were soldiers' daughters who had previously been employed in Army schools as pupil teachers and monitoresses, but there was further concern when it was suggested that pensions would shortly also become available to civilian schoolmistresses.[23]

The Army schoolmistresses appointed from the pupil teachers were generally reasonably well educated and qualified for teaching infants. It was however important to obtain a nucleus of more highly educated and better trained mistresses for employment in the elder girls' schools, which were established during the 1890s in some of the larger garrisons such as Aldershot, Woolwich, Chatham, and Gibraltar. Efforts continued to be made from time to time to attract candidates from the civilian training colleges, but with little success and the War Office feared that none would be attracted once pensions were available for school mistress in the civilian elementary schools. It would then become necessary to revert to an earlier system of paying the costs of sending a number of promising girls to a teacher training college before employment as Army schoolmistresses.[24]

The reports by the Director-Generals of Military Education in 1894 and 1896 give very little detail about the organisation of the garrison schools or the operation of the regimental schools that continued in India. They did however indicate that the schoolmasters and mistresses at the home stations faced a heavy workload. The high level of demand by soldiers wishing to attend school in order to obtain the Educational Certificates required for promotion was such that the War Office issued a regulation providing for a second adult session of instruction by the schoolmasters each day. The schoolmistresses were ordered to provide instruction for pupil teachers and monitoresses out of school hours. These regulations extended the working day

---

22   *Fifth Report by the Director-General of Military Education on Army Schools*, pp. 22-3.
23   *Sixth Report by the Director-General of Military Education on Army Schools*, pp. 21-4.
24   *Sixth Report by the Director-General of Military Education on Army Schools*, pp. 14, 21-2.

for schoolmasters and mistresses, and the War Office terminated Saturday morning school as a concession in response to an increasing work-load.

There were indications by 1893 that some of the garrison schools had become very large. The War Office authorised a staffing establishment of schoolmasters, probationary schoolmasters, and soldier assistants for the instruction of the adults and elder children at each garrison school. This was based on the average attendance during one month of the largest class at the garrison, irrespective of whether this class consisted of adults or children. The War Office introduced an extra payment for schoolmasters in charge of the 13 largest garrison schools in recognition of their managerial responsibilities and there were plans to extend the payments to the masters in charge of a further 19 schools.[25]

The provision of suitable accommodation for the Army's schools had long been a problem, especially in the older barracks. In the 1890s The Director-General reported that at some barracks classes were being instructed simultaneously by a number of teachers in a single schoolroom. The noise was distracting for both the teachers and their pupils and additional classrooms were required if the pupils were to make satisfactory progress.[26] In his report in 1896 the Director-General acknowledged that the long hours of teaching made 'heavy demands on the physical and mental powers of most Army schoolmasters' and warned that a 'regular and steady life' was essential if they were to achieve good results at the periodical inspections.[27]

Many years later, W. Blackman, reflected on his working day as an Army assistant schoolmaster at the Aldershot Garrison School in January 1898. There was an Army schoolmaster in charge of the whole school and four schoolmasters of warrant rank, two masters on probation, three NCOS attached as School assistants and School Orderly. There were between 70 and 80 boys who assembled each morning in the playground at 0900 and their hair, hands and boots were inspected, before they marched into the main schoolroom for hymns, prayers and scripture lessons. At 0930 the boys dispersed to various classrooms where they were taught until 12.30. Afternoon classes for the boys began at 1400 and finished at 1515. At 1525 Blackman assisted in one of the adult classes of men working for an educational certificate This ended at 1645, but men who could not attend this lesson because of other duties attended a second session of adult classes at which Blackman was expected to assist from 1800 to 1915 on every evening except Wednesday.[28]

The working week overseas could be equally demanding. A senior schoolmaster serving in India in 1914 recalled that his daily programme began at 0900 and ended at 1915, five days a week, whilst Saturday morning was taken up with organised sports

25 *Fifth Report by the Director-General of Military Education on Army Schools*, pp. 16, 18 (appendix V, p. 35)
26 *Sixth Report by the Director-General of Military Education on Army Schools*, p. 5.
27 *Sixth Report by the Director-General of Military Education on Army Schools*, p. 18.
28 W. Blackman, 'Reminiscences of the Retired', *Army Education*, September *1946:* quoted in Williams, *Tommy Atkin's Children*, p. 108.

for the children.[29] Although the regimental schools were retained in India following the formation of garrison schools in Great Britain, the subsequent reports by Director-General of Military Education do not make any direct reference to these schools. During the 1890s around one third of the British Army was stationed in India. There were usually 52 battalions of infantry, nine regiments of cavalry, around 70 batteries of Royal Artillery and some 20 companies of the Royal Engineers.[30] In 1888 there were 82 Army schoolmasters and 81 Army schoolmistresses on the establishment in India. On 1 January 1896 this was little changed with 79 schoolmasters and the same number of school mistresses, which would suggest that the Army schools in India continued mainly to be organised on a regimental basis.

In the second half of the 19th century attempts were made to ease the living conditions for soldiers and their families in India. Troops were housed in cantonments sited outside the large towns, in part to preserve the health of the men and their families, by ensuring that they were supplied with clean water and piped sanitation. New barracks were constructed, which were more spacious than in the UK and their large rooms were cooled by a 'punkah-wallah', who by pulling on a rope activated a large swinging cloth fan in the roof. The cantonments generally contained larger open spaces for recreation and sports than were found at the schools in the towns in the British Isles.

Much depended on the location of the particular cantonment, but the climate generally presented difficulties for managing schools in India. Outside the hill stations and on the plains temperatures became so unbearably hot in the middle of the day that most serious work was undertaken in the early morning and in the cool of the early evening. The onset of the monsoon brought some relief, but often also the onset of fever. Despite the attempt to isolate the cantonments and attend to the barrack's sanitation and to ensure that families received pretty much the same food that they were accustomed to in Great Britain, nevertheless there were frequent bouts of sickness. These often included outbreaks of enteric fever, diphtheria and sometimes cholera.[31] Medical officers frequently advised the closure of the schools. The Director-General in 1896, without specifically referring to India, expressed concern about the frequent closure of the schools on account of sickness and the effects on the education of the children. He pointed to the regulations, which prescribed that the isolation of families was sufficient except where the disease attained an epidemic form.[32] Towards the end of the decade a number of units stationed in India commissioned photographs of their children's schools together with their teaching staff.

29   White, *The Story of Army Education*, p. 273.

30   J. Morris, *Pax Britannica* (London: Penguin Books 1987), p .405; T. A. Heathcote, *The Indian Army* (London: Davis& Charles 1974), p. 202.

31   French, *Military Identities*, pp. 103-4, 108, 122-23, 131; Heathcote, *The Indian Army*, pp. 66-7.

32   *Sixth Report by the Director-General of Military Education on Army Schools*, p. 14.

Regimental School of the 1st Battalion of the Northampton Regiment at Secunderabad
c.1898. (Reproduced by permission of the late Arthur Cockerill, Cobourg, Ontario, Canada)

The photograph of the infant and elder children schools of the 1st Battalion
Northamptonshire Regiment depicts 38 boys and girls. Mr Gould, the Army
schoolmaster, is seated at the front on the left and Miss Pinsent the schoolmistress
is seated at the front on the right. Standing next to the schoolmistress on her left is
the monitor. There are three Lance-Corporals who are serving as soldier assistants.
On the back row is 'The Munshi', an Indian teacher who was frequently employed
to teach Hindi and sometimes also Urdu–usually to the adults in the school. The
photo was probably taken in the main schoolroom. Most of the younger children in
the front row are holding slates and the older children text books. Geography had
an important place in the Army school's curriculum and the large maps on the rear
wall are of England and Wales and the Western and Eastern Hemispheres. This was
an advance of the state of affairs in the 1860s and 1870s, when the school inspectors
in India complained about the absence of maps and atlases in the children's schools.

The photos of the schools of other regiments contain a smaller number of children:
that of the 2nd Battalion of the Wiltshire Regiment at Quetta in Baluchistan in 1899
shows 25 children; whilst that of the 2nd Royal Irish Rifles at Poona in 1897 contains
only 15 children of various ages. All the photographs include the schoolmaster and
the schoolmistress, a pupil teacher or monitors, and a number of soldier assistants.

Regimental School of the Second Battalion Royal Irish Rifles, Poona 1897. (Reproduced by
kind permission of the Adjutant General's Corps Museum, Winchester)

The War Office attempted to ensure that the Army's Schools kept pace with
developments in public elementary schools so that soldiers' children would not be at
a disadvantage. The Kindergarten movement had started in England in 1854 and this
approach to pre-school education, which emphasized the importance of play and early
learning through practical activities was popularised during the 1870s. Kindergarten
methods were introduced in the publicly funded infant schools from 1877. The
Education Committee of the Privy Council exerted pressure on the managers of the
civil schools to adopt this approach and made the payments of some of its grants
dependent on its successful introduction. If the education in Army schools was to be
kept on par with that of the civilian elementary schools, some variant of kindergarten
instruction had to be introduced. A modified system was tried experimentally for six
months in the Model School at Aldershot and the Secretary of State approved the
introduction of some of the kindergarten methods alongside formal schooling in the
infant schools. The inspectors observed immediate benefits from this innovation. It
introduced variety into the children's day and made their work more interesting, and
they were generally less tired and more attentive during their five hours school day.
The Director-General reported in 1896 that the children's mental powers developed
more rapidly under the new system and that, when taken with the improvements in

the training of the teachers, the children in the infants' schools were now in general better prepared when they passed into the elder children's schools.[33]

In 1886 the curriculum for the elder children at the Army Schools had been assimilated to that in the public elementary schools as approved by the Education Committee of the Privy Council and contained within the Civil Code. In 1890 and 1891 amendments were made to allow Board School managers to make a wider choice in the subjects in the curriculum of their schools. The War Office had to decide whether it should make similar changes in Army Schools. In addition to lessons in reading writing and arithmetic, children in Army schools had regular physical exercise amounting to a quarter of an hour each day. This was considered essential for the children's health and physical development. There were compulsory singing and recitation lessons, which were considered important to overcome incorrect pronunciation. English Grammar, Geography and English History were selected as compulsory subjects from a list of additional subjects approved by the Civil Code. Needlework was compulsory for girls. The civil code added drawing to the core of compulsory subjects for boys and some parents of children at Army schools expressed wish that this subject should be taught so that their sons would not be disadvantaged compared with the sons of civilians in seeking employment. The Director-General was sympathetic to this request but decided not to proceed because class time would have to be taken from other subjects and there would be some additional expense in terms of models and materials.

The Civil Code contained a list of 'specific subjects', such as foreign languages, science and mathematical subjects which could be taught to the more able pupils. The War Office decided that it would be difficult to teach most of these subjects in the Army's schools and the choice for the more able boys were restricted to one subject from algebra, geometry and mensuration. The flexibility introduced within the Civil Code made sense for the civilian schools where many children passed all their elementary education in one school. Army children and their teachers however moved regularly between stations and the War Office decided the curriculum and system of instruction had to be uniform at home, in India and in the colonies so that there was continuity in the children's education no matter which school they were attending.[34]

The advantages of a uniform curriculum for Army schools were lucidly expressed some years later by Army schoolmaster A.L. Collinson:

> Each child in every Army school throughout the Empire had an arithmetic book and three readers, literary, geographical and historical, appropriate to his standard. And these were chosen not by the headmaster but by the War Office. This ensured that when Sergeant Brown was posted from Aldershot to

33   *Fifth Report by the Director-General of Military Education on Army Schools*, p. 13; *Sixth Report by the Director-General of Military Education on Army Schools*, p. 16.
34   *Fifth Report by the Director-General of Military Education on Army Schools*, pp. 10-11.

Jubbulpore or Jamaica or Hong Kong or Malta his son in standard IV would be able to enter standard IV in his new station and use the same text books. Moreover, the last examination of Jimmy Brown at Aldershot travelled with him to his new station for the information of his new headmaster, whose curriculum was identical to the smallest detail with that used at Aldershot.[35]

Separate classes for boys and girls in the large public elementary schools had become increasingly common by the 1890s. The system of regimental schools had made it very difficult to meet the preferences of some families for separate classes for girls and boys. At the larger stations the formation of garrison schools sometimes allowed the creation of separate classes. Following the practice in place for some years the girls at Chatham were taught by an Army Schoolmistress. This was considered a much better arrangement for teaching especially wherever the girls were taught needlework. Recently constructed barracks were equipped with separate classrooms for boys and girls, but mixed class had to be retained at the older barracks where there was not enough accommodation available for separate classes.[36]

The Director-General reporting on the elder children's schools in 1896 argued that, with the exception of the omission of 'drawing' (which still had not been introduced for reasons of cost), the curriculum at the Army's schools was broader than in many civilian elementary schools. Furthermore, the Army Schools were subject to periodical and surprise inspections and there was an annual examination by age of every child on the register. In civilian schools the tests were made by sample and a child might be examined in one subject only. An Army school had to satisfy the inspector of the standards achieved by each child appropriate to its age. In addition, Army schoolmasters and mistresses depended on a satisfactory report on the tone, discipline, and administration of their classes for their periodical incremental increases in pay. The inspection of the Army's schools was thorough and stricter than for the civilian schools and the Director-General concluded that the results produced were markedly good.[37]

In one matter it was necessary to enact legislation to ensure that Army children were not disadvantaged. Endowed charities in England and Wales had been prominent in the development of elementary schools and later what came to be referred as 'higher class schools' and subsequently as 'Secondary Schools.' The Charities Commission in their numerous schemes for the management of educational trusts had made liberal provision for children to gain admission from the public elementary schools to these 'higher class schools', through scholarships or the remission of fees for candidates

35   NAM: Records of the Royal Army Educational Corps Army, Educational Policy and Regimental School 1846-1920, Box 22127, A. L. Collinson, 'The Memoirs of an Army schoolmaster 1904-1927'.
36   *Fifth Report by the Director-General of Military Education on Army Schools*, p. 13.
37   *Sixth Report by the Director-General of Military Education on Army Schools*, p. 12.

who were successful in competitive examinations. In 1891 in order that children at the Army Schools should not be at a disadvantage, Parliament passed the Army Schools Act, which specified that an Army school should be deemed to be a public elementary school for purposes of participation in endowed charities. It was hoped that Army schoolmasters would follow the practice in the civilian elementary schools and prepare the brighter children for these scholarship examinations. The take up however was disappointing and in the two years to 1895, the only children benefitted from the legislation and gained scholarships, were 11 boys and three girls from the Royal Artillery at Woolwich.[38]

The Education Act of 1902 only served to highlight the isolation of the Army's schools from the civilian schools. The Act enabled local authorities to create and maintain entirely new secondary schools and to link them with elementary schools. Competition soon developed for the available places at these schools and army children were handicapped by movement of soldiers' families between stations at home and abroad. In 1904 the War Office invited the Board of Education to examine the Army's schools. The main emphasis of the subsequent report was on modernising an old-fashioned curriculum: there was no science or drawing and the schools did not possess pianos or any musical instruments. The teaching of existing subjects, such as history and geography, focused on mechanical memorising and rote learning. The investigating committee however was restricted from making recommendations that involved any significant expenditure and nothing was done.

The War Office did make efforts to remind parents of the long-term benefits for their children that would follow from regular attendance at the garrison schools. From 1891 a Certificate of Achievement was given to each child who passed the examinations at the annual inspection and the Director-General reported that these certificates were much appreciated by the children and their parents. There however was a long tradition of families keeping these children at home on one or two days each week to help with washing and other house work in the married quarters. In 1892 the elder children's schools were extended by half an hour per day from Monday to Friday and Saturday morning school was abolished. It was hoped that this would secure regular attendance on the five working days. COs were instructed to put pressure on parents and in 1896 the Director-General was able to report much more regular attendance at the children's schools.[39]

During the 1890s children from working class families mostly left elementary school for employment in their early teens, although invariably these children continued to reside with their parents. Soldiers' families were however migratory and with the exception of units embarking on active service, soldiers' families moved

38 *Fifth Report by the Director-General of Military Education on Army Schools*, pp. 12-13; *Sixth Report by the Director-General of Military Education on Army Schools*, p. 13.
39 *Fifth Report by the Director-General of Military Education on Army Schools on Army Schools*, pp. 13-14; *Sixth Reports by the Director-General of Military Education on Army Schools*, p. 14.

regularly between stations at home and abroad. For most of the Nineteenth century soldier's children had few career options once they reached the age to leave school, especially when a regiment was serving overseas. Soldiers' sons frequently enlisted as boy soldiers, whilst their daughters often married older men who were serving soldiers. In the 1880s and 1890s many of the pupils attending the elder children's schools were the sons and daughters of NCOs and Warrant Officers, who had themselves gained a fair standard of elementary education, much of it whilst in the Army. The Army was providing a good standard of elementary education and the War Office from time to time actively promoted employment opportunities that were open to the children from the Army Schools.

Special attention over a six-year period in the 1890s was given to establishing a uniform style of handwriting across all Army schools. This helped the children's progress as they moved from one school to another, and was also important because of large number of clerical vacancies that were regularly available in the Post Office and other businesses for young men and women who could write a clear and legible hand.[40] In 1893 the War Office drew attention to the opportunities that existed for boys of 14 years of age to prepare themselves in the Army's schools for entry as 'Boy Copyists' in the civil service and the schoolmasters were exhorted to offer every facility for boys to compete.

That same year, a circular was sent to the General Officers Commanding Districts regarding the opportunities that existed for soldiers' sons of good character and ability to apply for the post of pupil teacher at the DYRMS and the RHMS and subsequently to train as an Army schoolmaster. In order to encourage applications, boys who had passed Standard VII in the Army Schools Examination could be appointed as salaried 'School Assistants' in the place of soldier assistants provided that this did exceed the authorised number of teachers at the station. These boys would only assist in teaching the children and would continue their education by attending one of the adult schools and study under the schoolmaster. When they were of age they would compete for places as pupil teachers at the Army's two residential Schools.[41]

With an eye to addressing the difficulty in securing sufficient trained mistresses for the infant schools, the War Office emphasised this career opportunities for soldier's daughters. Girls who passed Standard V in the school examinations could be appointed as paid monitoresses in the infant schools. Throughout the1890s some 200-220 girls were employed in these salaried posts. The most successful were subsequently employed as pupil teachers with the prospect of being put forward after two years' service as candidates for the position of Army Schoolmistress. These girls were given special instruction after school hours to prepare them for the examination for Army schoolmistress. There were particular difficulties in recruiting to these posts in South Africa and some of the other colonies where there were good local

40   *Sixth Report by the Director-General of Military Education on Army Schools*, pp. 14 15.
41   *Sixth Report by the Director-General of Military Education on Army Schools*, p. 43.

employment opportunities, but these arrangements on the whole worked well and 62 pupil teachers were employed in 1896, which was double the number employed in 1892.The War Office stressed that the posts of Army Schoolmistress offered 'solid advantages' to soldiers' daughters. They provided a graduated pay scale and were pensionable. Moreover, the work was in a 'superior class' of employment and with shorter hours than was usually available to girls on leaving the civilian schools. This was a very attractive proposition for soldiers' daughters when their fathers' regiments were stationed in India.[42]

A group of Army School Inspectors c.1905. (Reproduced by kind permission of the Adjutant General's Corps Museum, Winchester)

There were no further inspection reports published by the War Office from 1896 to 1912, but the revised system of Army Schools that had been introduced following the recommendations of the Harris Committee in 1888 continued in place until the outbreak of the First World War. In 1912 there were some 300 Army schoolmasters and approximately 100 were below Warrant Rank. In addition, there were 20 Inspectors with commissioned rank.[43] The system was in practice highly decentralised. The post of Director of Military Education was abolished probably for reasons of economy in 1898 and with a short exception in 1902-1903, when there was a Director

42 *Sixth Report by the Director-General of Military Education on Army Schools*, pp. 14, 21.
43 Commissioned Inspectors had the rank of lieutenant and after ten years the rank of Captain. Adjutant-General's Corps Museum, Extract '*The Army List of early 1912: Corps of Army Schoolmasters*'.

of Military Education and training, the Army's schools were under the jurisdiction of the Adjutant-General, and from 1903 under the particular management of an Assistant Adjutant-General assisted by a retired officer. Successive editions of the Army School Regulations specified the detailed administration of the schools and the duties of the teaching staff. Every Military District had its own inspector whose duties were to see that the regulations were adhered to, and to observe the conduct, dress and appearance of each member of the school staff. The teaching staff were trained at the Army's own teacher training establishments or at civilian colleges and served a probationary period and passed an examination before substantive appointment. They were generally well regarded by regimental officers and the standard of their training impressed H M Inspectors of Schools.[44]

44 White, *The Story of Army Education*, pp. 42-43.

22

Some Notable and Pioneering Achievements

The Army educated many thousands of soldiers' children during the nineteenth century and has a good claim to be the pioneer of publicly funded elementary education in Great Britain. Fredrick Duke of York, the C-in-C at Horse Guards, established the system of regimental schools some 30 years before the first grants were made to the educational charities for school buildings and almost sixty years before William Gladstone's government began to establish a national system of elementary education for children in England and Wales. In contrast to the patchwork of grant maintained and local board schools that provided elementary education in the later Victorian years, the Army's schools formed a single uniform system across all the regiments and corps and its schoolmasters and schoolmistresses, unlike the teachers in civilian schools, were employed directly by the Crown.

The Duke of York's Order to the Army on 1st January 1812 explained that the regimental schools had been established to educate soldiers' children and made no mention of schools for serving soldiers. The Duke's correspondence with Viscount Palmerston, the Secretary at War, and the War Office's Circular to Colonels of regiments explained however that they were also for the education of young soldiers. Many COs were prepared to go much further and issued regimental standing orders insisting that private soldiers who were seeking promotion as NCOs must attend school until they were literate and numerate. The Army's schools were unique in that they also provided both beginners and continuing education classes for adults alongside those provided for children.

The reasons given for justifying the public expense of the providing schooling for the serving soldier shifted during the century. Rev George Gleig the Inspector of Military Schools from 1846 to 1858 brought something of early Victorian evangelicalism to the reorganisation of the Army's schools. His priority was the moral education of the private soldier and the subsequent improvements that this would bring to the character of the Army. His successors had less lofty ambitions and emphasized military efficiency and the practical need for the modern soldier to have a sound elementary education. There were however disagreements within the military departments about whether new recruits should be compelled to attend school. The British Army was a volunteer army and many recruits had little interest in returning to the classroom and there was always a need to avoid anything that might discourage recruitment. From 1870 it was expected that over time the national system of elementary schools would provide the typical recruit with an education of a standard that would enable him to effectively discharge his military duties both as a private soldier and as an NCO. This proved to be unrealistically optimistic. Boys left elementary school some six or more years before enlisting in the Army and the typical recruit in the years leading up to the Great War entered with a low standard of education. There was therefore a continuing need for classes for enlisted men alongside those for soldiers' children.

Throughout the century a substantial part of the Army were stationed in the various garrisons across the empire and a number of regiments were always in transit between barracks in Great Britain and overseas. Regiments retained at home moved at intervals across the British Isles and for much of the century were stationed to provide support for the civil authorities, especially in Ireland. Once the decision had been taken to provide schools for soldiers' children there was no practical alternative, but to deliver the provision through separate regimental rather than garrison schools. Circumstances changed in the 1870s with the introduction of short service enlistment and settled regimental depots to receive recruits and opinion moved in favour of establishing garrison schools, especially for soldiers serving in the Great Brtiain. The stationing of a large part of the Army in India and other colonial garrisons, and continuous movement of regiments, rendered it impractical to send the Army's children to civilian schools and this ensured the continuation of regimental schools for the soldiers' children. Moreover, COs were able to ensure that the children of soldiers with families living in barracks attended regularly at a regimental or garrison school.

Although the development of railways and the introduction of steam powered troopships reduced the disruption to schooling as regiments moved between barracks at home and abroad, the exigencies of military service had some unavoidable impact on the progress of pupils in the Army's schools. This did not always mean that the progress of soldiers' children was any less than that of the children in civilian schools. The 1870 Education Act did not introduce compulsory school attendance and it took a further ten years for the Education Department to commit to universal direct compulsion and longer still for local authorities to secure its implementation. Many parents depended on their children's employment to supplement what was often little more than a subsistence income and their attendance at school was irregular. It was not until the mid-1890s that there was a network of elementary schools throughout the country, and the majority of children had some experience, however brief, of attending school.[1]

---

1   Sutherland, *Policy Making in Elementary Education*, p. 340.

Emile Durkheim famously defined the purposes of education as '...to develop in the child a certain number of physical, intellectual and moral states, which are demanded of him both by the political society as a whole and the special milieu for which he is specifically destined.'[2] Majority opinion in the nineteenth century gave the moral element in education a specifically religious dimension and in Great Britain this led to rivalry between the different denominations that supported the civilian schools. Once there was an attempt to establish education as a responsibility of the state this created acute tensions and political divisions.

The instructions for conducting the regimental schools issued in 1812 explicitly stated that Army's children should be educated in the principles of the Established Church. The wording in the instructions was sufficiently broad to allow the regimental schools of the Scottish regiments to be conducted according to the principles of the Presbyterian Church in Scotland and the Protestant dissenting and non-conformist churches did not appear to have had any objection to the Army's schools. This indifference however was not shared by the Roman Catholic Church, which from the 1840s became increasingly assertive and protested that the children of Catholic soldiers should not be exposed to the teachings of the Anglican or any Protestant church. This had the potential to become a serious problem given the very large numbers of Irish Catholic soldiers in the Army. Many COs were aware of the dangers and had the good sense to allow parents to withdraw their children from morning prayers and from learning the Anglican catechism. This did not satisfy Archbishop Cullen and the hierarchy of the Roman Catholic Church in Ireland who were opposed to mixed schools in which Protestant and Catholic children were taught together in the same classes for secular subjects. The War Office however held its ground and confrontation was avoided by the appointment of Catholic Army Chaplains to attend to the religious education of the children of Catholic soldiers. The Board Schools established in England and Wales from 1870 prohibited denominational religious education and the War Office included a similar prohibition in the regulations for Army's schools. In the long run the Army was spared the bitter sectarian disputes that characterised political discourse about public funding of civilian schools but was not immune from the debate discussion about the extent of elementary education that was appropriate for the children of the working classes.

In terms of the curriculum, the War Office broadly followed the developments in the civilian schools. Infant schools and subsequently kindergartens were introduced for the younger children and an attempt was made to introduce industrial classes to teach practical skills to the older children that would be useful in their adult life. In later years there was a recognition that the ability to write legibly and intelligibly and have achieved a good standard in numeracy would qualify the children for entry into the expanding clerical and white collar occupation, but for most of the century the

2   Quoted in: Sutherland, *Policy Making in Elementary Education*, p. 1.

received opinion was that soldiers' children would mostly enter into manual work should not be over-educated for their future stations in life.[3]

The glaring weakness of the Duke of York's system of regimental schools was that it did not provide for the training of army schoolmasters and COs were ordered simply to select the most suitable men for promotion as schoolmaster-sergeants to manage the schools. Many COs struggled to find men who were suitable for appointment and in consequence there were considerable variations in the standards of teaching and the progress of pupils across the regimental schools. The half-yearly inspections of each military district at least ensured that COs appointed a schoolmaster-sergeant and endeavoured to maintain a regimental school, but the inspecting officers were not qualified to assess the standard of the education provided by the schools or the progress of the pupils.

All of this changed with the reforms introduced by Sidney Hebert and Fox Maule (Lord Panmure) at the War Office from 1846. The Normal School at Chelsea, which trained the Army's schoolmasters until 1887, was modelled on the teacher training institutions of the Anglican National Society for the Education of the Poor. The newly trained Army schoolmaster undertook his teaching practice with the boys of the RMA Model School at Chelsea, but he did not gain any practical experience in teaching adults and like his predecessors, the schoolmaster-sergeants, he learnt his craft at the chalk face during the early years of his career. Matters did not improve until the closure of the Normal School and thereafter the probationary army schoolmaster undertook teaching practice with classes of both children and adults under the supervision of qualified and experienced army schoolmasters at the Aldershot garrison schools.

The schoolmaster-sergeants looked to the women of their regiments to teach the girls needlework and other domestic crafts and often relied upon soldiers' wives and their older daughters to assist them in the classroom in managing the younger children. These women were untrained and largely unpaid, but their importance was acknowledged by the War Office as early as 1840, when a Royal Warrant was issued authorising the appointment and payment of army schoolmistresses. There is no information about the numbers appointed under the warrant until the publication of Lieutenant Colonel Lefroy's report on the Army's schools in 1859. Their importance however increased from the 1850s, when the Army Schools' Regulations established separate Infant Schools and also Industrial schools to teach soldiers' daughters sewing and other domestic subjects. The War Office does not appear to have considered establishing its own 'normal School' in Great Britain for training the Army's schoolmistresses and instead relied on recruiting trained civilian teachers. Unsurprisingly many unmarried qualified civilian teachers were reluctant to consider Army life and although a training facility was established at Aldershot, there were never enough trained schoolmistresses and the regimental schools continued to depend on soldiers' wives and their daughters working as classroom assistants.

---

3   *Second Report of the Royal Commission on Military Education 1870*, pp. 183-6.

Once there were a sufficient number of trained army schoolmasters it was possible to appoint some of the best and most experienced to inspect the regimental schools and assess the educational progress of the pupils. The civilian teachers and Army's schoolmasters and mistresses each taught under their respective school regulations and were subject to periodic visits by their own inspectors. The reports by HMIs on the civilian elementary schools were often mechanical and contained little that was stimulating or supportive of the teachers' professional development. There is no indication that the reports by the Army's inspectors on individual schoolmasters were markedly different, but when aggregated they recorded a broad satisfaction with the work of the garrison and regimental schools. Outside the larger garrisons the army schoolmasters and mistresses often worked in the same isolation as did their contemporaries in the many village schools throughout the British Isles, but they were at least spared the system of payments by results and the level of anxiety that was experienced by the civilian teachers when the HMIs visited their schools.[4]

There is wide agreement that the regimental system was the essence of the British Army in the nineteenth and twentieth centuries and that the forging of regimental identities was the 'principle vehicle of the nation's military culture.'[5] Although there were always some garrison schools, it was each regiment's school that was responsible for providing most of the elementary education for the British soldier and his children during the 19th century and this contributed to strengthening regimental identity.

Whilst 'the regiment' has been seen as a source of the Army's strength it also has been accused of fostering a culture of amateurism that became increasingly out of place as the century progressed. The staffing of the Army's schools by untrained schoolmaster-sergeants appointed by the CO from within the ranks and assisted often by soldiers' wives and daughters contributed to a developing sense of regimental identity during the first half of the century, but its amateurism resulted in ineffective schooling and arguably was a waste of tax payers' money. The creation of a body of trained schoolmasters and schoolmistresses was designed to address this. A corps of trained teachers drawn from outside the ranks of the regiment and with its own pay scales and career structure would however inevitably develop a separate professional identity within the Army. Nevertheless, whenever it was necessary to retain the regimental schools, trained schoolmasters and mistresses were assigned to and served with a particular regiment. In this regard their working life differed little from that of their untrained predecessors in the first half of the century, working often in relative isolation in barracks and cantonments in the various military stations across the British Empire. They shared their postings with the NCOs and enlisted men and their families and their work deserves special recognition in any history of the British Army during the 19th century.

4   Sutherland, *Policy Making in Elementary Education*, pp. 65-68
5   J. Keegan, 'Regimental Ideology', in G. Best and A. Wheatcroft (Eds.), *War, Economy and Military Mind* , (London: Croom Helm1976), p. 16.

The history of public policy and administration in Great Britain has often focused on the dynamic contribution made by prominent public servants in shaping initiatives and effecting reform. Subsequently there has been recognition of the crucial contribution made by the political heads of the relevant government departments in effecting change and the wider political context in which policy emerged. There has also been recognition that successive reforms were often the practical response to the problems of the implementation and administration of earlier policy.

In the case of the history of the British Army's schools, the literature has focused on the part played by Frederick Duke of York in establishing a uniform system of regimental schools across the Army. Little attention has been given to the Duke of York's motives for establishing the system of regimental schools immediately after he resumed command at the House Guards in 1811, or the crucial contribution made by Viscount Palmerston at the War Office in securing the necessary funding. Although York's plan did include training for some of the first cohort of designated schoolmaster-sergeants, together with written guidance on the curriculum and pedagogy that was to be adopted, there was no attempt in the post war years to establish a permanent facility to train the schoolmaster-sergeants. The political climate of the day would not have easily accepted such a proposal, but the literature hitherto rarely mentions the problems faced by commanding officers in appointing competent schoolmaster-sergeants to staff the schools, or the difficulties experienced by these schoolmasters in keeping their schools open as their regiments moved between stations throughout the Empire.

Rev George Gleig has been given the credit for persuading the War Office to establish a training school for army schoolmasters at Chelsea in 1846 and the literature has emphasised his inspirational and dynamic contribution in the following years to the reform of the regimental schools. It was also especially fortunate that in the 1840s and 1850s there were a succession of ministers at the War Office who were sympathetic to the reform of the Army's schools, but the literature hitherto has given little weight to their contributions and in particular to the work of Sidney Herbert (Baron Lee) and Fox Maule (Lord Panmure) in ensuring the successful implementation of the reforms.[6]

Military administration in Great Britain and Ireland during the first decades of the nineteenth century was shared between the various military departments and there were always tensions over matters of command the Army between the government ministers in charge of the War Office and the C-in-C at the Horse Guards. The supremacy of the War Office was firmly asserted in the second half of the century and the introduction of trained army schoolmasters and the consequent reforms in the

6   The Harris Committee (1887) recorded that Herbert and Fox Maule had taken a particular interest in the training of the Army's schoolmasters and had regularly visited the Normal School and observed lessons.

Army's schools by Sidney Herbert and Lord Panmure was an early milestone in this development in military administration.

The legacy of the reforms in army education continued in the years following the First World War. In June 1920, a Royal Warrant established the *Army Educational Corps* (AEC) with an initial establishment of 400 officers, 595 Warrant Officers and NCOs and 289 Army schoolmistresses. The Corps assumed responsibility for some 5,000 children in 190 Army schools, the majority of which were overseas, mainly in India, the Mediterranean and the Middle East.[7] In November 1946, in the centenary year of Queen Victoria's warrant that formed the basis for the subsequent development of Corps of Army schoolmasters, King George VI granted the Army Educational Corps a 'Royal Title' in recognition of its work with serving soldiers across all theatres during the Second World War.

The responsibilities on the Royal Army Educational Corps (RAEC) grew in the immediate post-war years. By 1948 Britain's war-time force had been reduced to 700, 000, which included 150,000 colonial and Gurkha troops, but National Service provided about 100,000 recruits annually and many had a low standard of education. Military commitments were wide spread and there were large forces permanently stationed in the British Zone of Germany and though the Army left in India in 1947, there were 115,000 men outside Europe, mainly in the Middle East and Malaya. In addition to making provision for enlisted men, some provision had to be made for the children of married men at home and in the overseas garrisons.[8]

The 1944 Education Act had given the Local Education Authorities (LEAs) wide powers and duties in England and Wales over a new structure of education organised in three successive stages of primary, secondary and further education. The War Office was faced with responsibility for implementing the Act in the Army's schools in Great Brtiain and in ensuring that children of troops stationed overseas enjoyed the benefits and opportunities of the Education Act.

At home the Ministry of Education asked each LEA to accept the responsibility for the education of army children in its area. All accepted and by the end of 1948 all the army's children's schools had been taken over by their local LEAs, except for the Duke of York's Royal Military School at Dover and the Queen Victoria's School at Dunblane. For the first time since the regimental schools had been established in 1812, the Army relinquished direct responsibility for educating soldiers' children in Great Britain, and a number of the remaining Army's Schoolmistresses were seconded to LEAs.[9]

---

7   St John Williams, *Tommy Atkins' Children*, pp. 122-6. Army Schoolmistresses were employed and served under a separate Royal Warrant, and from 1927 were designated as Queens Army Schoolmistresses (QAS). None was recruited during World War II, nor after 1945.

8   St John Williams, *Tommy Atkins' Children*, pp. 161-2.

9   St John Williams, *Tommy Atkins' Children*, p. 156.

There was no alternative but to establish forces schools for the families of soldiers stationed in the overseas garrisons. These were organised with the involvement of all three armed services with a Director of Army at the War Office having responsibility for the Army's schools. The decision was taken to staff the schools with civilian teachers. The majority were Great Britain based teachers on secondment from their LEAs, together with locally recruited civilian teachers and a very small and decreasing number of the Army Schoolmistresses. In June 1969 there were 53,040 children in 147 schools with 2,512 civilian teachers across the Army's overseas Commands.[10]

In the following years successive British governments withdrew the armed forces from many of the overseas stations and there was gradual closure of the Army's schools. There were also significant reductions in the numbers in what had become was now a volunteer regular army and the decision was made to merge a number Army's supporting corps. In 1992 the RAEC became the Educational and Training Services (ETS) branch of the newly formed Adjutant General's Corps.

In 1896 the Army had an authorised establishment of 192,000 NCOs and men, and the regimental and garrison schools and the 265 army schoolmasters and 285 schoolmistresses taught some 27,000 adults and children on the school registers. The strength of the Regular Army at the time of writing stands at some 83,000 men and women and 30,000 trained personnel in the Army Reserve. Nevertheless, the Army today continues to attach great importance to provision of learning and development opportunities for all its serving personnel. The ETS is an all-officer and all-graduate branch and employs 300 regular and reserve personnel.[11] Although they do not teach soldiers' children, they follow in the footsteps of their 19th century predecessors by providing tuition in English and Maths and in preparing soldiers for promotion as NCOs and Warrant Officers. They continue into the 21st century the Army's pioneering work in the provision of adult education in the United Kingdom.

10   St John Williams, *Tommy Atkins' Children*, p. 215.
11   Spiers, *The Late Victorian Army*, p. 120; *Armed forces.co.uk*. <www.army.mod.uk> (accessed 20 January 2018).

Appendix I

Council of Military Education and Successors 1857-1904

Vice President of the Council of Military Education 1857-70[1]

Major General Duncan A. Cameron	April 1857 to January 1861
Major General Randal Rumley	January 1861 to October 1862
Major General Frederick. W. Hamilton	October 1862 to April 1866
Lieutenant General Sir William C. E. Napier	April 1866 to January 1870

Director General of Military Education 1870-1904

Lieutenant General Sir William C.E. Napier[2]	January 1870 to January 1875
Major General Evelin H.F. Pocklington	January 1875 to January 1878
Lieutenant General Charles. P. Beauchamp Walker	January 1878 to December 1884
General Sir Edwin Beaumont-Johnson	December 1884 to March 1888
Lieutenant General Sir Ralph Biddulph	March 1888 to January 1893
General Sir Wilbraham O. Lennox	January 1893 to January 1895
Major General Sir Charles W. Wilson	January 1895 to March 1898
Colonel Alexander M. Delavoye[3]	March 1898 to January 1903
Major General Sir Henry J.T. Hildyard[4]	January 1903 to January 1904

1   From 1857 until 1870 The Duke of Cambridge as Commander-in-Chief was ex officio President of the Council of Military Education. In reality the day to day work was done by the Vice President of the Council of Military Education.
2   The *Army List* continues to record Napier's appointed date as April 1866, even though in 1871 his title changed from Vice President of the Council of Military Education to Director General of Military Education.
3   Delavoye was not officially Director General. Between March 1898 and January 1903 there was no Director General, and Delavoye acted as Assistant Military Secretary for Education, having previously been Assistant Director of Military Education from July 1891
4   Hildyard had the new title of Director of Military Education and Training.

Appendix II

Instructions for Establishing and Conducting Regimental Schools

---

These instructions were circulated to all the regiments and corps in the British Army as an appendix to the General Orders issued by the Horse Guards on 1st January 1812. The Orders explain that the 'Instructions' had been approved by Dr Andrew Bell and were the best directions that His Royal Highness the Prince Regent could give for the conduct of the regimental schools.[1]

The introduction to the 'Instructions' explained that the great advantage of Bell's system of tuition was that 'by economising time' it provided the 'opportunity for establishing a drill', which was not only healthy for the children but would also implant in their minds at an early age a predilection for a career as a soldier. It was not envisaged that this drill would extend beyond teaching the children to hold themselves erect and march correctly in line and to form columns. They also should be encouraged to engage in 'manly games and pastimes' and generally in exercise that would produce the mental and physical attributes required of a soldier.

The 'Instructions' then move on to outline the interior economy of the schools and the practices in teaching and learning, using Dr Bell's system, which it was explained rested on the principle of tuition by the scholars themselves with the boys teaching one another under the superintendence of one master. The schools were to be organised in classes or companies with boys who appear to have made the same progress placed in each class. One of the boys from a higher class or at the head of his own class was to be designated as a 'sergeant teacher' for that class and the remainder was to be paired off into tutors and pupils, with the best trusty boys taking the worst pupils. Pupils were ranked according to attainment in each class and when a pupil had been ranked

---

1   The Rev. George Gleig, the future Principal Chaplain and Chaplain General to the Forces and Inspector General of Army Schools, believed that the 'Instructions' were prepared in 1811 by Dr Daley, who was the Chaplain to the Household Brigade and Gleig's predecessor as the Principal Chaplain at the War Office. They were issued with the approval of Dr Bell. See also, Gleig, *The Quarterly Review* LXXVII, Vol.154, March 1846, p. 542.

at the top of a class for some time, he was to be promoted to that the bottom of a superior class, but if he did not progress in his new class he was to be returned to his old class. Pupils who consistently failed were demoted to the top of an inferior class, but if he or she maintained a high ranking in this class he should then be returned to his original class.

The school day began in the morning with prayers, which took the form of a lesson in which the children were taught to repeat a small portion of the Lord's Prayer, the graces said before and after meals, other prayers and sections of the church catechism. The remainder of the morning was devoted to the teaching reading and writing. There was detailed guidance on teaching the alphabet commencing, with the copying of capital and small letters displayed on card by tracing with the forefinger in a tray of sand. The pupils were first taught to pronounce and spell words of one syllable and then to words of more than one syllable using *Mrs Trimmer's Charity Spelling Book (Part1)*. When the spelling book had been mastered, the scholar was thought to be qualified to read 'for practice and instruction' from a number of prescribed religious texts containing stories from the Old and New Testament of the Bible. Writing was taught by the pupils tracing letters in the sand and when acquainted with the forms of the letters, with chalk on a slate, and finally in a copy book with pen and ink.

Afternoon lessons were devoted to learning arithmetical tables of addition, subtraction, multiplication and division, which were spoken by the sergeant teacher and repeated by the children, until they had learned them by heart. Again, the pupils learned to recognise and write numbers by copying and tracing the outlines in sand and then with chalk on slates. They were then were the introduced to the simple and then the compound rules of addition, subtraction, multiplication and division. At each stage the teacher dictated sums, which were written down and solved by the pupils.

The pedagogy throughout the school was mechanical and dull by modern standards and relied on constant drill and repetition. However, the 'Instructions' specified that lessons or tasks of more than a quarter of an hour should never be set for the lower classes and of no more than half an hour for the higher classes. The rule of the school was: 'short, easy frequent and perfect lessons.'

The 'Sergeant Teacher' was to instruct and help the tutors in learning their lessons and teaching their pupils, to prevent idleness and examine the pupils' progress. At the end of each day the teacher of each class or the schoolmaster-sergeant in charge of the school recorded the number of hours of tuition and progress of each class in a register, which was to be inspected wherever possible on a weekly basis by the regimental commanding officer and the chaplain. The schoolmaster-sergeant was to superintend the whole school, directing and advising the teachers and regularly visiting their classes. He was to engage with the pupils and encourage the 'diffident, timid and backward; to check and repress the forward and the presumptuous; to bestow just and ample commendation on the diligent, attentive, and orderly, however dull their capacity or slow their progress' and to deal out praise and encouragement and displeasure and censure according to the disposition and progress of the pupil.

The 'Instructions' concluded by explaining that the principles of morality and religion could be taught in the same way as reading, writing and arithmetic, by frequent short and easy lessons. The schoolmaster-sergeant or a chaplain would specify the part of the catechism or other religious book to the sergeant teacher, which he was to explain to the tutors, who would then explain it to the pupils. Extracts from religious texts, which warned against 'lying, swearing, theft, and idleness, provoking conduct and the use of improper expressions, one towards another' and which impress the principles of the 'Established' religion should be selected for these lessons.

Appendix III

A Historiographical Footnote
The Strange story of the Rev George Gleig's Chance Meeting on a Thames River Steamer

---

Attributed to George Gleig, the articles on Army education reform in the 1840s first appeared in *The Quarterly Review*. That publication was noted for publishing articles that reflected Tory opinion and it was therefore surprising that an essay entitled 'National Education', which is widely accepted as having been written by Gleig, appeared in April 1852 issue of *The Edinburgh Review*, a publication usually associated with liberal and Whig views. The article read as follows:

> Sometime in the summer of 1846, two gentlemen met on the deck of a river steam boat, which was plying its usual course from the Nine Elms Pier to Hungerford Market. One was the late Lord Ashburton, better known in the monied (sic) and political world as Mr Alexander Baring; the other was the Rev G.R. Gleig, now Chaplain General of Her Majesty's forces and Inspector General of Military Schools. There had occurred not long previously some modifications in Sir Robert Peel's Government, by which the present Lord Ashburton, then Mr. William Bingham Baring, was transferred from the Board of Control to the Pay Office.[i.e. appointed the Paymaster-General of the Forces].[1]

During a conversation between the two gentlemen, the late Lord Ashburton explained that his son [Mr W. Bingham Baring] was not very pleased with his new post as Paymaster-General, because there was only a small amount of routine business to occupy his time. George Gleig then asked Lord Ashburton, whether his son would be prepared to undertake some 'great and difficult work.' Certainly was the reply, 'provided it is a useful one.'

---

1   Gleig, 'National Education', *The Edinburgh Review or Critical Journal*, Vol. XCV No.94, April 1852.

The author then introduced the reader to the Royal Military Asylum and outlined a little of its founding purposes and recent history and stated that according to its Commissioners the boys at the Asylum were happy and well cared for. However, the author asserted there were outward and visible signs that this was not the case and that all was not well at the Asylum. The author went on to explain:

> A few days after the conversation in the steam boat, noticed above, Mr Bingham Baring, then Paymaster-General of the Forces, called upon Mr. Gleig and the two gentlemen proceeded to the asylum. No announcement having been made of their intention to visit the place, they found it in what may be called its every day dress.

This was followed by a graphic description of the dismal conditions they found at the Asylum: boys engaging in heavy and dangerous domestic work around the building; cruel punishments and general maltreatment; chaos in the school room with the boys learning little from the coarse mannered and uneducated sergeant schoolmasters, who by their own admission were ignorant and totally unsuited to be teachers.

At this point the author declared that: 'The Paymaster-General had seen enough. He repaired at once to the War Office, over which Mr Sidney Herbert then presided, and Mr Gleig being called in *amicus curiae*, the work of reform began.'[2] The article asserts that these reforms, which included annexing a training institution for regimental schoolmasters to the boys' school, were strongly resisted by the Horse Guards and throughout the Army, however:

> [T]he liberal minded and thoughtful men, who had taken up a wise project, listened patiently to all of these objections and over-ruled them. The Asylum was remodelled. There was appended to it a training institution for regimental schoolmasters; and the experience of five years has exposed fully, and to the conviction we believe of all parties, the groundlessness to the alarm with which the undertaking was at the outset contemplated. Not only has discipline not been relaxed in the army...crime is less frequent; men's manners are softened, their very language taking a different tone...And we are happy to say that to be educated as grown in fashion.[3]

In the essay Gleig claims full credit for exposing the appalling conditions at the Royal Military Asylum and a great deal of the credit as the prime instigator of the whole

2   Gleig, 'National Education'.
3   Gleig, 'National Education'. The article includes testimony evidence on the progress of the reforms given by Fox Maule to the House of Commons' Committee on Military expenditure in February1850 (See Chapter 13) and concludes with an exhortation that the Army's success in developing an education, which was at the same time non-denominational and Christian should be extended to civilian schools.

reform package for the training of Army schoolmasters, but there is very little mention of the crucial and decisive part played by the political leadership at the War Office.

Gleig had certainly been making very critical comments about the poor standard of the boys' education at the RMA, albeit based on second-hand accounts since 1844. However, these criticisms focused on the continuing use of Andrew Bell's outdated system of instruction, the narrow curriculum at the Asylum, and the unsuitability of retired non-commissioned officers as teachers. There was no mention of the dismal conditions and harsh treatment of the boys that are described in detail in his article in *The Edinburgh Review*. Some of this detail had been publicised in Professor Moseley's April 1846 Inspection report, but there is no evidence that Gleig instigated Professor Moseley's inspection of the Asylum. Moseley's report was dated 7th April 1846, but Gleig claimed that his meeting on the Thames river steam boat and his unannounced visit the Asylum took place in the summer of 1846. The plan to re-organise the RMA was underway in May 1846 and was completed with the Royal Warrant and Gleig's conjoined appointment as Chaplain-General and Inspector of Army Schools in July 1846.

William Bingham Baring was a very shy and reserved man, and as the Paymaster-General of the Forces, he acted as Herbert's lieutenant in his dealings with the Commissioners of the RMA and the staff at the Horse Guards in the spring and early summer of 1846. It is possible that Baring accompanied by Gleig made a visit to the Asylum either immediately before or following the receipt Moseley's Report, but if so this would have been in the spring of 1846. Gleig may have had a slip of memory about the exact date of his unannounced visit, but as A.W. Cockerill has concluded this is unlikely, because in 1852 he was a healthy man and a prolific writer, who was only in his mid-fifties and was to continue as Chaplain–General until his retirement in 1875.[4]

George Gleig has been described as a creative writer capable of mixing fact and fiction in order to produce readable stories for the purpose of conveying a message and instructing the reader.[5] Whatever Gleig's motives, it is difficult to avoid the conclusion that in his article in *The Edinburgh Review* he falsified the record with regard to the exposure of the conditions at the RMA; and that he also judiciously omitted to mention either Henry Hardinge's early efforts to improve the regimental schools – of which he certainly was aware – or Sidney Herbert's singular achievement in securing the support of government to implement policies that would determine the framework for the provision of education for the rank and file in the British Army during the second half of the 19th century.

Gleig's 1852 essay in *The Edinburgh Review*, unlike those he published in the *Quarterly Review* during the 1840s, would merit little more than a foot note in

---

4   Cockerill, *Sons of the Brave*, p. 102.
5   D.M. Peers,'Gleig, Robert 1796-1888', *Oxford Dictionary of National Biography* <www.oxforddnb.com/> (accessed 11th January 2007).

the history of the Army's schools had it not been referred to prominently in the sparse historiography of the subject during the 20th century. A. C.E. Jarvis in his influential article: 'My Predecessor in Office, the Prebendary George Robert Gleig, M.A'. reproduced the essay in its entirety 'in order to accord Gleig his right place in the part he played in the series of events which lead up to a reformed system of education in the Army.' However Jarvis had explained earlier in his article that it was Sidney Herbert, albeit after Gleig had reported to him on the condition of the RMA, who started the work of reform by arranging Professor Moseley's inspection and who subsequently secured the acquiescence of the Duke of Wellington and the agreement of the Treasury to the re-modelling of the Asylum and the establishment of a Normal school for the training of army schoolmasters.[6]

Unfortunately, Jarvis did not mention the date of Moseley's inspection, nor to the chronology of the sequence of the discussions within government and between the military departments that lead to the reforms, other than that Gleig was appointed Inspector of Military Schools conjointly with post of Chaplain General in July 1846. This has caused most writers to conclude wrongly that Gleig's unannounced visit with Baring to the RMA resulted in the commissioning of Professor Moseley to inspect the institution.

Colonel A.C.T. White in *The Story of Army Education 1643-1963* and Colonel N.T. St John Williams in *Tommy Atkins' Children-The Story of the Education of the Army's Children 1675-1970*, both concluded that Gleig's chance meeting on the River Thames steamer boat and his unannounced visit to the RMA resulted in an official inspection 'ordered by the Privy Council' and that this resulted in a report [Professor Moseley's Report] that lead to the remodelling of the RMA.[7] These authors failed to identify the discrepancy between the date of Gleig's' unannounced visit to the Asylum (the summer of 1846) stated in his essay in the Edinburgh Review and the date of Professor Moseley's official inspection and report (April 1846). White observed that 'a chance encounter gave him (Gleig) the acquaintance of one of the Commissioners of the Asylum, Baring the Paymaster-General.' It is difficult to believe that Gleig was not acquainted with William Bingham Baring, who had been appointed Pay-Master General in February 1845 at the same time that Sidney Herbert had taken up post as Secretary at War. Moreover, William Baring was Chairman of the Board of Commissioner of the Royal Hospital Chelsea in which building George Gleig resided and served as Chaplain. Williams complicates the matter by stating that his chance meeting on the river steamer was with 'the Paymaster-General, who was one of the Commissioners of the Asylum' and he confuses Alexander Baring, first Baron Ashburton (1773-1848), the 'late Lord Ashbourne' referred to in the article

6   Jarvis, *Journal of the Royal Army Chaplains' Department*, Vol.IV, No.3248-949 (July 1931), pp. 48-53.
7   White, *The Story of Army Education 1643-1963*, pp. 31-32; St John Williams, *Tommy Atkins' Children-The Story of the Education of the Army's Children 1675-1970*, pp. 38-40.

in the 1852 *Edinburgh Review* with his son William Bingham Baring, second Lord Ashbourne (1799-1864), the Pay-Master General in Sir Robert Peel's government.[8]

A.W. Cockerill in *Sons of the Brave, the Story of Boy Soldiers* pointed out the discrepancy between the date of the commissioning and completion of Professor Moseley's report and the date of Gleig and Baring's 'unannounced' visit to the Royal Military Asylum and he also cautioned about Gleig's ability to combine fact and fiction in his writings. Subsequent research on the reforms of Army education in the 1840s nevertheless has continued to draw on the writings of Jarvis, White and Williams and has accepted the account given by Gleig in his 1852 essay in *The Edinburgh Review.*[9]

D.R. Jones, in *The Rev. G.R. Gleig and Early Victorian Education* (which is referenced in the Oxford National Directory of Biography) and E.A. Smith in *The Army Schoolmaster and the Development of Elementary Education in the Army 1812-1920* accept the veracity of Gleig's1852 account of the events leading up to the reorganisation of the RMA described in *The Edinburgh Review*, but both writers complicate the matter by misquoting from the essay and give the date of the unannounced visit to the Asylum as in the summer of 1845.[10] Jones speculated on why Gleig waited until 1852 until publishing an account of the conditions at the RMA. He was charitable about Gleig's motives and suggested that Gleig may have suppressed the material for official reasons in 1845-6 and published them in 1852 to belittle the previous administration's contribution to the reform of army education and so strengthen his position as Chaplain- General and Inspector-General of Schools to undertake further reforms.[11]

Whatever the veracity of Gleig's account in the *Edinburgh Review* of the events leading to the re-organisation of the RMA and the establishment of the Normal School for the training of army schoolmasters at Chelsea, it has nonetheless been accepted by successive authors and has enhanced his reputation as the principal architect of the 1846 re-organisation of the RMA and the subsequent reforms of education in the Army. This is an unfortunate simplification which neglects the broader context for these reforms, including the problems faced by COs in finding and retaining suitable soldiers to staff the regimental schools and the need for trained schoolmasters, who

8   St John Williams, *Tommy Atkins' Children*, p. 38; White, *The Story of Army Education*, p. 32. Both writers state that Gleig was appointed Chaplain-General in 1844, whereas his appointment at that date was as Principal Chaplain. He was made Chaplain-General when that post was revived in July 1846.

9   Cockerill, *Sons of the Brave-The Story of Boy Soldiers*, pp. 100-2.

10   Jones, 'The Rev. George Gleig and Early Victorian EducationSmith, 'The Army Schoolmaster and the Development of Elementary Education in the Army 1812-1820', pp. 80-81; M. Peers, *Gleig, Robert 1796-1888*, Oxford Dictionary of National Biography, Oxford 2004 accessed 11 January 2007.

11   Jones, 'The Rev. George Gleig and Early Victorian Education', pp. 82-87. This explanation is taken from: T. Bowyer-Bower, 'The development of educational ideas and curricula in the Army during the 18th and 19th centuries'(MA. Thesis, University of Nottingham, 1954) pp. 80-81.

would with the assurance provided by a system of professional inspection, deliver schooling to an acceptable standard throughout the Army.

Hew Strachan has pointed out that in order to fashion and implement a workable scheme of reform in the 19th century two levels of government were involved: the subordinate members of the departments responsible for the administration and the political heads of those departments, whose support was essential for its success.[12] The achievement of any reform in the Army at this date was complicated by the division of responsibilities at the administrative and political level principally between the Horse Guards and the War Office. The Army was certainly fortunate that Rev George Gleig began to take an interest in regimental schools shortly after his appointment as Principal Chaplain and he deserves credit for proposing that the Army should establish its own normal school for training its schoolmasters, but the political leadership of Sidney Herbert and his successor Fox Maul at the War Office was the deciding factor in making reform government policy and in securing the support or at least the acquiescence of the Horse Guards for the re-organisation of the RMA into a Normal and a Model School and the formation of a trained corps of army schoolmasters.

12   Strachan, 'The Early Victorian Army and the Nineteenth-century Revolution in Government', p. 801.

Bibliography

Adjutant-General Corps Museum, Winchester
Army schoolmaster William Bartram, family history
Army Lists, serving schoolmasters

British Library (BL), London
Hardwicke Papers Add.MS35774
India Office Records (IOR), East India Company General Correspondence1602-1859
India Office Records (IOR), Marriage Records of the Bengal Presidency
India Office Records (IOR), Records of the Military Department 1708-1957
Windham Papers Add.MS37880

Claydon Archives, Claydon House, Buckinghamshire
Papers of Sir Harry Calvert

National Archives (TNA) London
Calendar of State Papers: Domestic Series, 1661–78, Entry Book 47Home Office
HO 100/174/157/167/176: Militia Embarkation Returns

Education Department
ED17: Committee of the Privy Council on Education, Administrative History

War Office
WO 1/628: War Office in letters and papers 1804
WO 1/902: War Office in letters and papers, Proposals for enlistment 1804
WO 3/ 17: Commander in Chief, Out-letters 1797/98
WO 3/54: Commander in Chief Out-letters 1811
WO3/59: Commander in Chief   Out -letters 1813
WO 4/347: Administrative History of the Chaplains' Department
WO 4/348: Secretary at War, Out- letters, Chaplain General
WO 12: General Muster Books and Pay Lists
WO 13: Militia and Volunteers, Muster Rolls and Pay Lists
WO 25/1146: Embarkation returns

WO 27: Inspection Reports and Returns for Regiments

WO 30/39: Report ordered by the Secretary of State to consider the Precedence and Command of Warrant Officers and NCOs, 1881

WO 32/6952: Committee appointed to enquire into certain questions affecting Army Schools and Schoolmasters (Harris Report)

WO32/6079: Second Report of the Royal Commission on Military Education

WO 33/3: A Memorandum on Question of Army Education

WO 33/3B: War Office Reports and Memoranda

WO 33/29: Report of the Committee on Boy Enlistment, 1876

WO 33/39: Report of the Committee on the Royal Hospitals at Chelsea and Kilmainham, Royal Military Asylum, Chelsea, and the Royal Hibernian Military School Dublin, (The Morley Committee)

WO 43/361: Secretary at War, Adult Pupils to pay charges, 1844-45

WO 43/513: Army School Regulations, 1854

WO 43/535: Secretary at War, Post of Chaplain General to be abolished1830-43

WO 43/668: Secretary at War Regimental Pay and Allowances and Royal Warrants 1837-1846

WO43/740: Secretary at War, appointment of Rev G. R. Gleig as Principal Chaplain

WO 43/752: Secretary at War, appointment of schoolmistresses throughout the Army

WO 43/796: Chelsea Royal Military Asylum, Decision to upgrade following critical report by Privy Council

WO 43/807:   Secretary at War, Training of Army Schoolmasters at RMA Chelsea

WO 43/819: Proposal to provide Chapels in Barracks

WO 44/647: War Office Circular 79, 1811; Letter from Lt. Colonel Rottinger to the Board of Ordnance,24th July 1812; General Orders and Instructions for Establishing and conducting Regimental Schools,1812

WO47/59: Board of Ordnance, Minutes of Surveyor General, January 1762

WO 76/106: Records of Officers' Services 95th Nottingham and Derby Regiment (45th and 95th Foot) 1825-1878

WO 97: Royal Hospital Chelsea, Soldiers' Service Documents

WO 100/ 106: Peninsular Medal Roll

WO 143/6: Minutes of the Commissioners of the Royal Military Asylum, 1801-1812

WO 143/8: Minutes of the Commissioners of the Royal Military Asylum, 1813-1821

WO 143/9: Minutes of the Commissioners of the Royal Military Asylum, 1821-1832.

WO143/10: Minutes of the Commissioners of the Royal Military Asylum, 1833-1846

WO 143/18: Royal Military Asylum, admission of children, 1826-1880

WO 143/21: Discharges of Male Children, 1825-1867

WO 143/27: Royal Hibernian Military School, Boys' Index Book, 1803-1819

WO 143/28: Royal Military Asylum Commissioners' Letter Book, 1801- 1827

WO 143/30: Royal Military Asylum Commandant's Letter Book, 1818-1827

WO 143/38: Royal Military Asylum, Correspondence, Reports and Memoranda, 1832-1845

WO 143/39: Royal Military Asylum, Correspondence, Reports and Memoranda, 1846-1852
WO 143/47: Royal Military Asylum, Normal School Letter Book, 1853-1859
WO 143/48: Royal Military Asylum, Normal School Letter Book, September 1859
WO 143/49: Royal Military Asylum, Register of the Normal School, 1847-1851
WO 143/51: Royal Military Asylum School Committee Proceedings, 1847-1859
WO 379/1: Disposition of the Army, 1737-1950
WO 379/2: Stations of Regiments, 1818-1859
WO 379/6: Disposition and Movements of Regiments, 1803-1827
WO 379/7: Disposition of the Army, 1828-1856
WO 380/3:   Establishments and Stations of Regiments, 1803-1881

National Army Museum (NAM) London
Records of the RAEC: Army Education before 1846, Box 22125
Army Educational Policy and Regimental Schools 1846-1920, Box 22126
Army Educational Policy and Regimental Schools 1846-1920, Box 22127

National Library of Ireland (NLI) Dublin
The Kilmainham Papers

Parliamentary Papers, Great Britain and Ireland: House of Commons Debates and Speeches
Account of finally Audited Receipt and Expenditure for Army and Militia Services: 1843-1844 (1845)
Accounts and Papers Part III, East Indies (Education), Bombay, 1859.
Fifth Report by the Council of Military Education on Army Schools, Libraries and Recreations Rooms, 1868
Fifth Report of the Director-General of Military Education on Army Schools, 1893
First General Report by the Council of Military Education, 1860
First Report by the Council of Military Education on Army Schools, Libraries and Recreations Rooms, 1862
First Report of the Director-General of Military Education on Army School, Libraries and Recreation Rooms, 1872
Fourth Report by the Council of Military Education on Army Schools, Libraries and Recreations Rooms, 1866
Fourth Report of the Director-General of Military Education on Army Schools Libraries and Recreation Rooms, 1889
Papers Relating to Military Bands, House of Commons Sessional Papers, 15th February 1858.
Parliamentary Papers, Great Britain and Ireland: House of Commons Sessional Papers, Reports and Returns
Report of Commissioners Appointed to Consider the Best Mode of Reorganising the System for Training Officers and for the Scientific Corps, 1857

Report of the Commissioners appointed to enquire into the State of Popular Education in England. (Newcastle Commission), 1861

Report of the Commissioners of the Board of Education in Ireland, 1812

Returns relating to Military and Regimental Schools, 19th March 1852

Second Report by the Council of Military Education on Army Schools, Libraries and Recreation Rooms, 1865

Second Report from the Commissioners of Irish Education Inquiry1826, Army Estimates, 1828

Second Report of the Commissioners for Auditing Public Accounts in Ireland, 1813

Second Report of the Director-General of Military Education on Army School, Libraries and Recreation Rooms, 1874

Second Report of the Royal Commission on Military Education, 1870

Sixth Report by the Council of Military Education on Army Schools, Libraries and Recreations Rooms 1869

Sixth Report of the Director-General of Military Education on Army Schools 1896 House of Lord Sessional Papers: Correspondence with regards to changes in the transactions of business relating to the Administration of the Army, 7th April 1854

Third Report by the Council of Military Education on Army Schools, Libraries, and Recreation Rooms, 1866

Third Report of the Director-General of Military Education on Army Schools Libraries and Recreation Rooms, 1877

XIX Report of the Commissioners of Military Inquiry, House of Commons, 1812

Private Collection
Colonel J.B .Crowther, US Army, San Antonio, Texas: Crowther, Elizabeth, 'Description and Observation Book, 9th March to 14th July 1838' (Dublin: Kildare Place Society, Model School, Kildare Place, Dublin)

Regimental Records and Archives
1st Foot Guards, Order Books, Regimental Headquarters Grenadier Guards, Wellington Barracks, London

2nd Foot Guards, Order Books, Regimental Headquarters Coldstream Guards, Wellington Barracks, London

3rd Foot Guards, Order Books, Regimental Headquarters Scots Guards, Wellington Barracks London

King's Dragoon Guards, Standing Orders 1840, Firing Line, Museum of the Queens Dragoon Guards and the Royal Welsh, Cardiff Castle, Cardiff

Queen's Dragoon Guards, Standing Orders 1795, Firing Line, Museum of the Queens Dragoon Guards and the Royal Welsh, Cardiff Castle, Cardiff

10th Light Dragoons, Standing Orders 1797, Horsepower Museum, Winchester

10th Hussars, Standing Orders 1833, Horsepower Museum, Winchester

5th Regiment of Foot, Records of Service of Officers, Sergeants and Corporals, Northumberland Fusiliers Museum, Alnwick

12th Regiment of Foot, Standing Orders 1817, Suffolk County Archives, Bury St Edmunds.

14th Regiment of Foot, Register of Marriages 1807-1831, York Army Museum, York

22nd Foot, Digest of Service, Cheshire Military Museum

25th Foot, Miscellaneous Returns Book 1811-1817, Standing Orders 1834, Museum of the King's Own Scottish Borderers, Berwick on Tweed

30th Regiment, Standing Orders 1850, Lancashire Infantry Museum, Fulwood Barracks, Preston

40th Foot Regimental Order Books 1824-6, Lancashire Infantry Museum, Fulwood Barracks, Preston

47th Regiment Standing Orders 1834 Lancashire Infantry Museum, Fulwood Barracks, Preston

49th Regiment, Diary of William Comerford, Rifles Museum, Salisbury.

81st Regiment, Standing Orders 1808, Historical Record of the 81st Regiment 1872, Lancashire Infantry Museum Fulwood Barracks, Preston

82nd Regiment, Regulations 1844, Lancashire Infantry Museum, Fulwood Barracks, Preston

83rd Regiment Order Books, Royal Ulster Rifles Museum, Belfast

87th Regiment Standing Orders 1827, Royal Irish Fusiliers Museum, Armagh

Wiltshire and Swindon History Centre
Sydney Herbert Papers

Newspapers and Directories
Asiatic Journal, Madras, 1828-1829
Athenaeum, No. 974, 27th June 1846
Bengal Presidency and Asiatic Register, Calcutta 1835
Faulkner's Journal, 10th December 1795
Illustrated London News, 21st January 1865
Lloyds Weekly Newspaper, 30th December1855
Naval and Military Gazette, 6th May 1843, 15th July 1843, 19th September 1846, 21st October 1857
The Bombay Calendar and Almanac, 1856
The Irish Times, 1st September 1868
The Observer, 10th November 1846
The Times Newspaper: 21st August 1851, 19th July 1852, 31st July 1860, and 31st July 1861

Contemporary Works (Pre-1900)
Journals

Anon., 'Memoir of General Sir Harry Calvert', *The United Service Journal Part I* (1829), pp. 26-30

Gleig, G., 'National Education', *The Edinburgh Review or Critical Journal*, Vol. XCV, No. 94, (April 1852), pp. 321-357

Gleig, G., 'Moral Discipline of the Army', *The Quarterly Review* LXXVI, No. 152 (September 1845), pp. 387-424

Gleig, G., 'Education and Lodging the Soldier', *The Quarterly Review LXXVII, No. 154,*(March 1846), pp. 526-563

Gleig, G., 'Military Education', *The Quarterly Review LXXXIII*, No. 166, (September 1848), pp. 419-450

Books

Aitchison, J.W., *A General Code of the Military Regulations in Force under the Presidency of Bombay* (Calcutta: Adjutant-General Bombay Army, 1824)

Army List (London: War Office February, 1874)

Bell, A., *An Analysis of the Experiment in Education made at Egmore near Madras* (London: Cadell & Davies, 1808)

Cannon, R., Historical *Records of the 2nd or Queen's Royal Regiment* (London: Clowes and Sons, 1836)

Cannon, R., *Historical Record of the 20th or East Devonshire Regiment* (London: Parker Furnival & Parker, 1848)

Cannon, R., *Historical Records of the 22nd Regiment of Foot* (London: Parker Furnival & Parker, 1849)

Cannon, R. *Historical Records of the 31st, or the Huntingdonshire Regiment* (London: Parker Furnival & Parker, 1850)

Cannon, R. *History of the Cape Mounted Riflemen* (London: Parker Furnival & Parker, 1837)

Carter, T.R., *Historical* Records of the *26th or Cameronian Regiment* (London: Privately published, 1867)

Census of England and Wales (London: Census Office, 1871)

Cullen, P., *Letter to Lord St. Leonards on the Management of the Patriotic Fund and the application of public money to proselytising purposes* (Dublin: James Duffy, 1857)

Cullen, P., *Two Letters to Lord St. Leonards on the Management of the Patriotic Fund and the Second Report of the Royal Commissioners* (Dublin: James Duffy, 1858)

Cuncliffe, M., *The Royal Irish Fusiliers* (Oxford: Clarendon Press, 1859)

Duncan, F., *History of the Royal Regiment of Artillery* (London: John Murray, 1872)

Dupin, C., A *View of the History and Actual State of the State of the Military Forces of Great Britain* (London: John Murray, 1822)

First Report of the Statistical Society of London on the Condition of Education in the London District of Westminster in 1837 (London: Royal Statistical Society, 1838)

Gleig, G.R., *The Life of the Duke of Wellington* (London: Longman Green Longman Roberts and Green, 1864)

King's Regulations (London: Adjutant General Horse Guards, 1822)

Kings Regulations (London: Adjutant General Horse Guards, 1837)

Lamb, R., *Memoir of His Own Life* (Dublin: privately published, 1811)

Lefroy, J.H., *Report on the Regimental and Garrison Schools of the Army* [The Lefroy Report] (London, Stationary Office for the War Office, 1859)

Lady Lefroy (ed.), *The Autobiography of General Sir John Henry Lefroy* (London: privately published, 1895)

Lawrence, H.M., *The Lawrence Military Asylum, being a brief account of the past ten years of the existence and progress of the institution established in the Himalayas by the late Sir. H. M. Lawrence for the Orphan and other children of European Soldiers* (Sanawar: privately published, 1858)

Larpent, G. (ed.), The *Private Journal of Judge Advocate Larpent* (London: Richard Bentley, 1854)

Lushington, C., *History, Design and Present State of Religious, Benevolent and Charitable Institutions founded by the British in Calcutta* (Calcutta: Hindostanee Press, 1824)

Moosom, W.S., *Historical Record of the Fifty-Second Regiment* (London: Richard Bentley, 1860)

Moseley, H., '*Report on the Normal School for Training Regimental Schoolmasters, and on the Model School at the Royal Military Asylum, Chelsea ,24th August 1849*' (London: Minutes of the Committee of Council on Education, 1848-50, Vol.2)

O' Donnell, H., *Historical Records of the 14th Regiment* (Devonport: A. H. Swiss, 1892)

Oxford Dictionary of National Biography, 1st Ed. (Oxford: Clarendon Press, 1885-1900)

Queen's Regulations (London: Adjutant General Horse Guards, 1871)

The National Society for the Education of the Poor in the Principles of the Established Church throughout England and Wales, *First Report* (London: National Society, 1812)

The National Society for the Education of the Poor in the Principles of the Established Church throughout England and Wales, Second Report (London: National Society, 1814)

Regulations and Orders for the Army (London: Adjutant General Office Horse Guards 1881 and 1816, facsimile edition published by Frederick Muller Ltd, 1970)

*Regulations for the Army Hospital Corps (*London: War Office, August 1857)

Regulations for the Management of Army Schools (London: War Office, May 1863)

Regulations for Military Prisons (London: War Office, April 1863)

Rogers, S., *Historical Record of the 81st Regiment* (Gibraltar: Twenty-Eighth Regimental Press, 1872)

Royal Warrant Authorising the Commissioners of Affairs of Barracks to appropriate and fit up Barracks Rooms for Regimental Schools (London: War Office, 24th July, 1812) [See also Parliamentary Papers, '*The Lefroy Report*', Appendix 11 No. 3]

Simes, T., *The Military Medley* (Dublin: S. Powell, 1768)

Simes, T., *A Military Course for the government and conduct of a Battalion* (London: Privately published, 1777)

Sinnott, J., *A Military Manual of Light Infantry and other Duties* (Chester: privately published, 1845)

Smythies, R.H.R., *Historical Records of 40th (2nd Somersetshire) Regiment* (Devonport: privately published, 1896)

Southey, R., *The Life of the Rev. Andrew Bell* (London: John Murray, 1844)

Standing Orders of the 2nd Dragoons (Dublin, 1839)

Strange, T.B., *Gunner Jingo's Jubilee* (London: Remington and Co 1896)

Taunton, W.P., *Reports and Cases in the Court of Common Pleas 1781-1813* (London: I. Riley, 1816) pp, 67-6

The Importance of Promoting the General Education of the Poor (London: Philanthropist, 1811)

The 12th-14th Reports of the Society for Promoting the Education of the Poor in Ireland (Dublin: unknown 1826, 1827)

The Twenty –Fourth and Twenty-Fifth Reports of the Society for Promoting the Education of the Poor within the Government of Bombay (Bombay: Bombay Summacher Press,1839-40)

War Office, Circular 566, 10th March 1860

War Office, Circular 753, 1st May 1862

War Office, Circular 783, 17th September 1862

War Office, Circular No. 795, 2nd December 1862

War Office, Circular No. 485, 25th May 1863

War Office, Circular 360, 10th August 1863

War Office, General Order G100, 1st October1869

War Office, General Order G 70, G 71, G 73, 1st October 1870

War Office, *General Orders*, 1887

War Office, *Instructions for the Guidance of Candidates for Admission to the Army as Schoolmasters and for Admission into the Duke of York's Royal Military School and the Royal Hibernian Military School as Pupil Teachers*, 1894

War Office, *Report of the Inter-Departmental Committee on Army Schools* (Dassent Report), 1901

Post-1902 Works
Journals

Anon., 'Notes on School of 52nd Regiment of Foot 1807', *Journal of the Society for Army Historical Research,* Vol 27 (Summer1949), p. 87

Baule, S.M., 'Drummers in the British Army During the American Revolution', *Journal of the Society for Army Historical Research,* Vol. 86 (Spring 2008), pp. 24-28

Bonner, R., 'Hulme Cavalry Barracks, Manchester', *Journal of the Society for Army Historical Research,* Vol.91, (Autumn 2013), pp. 206-225

Bowyer-Bower T.A., 'Some Sources for the History of Education in the British Army during the 19th Century', *British Journal of Educational Studies,* Vol.4. No. 1 (Nov.1955), pp. 71-77

Bowyer-Bower, T: 'Some Early Educational Influences in the British Army', *Journal of the Society for Army Historical Research,* Vol. 33 (1955), pp. 5-12

Hagist, D.N., 'Unpublished Writings of Richard Lamb', *Journal of the Society for Army Historical Research*, Vol. 90 (Summer 2012), pp. 86-88

Jarvis, A.C.E., 'My Predecessor in Office, the Prebendary George Robert Gleig, *Journal of the Royal Army Chaplains' Department*, Vol. IV (July 1931), pp. 42-49

MacArthur R., 'British Establishments during the Napoleonic War', *Journal of the Society for Army Historical Research*, Vol. 87 (Summer 2009), pp. 155-159

O' Keefe. E., 'The Old Halberdier: From the Pyrenes to Plattsburgh with a Welshman of the 39th (Memoirs of the 39th Foot, 1808-1814)', *Journal of the Society for Army Historical Research*, Vol. 95 (Summer 2017), pp. 158-159

Smith, E.A., 'Educating the Soldier', *Journal of the Society for Army Historical Research*, Vol. 6 (Spring 1988), pp. 35-45

Strachan, H., 'The early Victorian Army and the Nineteenth-century Revolution in Government', *English Historical Review* (October 1980), pp. 782-509

Watts, A.E., 'An Early Instance of Civilian Assistance to Army Education', *Journal of the Royal Army Educational Corps*, Vol. XXIV, No.3 (September 1950), pp. 106-110

Webb Carter B. W. (ed.), 'Colonel Wellesley's Standing Orders to the Thirty-Third Regiment 1798', *Journal of the Society for Army Historical Research*, Vol.50. (Summer1972), pp. 65-77

Books
Army List 1912 (London: War Office, 1912)

Bannatyne, N., *History of the XXX Regiment 1689-1881* (Liverpool: Litlebury Bros., 1923)

Bart G. D & Ramsey G.D.(ed.), *The Panmure Papers* (London: Hodder & Stoughton, 1908)

Bartlett, T. & Jeffrey, K., *A Military History of Ireland* (Cambridge: Cambridge University Press, 1997)

Beamish, N.L. *History of the King's German Legion*, Vols. I & II (East Sussex: Naval and Military Press, 1997)

Best, G. & Wheatcroft, A. (Eds.), *War, Economy and Military Mind* (London: Croom Helm, 1976

Bourne, K., *Palmerston: The Early Years 1784-1841* (London: Allen Lane, 1982)

Canadine, D., *Victorious Century: The United Kingdom, 1800-1900* (London: Allen Lane, 2017)

Clarke, H.R., A *New History of the Royal Hibernian Military School Phoenix Park Dublin 1765-1924* (Yarm: Privately published, 2011)

Cockerill, A.W., *Sons of the Brave – The Story of Boy Soldiers* (London: Secker &Warburg, 1984)

Cockerill, A.W., *The Charity of Mars-a History of the Royal Military Asylum* (Cobourg, Ontario: Privately published, 2002)

Colledge, J. J., *Ships of the Royal Navy* (London: Greenhill Books, 1987)

Cookson, J.E., *The British Armed Nation1793-1815* (Oxford, Clarendon Press, 1997)

Cruickshank, D., *The Royal Hospital Chelsea* (London: Third Millennium Publishing, 2004)

Curtis, S.J.and Boultwood, M.E.A., *An Introductory History of English* Education (London: University Tutorial Press, 1966)

Dalrymple, W., *The Last Mughal* (London: Bloomsbury Publishing, 2006)

Devine, T. M. *The Scottish Nation –A Modern History* (London: Penguin Books, 2012)

Dickson M., *Teacher Extraordinary: Joseph Lancaster 1778-1838* (Sussex Lewes: Privately published, 1986)

Douet, J., *British Barracks 1800-1914*(London: English Heritage, 1998)

Fay, E., *Original Letters from India (*London: The Hogarth Press, 1986)

Firth, C.H., *Cromwell's Army* (London: University Paperbacks, Methuen and Co, 1962)

Fortescue, J.W., *A History of the British Army*, Thirteen Volumes (East Sussex: Naval and Military Press, 2004)

Fortescue, J.W., *The County Lieutenancies and the Army1803-1814 (*East Sussex: Naval and Military Press, date unknown)

French, D., *Military Identities* (Oxford: Oxford University Press, 2005)

Gilmour, D., *The British in India* (London: Alan Lane, 2018)

Gleig, M. (ed.), *Personal Reminiscences of the First Duke of Wellington* (Edinburgh and London: Blackwood &Sons, 1904)

Gordon, A. H., *Sidney Hebert: Lord Herbert of Lea, a Memoir* (London: John Murray,1906)

Groves, P., *Historical Record of the 7th or Royal Regiment of Fusiliers* (Guernsey: F. B. Guerin, 1903)

Guy A. J. & Boyden P. B., *Soldiers of the Raj: Indian Army 1600-1947* (London: National Army Museum, 1997)

Hansard, 1st, 2nd and 3rd series

Hawes, C.J., *Poor Relations: The Making of a Eurasian Community in British India, 1773-1833,* (London: Curzon Press, 1996)

Haythornthwaite, P.J., *The Armies of Wellington* (London: Brockhampton Press, 1998)

Heathcote, T.A., *The Indian Army: The Garrison of British Imperial India 1822-1922* (London: David & Charles, 1974)

Hilton, B., *A Mad, Bad and Dangerous People?* (Oxford: Oxford University Press, 2008)

Hopen, K.T., *The Mid-Victorian Generation 1846-1886* (Oxford: Oxford University Press, 2008)

Houlding, J.H., *Fit for Service (Oxford: Clarendon Press,* 2000)

Johnson, J., *From Bailey to Bailey: A Short History of Military Buildings in Sheffield* (Sheffield: privately published, 1998)

Jones, M.G., *The Charity School Movement* (Cambridge: Cambridge University Press, 1938)

Leask J.C. and Mcmance H.M., *The Records of the Royal Scots* (Dublin: Alexander Thom & Co., 1915)

Longford, E., *Wellington: Pillar of State* (London: Weidenfeld and Nicholson, 1972)

Lucy, John, *There's a Devil in the Drum* (East Sussex: Naval and Military Press, 1993)

McAnally, H., *The Irish Militia 1793-1816* (Dublin: Clonmore and Reynolds/Eyre and Spottiswoode, 1949)

Mokyr, J., *The Enlightened Economy: An Economic History of Britain 1770-1850* (Yale: Yale University Press, 2009)

Morris, J., *Pax Britannica* (London: Penguin Books, 1987)

Porter, A.(ed.), *The Oxford History of the British Empire, Vol.III: The Nineteenth Century* (Oxford: Oxford University Press, 1999)

Porter. R., *English Society in the Eighteenth Century* (London: Penguin Books, 1991)

R. Vinen, *National Service: A Generation in Uniform 1945-63* (London: Penguin Books, 2014)

Regulations and Orders for the Army 1811 and 1816 (London: Adjutant General's Office Horse Guards, facsimile edition published by Frederick Muller Ltd, 1970)

Rigby, B., *Ever Glorious: The Story of the 22nd (Cheshire) Regiment* (Chester: W.H. Evans, 1982)

Rogers, H.C.B., *Troopships and their History* (London: Seeley Service, 1963)

Royle, T., *Crimea* (London: Little, Brown Company, 1999)

Rudd ,L., *The Duke of York's Royal Military School* (Dover: St George's Press,1935)

Rumsby, J.H., *Discipline, System and Style: The Sixteenth Lancers and British Soldering in India 1822-1846,* (Solihull: Helion & Company, 2015)

Salmon, D., *Joseph Lancaster* (London: Longmans& Co, 1904)

Shipp, John, *The Path of Glory*, ed. C.J. Stranks (London: Chatto & Windus, 1969)

Silva, R.K., *Early Prints of Ceylon* (London: Serendib Publications 1985)

Smith, John, *In this Sign Conquer* (London : A.R .Mowbray & Co.,1968)

Spiers, E.M., *The Late Victorian Army 1868-1902* (Manchester: Manchester University Press, 1992)

Strachan, H., *Wellington's Legacy*: *The Reform of the British Army, 1830-1854* (Manchester: Manchester University Press, 1986)

Sutherland, G., *Policy Making in Elementary Education 1870-1895* (Oxford: Oxford University Press, 1973)

Sutherland, G., *Elementary Education in the Nineteenth Century,* (London: The Historical Association, 1982)

Sweetman, J., *War and Administration* (Edinburgh: Scottish Academic Press, 1984)

Urban, M., *The Man Who Broke Napoleon's Codes* (London: Faber and Faber, 2002)

Watson, J. Steven, *The Reign of George III* (Oxford: Clarendon Press, 1960)

Webb, E.H.B., *A History of the 17th (The Leicestershire Regiment* (London: Vacher & Son, 1912)

Webb, A.H., *History of the 12th (Suffolk Regiment)* 1683-1913 (London: Spottiswoode & Co, 1914)

White, A.C.T, *The Story of Army Education 1643-1963* (London: George G. Harrap & Co, 1963)

Williams, St John, N.T., *Tommy Atkin's Children: The Story of the Education of the Army's Children 1675-1970* (London: Ministry of Defence, 1971)

Unpublished Works

T.A. Bowyer-Bower, 'The development of educational ideas and curricula in the Army during the 18th and 19th centuries' (MA Thesis. Nottingham: University of Nottingham, 1954)

E.A. Smith, 'The Army Schoolmaster and the Development of Elementary Education in the Army, 1812-1920' (PhD Thesis. London: Institute of Education, University of London, 1993)

D.R. Jones, 'The Rev. G.R. Gleig and Early Victorian Education'(MA Thesis. Belfast: Queen's University Belfast, 1983)

Electronic Sources

Armed forces.co.uk <http://www.armedforces.co.uk/>
Army.mod.uk <https://apply.army.mod.uk/?cid=semp4928676829&ef_id=EAIaIQob ChMIjv-1ttT17AIVF-DtCh1B8gWtEAAYASAAEgJFs_D_BwE:G:s&s_ kwcid=AL!8141!3!323097708620!e!!g!!army mod uk>
Bexhill Hanoverian Study Group <info@bexhillhanoveriankgl.co.uk>
Hannover Stadtmuseum <historishes.museum@hannover-stadte.de>
Oxford Dictionary of National Biography <oxforddnb.com>

Index

The period 1815-1914 is sometimes called the long century of peace. It was in reality very far from that. It was a century of civil wars, popular uprisings, and struggles for Independence. An era of colonial expansion, wars of Empire, and colonial campaigning, much of which was unconventional in nature. It was also an age of major conventional wars, in Europe that would see the Crimea campaign and the wars of German unification. Such conflicts, along with the American Civil War, foreshadowed the total war of the 20th century.

It was also a period of great technological advancement, which in time impacted the military and warfare in general. Steam power, electricity, the telegraph, the radio, the railway, all became tools of war. The century was one of dramatic change. Tactics altered, sometimes slowly, to meet the challenges of the new technology. The dramatic change in the technology of war in this period is reflected in the new title of this series: From Musket to Maxim.

The new title better reflects the fact that the series covers all nations and all conflict of the period between 1815-1914. Already the series has commissioned books that deal with matters outside the British experience. This is something that the series will endeavour to do more of in the future. At the same time there still remains an important place for the study of the British military during this period. It is one of fascination, with campaigns that capture the imagination, in which Britain although the world's predominant power, continues to field a relatively small army.

The aim of the series is to throw the spotlight on the conflicts of that century, which can often get overlooked, sandwiched as they are between two major conflicts, the French/Revolutionary/Napoleonic Wars and the First World War. The series will produced a variety of books and styles. Some will look simply at campaigns or battles. Others will concentrate on particular aspects of a war or campaign. There will also be books that look at wider concepts of warfare during this era. It is the intention that this series will present a platform for historians to present their work on an important but often overlooked century of warfare.

Submissions

The publishers would be pleased to receive submissions for this series. Please contact series editor Dr Christopher Brice via email (chrismbrice@yahoo.com), or in writing to Helion & Company Limited, Unit 8, Amherst Business Centre, Budbrooke Road, Warwick, Warwickshire, CV34 5WE.

Books in this series:

1. *The Battle of Majuba Hill: The Transvaal Campaign 1880–1881* John Laband (ISBN 978-1-911512-38-7)*

2. *For Queen and Company: Vignettes of the Irish Soldier in the Indian Mutiny* David Truesdale (ISBN 978-1-911512-79-0)*

3. *The Furthest Garrison: Imperial Regiments in New Zealand 1840-1870* Adam Davis (ISBN 978-1-911628-29-3)*

4. *Victory over Disease: Resolving The Medical Crisis In The Crimean War, 1854–1856* Michael Hinton (ISBN 978-1-911628-31-6)*

5. *Journey Through the Wilderness: Garnet Wolseley's Canadian Red River Expedition of 1870* Paul McNicholls (ISBN 978-1-911628-30-9)*

6. *Kitchener: The Man Not the Myth* Anne Samson (ISBN 978-1-912866-45-8)

7. *The British and the Sikhs: Discovery, Warfare and Friendship (c.1700–1900)* Gurinder Singh Mann (ISBN 978-1-911628-24-8)*

8. *Bazaine 1870: Scapegoat for a Nation* Quintin Barry (ISBN 978-1-913336-08-0)

9. *Redcoats in the Classroom: The British Army's School for Soldiers and Their Children During the 19th Century* Howard R. Clarke (ISBN 978-1-912866-47-2)

* Denotes books are paperback 246mm × 189mm.